JAPAN IN THE
AMERICAN CENTURY

JAPAN

IN THE

AMERICAN

CENTURY

KENNETH B. PYLE

THE BELKNAP PRESS OF
HARVARD UNIVERSITY PRESS

Cambridge, Massachusetts
London, England
2018

Library of Congress Cataloging-in-Publication Data
Names: Pyle, Kenneth B., author.
Title: Japan in the American century / Kenneth B. Pyle.
Description: Cambridge, Massachusetts : The Belknap Press of Harvard
University Press, 2018. | Includes bibliographical references and index.
Identifiers: LCCN 2018012405 | ISBN 9780674983649 (alk. paper)
Subjects: LCSH: Japan—Civilization—American influences. | Japan—Foreign
relations—United States. | Japan—Foreign relations—1945– | Japan—
History—1945– | Japan—Politics and government—1945– | United States—
Foreign relations—Japan. | United States—Foreign relations—20th century.
Classification: LCC DS821.5.U6 P95 2018 | DDC 952.04—dc23
LC record available at https://lccn.loc.gov/2018012405

For Anne

Contents

JAPAN IN THE
AMERICAN CENTURY

Introduction:
An Unnatural Intimacy

N o nation was more deeply impacted by America's rise to world power in the twentieth century and its creation of a new international order than Japan. This book is about the extraordinary relationship of two peoples who in many ways stood at opposite poles in the values that their contrasting national experiences had implanted, thrown together by events that intertwined their histories in the closest ways. It is about what the diplomat-historian George Kennan aptly termed "an unnatural intimacy" between the Japanese and their American conquerors. In a little-noticed collection of essays on American foreign policy that he wrote in 1977, Kennan perceptively observed how events had thrust Japan and the United States together in an unpropitious way:

> They are very different people from ourselves; and if the recent War of the Pacific had not intervened, I would have been tempted to say . . . let us not push an unnatural intimacy too far and too fast. But the war did intervene. We were, as a result of it, thrown into contact with the Japanese in the closest way in the post-hostilities period. And out of this there did come a species of intimacy—an intimacy born of conflict and much agony, particularly on the Japanese side, but an intimacy nevertheless. We learned a good deal about each other, good and bad, in those unhappy years. That is the nature of all intimacies.[1]

In this "unnatural intimacy" and the intertwining of our modern histories, a prevailing American liberal tradition encountered a deeply resilient Japanese conservative tradition. The values of American civilization, the child of the Enlightenment, were utterly at odds with Japanese conservative orthodoxy. Liberal norms that the United States pursued in constructing world order conflicted with the values and collectivist norms of solidarity, consensus, community, and respect for hierarchy and status long embedded in Japanese culture. America's republican heritage of liberty, democracy, and individual rights stood in sharp contrast to a nation that had never experienced a democratic revolution and prized its communitarian values. A society of immigrants that depended on adherence to a liberal creed for its cohesion encountered one that had known no immigration for nearly two millennia and found its identity in ethnic community. Nevertheless, making light of Japan's conservative heritage, Americans occupied Japan with the intention of remaking Japan in their own image to fit into a new liberal world order. The resulting unnatural intimacy between these two nations, born of an unprecedentedly destructive conflict between them, reveals much about the character of the American world order as well as the unique course of postwar Japanese history.

The Asia Pacific War had its origins not in the 1930s, as often thought, but rather from the first years of the twentieth century when both Japan and America were ambitious, rising imperialist powers engaged in a contest for supremacy in the Pacific. The book begins with the central issue in their rivalry—sharply divergent visions of how the Asia Pacific region should be ordered. Similar in some ways to the emerging Sino-American competition early in the twenty-first century, both countries wanted a regional order to accord with their own values and interests. After World War I, America established a short-lived multilateral order designed to contain Japanese expansionist goals pursued at the expense of a weak and divided China. This flawed American-led order enshrining liberal principles of self-determination, free trade (the Open Door), naval arms limitation, and collective security failed to provide any enforcement mechanism. Japan, as Asia's first rising power, bringing historical traditions quite at odds with Western civilization and prefiguring the rise of other Asian powers in our own time, soon challenged the American order. Japan held that it had proved that its civilization's achievements destined it to expel Western power and create a new Asian order. Their rivalry to determine the regional order, stoked by mistakes and misper-

ceptions, intensified by rampant nationalism and racial animosity, resulted in the greatest conflict Asia has ever known.

In World War II, following the Japanese attack on Pearl Harbor, the
United States mounted a crusade to rid the world of fascism and militarism. Driven not only by the particular goals of national interest but also
by a will to create a lasting world order that would embody American
values and establish a lasting peace, President Franklin D. Roosevelt insisted on a policy of unconditional surrender of the fascist powers so as
to have a free hand to create a new American-centered world order. The
wisdom of unconditional surrender policy as it was applied to the Asia
Pacific War is questionable. World War II was the only foreign war in
American history waged to achieve unconditional surrender. Every
other war was fought to a negotiated peace. But this time the Americans
chose an ambitious alternative. Rather than simply drive the Japanese
back to their original borders, the Americans demanded the right to reform and remake Japan from root to branch. The unconditional surrender
policy came at a high price in human life and destruction. It provoked
last-ditch resistance from the Japanese military leaders and set the stage
for the calamitous ending of the war. It lengthened the war and required
the horrific battle of Okinawa, the firebombing of more than sixty Japanese cities, and the use of the atomic bomb.

Often called "the most controversial decision any president has
made," the use of the atomic bomb has long been a sensitive and unresolved issue between Japanese and Americans. For Japanese, it gave rise
to their sense of victimhood often to the exclusion of a consciousness of
the devastation and brutality their military had wreaked in Asia. As the
only people to have experienced nuclear holocaust it became a central
part of their postwar national identity. Most Americans have preferred
to believe that the bombs were necessary to avert an invasion of Japan
and save lives, but the fact of being the only nation to have used the
atomic bomb has left a sense of unease for a people accustomed to a self-
image of national virtue. The course of atomic decision making and the
momentum created by Roosevelt's unconditional surrender policy led
almost inexorably to the bombing of Hiroshima and Nagasaki. A devastated and occupied Japan was left in long-term subordination to the
United States. What motivated our uncompromising goals in the Asia
Pacific War was our determination to undertake the total transformation

of Japan as essential to our larger purpose of creating a new world order. Japan was to be made a permanently disarmed liberal democratic state that would conform with that order. For these reasons, I argue that the history of postwar Japan and an understanding of its unique course must begin with America's unconditional surrender policy.

The consequences for Japan were huge and long lasting. Seeing the American world order through the prism of US-Japan relations, the theme of this book, reveals much of its character as well as the unique course of postwar Japan. The essence of the new order lay not only in America's commanding world power but also in our belief in the universalism of American institutions and values. Confident that the values and institutions from our history provided the template for how world order should be organized, our distinctive approach to the world was to tutor other peoples in the ways of our national experience. The Pax Britannica had claimed to create "peace, order, and justice" in its imperial rule, but our plans were always set in a "tutelage framework."[2] Reinhold Niebuhr characterized the American purpose when he wrote that "except in moments of aberration we do not think of ourselves as the potential masters, but as the tutors of mankind in its pilgrimage to perfection."[3] We would use our power and influence to conduct a kind of global tutorial on our principles of representative government, the rule of law, free trade and market capitalism, individual freedom, and the values of Judeo-Christian civilization. The American world order gave birth to the United Nations, the Bretton Woods system for promoting international trade and economic development, and a multitude of new institutions including the International Monetary Fund, the World Bank, the General Agreement on Tariffs and Trade, and the Universal Declaration of Human Rights.

To remake Japan to conform to this new order, the American Occupation undertook the most intrusive international reconstruction of another nation in modern history. It was the most extreme of a great many American interventions in the domestic affairs of other countries, and its perceived success encouraged later US interventions elsewhere in the world.[4] Our persistent belief in the United States as a chosen nation with a unique role in world history found its most elaborate fulfillment in the opportunity to remake Japan's ancient and complex civilization. Undeterred by our deep cultural differences with Japan, we set out to refashion the political, economic, and social order of Japan and even its ways of thought and behavior to match America's own institutions and values. A defeated Japan was denied the opportunity to reform its institutions in accordance with its own cultural values. For Americans, the high moral purpose with which we approached the making of world order justified the contradictions of imposing democracy and overriding traditional liberal principles of self-determination.

The Occupation, however, immediately made compromises with the reality in Japan—compromises that bring into question the wisdom of having stubbornly adhered to the unconditional surrender policy. We kept the emperor and the powerful conservative bureaucracy as necessary to implement the revolutionary reforms in the first years of the Occupation. Still more compromises with the unconditional surrender policy came when the Cold War disrupted the American design of a unified world order. The United States abandoned its ill-considered wartime goal of a permanently disarmed Japan. To meet the challenges of the bipolar conflict, reforms were sharply curtailed and American policymakers began working closely with Japanese conservative leaders, even including former designated war criminals, to rehabilitate and remilitarize Japan to serve as America's chief ally in Asia.

The United States created new international institutions for the Cold War. In Europe, the most important was the North Atlantic Treaty Organization. In Asia, it was the US-Japan alliance. Japan was subordinated in the American Cold War order. Yoshida Shigeru, Japan's shrewd postwar leader, privately contrived to accept a long-term military alliance and US bases in Japan in return for an end to the Occupation. This hegemonic alliance subordinated Japan in the US-led struggle against the Soviet bloc and powerfully shaped the course of postwar Japan. Although the Occupation officially ended in 1952, Secretary of State John Foster Dulles privately described the alliance as, in effect, a continuation of the Occupation. Japan's sovereignty was lastingly compromised.

For Japanese of all persuasions, incorporation into the American Cold War system was an unhappy reality. What they sought more than anything was economic recovery, restoring their good name in the world, and regaining their national independence. Still deeply traumatized by memories of wartime suffering and sacrifice, the Japanese people feared being drawn into the bipolar conflict by the military alliance and the presence of US bases. Spontaneous public uprisings erupted in the 1950s against American hydrogen bomb testing in the Pacific, US bases in Japan, and continuation of the alliance. Popular goals of peace and neutrality in the Cold War culminated in massive outpouring of public opposition to Prime Minister Kishi Nobusuke, once a suspected war criminal but now supported by the Americans because of his commitment to rearmament and anticommunism. Millions of Japanese joined in the often violent uprising. It became a struggle over the nation's future, its democratic politics, its role in the world. It became a struggle for the soul of Japan. Although not successful in preventing renewal of the alliance, the popular demonstrations shaped Japanese politics for decades, demonstrating a massive popular embrace of pacifism and an opposition to involvement in the Cold War and positioning Americans in the awkward and ironic support of a conservative and unpopular Japanese leadership in apparent disregard for Japanese democratic aspirations.

The alliance became a twisted and contradictory one, lacking common purpose. For the Americans, it became a means to control Japanese foreign policy, ensuring that Japan did not choose neutrality in the Cold War and that it allow American military bases so critical to the US doctrine of forward deployment. Japanese leaders found ways to successfully adapt to their subordination in the American Cold War order. They formulated a unique strategy of pursuing their economic interests while passively deferring to American military and political domination. Depending on the security guarantee provided by American bases and on generous US aid, technology, and market access, the Japanese devoted their own resources and energies to building an economic powerhouse that restored Japan to international influence and prestige, while steering clear of active involvement in America's Cold War struggles. That they could legitimate their passive role by the no-war clause in the US-authored constitution contributed to mounting American frustration.

The Japanese engaged in a long struggle to rework and implement the US-imposed liberal economic, social, and political institutions to fit with their historical circumstances and cultural preferences. Despite Americans' confidence in the universality of their values and belief that progress would inevitably move Japan to converge with the model of the US institutions, Japan adhered to a different course and shaped its own path to modernity. Rather than adopt the principles of classical economics and the free market laws and institutions established in the Occupation, Japanese economists instead formulated a brilliant economic strategy to take advantage of the free trade principles of the new international economic order. Flouting those very principles, they fashioned a high-growth strategy of economic nationalism and state-led capitalism to catch up with the advanced industrial nations. Their strategy proved so successful that it became a model for other later developing economies and a challenge to the liberal economic paradigm and led to a series of bilateral US-Japan trade conflicts.

In the most ambitious and audacious aspect of its reforms, the Occupation set out to remake the values and institutions of Japanese society, even to change the ways of Japanese thought. As Kennan observed, "We . . . somewhat brashly undertook to show them how to live, in this modern age, more happily, more safely, and more usefully, than they had lived before."[5] Since its first full encounter with the West in the Meiji period, Japan had been resistant to any shared belief in universal moral values. Moral values were the values of the community to which one belonged. Through new laws and principles of education, Americans sought to reshape the most basic institutions in Japanese society, including the family, gender relations, and religious practice. Although Japanese have often found the new values liberating and have adopted some aspects of the liberal value system and its institutions, they have implemented them in their own distinctive ways. Japan has maintained its own unique social norms and patterns of behavior. Its society has not converged with American ideals of individualism, human rights, and gender equality.

Americans have often taken pride in bringing democracy to Japan. While it is true that the Occupation authored a democratic constitution to replace the imperial sovereignty of the Meiji Constitution, the reality is that democracy must be achieved to be viable. Like the Meiji Constitution of 1889, which was bestowed on his people by the emperor, the MacArthur Constitution was issued to the Japanese people. Japan never achieved a democratic revolution on its own. Japan became a democracy not through the imposed constitution but rather through an evolutionary process in which waves of popular movements in the postwar period made government increasingly accountable by demanding that it respect the welfare of the community rather than the special interests. In this process, democracy in Japan has acquired its distinctive communitarian characteristics. Despite the most intensive and intrusive intervention to reconstruct its society and political economy according to Western liberal values, Japan has maintained its own unique domestic order—even while slowly accommodating greater democratization. The weight of Japan's history and culture could not be overridden by claims of a supposed universal pattern of development.

Finally, we consider how early in the twenty-first century the American-dominated international order is eroding and how the postwar period of extraordinary American domination of Japan is passing. In Asia, power is in unprecedented flux. As power gravitates rapidly to the region's new emerging powers, the framework of rules and institutions established in the post–World War II era is challenged by China as outdated and not reflective of the changing distribution of international power. The American-led world order is undergoing fundamental changes in ways that test American primacy in the Asia Pacific region and make a new and more reciprocal relationship with Japan critical to the US strategy to maintain its capacity for leadership. Responding to the uncertain future of regional order, Japan is undergoing a sea change in its foreign policy. Its leaders have reinterpreted their constitution to allow for collective defense, they have established a national security infrastructure, and they have adopted a proactive foreign policy. In the words of its nationalist prime minister, Abe Shinzō, in 2013, "Japan is back." In 2016, as he prepared to make a historic visit of reconciliation to the war memorial at Pearl Harbor in response to President Barack Obama's visit months earlier to Hiroshima, Abe said, "I want to be able to demonstrate that 'the postwar era' has come to a complete end."[6] In the twilight of the American Century, Japan is adopting a new activist role in international politics not seen since 1945.

1

Two Rising Powers

Victors in a war write its history—at least in the first instance. With victory comes the privilege of writing the master narrative of how the war came about, who was responsible, who were the heroes, who were the villains. The Asia Pacific War, according to victors' history, was brought on by Japanese military aggression in China and by the unprovoked attack on Pearl Harbor. In the Tokyo War Crimes Trials, the burden of the prosecution's case was formulated as an organized conspiracy to wage aggressive war to take over the Asian continent. The charge represented the victors' narrow view of history, according to which, beginning in 1928 with the first attempt to seize Manchuria, Japanese had step-by-step pursued a planned strategy of subduing its neighbors in disregard of treaties that had committed them to adhere to peaceful change and respect for the territorial integrity of other states. To explain the causes of the war as the product of a simple conspiracy, as the original narrative did, was to treat it in a vacuum.[1]

Historians have since described a much more complex reality. The Asia Pacific War had its roots in clashing visions of regional order between Americans and Japanese that were long standing. As Akira Iriye pointed out in his study of the origins of their estrangement early in the century, "The simultaneous development of Japan and the United States as empires was . . . crucial in determining their destinies."[2] The United States and Japan were both ambitious rising powers engaged in a contest for supremacy in the Pacific well before the 1930s. Soon after both countries acquired overseas empire for the first time, the contest took shape as a naval rivalry and as a competition for influence over a weak and divided China. The simultaneous emergence of the two countries as imperialists at the turn of the century ignited a sense of rivalry and inevitable conflict. The incipient rivalry was overlaid, as Iriye showed, by ideological and psychological factors, but "above all it was racial and cultural."[3] All of these factors crystalized in divergent visions of how regional order should be organized. Their opposing visions were rooted in sharply contrasting histories and values that marked their paths to power in the modern world. Understanding the contest between two rising powers as competing visions of regional order is at the heart of explaining what caused the Asia Pacific War and what came after.

The Ambitions of Rising Powers

At momentous times in modern history, a bit like the one in which we live in the early twenty-first century, which is experiencing the rise of China and India, the international system undergoes rapid change as newly powerful nations emerge and radically change the existing distribution of power in the world.[4] Nations rise and fall owing to changes in their relative wealth and power. Some states grow more rapidly than others as they find more effective ways to organize their societies and to introduce technological changes that make them more productive. History has taught us that such times often turn out to be disruptive of international peace and stability.[5] Rising powers often become troublemakers. They are ambitious. They expect to exercise greater influence, commensurate with their new capabilities. They challenge the existing order and the prevailing norms in the international system. They want to change international rules and practices in ways that favor their interests. Their new capabilities increase their goals and interests. They are tempted by opportunities to expand their access to new territories, by new sources of raw materials or markets, and by the lure of intangible gains in prestige. They increase their military spending. They are prone to excesses of nationalist pride. Buoyed, often intoxicated, by their growing power and wealth, they are driven to expand their influence and to gain their deserved place in the sun. Their rise challenges the prevailing balance of power. "The strong," Thucydides observed two millennia ago, "do what they have the power to do." The newly strong, we may add, do what they have the new power to do.

The dawn of the twentieth century was such a time in world politics. In Europe, Germany's rapid rise challenged British supremacy. In the Pacific, both Japan and the United States were new and still immature rising powers. Japan was Asia's first rising power. Becoming the first nation in Asia to industrialize and to modernize its institutions, Japan freed itself from the fetters of imperialism and set out to join the Western powers in their domination of the Asia Pacific region. With overseas colonies attained in the Sino-Japanese War of 1894–1895 and the Russo-Japanese War of 1904–1905 Japan joined the imperial powers. The United States was also a newly rising power in the Pacific. In a fateful turn of history, America acquired the Philippines and Guam in the Spanish-American War of 1898, a seemingly minor conflict. At the same time the United States also annexed Hawaii and thus at the turn of the century became a newly rising power in the Pacific.

At the turn of the century, conditions in both countries were optimum for their emergence on the world stage. Both had newly strengthened, centralized government structures whose leaders perceived their nation's new power and opportunities. Ambitious, prone to excesses of national pride, tempted to expand their influence, their coincident rise fated Japan and the United States to rivalry. Facing each other across the Pacific, Japan and the United States were both revisionist states determined to transform international order as they found it. They became locked in a struggle to create their own versions of a new order. Each had a different vision of what rules and norms and institutions should govern the region. Their clashing visions destined them to confront each other. It need not have led to conflict. Nothing is inevitable in history. Properly managed, the rise of new powers can be peaceful. Misconstrued and mishandled, it can have cataclysmic consequences.

Paths to Power: American Imperialism

At the time of its emergence in the world, the United States was a raw and immature power. Americans had expanded across their continent with a restless and unbridled energy that steadily pushed back the frontier until at last they reached the shores of the Pacific. Then, within the space of eighteen months in 1898 and 1899, the United States expanded into Hawaii, Guam, Wake Island, the Philippines, and Samoa. Abruptly, a new American frontier extended far out into the western Pacific to the edge of the Asian continent. Historians have struggled to explain why an Atlantic-oriented people acquired territory 10,000 miles from their nation's capital. It seemed "a great aberration"[6] from the anticolonial tradition stretching back to the foundation of the republic.

Americans never thought of themselves as being imperialists in the usual sense, but their westward movement across the continent in the nineteenth century was powered by notions of empire and their approach to Asia was a projection of their experience with a frontier. America owed its origins as a nation to a war for independence from an empire, and it always set itself against the imperialist ways of the Old World. If they kept the term for self-reference it would have a new, liberal meaning. Thomas Jefferson reveled in his vision of the North American continent becoming "an empire of liberty." Other founders contrasted their new empire with the old. Hugh Henry Breckinridge assured his fellow Pennsylvanians, "Oh my compatriots . . . you are now citizens of a new empire: an empire, not the effect of chance, not hewn out by the sword; but formed by the skill of sages, and the design of wise men."[7] They could foresee little effective resistance from the native peoples to expansion westward across the continent. The Jacksonian editor John L. O'Sullivan, who coined this expansion as a mission of "manifest destiny," foresaw "the far reaching, the boundless future will be the era of American greatness. In its magnificent domain of space and time, the nation of many nations is destined to manifest to mankind the excellence of divine principles."[8] The day would come when America could bring to bear these "divine principles" on the remaking of the world.

Expansion of America would bring the blessings of liberty, democracy, law, and Christian faith to other parts of the new world. In terms of their opportunities as well as their subsequent self-image, Americans were blessed with a vast wilderness into which they could expand and, "acting for all mankind," as Jefferson wrote, demonstrate "what is the degree of freedom and self-government in which a society may venture to leave its individual members."[9] Through their ideals and practice Americans would provide a template for world order.

The reality of their imperial expansion was never so morally elevated as Americans preferred to think. They were able to preserve their exceptionalist identity because the frontier was only lightly held by Native Americans, whose numbers were decimated by European diseases to which they lacked immunity. Although Americans did not see their experience in any way related to the imperialism of European nations, as they took Louisiana, Florida, Texas, California, and Oregon, in the historian Walter Nugent's harsh description, Americans acquired "habits of empire," whether through "diplomacy, filibustering, armed conquest, cheating and lying, ethnic cleansing, even honest purchase and negotiation."[10] Acquisition of new territory seemed American destiny. As the historian Charles Maier observes, "The United States benefited from many factors in its development—its founding on a continent that had no massive sedentary population north of Mesoamerica, its absence of most hereditary ranks, its access to 'free' land, its settling by emigrants from diverse societies, its religious pluralism, its opportunity to build political institutions afresh."[11] As they moved through the wilderness and crossed the continent, the faith in their exceptionalist beliefs took hold. Writing in 1850, Herman Melville expressed this faith that America was set apart by Providence for higher purposes of leading the progress of humankind when he wrote:

> We Americans are the peculiar, chosen people—the Israel of our time; we bear the ark of the liberties of the world. . . . The rest of the nations must soon be in our rear. We are the pioneers . . . ; the advanced guard, sent on through the wilderness of untried things to break a new path in the New World that is ours. . . . Long enough have we been skeptics with regard to ourselves and doubted whether, indeed, the political Messiah has come. But he has come in *us*, if we would but give utterance to his promptings.[12]

As John Winthrop proclaimed in 1630 in a sermon delivered on the eve of sailing to America, "wee shall be as a Citty upon a Hill, the eies of all people are upon us."[13] Americans were secure in a faith that Providence had set their land apart to be not just one nation among many but a nation marked by destiny, as Lincoln put it, to be the "last best hope of earth."[14] The theologian Reinhold Niebuhr observed, "We had a religious version of our national destiny which interpreted the meaning of our nationhood as God's effort to make a new beginning in the history of mankind."[15] Later, as immigrants from many nations arrived, it was these ideals that held the country together. The historian Richard Hofstadter once wrote that "it has been our fate as a nation not to have ideologies but to be one."[16] From the time of the nation's founding, the American revolutionaries claimed universal importance for their rebellion, asserting that their principles of liberty, equality, and free government were for all people. The American Revolution, as the historian Gordon Wood writes, "gave us our obsessive concern with our own morality and our messianic sense of purpose in the world. . . . Our conception of ourselves as the leader of the free world began in 1776."[17]

By the end of the nineteenth century continental expansion was virtually complete. In 1890 the US Census Bureau reported the closing of the American frontier. The century-long movement across the continent had come to an end.[18] Three years later, the American historian Frederick Jackson Turner gave his famous address on "the significance of the frontier in American history." His thesis became and remains one of the most influential, if controversial, pieces of historical interpretation of American national character. Turner observed that the frontier, "the meeting point between savagery and civilization,"[19] had promoted self-reliance, individualism, and democracy. With its continual promise of free land, opportunity, and new beginnings, the frontier shaped American character, giving it "that coarseness and strength combined with acuteness and acquisitiveness; that practical inventive turn of mind, quick to find expedients; that masterful grasp of material things . . . that restless, nervous energy; that dominant individualism,"[20] all of which made Americans distrustful and dismissive of centralized political power.

Five years after Turner's address, which interpreted the passing of the frontier as a watershed event, the Americans pushed out into the far Pacific, annexed Hawaii and Samoa, and in the Spanish-American War seized the Philippines and Guam when Admiral George Dewey defeated the Spanish fleet in the Battle of Manila. Woodrow Wilson, teaching at Princeton, embraced Turner's thesis that with the closing of the continental frontier "the first period of American history" had ended. The future president wrote in a 1901 essay in *The Atlantic* that America now had a new Pacific frontier.[21] In that same year, in a remarkable address marking the 125th anniversary of George Washington's crossing the Delaware to engage British and Hessian forces in the pivotal battle of Trenton, Wilson forecast a new era for the United States as revolutionary as the one that had begun the nation's history.

> This great pressure of a people moving always to new frontiers, in search of new lands, new power, the full freedom of a virgin world, has ruled our course and formed our policies like a Fate. It gave us, not Louisiana alone, but Florida also. It forced war with Mexico upon us, and gave us the coasts of the Pacific. It swept Texas into the Union. It made far Alaska

a territory of the United States. Who shall say where it will end? The census takers of 1890 informed us . . . that they could no longer find any frontier upon this continent. . . . We had not pondered their report a single decade before we made new frontiers for ourselves beyond the seas, accounting the seven thousand miles of ocean that lie between us and the Philippine Islands no more than the three thousand which once lay between us and the coasts of the Pacific. No doubt there is here a great revolution in our lives. No war ever transformed us quite as the war with Spain transformed us. No previous years ever ran with so swift a change as the years since 1898. We have witnessed a new revolution. We have seen the transformation of America completed. The little group of states, which one hundred and twenty-five years ago cast the sovereignty of Britain off, is now grown into a mighty power. That little confederacy has now massed and organized its energies. A confederacy is transformed into a nation. The battle of Trenton was not more significant than the battle of Manila.[22]

Wilson's assertion that the decisive battle that gave birth to the nation was no more important than the defeat of the impotent Spanish fleet is astonishing, but it is indicative of his excitement that America was to have a foreign empire. Wilson's rhapsodic address envisioned the western Pacific as America's new frontier, bringing new opportunities for trade and also for proselytizing American values and ideals.[23] He called the United States "the frontier nation." If the continental frontier was, as Turner described it, "the meeting place between savagery and civilization," America's new Pacific frontier was, for Wilson, the meeting place between backwardness and civilization.

The United States had long been interested in Pacific trade. Americans were participants in the system of informal imperialism that the British established in East Asia in the middle of the nineteenth century. Informal imperialism infringed the sovereignty of Asian countries for the purpose of trade and commercial advantage, while avoiding the burden of territorial and political controls. Americans were the face of this informal imperialism as the Japanese first confronted it. While the British focused their attention on opening China to trade, the Americans took the lead in Japan. Commodore Matthew Perry imposed an initial treaty in 1854 and Townsend Harris, America's first diplomatic representative in Japan, negotiated the Treaty of 1858, which was soon followed by similar treaties that the other Western powers imposed on Japan. The treaties forced open its backward economy for trade, placing its tariffs under international control and giving Western traders extra-territorial rights.

By the end of the nineteenth century, American interest in the Pacific entered a new era. American ambition for empire in the Pacific was a reflection of its burgeoning industrial power since the Civil War. In the 1880s the United States surpassed Britain as the world's leading manufacturing state. From 1870 to the eve of World War I, the American growth rate was 80 percent higher than Britain's. By 1900 the United States had 24 percent of the world's manufacturing output, while Britain had 18 percent.[24] At the turn of the century the strong presidencies of McKinley, Roosevelt, Taft, and Wilson translated this industrial might into ambition for world influence. "God," Senator Albert Beveridge assured his colleagues in 1900 after returning from travel in Asia, ". . . has made us the master organizers of the world to establish system where chaos reigns. He has given us the spirit of progress to overwhelm the forces of reaction throughout the earth. He has made us adepts in government that we may administer government among savage and senile peoples. . . . He has marked the American people as His chosen nation to finally lead in the regeneration of the world."[25]

In the nineteenth century, pride in their institutions was typically expressed in a belief that America should be an example for the rest of the world—the Puritan ideal of a city on the hill. It was the virtue of America's foreign policy, John Quincy Adams said in his Independence Day address in 1821, that America "has abstained from interference in the concerns of others, even when conflict has been for principles to which she clings. . . . She goes not abroad in search of monsters to destroy." The United States would not use military force to intervene abroad. "She is the well-wisher to the freedom and independence of all. She is the champion and vindicator only of her own."[26] In the new century, America was to take on the responsibility of actively spreading and encouraging the acceptance of its institutions abroad. As president, Wilson would insist that American principles were "not the principles of a province or of a single continent . . . [but] the principles of a liberated mankind."[27]

Paths to Power: Japanese Imperialism

Japan, as Asia's first rising power, followed a path to power radically different from that of the United States. Like other Asian nations, Japan entered the international system as both economically backward and a victim of Western imperialism. Few countries had enjoyed the degree of isolation, self-sufficiency, and free security that Japan enjoyed for its entire history up to the mid-nineteenth century. This free security gave rise to a unique civilization and a fierce sense of a distinctive identity. Because Japan is a natural nation-state, its borders determined by the sea rather than treaties, its history up to the middle of the nineteenth century was lived almost entirely within the islands. Japan's submission to the Western imperialist system deprived the Japanese of their security, their independence, and their unchallenged sense of self. The infringement of their sovereignty sparked the overthrow of the old Tokugawa government in 1868 and set Japan on a determined course to acquire power equal to the Western imperial nations and to restore its independence.

The nature of a nation's modern revolution tells a good deal about the character of its subsequent history. The Meiji Restoration of 1868, Japan's modern revolution, was unlike other great revolutions of modern history in that it had no mission to remake humanity. It made no assertion of an egalitarian ethos rooted in universal values. It was not a democratic revolution. Had Japan's modern revolution been carried out by a rising middle class overthrowing the old elite in the name of new values and political rights, its modern history would have taken a different direction. But this was not the case. The Meiji Restoration was carried out "from above," by a party within the old ruling class. Led by young, low-ranking members of the traditional samurai elite, it was not a change in the name of new values such as liberty, equality, and inalienable human rights. Rather, it was motivated by the values inherited from Japan's long feudal period—values of power, status, realism, and respect for hierarchy.

The Meiji Restoration left modern Japan a legacy of social conservatism. The old order bequeathed three pillars of conservatism: six centuries of feudalism, the communal village in which the great majority of Japanese lived, and the institution of the extended family. The Meiji Restoration restored the emperor to the center of power and maintained the traditional respect for social hierarchy. There was no redistribution of land as occurred in many modern revolutions that tore apart existing social orders in a knock-down, drag-out struggle. What the restoration did do in the way of revolutionary social change was to open positions of leadership in the social hierarchy to those who mastered the new modern knowledge imported from the West. The resulting meritocratic principles brought new blood into the government—a bright, young, and highly motivated elite determined to create a powerful nation-state.[28] The new elite grasped the reality of the competitive struggles that must be waged for the nation's survival. They responded to the challenges of Western imperialism not with resistance but with a marked realism, pragmatism, and opportunism that led the Japanese alone among Asian peoples to accommodate quickly to the norms, principles, and mores of the imperialist system.

The essential purpose of Japan's modern revolution was to adopt modern knowledge, science, and technology to strengthen the nation and seek to make it the equal of the advanced military and industrial powers. It was a nationalist revolution designed to adapt to the international system. Attentiveness to power and the disposition to strengthen the nation at whatever cost legitimated a cultural revolution unique in modern world history. As one historian put it, the importing of Western culture during the Meiji period (1868–1912) "still stands as the most remarkable transformation ever undergone by any people in so short a time."[29]

The Meiji leaders thus set out to organize the nation internally so as to achieve its external goal of catching up with the West. They shrewdly created the most highly centralized state in the nation's history and adopted a broad program of reforms to enhance its power. Universal conscription, a universal system of compulsory education, an efficient new land tax, and a modern banking system all came in rapid order. The new leadership instituted an industrial policy designed to rapidly import the most advanced technology that the West could offer. Showing an astonishing readiness to emulate the practice of the advanced industrial countries, the government hastened the adoption of the new technology and new institutions by hiring more than 3,000 foreign advisors over the course of the Meiji period. The Meiji leaders adopted Westernized legal codes and a Prussian-inspired constitution to impress on the powers the civilized progress of Japan. The Meiji Constitution of 1889 and the opening of a parliament (Diet) with an elected lower house were crowning achievements. These policies meant, ultimately, not only the pursuit of industry but also of empire. Foreign Minster Inoue Kaoru summed up Meiji policy in 1887 as follows: "What we must do is to transform our empire and our people, make the empire like the countries of Europe, and our people like the peoples of Europe. To put it differently, we have to establish a new, European-style empire on the edge of Asia."[30]

In sharp contrast to the United States, whose power was bestowed on it by a vast continent rich in the resources required to feed its burgeoning industry, Japan's power was achieved by a feat of national will and a single-minded determination to overcome the obstacles posed by a stingy environment, a backward economy, and an infringed sovereignty. Japan made the best of the advantages it inherited from the pre-Meiji era—a productive agriculture, a literate and healthy population, and a well-ordered system of administrative governance. Drawing on the powerful conservative legacy, the government mobilized the people with nationalist goals and an ideology that inculcated loyalty to the emperor and service to the state. Japan's strength was the discipline with which it marshaled its limited resources. Its greatest assets were social coherence, an efficient bureaucracy, and a well-trained military. National power was to be achieved by unremitting hard work, unity, and the sacrifice necessary for the long march to industrial and military power. Lest the adoption of Western culture cause a loss of national identity, Shinto, a simple agrarian faith, was reworked to focus worship of the imperial institution. Descended from the Sun Goddess Amaterasu, the emperor was the head of the family state having a unique blood and spiritual relationship with his people. This ideology was at the heart of a unique Japanese polity or *kokutai* and nationalist ideology that was inculcated through education, the military, and a myriad of state-sponsored organizations.

Because the Meiji Restoration did not radically disrupt society and left intact a respect for authority, Japan had both a strong society and a strong state to pursue its policies of industrial and military strength (*fukoku kyōhei*). These policies bore fruit by the turn of the century as the nation completed a modern constitutional state, reformed its laws, made the transition to an industrial economy, and succeeded in ending Western infringements of its sovereignty. Adapting to the prevailing mores of the imperialist system, the Meiji state was ready to overcome challenges to its regional security. The Sino-Japanese War of 1894–1895 drove out Qing influence on the Korean peninsula, gave Japan colonial possession of Taiwan and commercial treaty concessions in China, and brought Japan fully into the imperialist system as a new power.

Meiji imperialism was initially defensive and preemptive. The power vacuum in East Asia and the encroachment of the imperial powers made it imperative that Japan look to its strategic interests. The prevailing political instability of East Asia outside of Japan created both problems and opportunities. Japan's more rapid development, together with the institutional backwardness of other countries in East Asia and the fear that these weak governments were giving Western powers control, impelled Japan to assert its influence over its neighbors. Western encroachment on old impotent governments in Korea and China at the end of the nineteenth century jeopardized Japan's security as well as access to the raw materials and markets of East Asia. To ensure its dominance of the Korean peninsula and thwart Russian influence in Manchuria, the Russo-Japanese War of 1904–1905 set Japan on a path to colonize Korea and to establish its sphere of influence in Manchuria.

Meiji imperialism scrupulously adhered to the practices of the Western powers and depended on British and American financing. Accommodating to the liberal international economic order, Japan adopted the Gold Standard in 1897, which opened access to massive borrowing in London and New York to finance the Russo-Japanese War, industrial development, and the carving out of a continental empire in Korea and China. A prominent economic historian labels its expansion prior to World War I as "dependent imperialism."[31] Later, the constraints of the Gold Standard on domestic policy came to be seen as part of the hegemony of the Western liberal world order from which nationalists sought to free Japan. But at the turn of the century, adoption of the Gold Standard was a mark of Japan's rising international prestige and its entry into the company of the great powers.

No event contributed more to this prestige than the Russo-Japanese War. Impressed by Japan's new power, President Theodore Roosevelt wrote to Senator Henry Cabot Lodge in 1905, "As for Japan, she has risen with simply marvelous rapidity, and she is as formidable from the industrial as from the military standpoint. She is a great civilized nation."[32] In the aftermath of this war, which his mediation ended, Roosevelt came to see Japan's rising power as a challenge to American influence in the Pacific.

A Contest for Supremacy

Today, in the twenty-first century, the United States is engaged in "a contest for supremacy"[33] in the Asia Pacific region with the rising power of China. It is a contest that bears some resemblance to the contest with

Japan a century earlier. A major difference, however, is that in the twentieth century both the United States and Japan were rising powers intent on changing the international system, whereas today the United States is a status quo power in relative decline and defending an international order that it had already created.

Japanese-American rivalry was a contest between two willful and ambitious powers. It began at the outset of the twentieth century as British power in East Asia began to wane. Britain had ruled the waves since the Napoleonic Wars, but, faced with the rise of Germany in its own neighborhood, quietly decided to scale back its naval power in the Far East. The Anglo-Japanese Alliance, signed in 1902, marked a triumph for Japan, while for England it provided support of its interests even while drawing down its power in East Asia.

The upshot of the British drawdown was that when the Russo-Japanese War ended in 1905, the United States and Japan confronted each other across the Pacific, bent on using their growing power to gain command of the Pacific, dominate its commerce, and influence the fate of China. It was a clash of national wills that played out in a variety of issues that arose in the years immediately after 1905. Expansionism was expressed not only through conquest and colonization but also through migration, tourism, trade, foreign investment, and the spread of cultural values.

The American thrust into the far Pacific created a security dilemma with Japan. Both states, by seeking to ensure the security of their interests and by taking measures to enhance their power, aroused the suspicion, distrust, and insecurity of the other, thereby stimulating an ongoing competition for power and security.[34] The US Navy drafted a strategy in 1906, known as War Plan Orange (orange was the code name the Navy assigned to Japan), to combat the hypothetical threat. The US Navy therefore hypothesized Japan as its number one potential enemy.

Roosevelt, who more than anyone had been responsible for the acquisition of the Philippines, now recognized the vulnerability of the new colony. Its distance from the United States, the president wrote in a 1907 letter to Secretary of War William Howard Taft, made the Philippines "our heel of Achilles. They are all that make the present situation [with Japan] dangerous."[35] With his keen sense of the balance of power, Roosevelt saw Japan's growing power after the Russo-Japanese War as a threat to American interests and dispatched the American fleet of sixteen battleships on a round-the-world tour principally to impress the Japanese with US power.

In 1907, the Japanese Navy designated the US Navy as its principal hypothetical enemy and in a document that mirrored War Plan Orange set forth a policy to ensure Japanese "supremacy in the Western Pacific and prevent the United States from forceful intervention in China."[36] Although the earlier motivations of Japan's leaders were primarily defensive and preemptive, the drive for more advantage and influence now took on an offensive strategy. The strategic requirements of the empire included both insular possessions and continental territory. The rising Army leader Tanaka Giichi wrote in 1906, "We must disengage ourselves from the restrictions of an island nation and become a state with continental interests."[37]

In these years, no one thought more deeply about the implications of the two rising powers than the American naval strategist Alfred Thayer Mahan. In 1910, Admiral Mahan, whose 1890 book *The Influence of Sea Power on History* had attracted as much attention in Japan as in the United States, identified Japan as "the problem state of Asia." His views were sought not only by Theodore Roosevelt but also by his young cousin Franklin Roosevelt. Mahan became convinced that America's next war would be with Japan because of rivalry for influence over China, the "inflammable" issue of Japanese immigration in the United States, and the exposed position of Hawaii and the Philippines.[38] To the young Franklin Roosevelt, who in 1913 was appointed assistant secretary of the navy, Mahan wrote that Japan's ambition in China might develop "that sense of proprietorship" that "easily glides into the attempt at political control that ultimately means control by force."[39] Franklin Roosevelt was greatly influenced by Mahan's writings, and his position in the Wilson administration left him with an attachment to the navy and a keen interest in the contest for supremacy with Japan. His interest went deeper because of his maternal grandparents' activity in the early American China trade. His close associates later recalled his fondness for describing this family connection, which gave him the "deepest sympathy for the Chinese" in their relations with Japan.[40]

In addition to the naval rivalry, the other fundamental contest between Japan and the United States was the future of a weak and divided China. Although US trade and investment in China were very small and remained so, Americans saw in China the prospect of a future market for their goods. Secretary of State John Hay in 1899 and 1900 sent notes to the other imperial powers asking for their agreement to maintain the "open door" to trade and to refrain from partitioning China. US export trade with China by 1920 was less than 2 percent of total US export trade. The entire US foreign investment in East Asia in the 1930s was only 5 or 6 percent of its total investment abroad. Typically, the US exported five times more goods to Japan than to China.[41] It was the prospect of future gains that swayed US business interests.

More influential than the economic prospects was the sentimental interest in China. In the progressive politics of the first decades of the twentieth century, Americans were excited by the overthrow of the Qing dynasty in 1911 and the establishment of a republican government that looked to America for support. Its leaders, including Sun Yat-sen, proclaimed democratic ideals and cited Abraham Lincoln as their model. The Chinese Republic came to be regarded as a younger brother or ward of the American people. Mingled with this political attraction was the missionary impulse. Of the 3,800 Protestant missionaries that America sent abroad in the early twentieth century, 3,100 went to China.[42] While Japan had been noticeably less receptive to Christian proselytization, China seemed to hold endless prospects for conversion. Most American churches maintained connections to at least one missionary in China. The influence of American missionaries on public opinion was deep and abiding. George Kennan, reflecting later in his life on "the unnecessary war with Japan," was inclined to lay a great deal of blame on "the American missionary movement, with its powerful pro-Chinese and anti-Japanese bias."[43] Among Americans the contest for supremacy was profoundly shaped by attitudes and perceptions, and it was this sentimental interest together with the dream of a China market that swayed American sympathy. China became, as the Stanford historian David Kennedy observed, "the central paradox of America's Asian diplomacy: the United States wanted to champion Chinese sovereignty and to control developments in Asia, even in the absence of any substantial American interests on the ground; at the same time, Washington resisted the commitment of any appreciable economic, diplomatic, or military resources to the region. Here was a perilous disconnect between American aspirations and American means, a gap between the national wish and the national will." Time and again, American policies were founded on attitudes rather than clearly conceived strategy;

and "attitudes were dangerous guides to foreign policy, especially when they were premised on morally charged and uncompromisable principles rather than on negotiable material assets."[44]

On the other hand, for the Japanese, their weak neighbor seemed a natural place in which to extend its growing power and influence.[45] As Asia's first rising power, the Japanese believed they had a mission to teach the lessons of modernization and reform that they themselves had recently mastered. The belief that Japan was the natural leader of Asia was long held, and as its successful modern reforms were accomplished, the belief grew stronger. The great apostle of liberal reform Fukuzawa Yukichi recorded his inner ambitions for Japan in a highly revealing moment in 1882:

> Whenever I go abroad and stay in Europe or in the United States, I frequently have unpleasant experiences because the peoples of these nations tend to treat me less than cordially. Recently I took a voyage across the Indian Ocean. During that trip, I saw the English officers land on many places in China and elsewhere that they controlled. They were extremely arrogant and their attitude to the natives was so brazen that it was not possible to believe the English were dealing with the same human beings. In seeing all of this, my reaction was a mixture of pity for the natives and of envy for the English. Even now I cannot forget the promise I made secretly in my heart. We are Japanese and we shall some day raise the national power of Japan so that not only shall we control the natives of China and India as the English do today, but we shall possess the power to rebuke the English and to rule Asia ourselves.[46]

The Japanese regarded Western nations, especially now the United States, as interlopers, while Japan as an Asian nation had a legitimate role of leadership. World War I and the preoccupation of the Western powers with the conflict in Europe tempted a new generation of Japanese leaders to a bold expansion of its influence in China. When war broke out in August 1914, citing its alliance with England, Japan seized German-held islands in the Pacific (the Carolines, Marianas, Marshalls, Palau, and Yap) as well as the German sphere of influence in Shandong. Still more boldly, in January 1915, Japan announced a set of twenty-one demands that would establish hegemony over the weak new Chinese Republic. Facing strong Anglo-American opposition as well as internal disagreement, the Japanese backed down, but their ambition was clear for all to see.

When America entered the war in 1917 and the great powers were preoccupied in Europe, Prime Minister Terauchi Masatake (1916–1918) saw the war as an opportunity to restrain the "haughtiness" of the Europeans and make clear that "eventually, all of Asia should be under the control of our Emperor."[47] To achieve financial independence, Japan went off the Gold Standard and resumed an aggressive expansion. At the end of the war, under Terauchi's leadership Japan dispatched more than 70,000 troops into Siberia, ostensibly to counter Bolshevik influences. Japan's opportunistic attempts to expand, however, left it isolated and distrusted among the Western powers when the war ended.

Contending Visions of Order

World War I intensified the naval rivalry and the competition for influence over China, and gave rise to deeply divergent views of Asia's future. Both the United States and Japan were revisionist powers. Both sought to change the international order. Both held visions of how order in the Asia Pacific should be organized. While Japan was now a great power in Asia, America emerged from the war as the world's most powerful nation. The US economy was nearly triple the size of Britain's. With its burgeoning industrial output, financial capital, agricultural production, and sufficiency of raw materials, America's economic capacity was unrivaled. This preeminence, together with the decisive part it played in ending the European conflict, allowed it to dominate the peace settlement and introduce an American agenda for transforming international affairs.

Woodrow Wilson was the seminal figure in shaping the American people's dominant and lasting school of thought about their role in the world. He tapped into their distaste for the policies of the Old World. Wilson set out not simply to reform the old international system but rather to transcend it in accord with revolutionary ideals growing out of American history. He brought to the international stage a messianic version of American exceptionalist ideology. It was an ideology of international liberalism. The United States was to be a missionary for the principles of a new world order. Disdaining concepts of balance of power, alliances, spheres of influence, and secret agreements for the conduct of international relations, he advanced liberal ideals of self-determination and the sovereign rights of every people, accountable government, and the rule of law as the appropriate bases for international order. In Asia, Wilson's "new diplomacy" stressed opposition to international power rivalries at China's expense. Wilson later told his European counterparts at the Versailles Peace Conference in 1919 that there was "nothing on which the public opinion of the United States of America was firmer than on this question that China should not be oppressed by Japan."[48] The competition among the imperialists in East Asia, Wilson believed, would have to be replaced by a new order in which all would refrain from military and political expansion.

Wilson proposed a triad of liberal principles for world order. The first principle, the self-determination of all nations, was an essential condition of world peace. Empires must be replaced by democratic governments, which would adhere to the principle of national self-determination. The second principle, arms control, was new in Wilson's day. In his view the accumulation of weaponry was itself a cause of war. He proposed the reduction of all armaments to the lowest level consistent with national safety. The third principle was the open door, the removal of restraints on international trade. Where free trade was practiced, peace would prevail; nations joined in trade would share a common interest in preserving prosperity from the destruction of war.

Finally, if this triad was to endure, the key to a new international order was an institution that would reinforce these three principles and ensure peaceful settlement of disputes. The centerpiece of his agenda was the institution of collective security. Peace could be maintained by constructing a "community of power, not organized rivalries but an organized peace."[49] Anarchy in the international system would be overcome by an association of nations committed to these principles and that would provide mechanisms for dispute resolution and mutual security obligations.[50]

International liberalism was still embryonic in Wilson's day, but it resonated deeply with the American worldview taking shape in the early twentieth century. Such idealism could give birth to great military power to achieve its goals, but it was bound to bring disillusionment, as it soon did with the Americans' lapse into isolationism between the two world wars. Nevertheless, Wilson's international liberalism retained its hold on the American sense of mission in the world and became the dominant school of American foreign policy. For the realist Henry Kissinger, Americans lacked both the theoretical and the practical basis for the European-style diplomacy of constant adjustment of the nuances of power from a posture of moral neutrality for the sole purpose of preserving an ever-shifting balance. . . . Wilson . . . tapped his people's emotions with arguments that were as morally elevated as they were largely incomprehensible to foreign leaders.[51]

The Wilsonian approach to world order was anathema to the conservative values that came out of the Meiji Restoration and to the ambitions of Japan as a rising power. To the majority of Japanese leaders, the assertion of self-determination, territorial integrity, and the open door as principles of universal validity flew in the face of reality when applied to a weak and chaotic Asia. When told by an elder statesman that these principles would mean that Japan would have to fundamentally revise its policies on China, the future prime minister Inukai Tsuyoshi asked incredulously, "Are you saying that apart from economic relations Japan should desist from [territorial] expansion?"[52] The very idea that a nation must be governed by abstract principles equally applicable to all societies was scarcely credible and was met with a combination of skepticism and cynicism. The Japanese had no legacy of transcendental and universal values through which to understand international liberalism. To Japanese leaders, bred in a deep conservative tradition of realpolitik, the American rhetoric of international liberalism represented a guise for the preservation of the status quo in Asia.[53]

A Flawed American Order in Asia

The United States was not only a new rising power but also the primary world power, owing to the destruction wreaked on Europe during World War I. The United States, however, proved unwilling to fulfill the responsibilities in the international system that came with such preeminence. It used its wealth and power in an ineffective and inconsistent way. While boldly asserting abstract moral and legal principles that should govern international behavior in the region, the United States soon proved unwilling to maintain a balance of power to compel compliance with these principles.[54]

Although Wilson's vision of a new world order was shattered by the US Senate's rejection of the Versailles Treaty and of US membership in the League of Nations, Wilsonian principles survived in a postwar US initiative to establish a new regional order in Asia. Japan's rising military power since the Russo-Japanese War and unilateralism during World War I had provoked American distrust. The new Warren Harding administration was, if anything, more determined than Wilson to curb Japanese power. Republicans, no less than Democrats, were hostile to Japanese ambitions. The chairman of the Senate Foreign Relations committee, Henry Cabot Lodge, characterized Japan's expansionist ambitions as "the coming danger of the world."[55] Two years after Versailles, the United States convened the Washington conference of 1921–1922 to provide a new set of principles and institutions to guide the workings of the international system in East Asia. The United States pressed Japan to accept its concept of regional order in a set of treaties based on the Wilsonian principles of self-determination, disarmament, free trade, and collective security. The treaties were designed to contain further Japanese expansion in Northeast Asia and especially encroachment on China.

The most immediate and pressing issue at the conference was the emergent naval arms race.[56] The new secretary of state, Charles Evans Hughes, believed that stability required linking a political arrangement with a naval settlement. Hughes achieved a series of agreements. First was a naval arms limitation agreement. The Japanese agreed to a limitation on capital ships at 60 percent of the American and British fleets in return for which the British and Americans agreed not to fortify any islands between Singapore and Hawaii, in effect giving Japan naval supremacy in the western Pacific. The second was a nine-power treaty that committed the United States, Japan, Britain, and the other signatories to respect the territorial integrity, self-determination, and open door in China. Third, the United States pressed Britain to end the Anglo-Japanese alliance and replace it with a weak and harmless collective security treaty that simply provided for the United States, Japan, Britain, and France to consult should there be any threats to peace in the Pacific. It defined no particular obligations.

There were many flaws in the Washington Treaty System, as this regional order came to be known. The nonfortification agreement meant that the United States would be hard-pressed to keep its treaty commitment to uphold Chinese sovereignty should Japan choose to encroach on it. Here was a dangerous gap between commitment and capability. The Washington system lacked a viable enforcement mechanism to ensure compliance with its provisions. It had no institutional machinery or viable great power management to enforce its norms. Hughes seemed to believe that the agreements would be self-enforcing based on a cooperative approach, an agreed-on set of rules, and norms restraining the exercise of power.

The United States had made a treaty commitment to uphold the territorial integrity of China, but lacked the power and, as it would turn out, the will to maintain it. The Americans made clear their limited liability. As President Harding assured the Senate regarding the Washington agreement, "There is no commitment to armed force, no alliance, no written or moral obligation to join in defense." Accordingly, the Senate in ratifying it stipulated that it entailed no American commitment to use force to compel compliance to the treaty. Signing the treaty, Harding announced that it achieved the protection of the Philippines and that any aggression in the Pacific would be deterred by "the odiousness of perfidy" that the court of world opinion would render.[57] Americans naively believed that their principles were so incontrovertible that they would be self-enforcing through the moral suasion of world opinion. The Americans preferred to avoid costs and commitments implied by their stated goals. As a result, the agreements were dependent on the durability of moderates in the Japanese government who held that Japan's interests were best served by maintenance of friendly ties with the Americans. For the time being the moderates in Japan held power, but rising nationalist sentiment viewed the agreements as obstructing Japan's legitimate goals of leadership in Asia.

Pride and Prejudice

The skepticism that Japanese leaders felt toward the new American-led order in the Pacific was stirred by the racial prejudice so pervasive in American society. From the turn of the century, the racial antagonism that Japanese immigrants encountered on the West Coast of the United States as well as within other Anglo-Saxon countries was deeply wounding to nationalist pride. The highly developed and elaborate culture of honor that was the legacy of their long feudal experience made the Japanese hypersensitive to the discrimination against their migrant workers.

Racist views were found in every quarter of American society, even among the most sophisticated intellectual leaders. The highly respected

Archibald Cary Coolidge, professor of history at Harvard and a member of the American Peace Delegation in Paris, wrote that "the Japanese have entered so whole-heartedly into European civilization, and have proved themselves such adepts at it, that we can imagine their being regarded as one of the white peoples." Nevertheless, like hybrid dogs, they were unassimilable, for "if kinds that are too alien to one another are bred together, the product is a worthless mongrel." Coolidge, who in 1922 became the first editor of the elite journal *Foreign Affairs,* favored complete restriction on Japanese immigration.[58]

Japan's unhappy experience at the Versailles Peace Conference left a deep bitterness. Representing the only non-Western nation among the five great powers, it was ill at ease in a setting of Western leaders who sometimes treated it as a strange intruder. French prime minister Clemenceau was heard to remark to his foreign minister during one long meeting, "To think that there are blonde women in the world; and we stay closed up here with these Japanese, who are so ugly." No American was more sensitive to Japanese feelings, their aspirations as a rising

Anti-Japanese racial prejudice was rampant in prewar America. In 1923, the Hollywood Association started a campaign to expel Japanese from the California community. Bettmann / Getty Images / 514689290.

power, than Wilson's foreign policy advisor, Colonel E. H. House, who described the Japanese delegates at Versailles as "silent, unemotional, watchful."[59] House had written Wilson before the conference that Japanese interests must somehow be accommodated if they were to be successfully drawn into accepting the new order:

> We cannot meet Japan in her desire as to land and immigration, and unless we make some concessions in regard to her sphere of influence in the East, trouble is sure sooner or later to come. Japan is barred from all the undeveloped places of the earth, and if her influence in the East is not recognized as in some degree superior to that of the Western powers, there will be a reckoning.[60]

Recognized as one of the five great powers, Japan sought reassurance that it would be treated equally by the others in the new international order. Japanese delegates proposed a clause in the charter of the League of Nations that would endorse "the principle of the equality of nations and just treatment of their nationals." It was not, as it is often mistakenly interpreted, meant to express a universal principle.[61] Japan did not intend the principle to apply to Koreans, Chinese, or other non-Western peoples, for whom the Japanese themselves were surely not disposed to treat on the basis of equality. Instead, it was meant to ensure equal treatment of Japanese. As the historian Naoko Shimazu bluntly concluded in her study of the issue, "The Japanese sought to gain the status of honorary whites and nothing more."[62] Oblivious to their own version of racial supremacism, the Japanese were deeply offended by the failure of the United States and Great Britain to support the racial equality clause proposal for the League covenant. The young aristocrat Konoe Fumimaro, returning from Versailles, wrote in 1920:

> The causes of the anti-Japanese movement are various, but racial prejudice is one of them. That the white people—and the Anglo-Saxon race in particular—generally abhor colored peoples is an apparent fact, so blatantly observable in the U.S. treatment of its black population. I for one felt a sort of racial oppression more in London than in Paris, and furthermore, that sense was heightened upon my arrival in New York.[63]

From top to bottom, American society was pervaded by a strong sense of racial hierarchy. The young Franklin Roosevelt, to cite a particularly important example, held strong racist views. Much like his admired Mahan, who believed that Japanese immigrants were unassimilable,[64]

Roosevelt regarded racial mixing as unhealthy and argued that restriction of Japanese immigration was morally justifiable because it was reciprocal. In a 1923 article he wrote: "I do not believe that the American people now or in the future will insist upon the right or privilege of entry into an oriental country to such an extent as to threaten racial purity or to jeopardize the land-owning prerogatives of citizenship. I think I may sincerely claim for American public opinion an adherence to the Golden Rule."[65] It was certainly true that Japanese did not want Americans migrating to Japan, intermarrying, buying land, or seeking citizenship. But such goals were never consequential to Americans. The important point was that Americans' unwelcoming attitude toward Japanese immigrants was filtered through the Japanese strong feelings of honor and status and their sense of insecurity and vulnerability in a world dominated by the Anglo-American powers.

When Congress singled out the Japanese for exclusion in the Immigration Act of 1924, it seemed to affirm that racial discrimination was a national policy. This law deeply embittered the Japanese. Kaneko Kentarō, a Harvard graduate and friend of the Roosevelts, resigned as president of the America-Japan Society, regarding it as "a great insult to Japanese national honor." Nitobe Inazō, a graduate of Johns Hopkins, married to an American woman, and serving as undersecretary general of the League of Nations, resolved not to visit America unless the act was revised.[66]

In 1925, Roosevelt visited Warm Springs, Georgia, for treatment of his legs, which had been paralyzed by polio. While there, he wrote a column in the *Telegraph* (Macon, Georgia) newspaper justifying resistance to Japanese immigration on the West Coast and passage of the Japanese exclusion act as a step in preventing "the undesirability of mixing the blood of the two peoples":

> Californians have properly objected on the sound basic ground that Japanese immigrants are not capable of assimilation into the American population. . . . Anyone who has traveled in the Far East knows that the mingling of Asiatic blood with European or American blood produces, in nine cases out of ten, the most unfortunate results. There are, throughout the East, many thousands of so-called Eurasians—men and women and children partly of Asiatic blood and partly of European or American blood. These Eurasians are, as a common thing, looked down on and despised, both by the European and American who resides there, and by the pure Asiatic who lives there.[67]

The United States failed to engage a proud and sensitive nation, which it had neither the interest nor inclination to understand or appreciate. The treatment of the immigration issue was a continuous source of antagonism that played into Japanese nationalist feeling. Rising states present a special challenge to a system. As one writer observes, "The status quo powers must exhibit empathy, fairness, and a genuine concern not to offend the prestige and national honor of the rising power."[68] The Anglo-American powers had not done this. They failed to reach out to, much less understand, this proud but highly vulnerable and insecure new power. Driven in their national life by a complex psychology of ambition, pride, self-doubt, and anger, many Japanese came to believe that their goals could be fulfilled only when they were strong enough to create their own international order. On December 8, 1941, the prominent writer Itō Sei recorded in his diary his impression of the momentous events: "It is our destiny (*shukumei*) that the only way we will feel ourselves a first-rank people in the world (*sekai ichiryū-jin*) is by going to war with the first-class white nations."[69]

Japanese Revisionism

As they become stronger, rising powers expect to exercise a greater influence, commensurate with their new capabilities. They may be tempted by opportunities offered them, where obstacles are surmountable, to expand their access to new territories or new sources of raw materials or markets or the lure of intangible gains in prestige, leadership, and security. Depending on many factors, including the degree of their alienation, the nature of their domestic politics, and the willingness and skill of the other powers to cope with this dissatisfaction, the rising power may be prepared to seek the overthrow of the existing international system. In the 1930s Japan reached this point. As the first non-Western nation to emerge from imperial subjectivity and to industrialize, Japan pursued a vision of regional hegemony as a matter of self-realization.

The Washington Treaty System, which sought to contain Japanese expansion and stabilize the regional status quo, provoked a split among the Japanese political and military elites. In the 1920s moderates held the upper hand, believing that the nonfortification agreements ensured Japanese naval superiority in their home waters and that America's more powerful industrial economy and Japan's trade dependence required good bilateral relations. For the duration of the 1920s, moderates held to this course, limiting Japanese ambitions in China to economic advancement.

Throughout the decade, the turbulence of the Japanese economy encouraged moderates seeking stability to restore the Gold Standard and adhere to Western liberal orthodoxy. In 1930, Finance Minister Inoue Junnosuke, a loyal adherent to the liberal international economic order, returned Japan to the Gold Standard in what was "perhaps the greatest economic policy mistake in Japan's modern history."[70] Coming in the midst of the worldwide Great Depression, at the very moment that America and England chose a protectionist path that devastated the Japanese export market, Inoue's deflationary policy deepened the suffering of industrial and farm labor.

The social crisis provoked by the Depression provided the opportunity for a latent opposition determined to challenge the status quo and revise the framework set in place at the Washington conference. Even as the Naval Arms Limitation Treaty was signed, Katō Kanji, representing junior, hard-line naval officers at the conference, railed at its restrictions: "As far as I am concerned, war with America starts now. We'll take revenge on her. We will!"[71] These "revisionists" expressed a growing resentment of the Anglo-American powers that had their imperial domains but that denied Japan pursuit of its legitimate interests in East Asia. Naval officers found the arms limitations unacceptable and demanded the right to build beyond these restrictions.

The revisionist sentiment in the navy was matched by strategic thought in the army that held that Japanese autonomy required a self-sufficient industrial base and access to the resource-rich Manchuria, where Japan had acquired treaty rights in the Russo-Japanese War. To Ishiwara Kanji, the army's influential strategist, control of Manchuria was necessary because war with America was "inevitable."[72] When Japan's army unit that was stationed in Manchuria to protect its concessions found the right moment to seize the sprawling region in September 1931, the Washington System and US treaty commitment to uphold Chinese territorial integrity and the open door were put to the test. Distracted by the problems of the Great Depression, the United States and Great Britain abandoned their liberal tenets in favor of protectionist measures. Secure between two great oceans, Americans steadily withdrew from Wilsonian concerns for world order. Americans were not prepared to take any decisive action to support the regional order they had established. President Herbert Hoover told his cabinet, "Neither our obligation to China, nor our own interest, nor our dignity requires us to go to war" over Manchuria. Hoover allowed that he "would fight for the continental United States as far as anybody, but he would not fight for Asia."[73] Failing to get either Hoover or the British to take concerted action against the Japanese, Secretary of State Henry Stimson expressed moral condemnation of this "breaking of international law" and announced that the United States would not recognize the new puppet state of Manchukuo.[74]

The fundamental weakness of the international order in the Asia Pacific region was now laid bare. The Americans had made many missteps in Asia, which demonstrated that they were not prepared for the role of world leader. For an international system to be stable and enduring, the most powerful states must be committed to upholding its governing institutions and norms, through their prestige and their willingness to use force to preserve it. The Americans and the British broke with the liberal economic order they had created, and they failed to tend to the balance of power, much less recognize its validity as the basis for order. While declaring ratios of naval strength the United States neglected to maintain these ratios, while Japan built up to and beyond the agreed-on ratios. The dangerous gap between stated principles and the will to act embedded in the Washington System was now apparent. It was a critical moment. The success of the Manchurian Incident tipped the balance of power in Japanese politics. Revisionists were emboldened by the lack of effective resistance on the part of the Anglo-American powers and gained the upper hand in politics. As Ogata Sadako concluded in her study of the Manchurian Incident, "The absence of international opposition with teeth . . . drove [Japanese] foreign policy toward adventurism."[75] Moreover, the new Japanese colony of Manchukuo ignited a wave of populist nationalism. Through the media and popular culture, with the dispatch of hundreds of thousands of Japanese settlers to the new territory, as well as through tens of thousands of professionals taking up the work of economic development, empire building became a popular enterprise. The entire society was invested emotionally and materially in the new colony. As the historian Louise Young concludes, "By the end of the decade [after the Manchurian Incident] the Japanese commitment to Manchukuo

Following the Manchurian Incident of September 18, 1931, Japanese troops
seized the vast region and established the puppet state of Manchukuo.
Keystone / Getty Images / 2696432.

had escalated to a scale and complexity that left policy makers with few
options for retreat."[76]

The ambitions of rising powers are fed by nationalism that is typically sponsored by leaders but that often slips out of their control. This
was particularly so in Japan, where decades of indoctrination had mobilized a populace highly receptive to the appeal of the most extreme
nationalist slogans. In the aftermath of the Manchurian Incident, Japan
withdrew from the League of Nations in 1933, and revisionists in the
army and navy were emboldened to pursue their expansionist goals, no
longer restrained by the discredited Washington treaties. It was not solely
in the military, or even in the zealous right-wing extremist organizations, that ultranationalism held sway. Elite bureaucrats drew on
European fascist state planning that they believed would not only over-

come liberal capitalist inefficiency but enable Japanese regional hegemony by mobilizing all the resources of the nation.[77] Japan left the Gold
Standard and embarked on policies of economic nationalism and state
control that insulated Japan from the international financial system. Extremes of nationalist ideology gripped every part of Japanese society.

Official indoctrination characterized Anglo-American values of individualism, liberalism, and capitalism as motivated by materialism and
egocentrism. In contrast, Japanese society had its foundations in spiritual commitments of selfless loyalty to the entire community. As a result,
society attained a natural harmony and solidarity in which everyone
found their proper place. This moral order had divine origins in the
unique imperial line, and Japan consequently had a mission to extend
its blessing to other peoples.

In the sharpest possible contrast to the American self-image of
exceptionalism, the Japanese thought of their society as unique.[78] In a
profoundly conservative statement of Japan's uniqueness (*mezurashisa*),
the Kyoto University philosopher Watsuji Tetsurō, who shaped the official ideology in the 1930s, stressed the precedence accorded society over
the individual. The Japanese spirit was embodied in social solidarity
found first in the family, "a cooperative group of selfless human beings,"
and in a further ethical sense of service to the larger society, the state,
and the emperor. Other states in Asia had a sense of such solidarity, but
Japan, in its devotion to its emperor, had carried this achievement to its
highest level. The result was that Western individualism, materialism,
and rationalism and their political outgrowths of parliamentary democracy and radical social movements of rebellion and resistance were neither appropriate to Japan nor in any way morally superior. By their racial purity and collective loyalty to an emperor descended from the
gods, the Japanese were "the leading race" (*shidō minzoku*), destined to
organize other Asian peoples, free them from the oppression of Western
imperialism, and create a new regional hierarchy in which every people
could find their "proper place."

Anglo-American complacency left the regional system in an anarchic
condition, opening the way for Japanese opportunism. Foreign Minister
Hirota Kōki announced in the Diet on February 22, 1934, that Japan
would undertake responsibility for creating a new regional order. "The
path of a rising nation," he said, "is always strewn with problems. . . .
Japan, serving as the only cornerstone for the edifice of peace in East

Asia, bears the entire burden of its responsibilities."[79] In an atmosphere dominated by rabid nationalist sentiment and demands for fulfilling its imperial destiny, under erratic leadership, Japan blundered into all-out war with China in 1937. The new prime minister Konoe Fumimaro, long a proponent of revisionism, foolishly underrated Chinese nationalism and regarded the government of Chiang Kai-shek as an obstruction that could be readily overcome on the way to a new order. The atrocities committed by the Japanese army as it undertook all-out military action to subdue Chinese resistance belied the pan-Asian claims of Japanese slogans. The brutal rape and massacre of many tens of thousands of Chinese in a rampage by Japanese troops in the capital city of Nanjing in 1938 left a lasting outrage against the invaders.

Japan increasingly made common cause with Germany and Italy, which like Japan were intent on creating a new order. In the autumn of 1940, as Holland and France fell to Germany and invasion of England seemed imminent, their Asian colonies became targets of opportunism. Foreign Minister Matsuoka Yōsuke announced plans to create a Greater East Asian Coprosperity Sphere. Japan entered into the Tripartite Pact with the fascist powers in Europe, by which the signatories pledged to aid one another if attacked by a power not currently involved in the European war or the fighting in China. Tokyo thereby hoped to isolate the United States and dissuade it from resisting Japanese seizure of European colonies in Southeast Asia.[80] In a monumental misreading of the consequences, the reckless and unstable Japanese foreign minister Matsuoka Yōsuke believed that the pact would keep the Americans out of conflict with Japan, but it had the opposite effect.

The Americans at last began to awaken to their mistakes of abandoning the Washington Treaty System together with the liberal economic order, both of which they had created. America now saw the fascist challenge in Asia and Europe as linked and faced the specter of confronting hostile hegemonies in both regions. The fateful signing of the Axis Pact greatly diminished the possibilities for peacefully resolving the historical differences that had accumulated between the two rising powers since the turn of the century. US interests in the region were not so great as to warrant total war, but when the issues in Asia were linked to the issues in Europe they grew more intractable. The historian Hata Ikuhiko describes the pact as "the point of no return" in which "the already narrow range of choices narrowed even further."[81] Avoiding

conflict now would require the most skillful diplomacy, of which neither country proved capable.

At this late hour, the Americans stiffened their resolve, confident—
overconfident—that Japan could be brought to heel because of its heavy
dependence on the United States for machine tools, raw materials, and,
above all, oil. The Roosevelt administration imposed crippling economic
sanctions and an embargo. As the president conceived it, the United
States would "slip the noose around Japan's neck and give it a jerk now
and then."[82] Assistant Secretary of State Dean Acheson, who helped
tighten the embargo beyond what the president intended, was certain
that it would not lead to war because "no rational Japanese could believe that an attack on us could result in anything but disaster for his
country."[83] Roosevelt later said he only wanted "to bring Japan to
its senses, not to its knees."[84] George Kennan, along with many historians, subsequently faulted the mishandling of the embargo with pro-
voking war.[85]

Negotiations between Secretary of State Cordell Hull and Japanese
ambassador to Washington Nomura Kichisaburō over the standoff
foundered in a morass of misperception and ineptness. To lift the embargo, Hull repeatedly insisted on returning to the principles of the
Washington System. For a time, Roosevelt toyed with the idea of a modus
vivendi with the Japanese, but ultimately he sided with Hull's principled stance and reliance on economic pressure to bring about Japanese
submission. As the historian Christopher Thorne observed, "Where only
step-by-step, practical bargaining might just conceivably have succeeded,
Hull based his approach in 1941 on sweeping general principles, admirable in themselves, but inappropriate if the aim were to secure a *modus
vivendi.*"[86]

In a summary, "astringent"[87] note to the Japanese on November 26,
Hull insisted that in order for the crippling embargo to be lifted, Japan
must withdraw its forces from Southeast Asia and China, accept the
Open Door, and renounce the Tripartite Pact. The Japanese leaders
viewed the American demands in Hull's note as a humiliating ultimatum. To them, as the historian Eri Hotta writes, "it was as if the
United States were demanding an unconditional surrender without
having fought and won a war with Japan."[88] In fact, Hull's note did fore-
shadow the uncompromising approach that Roosevelt subsequently
adopted in his unconditional surrender policy. The Americans failed to

Secretary of State Cordell Hull with Japanese ambassador Nomura Kichisaburō (left) and Special Envoy Kurusu Saburō as they arrive at the White House for negotiations, November 17, 1941. Underwood Archives / Getty Images / 142629620.

negotiate in a step-by-step process that might have averted conflict. As war in both Europe and Asia now loomed, the greatly enlarged international context in which US-Japan differences were now treated in Washington made the resolution of issues far more difficult. The historian Waldo Heinrichs, in his meticulous study of the complex context in which decisions were reached, concludes that compromise was rejected because of "growing American interest in forging and sustaining a coalition" to defeat the aligned fascist powers. In the employment of the embargo, "President Roosevelt failed to understand the desperation and determination of the Japanese, and like most Americans, severely underrated their capabilities."[89]

In a crisis of their own making, Japan's leaders equated American demands of withdrawal from China as jeopardizing Japan's survival.[90] The prime minister, General Tōjō Hideki, characterized American demands as denying the self-image that Japan had of itself as a great power and as a return to "little Japan before the Manchurian incident."[91] The preeminent historian of the naval rivalry Sadao Asada concludes: "American officials who engineered the embargo thought only in terms of deterring Japan . . . and were heedless of the fact that they had forced Japan's back to the wall until it felt compelled to strike."[92] Dean Acheson later admitted that "everyone in the [State] Department—and in the government generally—misread Japanese intentions. This misreading was not of what the Japanese military government proposed to do in Asia, not of the hostility our embargo would excite, but of the incredibly high risks General Tōjō would assume to accomplish his ends."[93] War with Japan, the Roosevelt historian David Kennedy concluded, was "one that more artful diplomacy in 1940–41 might have postponed or even avoided."[94] Whether in retrospect a conflict of so traumatic a character could have been avoided must remain a matter for counterfactual history, but there is good reason to believe that conflict might have been avoided by a more consistent long-term policy of firmness, patience, and understanding—that is, a policy in the 1930s designed to confront the Japanese with superior strength at every juncture where they might otherwise be inclined to encroach on the vital interests of a stable and peaceful region, and to do this in a consistent manner so that its basic purposes would not be subject to misinterpretation.

It was not inevitable that the contest for supremacy should lead to war. Despite their naval rivalry, American interests in the western Pacific were not so great as to justify all-out war with Japan. Similarly, Japan's interests were best served by maintaining good relations with the United States, its main trading partner. But both the United States and Japan miscalculated and misconstrued the intentions of their rivals. Midlevel officers in the Japanese military, long the source of uncompromising nationalism, demanded war. As the historian Hotta writes,

"None of the top leaders . . . had sufficient will, desire, or courage to stop the momentum for war. Particularly for the chiefs and vice chiefs of the general staff, it proved much easier to go along with the calls for war preparedness initiated by the [middle ranking military planners] than to try to restrain them."[95] Japan's leaders determined on a bold and crippling blow to the main US battle force in the Pacific. On the face of it, Japan's decision for war appears to fly in the face of realism. To declare war on a power with no less than eight times the material power might seem a rash and reckless act. Yet, in analyzing under what circumstances a state may decide to attempt a change in the international order and the way in which the elite perceives the relative costs and benefits and the price it is willing to pay, one has to take account of the historically formed perceptions of the leadership.[96] As Kissinger observed in a different connection, "No nation will submit to a settlement, however well-balanced and however 'secure', which seems to totally deny its vision of itself."[97] Seen in this light, the decision for war was less a reckless, irrational gamble than a choice between two equally "repugnant alternatives": war with a nation of vastly greater wealth and power or return to an international order that would require not only relinquishment of an empire but the destruction of what had come to constitute the nation's very self-image.[98] Japanese leaders would gamble all that Japan had achieved in the past century to preserve Japan's self-image. Moreover, they would do it in a way that so angered the Americans that it would lead to total, uncompromising warfare.

2

Unconditional Surrender Policy

T HE SURPRISE ATTACK ON PEARL HARBOR, in which some 2,400 Americans died and which destroyed the largest part of the Pacific Fleet, enraged and aroused a nation that had for many years turned its back on foreign affairs. Because the United States was a nation that had always enjoyed a free security, situated between two great oceans and without powerful neighbors, Pearl Harbor represented an unprecedented threat to its security. It was testimony to the depth of isolationism of the American people that they had to be bombed to return to an active role in international affairs.

In the months before the surprise attack, President Roosevelt had sought ways to stir the American people from their complacency. Alarmed by the growing threat to America's security, he had maneuvered to bring the United States to the side of Britain as it faced German air raids. In the months before Pearl Harbor as Hitler overran the European continent, as the fate of England hung in the balance, and as American negotiations with Japan foundered, American entry into global war was imminent. Events forced Roosevelt to ponder what might be American war goals. He had been discussing his views for many months with his longtime confidant Sumner Welles, now undersecretary of state, and his momentous meeting with Winston Churchill off the coast of Newfoundland in August 1941 was arranged at Roosevelt's urging primarily for this purpose.[1] He wanted, he told the prime minister, a joint declaration of war aims "relating to the civilization of the world." It was to be a set of "broad principles which should guide our policies along the same road."[2]

The meeting marked the moment at which the United States returned to Wilsonian principles and the goal of remaking the world order. The Atlantic Charter, issued at the end of their meeting, committed the two leaders to work for self-determination, disarmament of aggressors, free trade, freedom of the seas, and "establishment of a wider and permanent system of general security."[3] To these Wilsonian goals were added international collaboration to achieve New Deal–style reforms: the advancement of labor standards, employment security, and social welfare. The principles espoused in the charter, Roosevelt said in a message to Congress, were so "clear cut" that "a willingness to accept compromise" was out of the question.[4]

The draft of Roosevelt's six-minute address to Congress on December 8, 1941, began, "Yesterday, December 7, 1941—a date which will live in world history—the United States of America was suddenly and deliberately attacked by naval and air forces of the Empire of Japan." When he reviewed the draft he amended it to read "a date which will live in infamy."[5] And so began one of American history's most famous speeches. Roosevelt's address to Congress called on Americans to avenge "an unprovoked and dastardly attack."[6] It was significant that rather than a careful delineation of the circumstances that had led to the attack—the threat to US interests and an appeal to US idealism to wage a just war—in the fashion that Woodrow Wilson had addressed his war message to Congress in 1917, FDR made a short, rousing speech that emphasized both Japanese deceit and treachery and American innocence and resolve. In his final draft, foreshadowing the unconditional surrender policy, Roosevelt penned these stirring words: "No matter how long it may take us to overcome this premeditated invasion, the American people in their righteous might will win through to absolute victory."[7] In the wake of this call for vengeance and determination, the isolationist sentiment collapsed. With only one dissenting vote, the US Congress declared war that day on Japan. Germany and Italy, in turn, declared war on the United States, and America entered the war in Europe and the Pacific.

From the outset and over the first year of the war, Roosevelt characterized the American goals in distinctive ways. First, beginning with his address to Congress, he described the war as a crusade, a struggle be-

President Franklin D. Roosevelt addresses a joint session of Congress on December 8, 1941, and asks for a declaration of war against Japan in response to the Pearl Harbor attack. AP Photo / 4112081494.

tween good and evil waged for the achievement of universal moral principles. Second, as a consequence, there could be no compromise: the war must be fought to total victory. Weeks after Pearl Harbor, in his Annual Message to Congress, he said the nation's purpose must be "to cleanse the world of ancient evils, ancient ills. . . . No compromise can end that conflict. There never has been—there never can be—successful compromise between good and evil. Only total victory can reward the champions of tolerance, and decency, and freedom, and faith."[8] Rather than fight the war to an armistice and a negotiated peace agreement, as all other foreign wars in American history have been waged, Roosevelt announced in January 1943 that this war would be fought to unconditional surrender, and he ruled out any confidential discussion with the fascist powers as a basis for ending the conflict. Third, the goal was not simply turning back the enemies' expansionism. Rather, there would be a prolonged occupation of the enemy nations, the remaking of their domestic orders, and the reeducation of their people in the ways of democratic and peace-loving nations. Finally, Roosevelt cast the war not in terms of any specific goals of narrow self-interest but rather in pursuit of creating a new and peaceful world order.

Japanese leaders went to war with no clear strategy for war termination. Knowing that a protracted war with the United States could not be won, they believed that events would break in their favor—either the war in Europe would provide opportunities in Asia or, if they won decisive battles, the Americans could be persuaded to reach a compromise peace. Their sketchy plan was based on the belief that the United States, faced with war in Europe as well as the Pacific, would not have the determination to persevere in a prolonged conflict and would be ready to compromise. Japan could negotiate a settlement from a position of strength while occupying much of the Pacific and Southeast Asia.[9] America's unconditional surrender policy undermined this strategy.

Waging the war to unconditional surrender was an unprecedented goal. In his classic work *On War*, the Prussian military strategist Carl von Clausewitz (1780–1831) defined war as "an instrument of policy . . . a continuation of political intercourse, with the addition of other means."[10] The purpose of warfare is the achievement of concrete political objectives. "The political object is the goal, war is the means of reaching it, and means can never be considered in isolation from their purpose."[11] In other words, "War is a resort to violence to compel the enemy to accept a political objective that could not be obtained by peaceful means."[12] The Hull-Nomura negotiations in 1941 had sought to roll back Japanese expansion in China and Southeast Asia. But once war began, the United States greatly expanded its objectives. Rather than a war, as Clausewitz would have it, waged to achieve the concrete goals that diplomacy had failed to achieve, the war aims that the United States formulated after Pearl Harbor ultimately required the enemy to surrender its sovereignty, accept permanent disarmament, and have its leaders tried as war criminals, its government reengineered, and its society reeducated.

The consequences of Roosevelt's unconditional surrender policy for Japan were huge and long lasting. The policy determined not only how the war would be fought and how it would be terminated but also the long-range future of US-Japan relations to the present day. When the war was over and the Americans had achieved their all-out war goals, Japan was occupied, reconstructed, and incorporated into a new American world order. Understanding of postwar Japanese history and its dominant theme of American hegemony over many aspects of Japanese life must begin with the unconditional surrender policy.[13]

Total War

In the twentieth century, war became total war. Nations were fully mobilized for an all-out struggle. In one of his most dramatic fireside-chat radio addresses, two days after Pearl Harbor, the president described the conflict as total war in which the nation was "fighting for its existence and its life," and "every single man, woman, and child is a partner in the most tremendous undertaking of our American history."[14] World War II is the most extreme example of total war that the world has ever experienced. Not only were noncombatants at the home front mobilized, but enemy civilians were explicitly targeted and in the end the ultimate weapon was employed against them. War aims, which once had been concrete and focused, became vague and hyperbolic. All Americans must join in a crusade, the president said, "directed toward ultimate good as well as against immediate evil" in which the goal was a new, peaceful world order. "We Americans are not destroyers—we are builders. We are now in the midst of a war, not for conquest, not for vengeance, but for a world in which this Nation, and all that this Nation represents, will be safe for our children."[15] Japan's war goals were equally vague and hyperbolic. The Imperial Rescript declaring war on the United States said that the embargo caused Japan to fight for "self-existence and self-defense." This phrase, used over and over again, was never defined. The vague goals caused the Japanese historian Asada Sadao to conclude that "this was to be a war without war aims."[16]

In the past, wars had been fought over limited territorial objectives, but in the twentieth century war goals became focused on victory of ideologies more than on concrete and specific national interests. The French political theorist Raymond Aron observed that "it was no longer a question of shifting frontier posts a few miles. Only sublime—and vague—principles such as the right of peoples to self-determination or 'the war to end war' seemed commensurate with such violence, sacrifice, and heroism. It was technical excess that gradually introduced ideologies in place of war aims. Both sides claimed to know what they were fighting *about*, but neither said what it was fighting *for*."[17] That was certainly true in the Asia-Pacific War. Rather than clear and concrete war aims, Japanese and Americans were fighting for the triumph of their national ideologies.

In the early months of the war, the president made up his mind on unconditional surrender policy. A presidential committee on postwar foreign policy, composed of State Department officials and prominent private individuals, recommended in early 1942 that in light of the experience of World War I the United States should accept "nothing short of unconditional surrender by the principal enemies."[18] Roosevelt had discussed it with Churchill and mentioned it very briefly to the Joint Chiefs of Staff. As early as May 1942, Roosevelt privately determined that the war should be fought to unconditional surrender and not to a negotiated peace.[19]

Roosevelt gave his views of unconditional surrender to Canadian prime minister Mackenzie King in December 1942 during his visit to the White House. King recorded in his diary

> that [Roosevelt] thought what should be done was to defeat Germany first; demand unconditional surrender and then for the 3 powers: Britain, U.S. and Russia to turn to Japan and say: now we demand the same of you. If you want to save human life, you must surrender unconditionally at once. If not, the 3 of us will bring all our forces to bear, and will fight till we destroy you. Russia would then be persuaded to attack Japan. It would not take a year to bring about her defeat. He was not sure the Japanese would accept any unconditional surrender, and would probably seek to fight on.

But, he told King in a telling remark of later significance, "If the Japanese did not accept unconditional surrender then they should be bombed till they were brought to their knees."[20]

Then, on January 24, 1943, in his meeting with Churchill at Casablanca, he publicly made what Roosevelt biographer Frank Freidel described as "one of the most momentous and debatable pronouncements of the war,"[21] the sweeping concept of unconditional surrender. At the end of the conference, the president explained to the press: "I think we have all had it in our hearts and heads before, but I don't think that it has ever been put down on paper by the Prime Minister and myself, and that is the determination that peace can come to the world only by the total elimination of German and Japanese war power. . . . The elimination of German, Japanese and Italian war power means the unconditional surrender by Germany, Italy and Japan." Churchill, it appears,

Roosevelt with Prime Minister Winston Churchill in Casablanca, Morocco, on January 24, 1943, preparing to announce the unconditional surrender policy. AP Photo / 110502061226.

was ambivalent about such absolute war aims but chose not to say so publicly.[22]

After he returned to Washington, Roosevelt further explained in a press conference that he and Churchill "formally reemphasized what we had been talking about before, and that is we don't think there should be any kind of negotiated armistice, for obvious reasons. There ought to be unconditional surrender." No one in the press asked what were "the obvious reasons."[23] Days later he told White House correspondents that America would "fight this war through to the finish—to the day when United Nations forces march in triumph through the streets of Berlin, Rome, and Tokyo."[24] The eminent British military historian Michael Howard, in his study of wartime grand strategy, believed that the announcement at the Casablanca conference was made "without any of the forethought and careful consideration which should have gone to the framing of so major an act of Allied policy. . . . The question as to whether it would soften the enemy will to resist or to stiffen it does not appear to have been seriously considered at all."[25]

In his public addresses the president spoke only in the most general terms of what unconditional surrender entailed. Fundamental to the goal of uncompromising victory was Roosevelt's insistence on permanent disarmament of the enemy nations. "It is clear to us that if Germany and Italy and Japan—or any one of them—remain armed at the end of this war, or are permitted to rearm, they will again, and inevitably, embark upon an ambitious career of world conquest. They must be disarmed and kept disarmed."[26] Here the president foreshadowed the postwar disarmament of Japan, which was written into Article 9 of the Japanese Constitution.

Adding a legalistic approach to the goal of eliminating war and violence, Roosevelt emphasized conducting war crimes trials as part of unconditional surrender. The leaders of the Axis powers had engaged in a "lawless conspiracy" and must be arraigned, indicted, and subjected to due process of law: "We have made it entirely clear that the United Nations seek no mass reprisals against the populations of Germany or Italy or Japan. But the ringleaders and their brutal henchmen must be named, and apprehended, and tried in accordance with the judicial processes of criminal law."[27] Retribution against the conspirators must accompany the reformation of the people who had been misled.

In addition to disarmament and war crimes trials, he further added the goals of democratizing the political and economic structures and changing the way of thought of peoples in the fascist countries. They must be placed in political tutelage and reeducated. "They must abandon the philosophy and the teaching of that philosophy which has brought so much suffering to the world."[28] Both Churchill and Joseph Stalin had doubts about such totalistic goals, fearing that the policy would prolong the war by strengthening the determination of the Axis leaders to resist.[29] While publicly supporting the policy, Churchill from time to time privately urged modification of its terms. Stalin, while seeing the total destruction of Japanese power as in the Soviet national interest, cynically suggested that the Allies "agree to milder peace terms but once we get into Japan to give them the works."[30]

Although none of America's foreign wars had ever been fought to unconditional surrender, Roosevelt liked to root the concept in American history. He often explained that General Ulysses S. Grant had used the term in the Civil War and had even been called "Unconditional Surrender Grant." The president's comparison to the Civil War experience was not quite accurate. Grant had first used the term as a demand on Confederate forces at Fort Donelson. Furthermore, unconditional surrender in the Civil War applied to saving the union, the purpose of the war for the Union forces with which it was not possible to compromise. The unconditional surrender and remaking of a foreign state was something quite different. The American historian James McPherson describes Lincoln's unconditional surrender policy as intended not for a war fought against an enemy state but rather for the suppression of a domestic insurrection. "He never referred to Confederate states or to Confederates, but [rather] to rebel states and rebels."[31] Before World War II all of America's foreign wars had been settled by negotiation. Wars were fought until an armistice halted the fighting, and a subsequent peace treaty settled the political conditions between countries and ended the state of war. The United States had never demanded unconditional surrender. The American Revolution, the War of 1812, the Mexican War, the Spanish-American War, and World War I ended with negotiated peace treaties. Unconditional surrender was explicitly rejected as a goal when the Cold War began.[32] Both the Korean and Vietnam wars ended with negotiated peace agreements. The term "unconditional surrender" originally applied to a fighting unit in the field. But Roosevelt applied the term not only to the entire military forces of the Axis powers but also to the Axis nations themselves.[33]

Roosevelt's Reasons

Although the long-range consequences were never fully thought out, Roosevelt had many reasons for insisting on unconditional surrender. In the first place, he needed to mobilize American opinion behind the war effort and his leadership of it. Americans had only recently abandoned their isolationism and he wanted to rally the kind of unflagging support and sacrifice that a crusade would elicit from popular opinion. Unconditional surrender was a captivating slogan to unite and exhort the American war effort. It more than succeeded. As the political historian

Melvyn Leffler observed, Americans have habitually in times of national danger returned to the crusading ideals of their own revolution and in doing so have tended to overreach: "At times of heightened threat perception the assertion of values mounts and subsumes careful calculation of interests. Values and ideals are asserted to help evoke public support for mobilization of power; power then tempts the government to overreach far beyond what careful calculations of interest might dictate."[34]

Public opinion in the United States, reacting to the provocation of Pearl Harbor and Japanese atrocities and reflecting a deep racial antagonism, came to overwhelming support of unconditional surrender policy. "Probably in all our history," the distinguished American historian Allan Nevins wrote, "no foe has been so detested as were the Japanese."[35] But more than that, Roosevelt recognized that Americans would respond less to narrowly defined terms of national interest than to the mission to rid the world of political evil. Churchill and Stalin could think of national interest and the achievement of a favorable new postwar balance of power, but for Americans the war was to fulfill its national ideology.

This idealist fervor to protect democratic freedoms, it should be noted, did not protect the civil rights of over 110,000 Japanese Americans living along the Pacific Coast who were interned by Executive Order 9066. Roosevelt signed the order on February 19, 1942, authorizing the army to remove them to remote camps in the western United States. Most Americans could see no distinction between Japanese and Japanese Americans and were therefore supportive of this cruel and unjust measure. Internment represented a continuation of, actually an intensification of, pervasive racist sentiment in the prewar attitudes of Americans toward Japan and Japanese immigrants. Neither German Americans nor Italian Americans were subject to such mass internment.[36]

Although unconditional surrender may have had its origin partly as the rhetoric of propaganda, its repeated assertion soon became so embedded in policy and in popular consciousness that when the new and inexperienced Harry Truman took office as president in the last months of the war, he at once announced it as firm policy. The policy by then had taken on a life of its own.

A second motivation for unconditional surrender was Roosevelt's political determination to avoid what he regarded as the policy mistakes

Persons of Japanese ancestry arrive at Santa Anita Assembly Center in California before being sent to an internment camp, April 5, 1942. American Photo Archive / Alamy Stock Photo / HMBC4E.

that Wilson had made in World War I, which he had witnessed first-hand as Wilson's assistant secretary of the navy. The American commander in chief in Europe in 1918, General John Pershing had favored demanding unconditional German surrender.[37] Wilson was criticized as weak by his political opponents for his efforts to achieve "peace without victory" through an armistice and a negotiated peace. Germany was allowed to recover and pose a renewed challenge to peace and order. Wilson had paid a political price at home for his advocacy of an armistice and a negotiated peace.[38] FDR remembered the attacks on Wilson by the Republican hawks, including his cousin Theodore, who had favored all-out war against Imperial Germany and had charged the president with weakness in seeking an armistice and "peace without victory." Henry Cabot Lodge and the Republicans had seized on the concept of "unconditional surrender" as a shibboleth to attack Wilson as weak. As his biographer Robert Sherwood often observed, Roosevelt was "haunted by the ghost of Woodrow Wilson" and often during the war reminded the American people of the mistakes made after World War I.[39] Roosevelt explained to the American people that "after the

Armistice in 1918, we thought and hoped that the militaristic philosophy of Germany had been crushed; and being full of the milk of human kindness we spent the next twenty years disarming, while the Germans whined so pathetically that the other Nations permitted them—even helped them—to rearm. . . . It is my intention to do all I can as President and Commander in Chief to see to it that these tragic mistakes shall not be made again."[40]

The historian Ernest May observed that the president's stubborn adherence to unconditional surrender policy was based on the kind of "superficial reasoning" that policymakers often make, which is to draw false or simplistic lessons from the recent past. "Like generals preparing for the last war, American statesmen in World War II thought only in terms of the last postwar era." As FDR wrote to his secretary of war in 1944, "It is of the utmost importance that every person in Germany should realize that this time Germany is a defeated nation." Roosevelt's original formulation of unconditional surrender policy was entirely focused on the experience with Germany. It had nothing to do with Japan, which had been an ally in World War I.[41] (After the fascist government in Italy collapsed and Mussolini was deposed, the Allies accepted a conditional surrender from the new government.) Nevertheless, as the war against Germany was drawing to a close, Roosevelt made clear that the lessons drawn from the experience with Germany would be applied not only to Germany but also to Japan: "Practically all Germans deny the fact they surrendered in the last war, but this time they are going to know it. And so are the Japs."[42] In a statement hailing the landing of American troops in the Philippines on October 20, 1944, the president repeated the same uncompromising determination toward Japan:

> We have learned our lesson about Japan. We trusted her, and treated her with the decency due a civilized neighbor. We were foully betrayed. The price of the lesson was high. Now we are going to teach Japan her lesson. We have the will and the power to teach her the cost of treachery and deceit, and the cost of stealing from her neighbors. With our steadfast Allies, we shall teach this lesson so that Japan will never again forget it. We shall free the enslaved peoples. We shall restore stolen lands and looted wealth to their rightful owners. We shall strangle the Black Dragon of Japanese militarism forever.[43]

Still another motivation of his unconditional surrender policy was to hold together the wartime alliance with Stalin. If the new postwar order was to be achieved, Roosevelt believed it was necessary to unify the Allies and especially reassure Stalin that the United States would not reach a separate peace with Hitler. Roosevelt and Churchill were not ready to agree to an immediate invasion of Europe and the "second front" that Stalin wanted. They sought to assure him, however, that they would not reach a separate peace with Hitler. To his death, FDR remained committed to creating a postwar world in which Soviet-American cooperation was intact. Some kind of big-power cooperation would be necessary to keep the peace in the postwar world. Roosevelt told Soviet foreign minister Vyacheslav Molotov when he visited the White House in May 1942 that four powers—the United States, Russia, Britain, and China—might serve as "policemen" to maintain global security after the war.[44] Casting the wartime goals in vague and general terms served to stave off inquiries and bargaining about specific goals and peace terms. Moreover, as a matter of personal style, Roosevelt typically deferred decisions while he mulled the alternatives. There were in FDR's mind too many unanswered questions about the postwar situation and he wanted to keep his "freedom of action." He took care to maintain maximum flexibility by keeping foreign policy in his own hands.[45]

In addition to all these motivations, the deeper purpose of pursuing unconditional surrender was to have a free hand at the end of fighting to shape the postwar world. Roosevelt believed unconditional surrender of the Axis powers was necessary for the creation of a new postwar international order. Nothing less than total victory would satisfy the goal of achieving a new and permanent democratic and peaceful order. As the historian Warren Kimball writes, "The United States did not enter the war in order to reshape the world, but once in the war [a] conception of world reform was the assumption that guided Roosevelt's actions."[46] He came to believe that he would need "something akin to a tabula rasa," a clearing of the decks so far as the fascist powers were concerned.[47] Like Wilson, Roosevelt believed that the causes of war lay in the internal structure of states and that democratization would contribute to a peaceful international order. Though seemingly more hardheaded and realist in his policies, Roosevelt held an idealistic vision much like Wilson. Just as Wilson had described the Great War as "the culminating and final war for human liberty,"[48] so did FDR believe that it was possible to finally fulfill the American aspiration for a peaceful, democratic, rules-based world. Churchill and Stalin had historical geopolitical purposes as their wartime goals, but for the United States the war would be fought for universal humanitarian ideals with less attention given to the distribution of power on which a postwar order might be established. Roosevelt envisioned a postwar order maintained by the wartime allies acting in concert to preserve the peace and avoid a possible rivalry among the victors.

Roosevelt believed that American public opinion must be convinced of the high ideals for a new international order if the United States was not once again to withdraw from foreign affairs.[49] Committees in the State Department were working on aspects of planning for a postwar organization to replace the League of Nations. Whereas the British had provided many of the details of the latter, the Americans took the lead this time.[50] Beginning in 1943 and continuing to the last days of his life, Roosevelt pressed the Allies to accept his vision. Returning from Yalta, where he had met with Churchill and Stalin in February 1945, he declared in his last address to Congress that the new order that he sought would "spell the end of the system of unilateral action, the exclusive alliances, the spheres of influence, the balances of power, and all the other expedients that have been tried for centuries—and have always failed. We propose to substitute for all of these, a universal organization in which all peace-loving nations will finally have a chance to join." In the same address, he reiterated that "the unconditional surrender of Japan is as essential as the defeat of Germany—if our plans for world peace are to succeed."[51]

Roosevelt wanted to create a tabula rasa from which international harmony would emerge to allow the creation of a new structure of peace. Instead of negotiating with regimes that he found abhorrent, Roosevelt and the Americans believed that building a peaceful society of nations demanded internal interventions of the most radical sort into the domestic affairs of the aggressor nations. Like Wilson, FDR held to the liberal belief that war was caused by domestic conditions. The domestic sources of militarism and aggression must be rooted out if there was to be peace. It would be necessary to have a free hand to reform the internal workings of the Axis societies. The high idealism with which America saw its wartime goals was well illustrated by the hopes held for the United Nations, the new international organization that was to keep the peace in the postwar era. Domestic reform and democratization of Japan were necessary if future threats to peace were to be eradicated.

Implications of the Unconditional Surrender Policy

The unconditional surrender policy had profound implications for how the Asia Pacific War would be fought and ended. It meant fighting until Japan as a nation conceded total defeat and gave the Allies—especially the United States, which bore the brunt of the war in the Pacific—the right to occupy and remake Japan. Such an extreme goal provoked die-hard resistance from the Japanese military and meant that the American military must plan for the likelihood of an invasion of Japan or, if that prospect was to be avoided, the resort to a strangling naval blockade and undertaking the most devastating, even unthinkable, bombings and destruction of civilian life to achieve unconditional surrender and complete control of the Japanese homeland. It foreclosed diplomacy and the possibility of a limited conflict with specific political goals. Since any negotiation with the enemy was ruled out, conduct of the war gave priority to military strategy. The problem with such a policy was that it suspended foreign policy concerns, which should have been the ends. It was precisely what Clausewitz had counseled against.

Many of the president's advisors had reservations about his unconditional surrender policy. Secretary of War Henry Stimson opposed application of the unconditional surrender policy to Japan. The venerable Stimson, who had been Taft's secretary of war, governor of the Philippines, and Hoover's secretary of state, was brought into the cabinet in 1940 to add a bipartisan cast to foreign policy. His extensive experience with Asia gave him sensitivity to the unique cultures of the region. While believing compromise with Nazi Germany was not acceptable, he opposed the policy of unconditional surrender, intended to reconstruct and rehabilitate Japan. As the historian Sean Malloy in his study of Stimson writes, he was "entirely uninterested in dictating the form of the postwar Japanese government."[52]

In the military there was a keen awareness of the strategic implications. The ramifications of making such a demand, however, were never explored with the Joint Chiefs of Staff, who feared that it would prolong the war.[53] Invasion or destruction of the Japanese homeland had to be full scale and could not be dragged out for fear that the American people's patience with the lengthy war effort would wear down. As one authority writes, "The policy of unconditional surrender greatly restricted the freedom of strategic choice, giving the American armed forces a task 'unnecessarily large' by requiring of them considerably more than simply beating the enemy."[54] It might involve prolonged blockade and bombing, or, given the imperatives of time, it likely involved the invasion of Japan, which the navy had long regarded as "folly" and which army leadership saw as immensely costly in casualties. Further, unconditional surrender policy crucially implied the urgent need for Soviet entry into the war against Japan. Stalin had signed a neutrality pact with Japan in 1941, which was set to end in 1946. The prospect of invading the Japanese homeland, which unconditional surrender policy would likely require, meant that the US military needed Soviet participation, which would allow Stalin the opportunity to pursue his ambitions in Asia.

Moreover, the unconditional surrender policy involved occupation of the enemy country for a prolonged period in order to conduct and enforce the envisioned domestic reforms. Army leadership was reluctant to become engaged in such "social engineering."[55] Army chief of staff General George Marshall on occasion grumbled about Roosevelt's inflexible adherence to unconditional surrender, observing that we are "up against an obstinate Dutchman who had brought the phrase out and didn't like to go back on it."[56] The State Department was also unenthusiastic about the implications of the policy. While Roosevelt was not concerned with details, the State Department recognized that there were issues involved in planning to so totally remake a defeated nation. As a department memo recognized, "Unconditional surrender of a state is an innovation which requires exact definition" and suggested that, in view of prevailing concepts of international law, authority to undertake internal reforms would have to be spelled out in the surrender document.[57]

Roosevelt, who typically monopolized foreign policymaking, gave little heed to his secretary of state before making this policy proclamation.[58] When he belatedly learned of it, Cordell Hull was personally opposed to it not only, as he later recorded, because "it might prolong the war by solidifying Axis resistance into one of desperation" but also because "the principle logically required the victor nations to be ready to take over every phase of the national and local Governments of the conquered countries, and to operate all governmental activities and properties. We and our Allies were in no way prepared to undertake this vast obligation."[59] Nevertheless, despite his private doubts about it, Hull fell in line with the president's directives.

Reflecting Roosevelt's personal domination of foreign policy, the State Department was generally without strong policy influence. The Japanese floated a variety of unofficial peace overtures through private as well as third-country channels, but none of these efforts got traction. They were informal offers to negotiate, but lacked credibility because they did not come from official sources. More important, American diplomats were not empowered to discuss any peace offers other than unconditional surrender.[60] The State Department's role in foreign policymaking was confused and sometimes haphazard. Policy planning recommendations often never made it to the White House, and, conversely, the department was often left in the dark as to what had been decided by the president at his major conferences with allied leaders.[61] Dean Acheson remembered the wartime State Department in which he served as "somnolent, with neither premeditated strategies nor any other ideas. It could only react to external events of the moment. Immobilized in addition by divisions among encrusted geographic baronies, the department . . . was utterly unprepared for war."[62] Lamenting the weakness and lethargy of the department, he singled out FDR's unconditional surrender policy as particularly flawed. "There was room," Acheson later wrote, "for something a little more modern and percipient than FDR's adoption of General Grant's 'unconditional surrender,'" but the department lacked the intellectual vigor to contribute to "the conduct of the war or to the achievement of political purposes through war."[63]

The War Department had much greater influence on policy than did State, and the military's postwar influence over postwar Japan would continue for many decades. Assistant Secretary of War John McCloy later reflected that the goal of unconditional surrender gave the military priority and that the result was to confine "large questions on the conduct of the war to purely military considerations." He felt that too often "the civilian leadership, out of deference to military judgment, ended up ignoring important political considerations."[64]

The Cairo Conference

At the Cairo conference in November 1943, Roosevelt turned explicitly to planning for postwar Asia. Once again, the president's personal domination of foreign policy was striking in this meeting with Churchill and Chiang Kai-shek. The State Department was neither represented nor consulted about the planning or the agreements reached. The department's small group of Asian experts was left in the dark about the conference.[65]

In Roosevelt's still-quite-rough thinking about postwar Asia, he had certain principles that related to his vision of a new international order. One was the future importance of China and another was an end to Western colonialism. Churchill, determined to preserve the British Empire, was opposed to both. In his famous 1942 speech he asserted that while Britain did not seek territorial expansion in the war, at the same time "we mean to hold our own. I have not become the King's First Minister to preside over the liquidation of the British Empire"—a broadside meant for the Americans among others.[66] Throughout the war, Roosevelt pressed him to make concessions on independence for India until finally Churchill wrote to the president that continued prodding on this point could lead to a break between them.[67] Similarly, he had no enthusiasm for Roosevelt's promotion of China as one of the four great powers. The president at the Cairo conference, he later wrote, "took an exaggerated view of the Indian-Chinese sphere . . . with the result that Chinese business occupied first instead of last place."[68]

As Robert Dallek writes, Roosevelt "looked forward to having China help the United States preserve peace in the Pacific after the war. Though she was now occupied and weak, he believed that her large population would eventually make her a Great Power."[69] China would help keep Japan in check after the war, and Roosevelt shared the great American popular attachment to China. Roosevelt's family's connections to the China trade, as Robert Butow's meticulous research shows, had given the president a longtime interest in and attachment to relations with China.[70] The public outpouring of admiration for Madame Chiang Kai-shek during her wartime visits to the United States led FDR to effuse that for over a century the people of China "have been, in thought and in objective, closer to us Americans than almost any other peoples in the world—the same great ideals. China in the last—less than half a century has become one of the great democracies of the world."[71] Partly he used the fiction of China as a Great Power, expecting that it would align closely with American interests.

In his meeting at Cairo, Roosevelt explored with Chiang Kai-shek China's future role in a trusteeship system for former colonies. Would China be willing to exercise trusteeship over French Indo-China? Chiang was reluctant to undertake that responsibility, but the most remarkable part of this freewheeling discussion of the future territorial settlement came when "the President then referred to the question of the Ryukyu Islands and enquired more than once whether China would want the Ryukyus. The Generalissimo replied that China would be agreeable to joint occupation of the Ryukyus by China and the United States and, eventually, joint administration by the two countries under the trusteeship of an international organization."[72] The future of the Ryukyus was left unresolved for the time being.

In a hastily drafted general statement known as the Cairo Declaration, the three leaders announced their intention to dissolve the Japanese empire and reaffirmed unconditional surrender policy:

> Japan shall be stripped of all the islands in the Pacific which she has seized or occupied since the beginning of the first World War in 1914, and that all the territories Japan has stolen from the Chinese, such as Manchuria, Formosa, and the Pescadores, shall be restored to the Republic of China. Japan shall also be expelled from all other territories which she has taken by violence and greed. The aforesaid three great powers, mindful of the enslavement of the people of Korea, are determined that in due course Korea shall become free and independent.

Stalin, not at war with Japan, privately approved the declaration before its issuance, and Roosevelt and Churchill also explored with him the concessions he would expect in return for eventually joining in the war against Japan, all of which prefigured his subsequent demands at the Yalta Conference.[73]

Japanese Reaction to the Unconditional Surrender Demand

When Japanese leaders in their desperate frame of mind determined to take their nation into war, they gambled all that had been achieved in the previous century to make Japan a world power. Some Japanese leaders foresaw the Armageddon that such a gamble would bring about.

No one was more perceptive than Admiral Yamamoto Isoroku himself, the planner of the Pearl Harbor attack. Knowing the United States better than all other military leaders, he was full of foreboding. He had attended Harvard from 1919 to 1921 and served as a naval attaché in the Japanese embassy in Washington from 1926 to 1928. He had traveled widely across the United States and, as an American naval officer who knew him well remembered, "he had been mightily impressed with the power manifest in the Pittsburgh steel mills, the Detroit auto factories, the Kansas wheat fields, and above all by the Texas oil fields."[74] He had a keen respect for American science and technology.

Yamamoto opposed the signing of the Tripartite Pact, saying, "To side with Germany, which is aiming at a new world order, will inevitably embroil Japan in a war to overthrow the old Anglo-American order."[75] In September 1941 he warned the chief of the Naval General Staff that a war would be protracted: "Ultimately we will not be able to contend with [the United States]. As the result of war the people's livelihood will become indigent . . . and it is not hard to imagine [that] the situation will become out of control. We must not start a war with so little chance of success."[76] Nevertheless, in his position as commander in chief of the combined fleet he believed that if told that war was unavoidable the only chance of success would be a surprise, crippling blow to the US Pacific Fleet. He promised that if the Pearl Harbor attack succeeded in incapacitating the US Pacific Fleet, he would "run wild for the first six months or a year, but I have no confidence for the second or third year."[77]

Japan did run wild in the first months of the war, conquering more territory in a shorter time than any nation in history.[78] The Japanese swept through Southeast Asia destroying the underpinnings of Western imperial power. Colonial governments in Hong Kong, Malaya, Singapore, the Dutch East Indies, the Philippines, French Indo-China, and Burma yielded to Japanese forces in rapid succession. By the end of 1942 Japan had established dominion over 350 million people, a population three-quarters the size of the British Empire, in a vast area from the Solomon Islands in the mid-Pacific to the borders of India, and from the rain forests of New Guinea to the icy shores of the Aleutians. Immediately after Pearl Harbor, the government announced that the war would be called the Great East Asian War "because it is a war for the construction of a new order in East Asia" and entailed the "liberation of East Asian peoples from the aggression of America and Britain."[79]

Admiral Yamamoto Isoroku, planner of the Pearl Harbor attack. Süddeutsche
Zeitung Photo / Alamy Stock Photo / C5008P.

The Japanese failed to establish the legitimacy of their new order.
They needed to legitimize their territorial expansion and explain the
principles, norms, and values that would govern Japanese leadership of
Asia. A successful order required a persuasive ideology, a universal message, to rally Asians and justify the exercise of raw power. Accustomed
to their own narrow inward-looking nationalism, the Japanese struggled to construct a legitimate order. From the beginning it was a poorly
contrived and artificial effort. The claim to liberate Asians from Western
imperialism was belied by the coercion and brutality with which Japanese established their rule. The well-being of other Asian peoples was
wholly subordinated to Japanese interests. Japan quickly demonstrated that it was itself a colonial power and not a wealthy one that

was capable of offering benefits to underwrite its regional order. As the Japanese historian Hata Ikuhiko wrote, everywhere that Japan acquired new territories it followed "a ruthless policy of local plunder, reminiscent of early Spanish colonial policy. Land was seized for the settlement of Japanese immigrants in Manchuria; on the Chinese mainland businesses and enterprises were confiscated; and Japanese forces fighting in China and later in the Pacific lived off the land. . . . In modern history there has been no other instance of a foreign expeditionary force's adopting a policy of local self-sufficiency from the very outset. It was a glaring demonstration of the enormous disparities between slogans and realities."[80]

In going to war, most Japanese leaders believed that the Americans could be brought to negotiate a peace that would serve Japanese interests. One midlevel naval planner wrote in his memoirs: "I saw this as a limited war" to be settled by negotiation once Japan had dealt the enemy heavy damage.[81] Japan would win early victories and undermine American morale. Japanese leaders knew that although war might go well for a time, ultimately it must be brought to a negotiated end if Japan was to avoid disaster. Their hope was that Japan could negotiate a settlement from a position of strength while occupying much of the Pacific and Southeast Asia.[82] Such hope was based on the belief that the United States, faced with war in Europe as well as the Pacific, would not have the determination to persevere in a prolonged conflict and would be ready to compromise.

Believing that an early victory in a decisive battle would demonstrate its military superiority and open the way for a negotiated settlement, Japanese leaders hoped to preserve Japan's dominance in Asia and the western Pacific. The memory of the Battle of the Japan Sea in the Russo-Japanese War was regularly cited as a powerful precedent. That epic battle destroyed the Russian fleet and led the Russians to accept a negotiated peace. Japan's resources were stretched to the limit, but that decisive battle led the Russians to accept Theodore Roosevelt's mediation of peace. It left a military legacy of how a definitive engagement could lay the foundation for a negotiated peace.[83]

Japanese leaders' sketchily drawn plans for an exit strategy were predicated on seizing lands that would give them the material resources required. They could then hold these acquisitions and bargain for a compromise peace. Having no concrete strategy for war termination, they clung to a vague notion that events would break in their favor, either the war in Europe would provide opportunities for Japan in Asia or the Americans would not have the heart for a protracted conflict, or both.[84]

By 1943, as the tide of war turned steadily against Japan, such hopes dimmed. When the Allies announced the Cairo Declaration in December, the implications of unconditional surrender terms began to sink in.[85] In a radio broadcast on December 8, the second anniversary of Pearl Harbor, Tōjō denounced the Cairo Declaration as evidence that the United States and its allies intended to reduce Japan to a third-rate nation while continuing their domination of Asia.[86] Japanese leaders were taken back by Roosevelt's unprecedented war aims. Unconditional surrender policy confounded Japan's expectations for war termination and left the Japanese leaders in the dark as to what it implied. It led the Japanese military to dig in its heels. The harsh reiteration of the unconditional surrender policy in the Cairo Declaration hardened Japanese attitudes.

Civilian leaders who favored negotiating an early end to the war were severely handicapped by the Allied refusal to talk. What exactly did this policy entail? How long did the Allies intend to occupy Japan? Would the emperor be tried as a war criminal? Might he possibly be executed and the imperial institution abolished? Would the nation as they knew it come to an end? Roosevelt's speeches referred vaguely to occupying and disarming Japan, conducting war crimes trials, reforming the structure of the political and economic system, and changing the thinking of the Japanese people. These sweeping and undefined war goals were tempered only by occasional promises not to enslave the Japanese people.

In such circumstances, the Japanese government was too divided to formulate a coherent plan for terminating the war. With only the broadest outline of what the Allies meant by this policy and with no backdoor channels to the United States to provide any clarification, the early hope for a negotiated settlement steadily gave way to a determined will in the army to dig in for resistance. The civilian government and the throne were often cowed by the military, especially by the army.

Unconditional surrender provoked unconditional resistance from Japan. The Japanese, known for their capacity for fanatical fighting, especially for their refusal to countenance surrender by individual soldiers or by military units, were stiffened in their resistance by the extreme war goals of the Allies. When Saipan in the Marianas fell in

July 1944, the home islands were now within the range of B-29 bombers. The Tōjō cabinet resigned and a mood of desperation set in. It was clear to all belligerents that the war was lost. Leaders in the planning division of the Japanese Army Headquarters concluded that "we can no longer conduct the war with any hope of success." They reached the "unanimous agreement that henceforth Japan will undergo gradual deterioration, so plans should be devised to end the war quickly."[87] Yet the war persisted for another year, during which firebombing of Japanese cities gradually intensified until more than sixty cities were devastated and more than a half million civilians perished. The military was determined to continue the struggle in the belief that if Japan could make the war so costly and bloody the Allies would eventually agree to negotiate a settlement that would preserve some part of its war aims.

Assessing Unconditional Surrender Policy

America's unprecedented policy of unconditional surrender became the critical starting point in the making of postwar Japan. It determined how the war in the Pacific would be fought, how it would end, and the long-range future of Japan as a subordinate state in an American world order. Thus, the policy deserves the historian's careful assessment. Not until the very end of the war was the unconditional surrender policy clearly spelled out for the Japanese. Instead, six general goals were repeatedly enunciated by the Americans: dissolution of the Japanese empire, occupation of the country, permanent disarmament, war crimes trials, reconstruction of the political and economic systems, and reeducation of the people.

Were such unprecedented wartime goals justified? Was unconditional surrender a wise policy in the Asia Pacific War? Would not a more flexible approach to war termination have brought an earlier end to the war against Japan? Was a negotiated peace possible and preferable to the mayhem, violence, and destruction required to achieve unconditional surrender? Would a negotiated peace that left a defeated Japan with a measure of independence and provided a basis for a balance of power in the region have been preferable? As Michael Doyle writes in his study of foreign interventions, "The Allies clearly had a right to end German and Japanese aggression and drive their armies back to their borders. But were they entitled to also reform Germany and Japan? . . . Alternatively, when instead should the victors relinquish the goals of unconditional surrender and peacebuilding in order to spare the lives that a campaign for total conquest will cost?"[88]

Whether a more flexible American approach to war termination might have brought an earlier end to the Asia Pacific War has been the subject of much subsequent debate. Most of the debate has focused on the last months of the war and the vexed issue of whether use of the atomic bomb might have been averted. But the influence of the sweeping character of the war goals extends beyond the termination of the war to include the formation of the postwar Japanese state and the regional order that were profoundly shaped by the unconditional surrender policy.

In his seminal work on Japanese surrender, Robert Butow observed that "there can be little doubt that the unconditional surrender demand sparked the imagination and perhaps even fired the resolve of many people on the Allied side. What is open to question, however, is the value of the concept as an instrument of policy with respect to the enemy."[89] The British military historian Michael Howard, reflecting on unconditional surrender policy, wrote: "Political warfare specialists might have quoted Sun Tzu's advice, about leaving one's enemy a golden bridge for retreat. . . . There was no opportunity for such counsels to be heard at Casablanca. Had it been otherwise, the Allied leaders might have reflected a little more deeply on the question whether total victory is necessarily the surest foundation for lasting peace."[90]

A definitive answer to these questions is, of course, impossible. A negotiated peace likely would have opened the door to Japanese demands for preservation of the emperor system, for qualifications of Allied demands for occupation, disarmament, and war crimes trials, and for retention of the Korean colony.[91] Compromising the demand for unconditional surrender policy in 1944 or early 1945 would have left Japan defeated but perhaps still with its sovereignty intact with sanctions to ensure that it would conduct reforms and demilitarization. Negotiations would surely have been problematic, but all other foreign wars in American history had ended this way.

One critique of unconditional surrender policy in the Asia Pacific War comes from writers in the just war perspective. An important question that they address is whether the policy that was devised primarily toward Nazi Germany applied so well to Japan. From the perspective of *jus in bello* theory, Michael Walzer observes that "the outer limit of what can legitimately be sought in war . . . is the conquest and political reconstruction of the enemy state, and only against an enemy like Nazism can it possibly be right to reach that far. . . . The right does not arise in every war; it did not arise, I think, in the war against Japan."[92] Hitler and Nazism defied compromise solutions. With Japan, compromises were possible. We know that because, once the Occupation of Japan began, the Americans made a succession of major compromises with their wartime goals. It was ironic that after insisting on unconditional surrender and while imposing many sweeping reforms, the Americans nevertheless decided to keep the emperor and the conservative bureaucracy, leave high levels of capital concentration and corporate power intact, restore the prewar conservative elite, and—most ironic of all—prod the Japanese to rearm and restore Japan's dominant influence in Southeast Asia. Elaborating on the difference with Nazism, Walzer argues that

> the Japanese case is sufficiently different from the German so that unconditional surrender should never have been asked. Japan's rulers were engaged in a more ordinary sort of military expansion, and all that was morally required was that they be defeated, not that they be conquered and totally overthrown. Some restraint on their war-making power might be justified, but their domestic authority was a matter of concern only to the Japanese people. In any case, if killing millions (or many thousands) of men and women was militarily necessary for their conquest and overthrow then it was morally necessary—in order not to kill those people—to settle for something less.[93]

The most trenchant and sustained criticism of the unconditional surrender policy comes from realist writers who regard the policy as utopian in its expectation that it would bring a final solution to world conflict. They have been critical of Roosevelt's uncompromising goals in the war, arguing that "insistence on the total defeat of Germany and Japan had profoundly destabilized the postwar balance of power."[94] In that vein, Ernest May wrote that Roosevelt and his advisors "should have considered alternative shapes which the future might take and at least speculated about a world in which, among other things, Germany and Japan were impotent" and unable to participate in international politics for a long time to come.[95] Hans Morgenthau and George Kennan argued that rather than the doctrine of unconditional surrender, the effective way to maintain peace and achieve international stability was through a balance of power and "the wary toleration of adversaries rather than, as a point of principle, their annihilation."[96] Morgenthau, often regarded as the founding father of the discipline of international relations, argued that framers of American policy failed to understand the continuing role of power and national interest in international politics, instead substituting pursuit of moral principles and utopian solutions.[97] He wrote that

> the United States flatters itself that in its dealings with other countries it seeks no selfish advantage but is inspired by universal moral principles. . . . Crush the enemy; force him into unconditional surrender; re-educate him in the ways of democratic, peace-loving nations; and with democracy established everywhere, peace and good will among nations will be assured. . . . For Churchill and Stalin the Second World War was the instrument of a foreign policy whose objectives had existed before the outbreak of hostilities and were bound to continue when the war had come to an end. For Roosevelt . . . the war was an end in itself, its purpose exhausted with total victory and unconditional surrender.[98]

Reflecting on the American tendency to apply moral and legal principles to foreign policy, Kennan observed that when

> indignation [against the lawbreaker] spills over into military contest, it knows no bounds short of the reduction of the lawbreaker to the point of complete submissiveness—namely, unconditional surrender. It is a curious thing, but it is true, that the legalistic approach to world affairs, rooted as it unquestionably is in a desire to do away with war and violence, makes violence more enduring, more terrible, and more destructive to political stability than did the older motives of national interest. A war fought in the name of high moral principle finds no early end short of some form of total domination.[99]

Writers of the realist persuasion imply that an earlier conclusion to the war in the Pacific that left Japan defeated but dependent on American restraint and surrounded by sufficient force to deter future adventurism would have been preferable. Such an outcome, before the bloodletting reached nihilist dimensions, would have changed the course of history. They contend that in its totalist approach of destroying Japanese power, unconditional surrender policy profoundly destabilized the postwar balance of power, allowing Stalin to reestablish his influence in Asia, and contributed to the rise of Chinese communist power and a divided Korea. Morgenthau held that American statesmen were under the "illusion that a nation can escape, if it wants to, from power politics into a realm where action is guided by moral principles rather than by consideration of power."[100] Isolationism in the interwar period and Wilson's and Franklin Roosevelt's so-called internationalism were "brothers under the skin" in their utopianism and failure to face and define national interests and political reality. "Both refuse to concern themselves with the concrete issues upon which the national interest must be asserted."[101]

In a less philosophical and more pragmatic critique, other writers have found fault with the effects of the policy. A strong case is made by many historians and military writers that unconditional surrender policy lengthened the war. In his important work on the politics of war termination, Leon Sigal writes, "Unconditional surrender remained open to a variety of interpretations. . . . Repeating the vague formula without spelling out its meaning may have postponed bickering over the spoils of war or the arrangements of peace, but it left Japan in the dark about the consequences of defeat. Imprecision could reinforce enemy intransigence and confound those in Tokyo trying to sue for peace."[102]

In the aftermath of the war, as the Cold War began, the *New York Times* war correspondent Hanson Baldwin described unconditional surrender policy as "perhaps the biggest political mistake of the war. . . . Unconditional surrender was an open invitation to unconditional resistance; it . . . probably lengthened the war, cost us lives, and helped to lead to the present abortive peace."[103] In his well-known study *Strategic Surrender,* the Rand Corporation political scientist Paul Kecskemeti concluded that the rigidities on both the Japanese and American sides prolonged the war. "Had direct and confidential channels of communication been established with the Japanese government, it is conceivable that the United States would have been able to clarify the situation and to disabuse the Japanese of their illusions." Although the Japanese put out feelers they never sent anyone abroad with official instructions to discuss surrender terms. "On the American side . . . confidential conversations with the enemy for the purpose of determining a possible basis for surrender were ruled out on principle." If the US had made a very determined effort to establish contact this "would have led to Japan's surrender before the Soviets entered the war, resulting in a far more favorable postwar balance of power in the Far East. But this approach was precluded by the prevailing rules of unconditionality."[104]

If, as Clausewitz urged, the purpose of war is to achieve concrete political objectives that could not be obtained by peaceful means, then unconditional surrender was an unwise policy. The war against Japan abandoned pragmatic political goals. Instead, the goal was left both vague and open ended: total destruction of the enemy and the remaking of its society. As a consequence the military was put in charge of the war at the expense of policymakers. Asserting a policy that could be fulfilled only by achieving total submission of the enemy was not what Clausewitz had argued was the purpose of war—namely, achieving goals that diplomacy had failed to achieve. That is, the challenge was to make force serve politics. The Hull-Nomura negotiations foundered on the US insistence that Japan withdraw from China and Southeast Asia. But rather than keep that goal, Roosevelt made total surrender and total remaking of Japanese society and politics the wartime purpose. Whatever the wisdom of the unconditional surrender policy, the long-term effect of this policy on postwar Japan and its capacity to recover its sovereignty proved profound. When the war ended, Japan was left in a prolonged state of dependence on the United States. Whether a negotiated peace might have been achieved and what the terms of a negotiated peace might have been is a matter for counterfactual history. What we do know is that the unconditional surrender policy led to the most extreme measures to achieve its goals and that the American people believed those measures were required to achieve a new and peaceful world order.

3

The Decision to Use the Atomic Bomb

THE AMERICAN DETERMINATION to achieve total victory led to the most extreme and uncompromising measures against Japan. The decision to use the atomic bomb is inextricably linked to unconditional surrender policy. It may be the most controversial decision any president has made.[1] At the turn of the millennium, in 1999, in a poll taken of prominent American journalists and scholars, the decision to use the atomic bomb on Hiroshima and Nagasaki was chosen as the most important event of the twentieth century.[2] This horrific event was at the center of the major developments of our time: it ended World War II, it began the atomic age, it established the Pax Americana, and it began the Cold War arms race.

The decision has aroused endless discussion and debate among historians. Historical controversy has revolved around several issues:

1. Was it necessary to use the bomb: was not Japan already defeated and on the verge of surrender?
2. Were there not viable alternatives such as a demonstration of the bomb or a naval blockade or modification of unconditional surrender policy or waiting for Soviet entry into the war?
3. Was the second bomb on Nagasaki necessary?
4. Did use of the bomb save lives by averting an invasion?
5. Were the bombs morally justified?

Historians have not come to any consensus on these issues. To these and many other questions, historians continue to offer many conflicting interpretations, leading the British military historian John Keegan to conclude laconically that "historians are committed to controversy as a way of life, and [the Hiroshima] controversy may never be settled."[3] The use of the atomic bomb left a lasting impact on postwar Japan and on Japanese-American relations. Japanese and Americans see this decision in very different ways. In 2015, on the occasion of the seventieth anniversary of the end of World War II, the Pew Research Center carried out a joint opinion poll that found that 79 percent of Japanese said the bombing was "not justified," while 56 percent of Americans considered it "justified."[4] Japanese believe that Japan was already defeated and on the verge of surrender, while a majority of Americans still hold that the use of the bomb was necessary in order to avoid a costly invasion.

One of the pillars of Japan's postwar national identity, about which virtually all Japanese (whatever their political persuasion) are agreed, is the belief that Japan, as the only nation to have suffered an atomic attack, has a unique mission to lead the world in banishing nuclear weapons. Japanese attitudes toward America's use of the bomb are complex. But hatred of America largely dissipated and, as Dower writes, "did not become a dominant sentiment in the weeks, months, and years that followed. The destructiveness of the bombs was so awesome that many Japanese initially regarded them . . . almost as if they were a natural disaster."[5] Literary historian John Treat observes that "despite the widespread reputation of atomic bomb literature [in Japan] as anti-American, in fact 'America' recedes from view in most examples of this genre." Rather than pursuing "the human hand that inflicted the suffering," the writings of novelists and essayists tend to treat the bomb as a human tragedy more than a Japanese tragedy. Nobel Prize novelist Ōe Kenzaburō, perhaps the most famous of the essayists on Hiroshima and Nagasaki, was sometimes criticized for seeming to ignore the human responsibility. Nevertheless, whatever the ambivalence and complexity of attitudes, the common Japanese sense of victimization remained dominant.[6]

Americans themselves remain unsettled by their use of the bomb. While a majority of Americans have found the decision justified by the lives saved in avoiding an invasion, they have nonetheless been uneasy over the morality of its use against civilians and deeply sensitive to expressions of opprobrium by those who found it otherwise. Being the first and only nation to use the bomb carried implications for Americans' own self-identity. Prone to regard themselves as a people of virtue and innocence occupying the moral high ground in international politics, Americans have been sensitive to the fact that theirs is the only nation to have used the atomic bomb.[7]

In 2003 when President George W. Bush announced the invasion of Iraq, former president of South Africa Nelson Mandela angrily questioned American self-righteousness in light of Hiroshima and Nagasaki. "Because they decided to kill innocent people in Japan, who are still suffering from that," Mandela said, "who are they now to pretend that they are policemen of the world?"[8] The leading Israeli scholar of modern Japanese history likened the bombing to the Holocaust in a lecture, reaching the judgment that "Auschwitz and Hiroshima . . . represented a new level of atrocity that human beings can perpetrate on each other."[9]

American politics have not permitted politicians to express regret. In 1991, on the fiftieth anniversary of Pearl Harbor, reporters asked President George H. W. Bush if an American statement of regret for Hiroshima might be forthcoming if the Japanese apologized for Pearl Harbor. "Not from this president," he replied. "I was fighting over there. . . . Can I empathize with a family whose child was victimized by these attacks? Absolutely. But I can also empathize with my roommate's mother, my roommate having been killed in action."[10] In Japan, Bush's response at once doomed the Diet's own consideration of whether it might make an apology for its wartime aggression on the occasion of the anniversary. Four years later, in 1995, on the fiftieth anniversary of the Hiroshima bomb, the Smithsonian Institution organized an exhibition for the occasion, which burst into a prolonged controversy over the narrative of the event written by American historians. Veterans protested to members of Congress that the narrative was unpatriotic in its neglect of Japan's treacherous attack that began the war, was dismissive of the suffering and sacrifices the GIs had made in the Pacific, and was oblivious to the massive American casualties that an invasion would have cost and that the bomb had prevented. In the end, the exhibition went forward with the *Enola Gay,* the plane from which the Hiroshima bomb was dropped, on display in the Smithsonian and little attempt to interpret the context of its fateful mission over Hiroshima.[11] President Bill Clinton at the time told the American Society of Newspaper Editors that America owed Japan no apology and that President Truman had made the right decision "based on the facts he had before him."[12]

Barack Obama cautiously broached the issue in the first foreign policy speech of his presidency, April 5, 2009, which was devoted to the need to strengthen the Nuclear Non-Proliferation Treaty. He observed that America was obligated to take the lead in ridding the world of atomic weapons, because "as a nuclear power—as the only nuclear power to have used a nuclear weapon—the United States has a moral responsibility to act." He was at once chided in a *Wall Street Journal* editorial for offering "a barely concealed apology for Hiroshima [which] is an insult to the memory of Harry Truman, who saved a million lives by ending World War II without a bloody invasion of Japan."[13] In a historic gesture of reconciliation, in May 2016 Obama became the first sitting US president to visit the Hiroshima Peace Memorial. He told the Japanese press that he did not intend to offer an apology because "I think it is important to recognize that in the midst of war, leaders make all kinds of decisions. It's a job of historians to ask questions and examine them, but I know as somebody who has now sat in this position for the last seven and a half years, that every leader makes very difficult decisions, particularly during time of war."[14] Presidential candidate Donald Trump at the time tweeted, "Does President Obama ever discuss the sneak attack on Pearl Harbor when he is in Japan?" and told a campaign rally that Obama's being in Hiroshima is "fine. Just as long as he doesn't apologize."[15]

The historical controversy has focused mostly on the motivation and deliberations of President Truman and his advisors during the summer months of 1945 after the fall of Okinawa and as an invasion of Kyushu loomed. If, however, the decision is studied in a broader perspective, Roosevelt's wartime goal of unconditional surrender policy can be seen as constituting such powerful momentum that some historians have found it difficult to believe that Truman ever, in fact, made a "decision."

The Manhattan Project and FDR's Legacy

America's decision to embark on a massive project to build an atomic bomb had little to do with Japan. On the eve of the Nazi invasion of Poland, Albert Einstein wrote a letter with the help of another Jewish émigré, physicist Leo Szilard, to President Roosevelt on August 2, 1939, describing the possible military applications of the achievement of nuclear fission and its likely use by Germany.[16] The letter engaged FDR's immediate attention and led to the largest scientific-industrial project in history. In a momentous coincidence of timing, Roosevelt set the United States on a course to build an atomic bomb in the months before Pearl Harbor.[17] He made this decision amid the greatest secrecy. The concern was not Japan but rather the alarming likelihood that Hitler was already pursuing the same goal.

It was not until late 1944 that the United States learned that the German nuclear project had made only limited progress.[18] But by that time, the US effort to make an atomic bomb, known as the Manhattan Project, had become a massive top-secret undertaking employing as many as 150,000 people at a staggering cost of $2 billion (more than $27 billion in 2017 dollars). It absorbed a large proportion of the nation's scientific and engineering talent, including some one hundred émigré physicists who had fled Germany and Austria in the preceding years.

The Manhattan Project was led by four men. There were two brilliant science administrators: Vannevar Bush, former dean of the MIT School of Engineering, who headed the newly formed Office of Scientific Research and Development, and James B. Conant, the president of Harvard, who came to Washington to head the National Defense Research Committee. The army was to be responsible for the project, and Brigadier General Leslie R. Groves was the officer in charge. The driving force behind the operational side of the project, Groves had been head of the Army Corps of Engineers and had just finished building the Pentagon when he was put in charge of the Manhattan Project. Less than six feet tall but almost 300 pounds, Groves was, according to his closest subordinate, "the biggest sonovabitch I've ever met in my life, but also one of the most capable individuals. He had an ego second to none, he had tireless energy . . . and he was absolutely ruthless in how he approached a problem to get it done. . . . I hated his guts and so did everybody else."[19] Groves chose as lead scientist in the project the complex and cerebral Robert Oppenheimer. Considering that Oppenheimer was already under suspicion for ties to the Communist Party, the two worked together remarkably well.[20] These four men ran the project; overall supervision was given to the venerable secretary of war Henry Stimson, a man of unquestioned integrity and rectitude and a pillar of the establishment.

As in the decision to pursue unconditional surrender, FDR's personal domination of policymaking in the decision to use the nuclear bomb was

Leaders of the Manhattan Project, General Leslie Groves and Robert Oppenheimer. Science History Images / Alamy Stock Photo / HRKN64.

striking. Roosevelt kept the critical policy decisions involved in the bomb's future use entirely in his own hands. As a consequence of his solitary decision and secrecy, careful, extended deliberation was put off and there never really was the broad attention to the important questions that so momentous an issue clearly deserved.[21] Roosevelt pondered the bomb's use largely in solitude when time might have permitted a deep and careful assessment of the new weapon.[22] A small circle of military and political leaders was privy to the details of the project but were not gathered by the president to consider the possible use of the weapon. Questions about the bomb's use were thus allowed to wait too long.

Britain shared in the details of the Manhattan Project, and in a secret aide-mémoire, which even Stimson did not know of, signed by the president and Churchill on September 18, 1944, they agreed that "when a 'bomb' is finally available, it might perhaps, after mature consideration, be used against the Japanese, who should be warned that this bombardment will be repeated until they surrender."[23] Three days later the president summoned Vannevar Bush to the White House for talks that included the future of the atomic bomb. They had an extended conversation over "whether the bomb should actually be used against the Japanese or tested and held as a threat. The two men agreed that the question should be carefully discussed, but Roosevelt also accepted Bush's argument that it could be 'postponed for quite a time' in view of the fact that certainly it would be inadvisable to make a threat unless we were distinctly in a position to follow it up if necessary."[24]

The aide-mémoire with Churchill was the only policy guideline FDR left behind when he died on April 12, 1945. Truman knew virtually nothing of the project until nearly two weeks after he became president. Some observers have wondered whether Roosevelt, had he lived, would have used the bomb. Other observers have wondered whether the bomb would have been used against Germany, suggesting its use against Japan was the result of the rampant racial prejudice at the time. General Groves recalls FDR telling him that "if the European war was not over before we had our first bombs he wanted us to be ready to drop them on Germany."[25] On another occasion, however, Groves told Stimson that "the target is and was always expected to be Japan."[26] Barton Bernstein, who has studied the issue as extensively as any historian, writes that "there is no substantial evidence, despite some spotty documents, that Roosevelt, had he lived, would have chosen to abstain from using the bomb on Germany, or on Japan." The war in Europe would be over before the bomb was ready, however, and planning for the use of the bomb had come to focus on Japan.[27] At the end of December 1944, Stimson and Groves informed Roosevelt that the uranium bomb, which did not require testing, would be ready by August 1, 1945, and the plutonium bomb would be ready for testing in July.

Targeting Civilians

The American determination to achieve unconditional surrender led to the most extreme measures, including the targeting of civilians, to break enemy morale. Americans saw this war as a crusade against evil, and so daunting was their industrial and technological capacity that they might well have felt that they had no reason to compromise. During the war, George Kennan worried that unconditional surrender policy would cause Americans to take the harshest measures possible against enemy populations "short of actual physical extermination" and to adopt "a ruthlessness now foreign to our troops."[28]

By 1944 the American war machine was on full display. Nothing symbolized the prowess of the war machine better than the B-29 that came into use in the last year of the war and did indeed lead to the most harsh and ruthless war measures ever taken by Americans. When Saipan fell to American troops in July 1944, the home islands came within range of the new B-29 super fortress. As Paul Kennedy observes, it was a turning point in the Asia Pacific War akin to Normandy in Europe[29] and allowed the firebombing of Japanese cities to begin.

The goal of unconditional surrender induced more and more extreme military measures, including the purposeful targeting of civilians. In 1939, prior to American entry into the war, FDR himself had publicly called on the combatants to avoid the bombing of civilians.[30] But by the latter part of the war, the US Air Force had crossed over from aiming at military targets to carpet bombing of cities. At first, they concentrated on military targets with mixed success. Soon, however, Major General Curtis LeMay, commander of the XXI Bomber Command, devised a strategy of firebombing that brought stunning results in 1945. Rather than flying at high altitudes, where the jet stream would blow bombs off target, LeMay had bombers fly at low altitudes and use a form of napalm to ignite fires in buildings, which were predominantly wood. At first, the bombing of civilians was justified by the necessity to hit military production, which was often subcontracted to small shops in civilian neighborhoods. But soon it was legitimated as necessary to break civilian morale and lead to an early end of the war. On the night of

March 9, 1945, 334 B-29s carried out a massive bombing of Tokyo in which upward of 100,000 residents of the Japanese capital died.[31] During the last year of the war, incendiary bombing extended to more than sixty other Japanese cities, which destroyed between 40 and 100 percent of those cities and took the lives of as many as half a million Japanese civilians. The postwar US Strategic Bombing Survey concluded that some of these cities had no industrial importance and "the preponderant purpose appears to have been to secure the heaviest possible morale and shock effect by widespread attack upon the Japanese civilian population."[32] Reflecting on the bombing long after the war, LeMay said, "I suppose if I had lost the war, I would have been tried as a war criminal. Fortunately, we were on the winning side."[33]

There is no record that Roosevelt had second thoughts about the expanded bombing mission.[34] In fact, when Churchill suggested at the Yalta Conference in February 1945 that it might be of "great value" if a four-power ultimatum were issued calling on Japan to surrender unconditionally, FDR dismissed the suggestion, observing that the Japanese "would be unlikely to wake up to the true state of affairs until all of their islands had felt the full weight of air attacks."[35] As the firebombing of Japanese cities intensified, Stimson was assailed by conflicting thoughts about indiscriminate attacks, as he wrote in his diary June 6, 1945: "First, because I did not want to have the United States get the reputation of outdoing Hitler in atrocities; and second, I was a little fearful that before we get ready [to use the atomic bomb] the Air Force might have Japan so thoroughly bombed out that the new weapon would not have a fair background to show its strength."[36]

Truman and the Momentum of History

FDR left a powerful but undefined momentum toward extreme solutions of war termination. In addition to his stubborn adherence to the policy of unconditional surrender, he had left his successor with the possibility of a frightening new weapon that could be used to subdue the enemy. By mid-1944 all belligerents knew that Japan had lost the war, but it lasted another year before it came to its catastrophic conclusion. To his last days, Roosevelt stubbornly insisted on unconditional surrender, and public opinion in the United States, reacting to the provocation of Pearl Harbor and Japanese atrocities and reflecting a deep racial antagonism, came to overwhelming support of his policy.

When FDR died on April 12, 1945, his own vice president knew little of the Manhattan Project.[37] Truman had met with FDR only twice since assuming the vice presidency. Shortly after Roosevelt's death, Stimson and Groves came to the White House and briefed the uninformed and inexperienced new president. Stimson told Truman: "Within four months we shall in all probability have completed the most terrible weapon ever known in human history, one bomb of which could destroy a whole city."[38]

Quite in contrast to Roosevelt, who characteristically kept his own counsel and dominated policymaking, the new president drew heavily on his advisors. Stimson asked the new president for authorization to appoint an interim committee to advise him on the use of the weapon. The committee, which Stimson chaired, included Bush; Conant; Karl Compton, president of MIT; and James Byrnes, soon to be the secretary of state.[39] A panel of several leading scientists—Oppenheimer, E. O. Lawrence, Arthur Compton, and Enrico Fermi—was also brought in to advise the committee. This was hardly an ordinary group of men. Rather, by human standards, these were the "best and brightest," who would deliberate on use of the ultimate weapon.

The rush of history was palpable. The new president was caught up in a surge of breathtaking events. Allied troops swept into Germany, and on May 8, after the suicide of Adolf Hitler, Germany surrendered. The battle of Okinawa had begun on April 1. The eighty-two-day battle was so bloody that a third of the entire Okinawan population of 450,000 people lost their lives, many at the hands of a Japanese military nominally defending them. In all, "234,000 people were killed, including 147,000 Okinawans, over 72,000 mainland Japanese, and more than 12,000 Americans. The US Navy lost more men at Okinawa than in any other battle in its entire history."[40]

At this late date, the end of May 1945, just weeks after Germany's surrender, with the invasion of the Japanese homeland imminent and with the bomb about to be tested, discussion of the weighty issues that ought to have been undertaken much earlier was about to take place. Should the Japanese be warned that the new weapon would be used against them if they did not surrender? Should there be a demonstration to impress the Japanese leaders? Should it be used against civilians, noncombatants? In a conversation with Stimson on May 29, 1945, General Marshall expressed concern that use against civilians would leave the United States with a burden of "opprobrium which might follow from an ill-considered employment of such force." He urged Stimson to consider that the bomb "might first be used against straight military objectives such as a large naval installation and if no complete result was derived from the effect of that, he thought we ought to designate a number of large manufacturing areas from which the people would be warned to leave."[41]

Two days later, on May 31, the Interim Committee came to the Pentagon for a momentous meeting to discuss how the bomb should be used. There, on Conant's recommendation, it was unanimously agreed that the bomb should be employed against Japan as soon as possible and that the target should be a vital war plant employing a large number of workers and closely surrounded by workers' houses. They briefly examined and ruled out the possibility of a warning or a demonstration. Oppenheimer could not think of a sufficiently spectacular demonstration other than "a real target of built-up structures." Furthermore, "if the Japanese received a warning that such a weapon would be exploded somewhere over Japan, their aircraft might create problems that could lead to the failure of the mission. If the test were conducted on neutral ground, it was hard to believe that the 'determined and fanatical military men of Japan would be impressed.'"[42] In retrospect, the Interim Committee's deliberations about the use of the bomb seem surprisingly brief.

Within days of receiving the Interim Committee's recommendation that the bomb should be used on Japanese cities with no prior warning or demonstration, the president also received the recommendation of the joint chiefs for the invasion of Japan. Not surprisingly, given the immense prestige of his predecessor, the new president was inclined to be faithful to Roosevelt's legacy and determined to adhere to its basic strategies. Most important, he accepted FDR's war goal. Unconditional surrender had become deeply implanted in American public opinion, institutions, and military strategy. A powerful momentum swept Truman forward. Memories of Pearl Harbor, the bitterness of fighting, Japanese atrocities, and wartime propaganda had built overwhelming public support for nothing short of all-out victory. Democracies in war—especially the Asia Pacific War—brought, as Michael Howard wrote, "an entirely new dimension of violent passion to which advances in technology could, unfortunately, give full rein. . . . They have repeatedly displayed a bellicose passion . . . vindictive in proportion to the shattering of their peaceful ideals."[43] In his first address to a joint session of Congress only four days after becoming president, Truman asserted that "our policy will continue to be unconditional surrender" and the entire chamber rose to its feet cheering. Congress reflected the overwhelming public sentiment. In polling undertaken on June 1, 1945, American opinion favored by nine to one an uncompromising stance of unconditional surrender over a negotiated peace, even though it meant a costly invasion of the Japanese islands.[44]

It was not only momentum of the popular support for the unconditional surrender policy that Truman accepted and that carried him along in his early decision making; it was the massive Manhattan Project's nearing its goal that propelled his decisions. Even though American intelligence learned in late 1944 that the Germans had not made progress on building an atomic bomb, having assumed that the war would be over before it could be achieved, the Manhattan Project could not be stopped. Many of the scientists who had worked on the project, motivated by a fear that Hitler might acquire the bomb, now had second thoughts. Albert Einstein said, "If I had known that the Germans would not succeed in constructing the atom bomb, I would never have lifted a finger."[45] A group of the scientists involved signed a document known as the Franck Report, which was delivered to Stimson and the Interim Committee. The document urged that a demonstration of the bomb be attempted and that, if it were subsequently to be used in the war, a clear warning be issued. Their effort, however, made no headway in the rush of events.

A targeting committee had been choosing cities where the bomb would make its greatest impact. Groves's favored target was Kyoto, the ancient capital with its cultural treasures. Surrounded by hills that would concentrate the explosive power, this city would maximize the psychological and physical impact of the new weapon. But Stimson, who was familiar with the city, would not hear of it and blocked every effort to keep it on the target list.

Unconditional surrender policy, with its moral fervor, commitment to attaining a new world order, deferral of political objectives, and the primacy it gave to military goals, contributed powerfully to the momentum that built for the use of the bomb. With negotiation ruled out, exerting "maximum force with maximum speed," as Stimson later explained, became the guiding assumption.[46] Conventional bombing and the new willingness to deliberately target civilian populations contributed to the growing momentum toward the use of the bomb. Escalating military pressure was accepted as the way to end the war early, and each branch of the American military was motivated to use its power to compel Japanese capitulation.

So powerful was Roosevelt's legacy that Truman's decision seemed a foregone conclusion to some of those closest to him. "At no time, from 1941 to 1945," Stimson later recalled, "did I ever hear it suggested by the President, or by any other responsible member of government, that atomic energy should not be used in the war."[47] Churchill likewise recalled "that the decision whether or not to use the atomic bomb to compel the surrender of Japan was never even an issue."[48]

Barton Bernstein observed that by the time Truman became president, an "implicit American decision—really a dominant assumption—had long existed: that the bomb would be used against a hated enemy. . . . Such powerful assumptions about the A-bomb use, and the presence of partial precedents in conventional bombing for such use, prepared the way for Truman. . . . The basic decision on using the bomb flowed from overwhelming, long-held assumptions."[49] General Groves later remarked that Truman's decision was "one of noninterference—basically, a decision not to upset the existing plans."[50] The new president, he added, was "like a little boy on a toboggan."[51]

Debating Modification of Unconditional Surrender

In the face of the momentum that had built for unconditional surrender policy and the use of the bomb to achieve it, in the months after Roosevelt's death a number of highly placed American leaders began to express doubts about the policy. With FDR's formidable domination of foreign policy gone, they raised the possibility of modifying the policy. The prospect of an immensely difficult and costly invasion of the home islands and the example of the human carnage that Okinawa demonstrated evoked the first real debate among the president's closest advisors. In April 1945, returning from a visit to Germany, Assistant Secretary of State John J. McCloy reported to Stimson that what he had seen there was "Hell on earth" and urged that adherence to unconditional surrender policy not be repeated in Japan.[52] By this time it was clear that the United States had the power to bring Japan to its knees and achieve ultimate victory, but several of the president's advisors in the summer of 1945 advocated a pragmatic and flexible approach. They tended not to be the New Dealers who were committed to Roosevelt's legacy. Instead, they were a more conservative group whose careers had been as bankers, lawyers, and diplomats and who were inclined toward achieving a postwar balance of power. They were especially wary of the growing clash of interest with the Soviet Union. They proposed modifying surrender terms. They could count on quiet support from voices in the military where there had always been deep misgivings about unconditional surrender policy because of the invasion of Japan that it might ultimately require.[53]

One of the most thoughtful voices in this debate was James Forrestal, a Wall Street investment banker appointed secretary of the navy in 1944. In this position, he became notable for exposing himself "to the dangers of warfare as no other United States official of his rank did in World War II."[54] Forrestal had gone ashore at Iwo Jima to witness first-hand the Marines' ferocious fighting against the 22,000 Japanese defenders, nearly all of whom died; and Forrestal had seen the raising of the American flag at Mount Suribachi. In the spring of 1945 in a meeting of the State War Navy Coordinating Committee, Forrestal raised issues that would ensue from total defeat of Japan and the effect this would have on the postwar international system. Forrestal feared that destruction of Germany and Japan would leave a vacuum and "seriously unbalance the international system." Writing in his diary on May 1, 1945, Forrestal recorded,

> I raised the question as to whether or not it was time to make a thorough study of our political objectives in the Far East and asked these questions:
>
> 1. How far and how thoroughly do we want to beat Japan. In other words, do we want to . . . destroy the whole industrial potential?

2. Do we want to contemplate their readmission to the society of nations after demilitarization?

3. What is our policy on Russian influence in the Far East? Do we desire a counterweight to that influence? And should it be China or should it be Japan?[55]

Forrestal's third question is especially interesting. Roosevelt, like Wilson before him, disdained the balance of power to keep the peace. Forrestal, like former United States ambassador to Japan Joseph Grew and others (whom we might label realists), thought that there would be a need to balance Russian power in the postwar period. Japan might be a better counterweight than China, which was still weak and chaotic. But that was not the dominant thinking in either the Roosevelt or the Truman inner circles. Forrestal later reflected after the war's end that diplomatic planning of the peace was far below the quality of planning that went into the conduct of the war. "We regarded the war, broadly speaking, as a ball game" to be finished "as quickly as possible" but with "little thought as to the relationship between nations which would exist after Germany and Japan were destroyed."[56]

Others joined in the debate in a critical meeting in the Oval Office on June 18, at which Truman approved Operation Olympic, the planned invasion of Kyushu, to begin November 1, 1945. Stimson and McCloy broached with the president a modification of unconditional surrender policy. Was not a diplomatic solution possible? Stimson said, "I do think that there is a large submerged class in Japan who do not favor the present war and whose full opinion and influence have not yet been felt. . . . I feel something should be done to arouse them and to develop any possible influence they might have."[57] McCloy later recalled that he argued for a political solution and added that "really, we should have our heads examined if we don't explore some other method by which we can terminate this war than just by another conventional attack and landing."[58] He urged the president to make an overture to the Japanese assuring them that the institution of the emperor could be maintained.

McCloy later reflected on how little extended discussion there was about the use of the bomb. Policymaking was largely left to the military. He noted that there was no representative of the State Department present at this Oval Office meeting. "There wasn't enough vigorous thinking going on in the State Department or for that matter in the White House at the time. At the June 18 meeting, it should not have been left up to [me] the assistant secretary of war to bring up the possibility of political settlement. . . . The White House came to rely perhaps too heavily on its soldiers for all advice."[59] The State Department was reduced to "almost an auxiliary arm of the military services."[60]

Some military leaders were, in fact, troubled by the unconditional surrender policy. In the same meeting, Admiral William D. Leahy, the president's senior military advisor (who had also been Roosevelt's advisor), "said that he could not agree with those who said to him that unless we obtain the unconditional surrender of the Japanese that we will have lost the war. He feared no menace from Japan in the foreseeable future, even if we were unsuccessful in forcing unconditional surrender. What he did fear was that our insistence on unconditional surrender would result only in making the Japanese desperate and thereby increase our casualty lists."[61] The issues being raised had to do not only with the casualties that Americans would suffer in the impending invasion, but also concern with the implications of dependence on Soviet entry into the war to make an invasion successful.

Truman listened sympathetically to the arguments for modifying surrender demands, but responded that he did not believe the American public was willing to end the war on any other terms. Truman said he had left the door open with congressional leaders to modify conditions, but it was clear the president was influenced by the momentum behind earlier policy decisions as well as the overwhelming views of public opinion on the issue.[62]

Another issue raised was whether insistence on unconditional surrender in order to occupy and remake Japan's domestic institutions was a wise policy. As was often the case, Stimson offered wise counsel. Not wanting to prolong the conflict and skeptical of remaking a culture so alien as Japan's, Stimson opposed trying to remake "the government of [Japan] as a whole in any such manner as we are committed in Germany. I am afraid we would make a hash of it if we tried."[63] Unconditional surrender was necessary for Germany, but not for Japan, where he believed there was substantial indigenous potential for postwar reform. Stimson could not accept the view that Japan was incapable of progressive reform after the war. He believed there was a potential for progressive leadership in Japan, which, once the military was defeated, could be counted on to revive progress toward democracy.[64] Stimson always believed that while unconditional surrender was a necessary prerequisite for Germany, the case of Japan was different and he dismissed what he called the "uninformed agitation against the Emperor in this country mostly by people who know no more about Japan than has been given them by Gilbert and Sullivan's 'Mikado.'" As the historian Sean Malloy concluded in his study of Stimson, Stimson's "basic conservatism left him unmoved by those who sought to use Japan's defeat as an opportunity to remake Japanese society in the Western image."[65]

What was significant about the June 18 meeting was that the possibility of modifying the unconditional surrender policy and of a political solution to the war was at last raised. But no channels to the Japanese were open, and little time or opportunity remained to explore the meaning of modified terms. At the conclusion of the meeting, Truman gave his approval to Stimson to draft a statement to the Japanese clarifying the terms of surrender.

President Harry Truman and Secretary of War Henry Stimson in the Oval Office on August 8, 1945, discussing prospects for Japanese surrender after the atomic bombing of Hiroshima. AP Photo / 450808038.

Drafting the Potsdam Declaration

Stimson took charge of drafting a statement for the president to take to Potsdam, outside Berlin, for his upcoming meeting in July with Churchill and Stalin. The "Big Three" would discuss and plan for the final phase of the war, and it seemed to be an appropriate time to issue a statement that might persuade the Japanese to negotiate surrender. Drafting this statement, Stimson was influenced by a group of specialists in the State Department, known as "the Japan hands." They had firsthand familiarity with Japanese politics and frequently consulted with George Sansom, the British historian of Japan assigned to the British embassy in Washington during the war. Sansom understood the deep cultural roots of Japanese society and the difficulty that an occupation force would have in transforming it. He counseled that the emperor should be kept, that some changes in the Meiji Constitution were necessary to give civilian control of the military and to increase the power of the Diet, but that reform should be left to the Japanese themselves. "The enforced adoption by Japan of a bill of rights would have little meaning as the ordinary Japanese is little aware of the real significance of personal liberties." He opposed any thought of the Allies assuming the governing functions in Japan, but rather said that they should work through the existing government, depending on sanctions to enforce reforms.[66] The latter suggestion from the deeply knowledgeable Sansom of the possible use of sanctions to ensure that Japan carried out reforms on its own was never seriously considered at the time by policymakers or since then by scholars.

The Japan hands in the State Department were likewise cautious and skeptical of imposing a sweeping liberal agenda. They were led by Undersecretary of State Joseph Grew, who had been US ambassador in Tokyo during the decade before Pearl Harbor. One of a handful of Americans with substantial firsthand knowledge of Japan, he held deep reservations about the success Americans could have in remaking Japanese institutions, for he believed that reform of Japan would have to come from within, depending not on imposed Western institutions but rather on indigenous change in accord with Japan's cultural traditions.[67] The patrician Grew had forged close, friendly ties with Japanese conservative leaders and believed that this elite was the best hope for the future. As it later turned out, many of his conservative elite friends, such as

Yoshida Shigeru, the postwar prime minister, did indeed reemerge and shape the course of postwar Japan.

Grew argued that giving assurance to Japan that it would be allowed to preserve the emperor as a constitutional monarchy would facilitate surrender and postwar reform, and it might terminate the war before the Soviet entry complicated matters. He likened the emperor to a queen bee: "To understand the position of the Emperor . . . it might be useful to draw a homely parallel. As you know, the queen bee in a hive is surrounded by the attentions of the hive, which treats her with veneration and ministers in every way to her comfort. . . . If one were to remove the queen from the swarm, the hive would disintegrate."[68] Grew thought, correctly as we now know, that the emperor would also be useful in getting the millions of Japanese troops overseas to lay down their arms. He feared a Carthaginian peace. Destruction of Japanese power would leave a vacuum in East Asia that the Soviets would fill, Japan and China would fall into the Soviet orbit, and "a future war with Soviet Russia is as certain as anything in the world is certain."[69] Grew fundamentally wanted Japan restored as a nation capable of taking an independent role in international politics. He believed the Japanese were best left "to determine for themselves the nature of their future political structure."[70]

The realists—Stimson, Forrestal, McCloy, Grew, and the Japan specialists—not only confronted a hostile public opinion, the product of a bitter war and widely held commitment to a punitive peace; they also faced strong opposition from New Dealers, whose sympathies lay more with China. They also adhered to the Roosevelt legacy of total military victory on the way to the creation of a new international order and to a democratic domestic politics as the key to such an order. In the State Department, they included Assistant Secretary of State Dean Acheson, who privately referred to Grew as "the Prince of the Appeasers,"[71] and the cerebral Assistant Secretary of State for Public Affairs Archibald MacLeish, who along with others argued that preserving the imperial institution with its "pernicious" emperor worship cult would be an obstacle to the rooting out of militarism and hence they opposed any compromise or negotiated settlement. As Leon Sigal observes, "To liberals who believed that Japan's aggressiveness was rooted in national character and tradition, it followed that extirpating that aggressiveness required no less than a fundamental transformation of Japanese social and political institutions."[72] Faith in the success of New Deal reforms at home against entrenched interests sometimes seemed to equate with a determination to renovate societies abroad that had disrupted world peace.[73]

Liberals like MacLeish and Acheson argued moreover that American public opinion was deeply set against any tampering with the unconditional surrender goal. So far as Truman and his newly appointed secretary of state James Byrnes were concerned, that was a powerful determinant. A Gallup poll at this time showed that 70 percent of Americans favored either executing or treating the emperor harshly.[74] The poll, however, failed to capture the considerable diversity and ambiguity in public discussion of the issue.[75] Acheson later admitted that he had been wrong and Grew right about the wisdom of preserving the imperial institution as a stabilizing force in postwar Japan. He recorded some years later that "Grew's view fortunately prevailed. I very shortly came to see that I was quite wrong."[76] Acheson belatedly regretted not only his view on the imperial institution but also the State Department's failure to devise any strategy better than unconditional surrender.

Five days before Truman was to leave for Potsdam, Stimson presented to him a proposed draft of a statement to be issued to the Japanese clarifying the terms of surrender. The draft included retention of the emperor and assumed that it would be signed by Churchill, Chiang Kai-shek, and Stalin, if Russia was ready to join the war on Japan. In an accompanying memo to the president that Stimson drafted with the help of the others, he made a remarkably dispassionate case for seeking a diplomatic solution. Stimson wrote that he feared that the determination to occupy Japan would inevitably call forth a fanatical last-ditch resistance that would incur warfare as bloody as Okinawa and "we shall have to leave the Japanese islands even more thoroughly destroyed than was the case with Germany." Stimson enumerated the overwhelming advantages that the United States and its allies now possessed, giving them the opportunity to persuade the Japanese to accept something other than unconditional surrender. In the conditions of the time, Stimson made a notable case for not only modifying unconditional surrender policy but also negotiating a settlement that would leave Japan intact and largely responsible for its own reforms and reconstruction:

> I believe Japan is susceptible to reason in such a crisis to a much greater extent than is indicated by our current press and other current comment, Japan is not a nation composed wholly of mad fanatics of an entirely different mentality from ours. On the contrary, she has within the past century shown herself to possess extremely intelligent people,

capable in an unprecedentedly short time of adopting not only the complicated techniques of Occidental civilization but to a substantial extent
their culture and their political and social ideas. Her advance in all these
respects during the short period of sixty or seventy years has been one
of the most astounding feats of national progress in history. . . . I think
she has within her population enough liberal leaders (although now submerged by the terrorists) to be depended upon for her reconstruction as
a responsible member of the family of nations. I think she is better in
this last respect than Germany was. . . . We have a national interest in
creating, if possible, a condition wherein the Japanese nation may live
as a peaceful and useful member of the future Pacific community.[77]

Stimson concluded, "I personally think that . . . we should add that we
do not exclude a constitutional monarchy under her present dynasty."

But having made what would seem a case for negotiation, providing
a thoughtful and dispassionate rationale of American interest in negotiating an armistice rather than mounting what was bound to be a costly
and bloody invasion, the memo went on to propose an ultimatum—a
public declaration of what surrender would entail and a warning of the
dire consequence of failure to accept the terms. "Following are our
terms. We will not deviate from them. They may be accepted or not.
There are no alternatives." Stimson was clearly of two minds. On the
one hand, the memo presented what would have been strong reasons
for negotiating an end to the war. But on the other hand, the memo and
the attached draft proclamation proposed an ultimatum, a nonne-
gotiable demand from which the United States would brook no exception. In the end, the draft ended up more an ultimatum rather than an
attempt to initiate a negotiated solution.

Potsdam

In July 1945 Stalin, Churchill, and Truman met at Potsdam in the last
of the "Big Three" wartime conferences to discuss the contentious issues of Russian occupation of Eastern Europe as well as how to bring
the war in the Pacific to an end. One of the consequences of unconditional surrender policy was the urgent need of Russian help in invading
Japan. Truman was intent on ensuring that Stalin, who had signed a
neutrality pact with Japan in 1941, would deliver on his earlier
promise to Roosevelt that he would enter the war against Japan approximately three months after the war ended in Europe. In return, it
was agreed that Russia would be compensated with the restoration of

the rights in Northeast Asia that it had lost in the Russo-Japanese War. Stalin was now ready to break the neutrality pact with Japan and seize the territorial gains Roosevelt had promised him. He assured Truman of his intention to enter the war, and the president wrote in his diary, "Fini Japs when that comes about," and to his wife, "I've gotten what I came for."[78]

While the Big Three were at Potsdam, Truman received word of the successful testing of the bomb at Alamogordo in the desert of New Mexico on July 16. As Churchill noted, the president was greatly energized by the news. Truman recorded in his diary, "Believe Japs will fold before Russia comes in. I am sure they will when Manhattan appears over their homeland."[79] During a break in their meetings, he casually mentioned to Stalin that the United States had developed a highly destructive new weapon. Stalin seemed indifferent, but we now know that he was fully aware from Soviet espionage precisely what the president was telling him.[80]

On July 26 Truman authorized the Potsdam Declaration, which he, Churchill, and Chiang Kai-shek (who was not present) signed. With the bomb successfully tested, Truman and his advisors were losing interest in Russia's joining the war. Stimson had urged the president to have Stalin sign the declaration. The impact of the Soviet signature, indicating its breaking of the neutrality pact and impending entry into the war, together with reference to a willingness to see retention of the imperial institution, Stimson thought, would offer the Japanese strong motivation to accept surrender terms. Churchill, as well, suggested that modification of terms might avert the need to invade and suffer massive casualties.[81]

Truman's new secretary of state, James Byrnes, persuaded him not to soften unconditional surrender policy and not to include the Russians. Stalin was not asked to sign the declaration, although he had come to Potsdam with a draft of such a joint statement that he had been led to expect he would sign demanding Japanese surrender. He wanted such a statement since, if rejected, it would provide pretext for breaking the neutrality pact with Japan and going to war to recover territory lost in the Russo-Japanese War and the strategic positions he sought for future security.

The Potsdam Declaration, issued as a public proclamation, called on Japan to surrender unconditionally or face prompt and utter destruction.[82] The Allies would occupy Japan to disarm it and establish a new order in accord with the freely expressed will of the Japanese people. There were three significant omissions: it made no mention of the bomb or of Russia's impending entry or of the fate of the emperor. Truman and Byrnes decided that it was politically unacceptable to abandon the policy of unconditional surrender. Byrnes advised the president that there would be terrible political repercussions and that public opinion would accuse the president of appeasement.[83]

Much misinformation exists about Truman's "decision." Generally, Americans have assumed that the Japanese were given a warning in the Potsdam Declaration of imminent disaster, and when they dismissed it the president made the decision to use the bomb. The use of this awful weapon, it is generally held, was justified by Japanese intransigence and by the lives, both American and Japanese, that were said to be saved by its use. The facts that Japan's desperate resistance was in reaction to the demand for unconditional surrender and the absence of any attempt to explore peace negotiations are often overlooked. But even before authorizing the Potsdam Declaration, Truman had given verbal approval to the military on July 24 to move ahead with plans to use the atomic bomb, apparently with the understanding that he could rescind the order if the Japanese accepted the ultimatum. Truman wrote in his diary the next day that the bomb would be used against Japan "between now and August 10th": "The target will be a purely military one and we will issue a warning statement asking the Japanese to surrender and save lives. I'm sure they will not do that, but we will have given them the chance."[84] Having already verbally given his approval of its use before the issuance of the Potsdam Declaration, he largely ceded control of the bomb and its use to the military.

Japan's *Ketsugo* Strategy

After the fall of Saipan in July 1944, bringing the homeland within range of the new B-29 bombers, the Tōjō cabinet resigned and a new weak and uncertain government faced mounting difficulties. In October, the epic battle of Leyte Gulf, the biggest naval engagement in history, ended in the destruction of the Japanese carrier fleet, and "the once mighty Japanese navy would never again play an important role in the Pacific War."[85] The remaining Japanese holdings in Southeast Asia were effectively cut off from the homeland. Desperation gripped the

Japanese leadership. It was not simply, as historians have often written, the rapidly deteriorating military situation that caused despair. Rather, it was increasingly the "domestic situation." The leadership was apprehensive over the growing unrest at home brought on by wartime controls, the shortage of food, and the devastation caused by American carpet bombing of cities. The records of the time are replete with reference to the unrest and disaffection of ordinary Japanese. "Police records from as early as 1942 convey a picture not merely of demoralization and mounting defeatism, but of growing contempt for existing authority extending even to the emperor himself. In the view of the Home Ministry's notorious Thought Police (*Tokkō,* literally Special Higher Police), as defeat grew closer and closer, Japan faced impending chaos and possibly even revolutionary upheaval."[86] In these circumstances a group of civilian leaders began cautiously and secretly discussing ways of terminating the war. Their major goal was preserving the imperial reign in the homeland, or what was simply known as the "national polity" or *kokutai.*

The clearest and most compelling evidence of this apprehension is found in the so-called *Yohansen* Incident of February 1945. "*Yo*" referred to the prominent diplomat Yoshida Shigeru, who was a leader of the effort, and "*hansen*" (anti-war) denoted an appeal to end the war. On February 14, Prince Konoe met with the emperor and presented a memorial that he had drafted with Yoshida asserting that defeat was "inevitable," expressing fear that a communist revolution might ensue because of popular discontent with the war, and urging direct negotiations with the Anglo-American powers. An imposing group of conservative civilian elite involved in drafting the memorial was convinced that Japan must surrender lest continuation open the way for a social revolution at home that might spell the end of the emperor's dynastic reign and the overthrow of the imperial system and its values—what was known as the *kokutai.* "I think there is no alternative to making peace with the United States," Konoe told the emperor. "Even if we surrender unconditionally, I feel that in America's case she would not go so far as to reform Japan's *kokutai* or abolish the imperial house. Japan's territory might decrease to half of what it is at present, but even so, if we can extricate the people from the miserable ravages of war, preserve the *kokutai,* and plan for the security of the imperial house, then we should not avoid unconditional surrender."[87] At the same time, Kido, the Privy Seal, was also warning the emperor that "the situation today has reached the point where people hold a grudge against the imperial house."[88]

Although the emperor replied that he agreed with Konoe, he nonetheless chose to procrastinate and side with the military in its strategy of fighting a decisive battle that would be so costly to the Allies that they would be willing to negotiate a peace. The emperor's failure to respond to this initiative from conservative civilian leaders at this time was a lost opportunity.[89] The Allied policy of unconditional surrender had always strengthened the hand of the hardliners. With only the broadest outline of what the Allies meant by this policy and with no backdoor channels to the United States to provide any clarification, Japan's early hope for a negotiated settlement steadily gave way to a determined will in the army to dig in for resistance. Those who favored negotiating an early end to the war were severely handicapped by the Allied refusal to talk as well as by the emperor's and the army's determination to fight on regardless of the cost to the livelihood of the people.

On April 5 the emperor approved the appointment of the aging admiral Suzuki Kantarō, his former grand chamberlain, to lead the government, and decision making was now placed in a Supreme War Council made up of the prime minister, foreign minister, ministers of war and navy, and the chiefs of staff of the army and navy. Known as the Big Six, they would make decisions by unanimous vote, occasionally meeting in the presence of the emperor. Within the Big Six, Suzuki, the foreign minister, and the naval minister were inclined toward finding a way out of the war, while the other three sided with the army's strategy of seeking a decisive battle, or *ketsugo*, that would so bloody the enemy that it would be compelled to negotiate a settlement. The *ketsugo* strategy was really the essence of what Japan's fallback strategy had always been. If it could not defeat the United States, then it would go on the defensive and demonstrate that if there was no longer any chance of winning, its enemy could not reach its aim either. The belief that Japan could sap the will of the Americans for a prolonged war and bring about a negotiated settlement had been a part of the military's strategy from the outset of the war, but by 1945 with allied invasion imminent, it had come to focus on a decisive battle in defense of the homeland.

Even after the German surrender on May 8 and the fall of Okinawa on June 22, the army remained wedded to the concept of *ketsugo*. It was

not entirely a fanatical or suicidal strategy. The army leaders knew what
Carl Clausewitz had theorized in his famous work *On War*. In the situation where the invader is intent on destroying the sovereignty of the
enemy, the defense can be superior to the offense even though the invader is far stronger. Clausewitz had written,

> In a war in which the objective of the attacker is the destruction of the
> defender's sovereignty, the difficulties for the attacker are increased by
> the inherently greater strength of the defender's political / policy motive.
> This is because the moral stakes for the defender are about existence,
> which is essential, whereas the attacker is concerned simply with
> gain which is discretionary. Moreover . . . the regular forces of the de-
> fender can be augmented by the actions of an aroused citizenry—that
> is, guerilla war. . . . A defender that is too weak to launch an offensive
> can still obtain favorable terms by discouraging the attacker through
> protraction of hostilities.[90]

The *ketsugo* strategy might have worked in the prenuclear age. In fact,
General Marshall worried that the American public might not have been
willing to tolerate the kind of massive casualties that would result from
an invasion and prolonged war. As American intelligence revealed the
growing strength of the Japanese buildup in Kyushu in the summer of
1945, it was unlikely, in the view of several historians, that Truman
would have gone through with the invasion (Operation Olympic) as
planned.[91] The atomic bomb solved the dilemma.

The emperor accepted the army's strategy and on April 8 approved
the *ketsugo* plan for defense of the homeland. The Japanese would be
readied for their Masada. The entire nation would be mobilized for this
final stand. Civilians, including women, would be trained. Kamikaze
would be prepared. Troops from Manchuria would be brought back in
massive numbers for an almost Armageddon last stand. The army prepared a massive mobilization of forces in the homeland to engage the
invasion. The military historian Richard Frank explains that the Japanese army now summoned supreme nerve for a battle in the homeland.
"If the initial assault could be repulsed, or even if its cost could just be
made prohibitive, Japan might yet extricate itself from the war with
honor."[92] With reinforcements from Manchuria the aggregate strength
of the homeland armies would be close to 3 million men. The mobilization of the civilian population and the further organization of suicidal
tactics were also part of the *ketsugo* strategy.

In the face of the army's intense determination, those within the Japanese leadership looking for a way out of the war had to be cautious. In a very real sense they were caught between the proverbial rock and a hard place. The Americans demanded unconditional surrender, and the army demanded unconditional resistance. The Americans had declared their sweeping goals in broad and unspecific terms: dissolution of the empire, occupation of the homeland, permanent disarmament of the country, war crimes trials of Japanese leaders, reengineering of the Japanese political and economic structure, and the reeducation of the people. The Japanese army had specified four contrary conditions as sine qua non for negotiation: preservation of the *kokutai* or imperial institution, no occupation, self-disarmament, and self-conducted trials.

In these circumstances, the effort to find a way out of this deadlock led the peace party down a strange and unlikely path. They turned to the Soviet Union to request its help in mediating a negotiated settlement. Foreign Minister Tōgō Shigenori recalled, "Had we not approached the Soviet Union, we would clearly have had to accept the terms of unconditional surrender. Only through Soviet mediation could we expect to turn unconditional surrender into conditional surrender."[93] On June 22, the day that Okinawa fell, the emperor sanctioned a direct approach to Moscow, despite the fact that the Soviet foreign minister had notified the Japanese government on April 5 that it would not renew the neutrality pact when it was due to expire a year hence. That fact alone should have discouraged an approach to Moscow. Ambassador Satō Naotake in Moscow was unambiguous in discouraging the approach, informing Foreign Minister Tōgō that it was unimaginable that Moscow would help in such an effort. Satō was extraordinarily direct in his criticism of the attempt, especially in light of the fact that Tokyo had not been able to come to any agreement on acceptable peace terms.

It is possible to see a glimmer of reason in Japan's peace feelers to Moscow. But it is a stretch. In general they were clumsy, farfetched, and naive. The Japanese were banking on the tensions between the Soviets and the Anglo-American powers to aid in their effort. The hope was that Moscow might be detached from the Allied side, persuaded to maintain its neutrality, recompensed with territorial concessions in the Chinese northeast, and induced to mediate a peace that would leave Japan intact. Moreover, the army was willing to accept this one diplomatic strategy while still maintaining its own *ketsugo* strategy. It was a measure of Japanese desperation that civilian leadership, with the support of the emperor and the wary acquiescence of the military, hoped the Soviets might provide an alternative to unconditional surrender.

The archival research of historian Yukiko Koshiro shows that certain Japanese strategists hoped to engage the Russians as a counterweight to the United States not only to mediate a peace agreement but also to forestall a postwar American regional hegemony that would disadvantage Japan. These strategists hoped that a balance of power in the region might provide a defeated Japan some leeway to preserve its autonomy.[94] How much influence these strategists may have had is difficult to gauge. Most critical wartime records were incinerated by the Japanese in the days after surrender and before the arrival of the Americans. It is noteworthy, however, that even during the war the Japanese were intrigued by the possibilities that Soviet-American rivalry could provide leverage for Japan in the postwar period.[95] We shall see that postwar Prime Minister Yoshida Shigeru seized on this rivalry to formulate a strategy for Japan's recovery.

Hiroshima and Nagasaki

Having broken both the civilian and the military codes of the Japanese, Washington was aware of the massive buildup for a battle of Armageddon as well as the attempt to persuade Moscow to mediate. When the Potsdam Declaration was broadcast, Prime Minister Suzuki, perhaps regarding the broadcast as propaganda, said that Japan would ignore it. He used the word *mokusatsu*, literally meaning to kill by silence, which was interpreted in Washington as rejection. On August 6, the uranium bomb, nicknamed "Little Boy," was dropped at 8:15 a.m. on the center of Hiroshima, a major depot of the Japanese army. Some 80,000 people are estimated to have died at once, and perhaps nearly that same number died later from radiation sickness and other injuries by the end of the year.[96] On August 8, Russia entered the war. The Red Army swarmed into Manchuria, routing the Japanese army there and then moving down the Korean peninsula. Some 700,000 Japanese were taken as prisoners back to Russia, where most were held in gulags doing forced labor for years.[97] Stalin pressed his generals to move at top speed to seize all the spoils he had been promised at Yalta. Additionally, Stalin hoped to occupy Hokkaido.

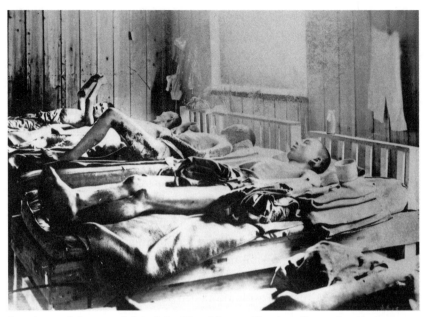

Survivors of the atomic bomb in Hiroshima suffer the effects of radiation, 1945. World History Archive / Alamy Stock Photo / D95NKX.

On August 9 at 11:02 a.m., a plutonium bomb, nicknamed "Fat Man," was dropped on Nagasaki, home of the Mitsubishi shipyards. An estimated 38,000 people were killed, and approximately that many more died by the end of the year. Rather than wait for Japanese reaction to the first bomb, General Groves had decided that hitting a second city swiftly would maximize the psychological impact. This decision was left to the military. In all, a great many more than 200,000 died from the two horrific bombs. The next city recommended as the target for the third atomic bomb was Tokyo. Moreover, the air force was preparing a list of several other cities for targeting as the atomic bombs became available.[98]

In the face of such utter disaster, an emergency meeting of the Supreme War Council was convened in the palace. With both the *ketsugo* strategy and the hope for Soviet mediation dashed, the emperor in unprecedented action broke the deadlock among the Big Six and expressed his will that the war be ended on the terms set forth by the Potsdam Declaration, with the sole reservation that the prerogatives of the emperor as sovereign ruler not be compromised.

When the Americans received this response, Secretary of State Byrnes wanted to reject it and adhere to the unconditional surrender policy. But in the end, Truman sent an ambiguous reply stating that the emperor would be "subject to the Supreme Commander of the Allied Powers" and "the ultimate form of government of Japan shall be established by the freely expressed will of the Japanese people." In the meantime, Truman ordered no more use of the bomb without his permission. He told his cabinet, as one member recorded, that "the thought of wiping out another 100,000 people was too horrible. He didn't like the idea of killing, as he said, 'all those kids.'"[99] In a second palace meeting with the Supreme War Council on August 14, the emperor insisted on accepting the reply from Washington. The next day at noon, in a recording of his Imperial Rescript calling on his people to "endure the unendurable," he announced acceptance of the Potsdam Declaration. Two days later in a second Imperial Rescript, he called on the Japanese armed forces throughout Asia to peacefully surrender and lay down their arms. Both Rescripts were almost universally accepted by the people and the military.

The emperor's extraordinary role in ending the war inevitably has raised questions of whether he could have prevented the war in the first place, whether he could have ended it sooner, and what, indeed, was the extent of his influence and the nature of his motivations. It seems clear that as a result of his upbringing and education he was consistently motivated by an obligation to preserve and protect the mythical sovereignty of the throne. Only occasionally did he intervene in politics, when it seemed necessary to safeguard the imperial system. His training was inescapably influenced by the elaboration of the imperial cult in modern times. Even its mythical symbols, the regalia, were essential to imperial legitimacy. After the war, he explained his sacred decision (*seidan*) in these terms:

> The main motive behind my decision at that time was that if we let matters stand and did not act, the Japanese race would perish and I would be unable to protect my subjects [*sekishi*, literally, infants, children]. Second, [the Privy Seal] Kido agreed with me on the matter of defending the *kokutai*. If the enemy landed near Ise Bay, both Ise and Atsuta shrines would immediately come under their control. There would be no time to transfer the sacred treasures [regalia] of the imperial family and no hope of protecting them. Under these

The Showa emperor (Hirohito) waves to a crowd at Hiroshima, December 7, 1947. In the background is the Atomic Bomb Dome. World History Archive / Alamy Stock Photo / EX6HEF.

circumstances, protection of the *kokutai* would be difficult. For these reasons, I thought at the time that I must make peace even at the sacrifice of myself.[100]

Hirohito shared the assumptions of Japan's nationalist ideology and imperial destiny, but he had been averse to going to war with the West, because such a conflict could risk the imperial system. In the end, however, he acquiesced in the decisions for war in the fall of 1941. The emperor placed a great deal of trust in Tōjō and his army faction to control the more fanatical elements of the military, and he supported the *ketsugo* strategy as the way to preserve the imperial system in the face of the unconditional surrender demand. Under the influence of the Imperial Court Ministry, the emperor was cautious and procrastinating, reluctant to inject the throne into politics and allowing opportunities to end the war to pass, expecting that the *ketsugo* strategy would prevail. Often unmentioned, the growing nervousness about domestic unrest as an additional threat to the imperial system weighed too on the Court and the elite. To the end, the emperor often seemed to value preservation of the imperial institution more than the well-being of his people.[101] Or perhaps he believed the two could not be separated. Too late, he finally acted only when the *ketsugo* strategy was checkmated by the atomic bombs and Soviet entry into the war.[102]

The Bomb's Legacy

One thing all historians may agree on. The decision was never subject to the careful and thorough deliberation that it should have had. For example, research by Sean Malloy shows that, while scientists knew of the lethal properties of the bomb's side effects, those who made the decision, including Truman, Byrnes, and Stimson, were not aware of the radiation effects and "that the weapon would continue to sicken and kill its victims long after use." The stove-piping of knowledge, together with the secrecy of the Manhattan Project, kept knowledge of the biological effects of radiation from the decision makers, who were only impressed by the blast potential of the bomb: "If American leaders had had even a rough understanding of radiation effects, that knowledge might well have affected decisions about *how* the bomb was used . . . such as the choice of targets, the possibility of an explicit warning or demonstration, and the pursuit of various diplomatic options."[103]

Most of the controversy among historians has swirled around the policies, motivation, and deliberations of President Truman and his advisors during the summer months of 1945 after the fall of Okinawa and as an invasion of Kyushu loomed. If, however, the decision is studied in a broader perspective, the momentum created by President Roosevelt's unconditional surrender policy should be understood as the source of Truman's "decision." Barton Bernstein, who has studied the issue as closely as any historian, concluded that "the basic decision on using the bomb flowed from overwhelming, long-held assumptions." "An implicit American decision—really a dominant assumption—had long existed: that the bomb would be used against a hated enemy."[104]

Confronted by surrender demands so antithetical to their values and self-identity, the Japanese military leadership determined on all-out resistance. Those Japanese leaders inclined toward ending the war were left in the dark as to what unconditional surrender would entail and were handicapped in their efforts to change the military's die-hard resistance. Unconditional surrender policy became deeply embedded in American public opinion.[105] By the time a new and inexperienced president came to office, a powerful momentum had built up in support of the unconditional surrender policy. The immense Manhattan Project itself only added to this momentum. In this context, as Reinhold Niebuhr wrote of Hiroshima, it is possible to see "historic forces more powerful than any human decision" at work.[106] That is, "since the Germans were at work on the bomb during the war, we had to develop it too; once built it was bound to be used if it would shorten the war."[107]

From the realist perspective discussed earlier, the American commitment to remaking world order and promoting democratization as essential to that pursuit led to extreme measures and utopian goals. With the unrealistic purpose of achieving a permanent peace, the United States demanded the right to reconstruct Japan and precluded any negotiations or compromise. Clearly, war fought to achieve idealistic goals fired the public resolve and galvanized support for the war effort. Understandably, the deadly surprise attack on Pearl Harbor and the appalling brutality of Japanese atrocities made it difficult to think of any peace short of total victory. Still, was it a well-conceived policy for conduct of the war? By its uncompromising character, it required either a bloody and costly invasion of the Japanese homeland or a protracted naval blockade to starve the Japanese people or continuation of the firebombing of cities—or, when it became available, the atomic bomb. The atomic bomb became the panacea for resolving the dilemmas that unconditional surrender policy created. With this weapon, invasion was no longer necessary, the ketsugo strategy was checkmated, and Russian involvement in the Occupation could be avoided. As French realist writer Raymond Aron noted, "American diplomacy itself had created a combination of circumstances which made resorting to the atom bombs almost inevitable by its demand for unconditional surrender, by its declaration to 'reform,' 'regenerate,' and democratize Japan, by the timidity of certain leaders not devoid of acumen, and by crusading slogans which precluded negotiations, even of a secret nature."[108]

If the purpose of war is to achieve concrete political objectives that could not be obtained by diplomacy, US policy abandoned the pragmatic political goals that had brought on war in the first place, namely, the insistence on Japanese withdrawal from the continent. Instead of that concrete aim, the goal became total submission of the enemy and the total remaking of its government, economy, and society. It had not occurred to the framers of American policy, wrote Hans Morgenthau, that "the business of war does not end with military victory but only with a viable distribution of power, the groundwork for which must be laid while the war is still in progress. Least of all did it occur to the framers of American policy that the Soviet Union might be destined to succeed Germany and Japan as a threat to the balance of power in Europe and in Asia."[109] To the end of his life, Roosevelt remained convinced that he could work amicably with Stalin and bring the Soviet Union into a new postwar order that would keep the peace. David Kennedy, in his magisterial history of the Roosevelt era, concludes that Americans might reflect "with some discomfort . . . on how their leaders' stubborn insistence on unconditional surrender had led to the incineration of hundreds of thousands of already defeated Japanese, first by fire raids, then by nuclear blast; on how poorly Franklin Roosevelt had prepared for the postwar era, on how foolishly he had banked on goodwill and personal charm to compose the conflicting interests of nations."[110]

While it is impossible, of course, to say whether a negotiated peace might have been achieved or what the terms of a negotiated peace might have been, we do know that a substantial portion of the Japanese conservative elite, fearing social revolution at home more than defeat in the war, was disposed to negotiate surrender. But while ending the empire, a negotiated peace might well have avoided the Occupation and left the Japanese to reform their own politics. It would have permitted the Japanese to find their own way back into the society of nations. Instead of having alien institutions imposed on them, the Japanese would have had to struggle to chart their own reforms.[111]

While Hitler and Nazism defied compromise solutions, we know that compromises with Japan were possible, because once the Occupation of Japan began, we made a succession of major compromises with our wartime goals. As we shall see, the American Occupation decided to keep the emperor. We also preserved in power the elite and powerful bureaucracy, left largely intact the huge oligopolies known as zaibatsu, and then—most ironic of all—prodded the Japanese to rearm and serve as our principal ally in Cold War Asia. In light of this postwar retreat from the unconditional surrender policy, it might well have been better to have had a less absolute set of goals, quite possibly averting the catastrophic casualties—American, Japanese, and other Asians—of the last year of the war, including those first victims of the atomic age.

4

An American Revolution in Japan

I N MODERN HISTORY, war has been a principal mechanism of change in the international system. It also transforms individual countries. World War II transformed America in many ways. But most profoundly it changed the way Americans related to the world. After its costly and misguided period of isolation and withdrawal from world affairs, the war experience made Americans ready to not only enter into the world but also take the lead in remaking it. Mobilization for the new war reawakened the Wilsonian ambition. The way in which Franklin Roosevelt cast the war as a crusade to remake the world according to American values and interests became the motivation that rallied the country to leave behind its isolationism.

In 1945 the United States was in a uniquely dominant position to reconstruct world order. The vacuum left by the wartime devastation suffered by all other major states, together with its own new power, gave the United States an opportunity to construct a new global framework of rules, institutions, and relationships within which states would operate. The United States was the principal architect of the United Nations, the International Monetary Fund, the World Bank, and an array of other institutions designed to establish a democratic capitalist world order. The Allied Occupation of Japan, which America controlled, set out to transform Japan into a permanently disarmed liberal democratic state that would support such an order.

Explicit in the unconditional surrender policy was the determination not to end the war with a negotiated peace that would leave the defeated nations a role in the international system. Japan would not be permitted to survive as a defeated and diminished power still able to play a role as a significant actor in international politics. Instead of a postwar order based on a balance of power to provide stability, as realists like Forrestal, Grew, McCloy, and others favored, the purpose was much more ambitious. The United States would assume the mantle of global leadership to order the world on the basis of the American model of democratic capitalism in accord with the values and institutions rooted in its own national experience.

By the war's end, Americans were, indeed, ready to remake the world. This time they had not only the power but also the will. In the last months of the war, Roosevelt evoked this will in a forceful and stirring radio address to the nation: "The power which this Nation has attained—the political, the economic, the military, and above all the moral power—has brought to us the responsibility, and with it the opportunity, for leadership in the community of nations. It is our own best interest, and in the name of peace and humanity, this Nation cannot, must not, and will not shirk that responsibility."[1]

Nowhere was American readiness to remake the world on clearer display than in Japan. Japan would be reconstructed as a liberal democratic state and kept in tutelage to ensure that it would fit into the new international order. The Americans set out to do what no conquering nation in modern history had ever attempted in so thorough a fashion. They would remake an ancient and complex civilization in their own image from top to bottom. President Truman was confident that it could be done. "We have emerged from this war," he said, "the most powerful nation in the world—the most powerful nation, perhaps, in all history."[2]

Indeed, the world had never seen the kind of preponderant power that the United States possessed at the end of World War II. "The United States," said Winston Churchill in 1945, "stand at this moment at the summit of the world."[3] America had unchallenged power and wealth. Unlike other major powers, its homeland remained untouched by the ravages of war. Its gross national product (GNP) had increased by 60 percent over the course of the war years and was three times that of the Soviet Union and more than five times that of Great Britain. Seven and a half million American service personnel were deployed abroad. America had half the world's shipping vessels and its navy patrolled the oceans of the world. Its industrial base produced 40 percent of the world's output and a third of the world's exports. Its treasury garnered two-thirds of the world's gold reserves. Its scientists had unlocked the explosive power in the heart of matter, and it was the sole possessor of the most powerful weapon the world had ever known. Little wonder that Americans' faith in themselves and in their values knew no bounds. Little wonder, too, that the United States would use this power and wealth in the service of its exceptionalist faith and missionary impulse to create a new international order.

Many observers saw that postwar America was on the way to becoming the successor to the British Empire. Americans did not want to be thought of as imperial. Such description would be contrary to their self-image. During the war, Roosevelt had insisted that America would be a great power but would not behave like one. Even as the Pax Americana was taking shape, Roosevelt was asserting that the age of imperialism was over. He envisaged the postwar world as postimperial. Ending European colonial empires was a priority of his plans for the postwar world.

The president favored a postwar arrangement whereby colonies would be given trusteeship status under international supervision that would prepare them for self-government. In its gradualism, the trusteeship scheme was decidedly paternalistic. Colonial peoples needed tutelage and training before gaining self-rule. Korea, for example, should be promised "ultimate independent sovereignty," but a training period of "perhaps forty years" would be needed.[4] Despite its gradualism, Roosevelt's anti-imperialist views collided with Churchill's determination to oppose interference with British colonies and especially with India, whose independence was a particular goal of the president.

FDR worked steadily during the war to formulate the concept of trusteeships, which he wanted written into the UN Charter and which he hoped would provide the impetus for decolonization. "When we've won the war," he declared, "I will work with all my might and main to see to it that the United States is not wheedled into the position of accepting any plan that will further France's imperialistic ambitions, or that will aid or abet the British empire in its imperial ambitions." Roosevelt chastised Winston Churchill, "You have four hundred years of acquisitive instinct in your blood and you just don't understand how a country might not want to acquire land somewhere else if they can get it." This was pure American sentiment. As *Life* magazine expressed it: "One thing we are sure we are *not* fighting for is to hold the British Empire together."[5]

Nevertheless, as the war in the Pacific entered its final stages, the Roosevelt administration was looking for bases by which it could secure its position in the postwar period. Secretary of the Navy Frank Knox told Congress in 1944 that all the islands that the League of Nations had mandated to Japanese trusteeship in World War I "have become Japanese territory and as we capture them they are ours."[6] Even as his joint chiefs were drawing up a shopping list of bases that the United States would want to control after the war, FDR, wanting to avoid any taint of imperialism, favored acquiring as US bases the formerly held Japanese islands by having them designated as administered under international trusteeship.[7] As Robert Dallek observed, "He saw a trusteeship system allowing the United States to establish long-term naval and air bases at strategic points in the Pacific and elsewhere. . . . While he sincerely hoped that a trusteeship system would lead to independence for former colonies, Roosevelt also wanted this idealistic approach to mask his concern with power."[8] If it was to be imperialism, it had to be liberal imperialism. A system of trusteeships would not only allow the United States to establish "long term naval and air bases at strategic points in the Pacific" but also allow formerly colonial people to acquire the first steps to self-rule while under the supervision of the new international organization that he envisioned. "In Roosevelt's judgment, this could provide a means of both aiding exploited peoples and creating a workable Pacific security system for at least twenty years."[9]

The British could see, if the Americans could not, how history was unfolding. By 1943 the British embassy in Washington reported "a fairly clear imperialist line" in US demands for postwar bases and commercial advantages in the Pacific.[10] No one could have a broader perspective than the historian of the rise and fall of civilizations, Arnold Toynbee, who thought he saw "the first phase of a coming American world empire." The transfer of global power to the Americans was recognized by other British writers such as the economist Harold Laski, who wrote that America would soon "bestride the world like a colossus, neither Rome at the height of its power nor Great Britain in the period of its economic supremacy enjoyed an influence so direct, so profound, or so pervasive."[11] In 1938, the United States had only fourteen military bases outside its continental borders. By 1945 it had tens of thousands of installations scattered across the globe. With postwar drawdown, the number had contracted to about 2,000 bases by 1948.[12] With its anti-imperialist self-image, America was becoming an empire in denial.

Occupation Authority

It was in Japan that this imperial realty was most clearly on display. The United States was prepared to behave very much in imperial fashion. Sovereign authority was in the hands of the Occupation. Japan would have no independent foreign policy or direct diplomatic relations. A new domestic order of things would be imposed on the defeated nation, and compliance would be ensured through coercion and the use of power.

The remaking of Germany was an Allied undertaking, but the re-making of Japan was entirely American. As such, it reflected America's liberal vision. Nowhere else could one find a more audacious example of their exceptionalist belief than the self-assurance Americans had in attempting to remake Japan's ancient and complex society in their own image. The persistent belief in the United States as a chosen nation with a unique role in world history found its most elaborate fulfillment in the opportunity to remake an Asian nation whose history and civilization were wholly at odds with America's. Just as the Americans had seen themselves in their national origins as beginning the world anew, so they believed that in Japan they could turn a new page in history and remake the country according to the values and institutions that they had perfected. Behind the obvious pretension and vanity was what Reinhold Niebuhr calls "our dreams of managing history."[13] America set out to put Japan on a peaceful course by imposing institutions from its own young civilization on another people whose history and habits were utterly different. The Occupation's agenda was underwritten by a claim to absolute virtue and faith in the meaning of American history and in the belief that America was the actualization of ideals and values inherent in the progress of human society. "The universalist impulse in America," Robert Dallek observed, ". . . of vastly different peoples and systems imitating U.S. institutions were the products not of rational thought or close attention to the external world but of ingrained parochialism or blind conviction that everyone wanted to follow the American lead."[14]

Unconditional surrender policy put the US military in charge of carrying out a reformation of Japan. Ted Cohen, a young New Deal lawyer in the Occupation, reflected with some abashment many years later:

> Nothing the United States had ever attempted in any other land, or even in its own, was as grand in conception. In retrospect, one trembles at American presumption. . . . On the face of it the great project was replete with paradox. The idea of democratizing by means of that least democratic of institutions, the Army, was patently illogical. . . . Entrusting the detailed reconstruction of the internal workings of an extraordinarily subtle and complex society, certainly the least known among the major nations to America, to a corps of officials very few of whom had even a smattering of Japanese history or language clearly invited ridicule.[15]

The revolutionary origins of the American nation have been a constant source of inspiration for American exceptionalism. The belief that America was in the vanguard of progress and that the ideals and institutions coming out of the American Revolution were a model for the world was captured in Emerson's poem declaring the battle of Concord began with "a shot heard round the world."

Americans plunged into nation building in Japan with little self-doubt. Yes, there were those like Henry Stimson, who feared that if Americans tried to remake Japan "we would make a hash of it."[16] The British scholar-diplomat George Sansom, who had lived for decades in prewar Japan and knew the intricacies and complexities of the ancient Japanese civilization, was skeptical of undertaking such an ambitious cultural transformation.[17] But for most Americans who approached the task, there was an enthusiasm born of experiences rooted in American history and the exceptionalist faith.

The United States therefore brushed aside the precedent of international law, which sets limits on what an occupying country was allowed to undertake. According to international law, a state so totally defeated that its institutions had disintegrated, such as Germany in 1945, gave the occupying power the right to construct new institutions.[18] But Japan was different. The Japanese government was still functioning when Japan surrendered. The Meiji Constitution and legal codes were all still intact. Article 43 of the 1907 Hague Regulations stated, "The authority of the legitimate powers having in fact passed into the hands of the occupant, the latter shall take all the measure in his power to restore and ensure, as far as possible, public order and [civil life], while respecting, unless absolutely prevented, the laws in force in the country."[19] Those restrictions had been the culmination of international law in the nineteenth century. As Michael Doyle sums up, under existing international law, occupiers were "not permitted to reform the laws, promote human rights not already recognized in local law, change the constitution, democratize, or promote social equity."[20] In other words, everything the Americans were about to do to transform Japan was prohibited.

But in the century of total warfare, Americans made light of those restrictions, presuming that Japan's "unconditional surrender" gave them legitimate authority and justification for ignoring the principles of international law. As Truman told General Douglas MacArthur after appointing him Supreme Commander of the Allied Powers, "Our relations with Japan do not rest on a contractual basis, but on an unconditional surrender. Since your sovereignty is supreme, you will not entertain any question on the part of the Japanese as to its scope."[21] With hundreds of thousands of American soldiers arriving, Japanese sovereignty had disappeared. For the first time in history, Japan was occupied by enemy forces.

Japan through an American Prism

Scarcely foreseen at the time of its announcement, the unconditional surrender policy would draw the United States across a threshold of unprecedented involvement in the affairs of another nation. It meant that the United States had to begin planning for the occupation of Japan and not only disarm the military and try its leaders, but also transform its political and economic structure, reform its society, and reeducate its people to ensure that Japan would not again be a threat to peace.

It was a task for which Americans were ill prepared. Still, during the war years a remarkable group of American social scientists came to Washington to begin study of Japanese culture and to advise in the formulation of policy. How could the Japanese be prodded to surrender unconditionally? What reforms would be required to transform Japanese state and society? How could the Japanese be motivated to accept radical social change?[22] In short, there was an urgent need to try to fathom a complex and subtle culture far older than the American and the result of a history that was profoundly different. Planning moved slowly since the expertise and the infrastructure were not in place to undertake the challenge of remaking another society, especially one so fundamentally alien. Nevertheless, by the last year of the war, a mobilization of outside advisors brought new thinking and ideas to Washington. Rarely was its knowledge about Japan deep, but it was the beginning of an American effort to account for and interpret Japanese behavior.

As the Occupation began, the writer who made the most poignant effort to help Americans understand the Japanese was the anthropologist Ruth Benedict. Her book *The Chrysanthemum and the Sword,* published in 1946, became "the most famous American social-science contribution to the Second World War."[23] Given that serious American study of Japan was in its infancy, it was perhaps inevitable that Benedict's interpretation should later be seen as ethnocentric and patronizing.[24]

Yet, there is no denying that the book became highly influential. It has had a huge audience in Japan, where it has sold nearly 2.5 million copies, has gone through more than one hundred printings, and is still widely discussed in Japanese school textbooks. The cultural anthropologist Aoki Tamotsu credits it with beginning the postwar obsession with Japanese identity and establishing American culture and values as everything that Japan was not and that it might be—a kind of negative identity.[25] The prominent Japanese psychiatrist Doi Takeo recalls first reading *Chrysanthemum:* "I still remember the vivid impression I had of seeing myself reflected in it. Time and again, as I turned the pages, I gave a nod of surprised recognition. At the same time the book stirred my intellectual curiosity as to why the Japanese and the Americans should be so different."[26]

The book was the product of an extraordinary life of study that brought Benedict to Washington, where she became one of the most thoughtful and sensitive of the group of social scientists assembled to help policymakers understand the unfamiliar countries with which the war had thrown Americans into contact. Benedict brought a formidable intellect and analytical experience to her task. Her earlier book *Patterns of Culture,* published in 1934, became "probably the most popular book

Anthropologist Ruth Benedict, author of *The Chrysanthemum and the Sword*.
MixPix / Alamy Stock Photo / D88E2A.

in anthropology ever published" in the United States.[27] In this and sub-sequent writings, Benedict helped redirect the field of anthropology away from its existing view of behavior as racially determined. Rather, behavior was the expression of customs, institutions, and ways of thinking inherited from the distinctive histories of different peoples.

In June 1944, she was assigned to the study of Japan. "I was asked to use all the techniques I could as a cultural anthropologist to spell out what the Japanese were like."[28] It was a challenge. Japan, she wrote, is "the most alien enemy the United States had ever fought in an all-out struggle."[29] She did not know the language and had never visited the country. But it was a challenge for which her career and her passions had prepared her. Her studies had shown her that there was an inherent logic of assumptions that bound all aspects of social behavior together, and that by studying diverse practices and institutions in a society one could find a pattern that integrated the whole culture. Therefore, drawing on "wildly assorted materials derived from wildly assorted sources (legends, movies, interviews with Japanese expatriates and prisoners of war, scholarly works, newspaper accounts, radio broadcasts, 'antiquarian papers,' novels, speeches in the Diet, military intelligence reports),"[30] she wove a compelling picture of the patterns of Japanese culture. The reports that she wrote for the government became the basis of *The Chrysanthemum and the Sword.*

A poet by avocation, gentle and thoughtful in her ways, and not comfortable with the mainstream of American life, she wrote with grace and simplicity, producing a sympathetic portrait remarkable for a time of deep bitterness toward the Japanese. Benedict set out to make Japan intelligible to Americans, to explain the cultural logic in terms they could understand. She attempted to make intelligible what Americans thought exotic by comparing it to the familiar. In fact, as one Japanese anthropologist observed, *Chrysanthemum* "presents a self-portrait of Americans by using the radically different culture of Japan as a mirror."[31]

The "we / they" description was later criticized as ethnocentric, but positioning the Japanese and Americans as a mirror image was her way of conveying an understanding for Americans. "The arc of life in Japan," she wrote, "is plotted in opposite fashion to that in the United States." Where Americans pursue freedom of choice during the course of their lives, "the Japanese rely on maximizing the restraints upon [them]."[32] Japanese are ever constrained in their behavior by their obligations, while Americans value spontaneity.

A main contrast between Japanese and American culture as Benedict described it was the Japanese confidence in hierarchy and the American devotion to equality. "Any attempt to understand the Japanese must begin with their version of what it means to 'take one's proper station.' Their reliance upon order and hierarchy and our faith in freedom and equality are poles apart and it is hard for us to give hierarchy its just due as a possible social mechanism. Japan's confidence in hierarchy is basic in her whole notion of man's relation to his fellow man and of man's relation to the State."[33] Sifting through the documents of Japan's wartime nationalist ideology, Benedict had no trouble finding repeated reference to the worldview that leaders described, universalizing domestic Japanese values as appropriate to the international system in East Asia where other Asian peoples were expected to take their proper station behind Japanese leadership. Such a view was bound to be anathema to Americans: "Equality is the highest, most moral American basis for hopes for a better world. It means to us freedom from tyranny, from interference, and from unwanted impositions. It means equality before the law and the right to better one's condition in life. It is the basis for the rights of man as they are organized in the world we know. We uphold the virtue of equality even when we violate it and we fight hierarchy with a righteous indignation."[34]

Although she was later criticized for not fully grasping their meanings, Benedict engaged in word studies that revealed deep cultural significance for which *Chrysanthemum* became famous. She showed remarkable sympathy and sensitivity for the Japanese sense of social interdependence, understanding that Japanese society was held together by a recognition that relationships were reciprocal and complementary. Accordingly, she stressed the indebtedness that pervaded social interactions. *On* was the sense of obligations passively incurred in the course of life from parents all the way to the emperor.[35] *Giri* was the obligation "to repay *on* to one's fellows." Japanese are taught to deeply feel a gratitude for the benefits they have received from others, whereas Americans, with their traditions of individualism, often overlook these benefits and take pride in being self-made: "Because Westerners pay such extremely slight attention to their debt to the world and what it has given them in care, education, well-being or even in the mere fact of their ever having been born at all, the Japanese feel that our motivations are inadequate. Virtuous men do not say, as they do in America, they owe nothing to any man."[36]

Where Americans find their guidance in universal principles, Japanese are guided by the proper behavior expected in different situations. Westerners had an absolute standard of values, she wrote, while Japanese were governed by situational ethics. She captured this contrast most famously in her comparison of shame and guilt cultures:

A society that inculcates absolute standards of morality and relies on men's developing a conscience is a guilt culture by definition. . . . True shame cultures rely on external sanctions for good behavior, not, as true guilt cultures do, on an internalized conviction of sin. Shame is a reaction to other people's criticism. A man is shamed either by being openly ridiculed and rejected by fantasying himself that he has been made ridiculous. . . . Shame has the same place of authority in Japanese ethics that "a clear conscience" "being right with God," and the avoidance of sin have in Western ethics.[37]

Japanese live within boundaries maintained by avoiding the shame of transgressing conventions prescribed by the time, place, and social position. Americans, in contrast, are motivated to avoid guilt felt in breaking internalized moral principles.[38]

To Benedict, the Japanese were a people of contradictions. They cultivated both beauty and violence, the chrysanthemum and the sword. They could be aggressive, as a result of childhood indulgence, or they could be gentle, as they were molded by the constraints of social patterns. She compared the social restraints on Japanese life to the careful positioning of chrysanthemums in flower arranging, even with its artifice in pruning and using hidden wires to keep the stems in place. Social life, with its intricate codes to govern shades of behavior in different situations, was a heavy burden: "The Japanese have paid a high price for their way of life. They have denied themselves simple freedoms which Americans count upon as unquestioningly as the air they breathe."[39] Despite her professional commitment to respect the essential worth of every culture, as one of her biographers put it, Benedict could not conceal "what she valued in American society: spontaneity and creativeness; a cautious adventurousness and enterprise; a respect for individuality."[40]

In many ways, the most important conclusion of Benedict's book for policymakers was that Japan could change—or, rather, Japan could be changed. Inherent in her approach was a belief that culture had to be relearned in each generation. Unlike racist dispositions, which believed behavior was biologically inbred, she implied that understanding Japanese culture would make possible fundamental reforms that would change Japanese behavior. "Under a new dispensation they will have to learn new sanctions. And change is costly. It is not easy to work out new assumptions and new virtues. The Western world can neither suppose that the Japanese can take these on sight and make them truly their own, nor must it imagine that Japan cannot ultimately work out a freer, less rigorous ethics. . . . [They] can, in a new era, set up a way of life which does not demand the old requirements of individual restraint. Chrysanthemums can be beautiful without wire racks and such drastic pruning."[41] In sum, the anthropologist Marilyn Ivy observed, Japan was "open to Americanized rehabilitation."[42]

Benedict has been much criticized for her failure to transcend her own cultural dispositions and to appreciate Japan simply on its own terms. Nevertheless, for her time, her sympathetic interpretation, whatever its shortcomings, was a remarkable achievement. She made this alien, enemy culture understandable to Americans in ways they could grasp.

MacArthur and the Liberal Agenda

The Occupation reforms in Japan represented the apotheosis—the very culmination—of American liberalism. Perhaps nowhere else in American history can one find a more extreme example of the commitment to what the political scientist Louis Hartz called "the liberal tradition in America" or what Gordon Wood called "the idea of America."[43] It was an irony of history that the agent for the liberal agenda to transform Japan was a figure identified with the right wing of the American political spectrum. This apparent anomaly is best understood as evidence of the pervasive hold of liberal ideals across the entire American political spectrum. The unlimited faith of Douglas MacArthur in the liberal credo was testimony to the depth of American faith in the universal claims of its values and institutions. His domineering role in Japan was the supreme example of America's post-1945 imperial role in the making of the new world order.

MacArthur had an ego bigger than life. It was not just his personal self-importance that made it so. His ego was inflated by his sense of American cultural superiority at a historical moment when that national self-assurance knew few bounds. It was perhaps fitting that an undertaking so grand and pretentious would be led by one of such ego. Although his military career included distinguished service in Europe during World War I and in Washington as army chief of staff (1930–1935), his life, more than any American general, was focused on the Asia

Pacific region.[44] Fresh out of West Point in 1903, MacArthur was posted in the Philippines, where his father had ruled as military governor for a brief period after it became an American colony. In 1905 he accompanied his father to Japan when the latter was designated as President Theodore Roosevelt's observer at the Russo-Japanese War. MacArthur made a grand tour of Asia with his father after the Russo-Japanese War and felt he had discovered "western civilization's last earth frontier."[45] Still, the general was less swayed by the overt racism of many Americans, but rather by a paternal view of Asians. In 1935 he returned to the Philippines as military advisor and then as the field marshal of the Philippine Army as the islands began to prepare for their independence.

MacArthur, like other Americans going back to Woodrow Wilson, saw his mission as bringing to Asia the same principles that had governed American expansion across the continent to the Pacific. It was a mission of spreading the principles of representative government, the rule of law, the freedom of the individual, and the values of the Judeo-Christian civilization. Americans believed that their history had prepared them for nation building.[46] Partly it grew from the founding of their own nation and from their experience of expanding across the continent and replicating institutions of self-government in newly acquired territories. This faith in their own preparation for tutoring backward countries was what had sparked the young Woodrow Wilson's enthusiasm for acquiring the Philippines. Writing in 1901, Wilson said that "Americans must help 'undeveloped peoples still in the childhood of their natural growth[,] . . . inducting them into the rudiments of justice and freedom.'"[47] The Filipinos would someday be independent but first must be tutored. "They can have liberty no cheaper than we got it. . . . We are old in this learning and must be their tutors." They must have tutelage in the institutions that Americans had mastered. "In brief, the fact is this, that liberty is the privilege of maturity, of self-control, of self-mastery and a thoughtful care for righteous dealings,— that some peoples may have it, therefore, and others may not."[48]

Wilson's disposition to teach other countries the lessons of America's history foretold the kind of presumption that Americans would later bring to the remaking of Japan. When Wilson observed of the Filipinos, "They are children and we are men in these deep matters of government and justice," he foreshadowed Douglas MacArthur's description of his tutelage of the Japanese in the Occupation. MacArthur believed that the Japanese had to be schooled in American ideals and institutions. Reflecting before a congressional committee on his experience in reforming Japan and the Japanese, he observed, "If the Anglo-Saxon was say 45 years of age in his development, in the sciences, the arts, divinity, culture, the Germans were quite as mature. The Japanese, however, in spite of their antiquity measured by time were in a very tuitionary condition. Measured by the standards of modern civilization, they would be like a boy of twelve as compared with our development of 45 years."[49] When his views later became known in Japan, MacArthur was sarcastically said to view Japan as "a nation of teenagers." But it was certainly true that the general's approach was nothing but paternal.

The general saw himself alone as the architect of the new Japan: "I had to be an economist, a political scientist, an engineer, a manufacturing executive, a teacher, even a theologian of sorts. I had to rebuild a nation that had been almost completely destroyed by the war. Whatever my ethical teachings had been, whatever my basic character was, whatever the concept of mankind that lay within my soul, I would have to bring into this political, economic, and spiritual vacuum concepts of honor, justice, and compassion."[50]

The mind-set of the Occupation sprang from two fundamental beliefs. One was ethnocentric and culture-bound: America, whatever its faults, was the most modern of all nations, and since all societies must develop along more or less the same lines, changes in Japanese society should be modeled after American institutions. In this belief was the American version of the Western presumption that there would be only one way for a non-Western society should it modernize: it must follow in the path laid out by the advanced Western countries. Among Americans in the Occupation it was an idée fixe that there was but one modernity—a single path of economic and political development. To the Americans, therefore, the whole modern system in Japan was distorted; because it had not developed along the lines of the United States, it was somehow abnormal, unhealthy, and premodern. Whatever the United States had become, the rest of the world could also attain if it followed in the American path. We shall see this theme repeatedly in postwar Japan's experience. The Japanese were confronted in their politics, society, and economy by the American contention that the path of development was unilinear and that all nations would converge on a liberal pattern represented best by the United States. MacArthur wrote in *Life* magazine in 1947 that the values and institutions that came out of the American experience "are no longer peculiarly American, but now belong to the entire human race."[51] So he set about remaking Japan after the image of his native country. "My major advisors now," he remarked in 1948, "have boiled down to almost two—George Washington and Abraham Lincoln. One founded the United States, the other saved it. If you go back into their lives, you can find almost all the answers."[52]

The other fundamental belief of the Occupation was the enduring tenet of the American liberal credo: if the people of a nation were given control of their destiny, they would choose a peaceful course out of their own self-interest. "War's genesis," MacArthur wrote in the *Life* article, "lies in the despotic lust for power. . . . Never has it originated in the voluntary action of a free people—never will a free people voluntarily associate itself with the proposition that the road to peace and well-being and happiness lies through the crucible of war." Whether aware of it, MacArthur was hearkening back to the ideas of the Founding Fathers and their belief that, unlike monarchies, whose narrow, vested interests provoked warfare, self-governing republics would be peace loving because a sovereign people would see its interests better served by commerce among nations. Thomas Jefferson, James Madison, and especially Thomas Paine all believed that "peace was therefore fundamentally a question of the establishment of democratic institutions throughout the world."[53]

Revolutionary Change

MacArthur organized the surrender ceremony aboard the USS *Missouri* in Tokyo Bay with a sense of high drama. Foreign Minister Shigemitsu Mamoru and Army Chief of Staff Umezu Yoshijirō signed the surrender document for Japan, followed by MacArthur, flanked by the frail figures of Generals Wainwright and Percival, who had surrendered to the Japanese at Bataan and Singapore, respectively, and been interned in Japanese prison camps. "A great tragedy has ended," the orotund MacArthur intoned. "A great victory has been won. The skies no longer rain death—the seas bear only commerce—men everywhere walk upright in the sunlight. The entire world is quietly at peace. The holy mission has been accomplished."[54] In a real sense, the holy mission was not over. When MacArthur entered Tokyo six days later and established himself in the Dai-ichi Building, overlooking the Imperial Palace, the Americans began an occupation of Japan that was characterized by a high sense of idealism and mission.

MacArthur was the recipient of directives from Washington, which usually provided broad contours of reform and were only occasionally detailed. In practice, he had a great deal of leeway in implementing these directives. The Occupation was overwhelmingly an American enterprise. There were international advisory groups, but they were weak and MacArthur often ignored them. The Occupation was a unified system of military control. MacArthur so dominated the proceedings that his title SCAP (Supreme Commander of the Allied Powers) came to refer to the entire Occupation.

In the first months of the Occupation, MacArthur moved resolutely to institute those revolutionary reforms—demilitarization, war crimes trials, a new democratic order, and reeducation of the people—that Roosevelt had promised and the Potsdam Declaration had defined. With missionary zeal the reforms were instituted in a peremptory succession of decrees. Beginning by disbanding the entire military, SCAP moved quickly to abolish all laws that restricted freedom of speech, thought, religion, and assembly and released all political prisoners, many of whom were communists. In addition, it disestablished State Shinto, which had been the religious backbone of prewar militarism, and declared that all ties between government and religion were forbidden.

Nothing better demonstrated American impatience to clear the way for a democratic order than the "purge" directive removing from eligibility for office anyone who had played a part in promoting "aggression or militant nationalism." Military officers, heads of overseas business organizations, colonial officials, and leaders of nationalist organizations were all purged. In short order, 220,000 persons were summarily removed from eligibility for positions in the new government.[55] A prominent American writer visiting Japan was stunned by the policy: "This use of the word 'purge' was new to me; I had never heard it in political talk except in connection with Russia." But SCAP reveled in its power and a joke circulated that asked, "What is the difference between Stalin and MacArthur? Stalin purges with trials, but MacArthur purges without trials."[56]

SCAP also moved resolutely to establish the war crimes trials that Roosevelt promised. The Tokyo Tribunal closely followed the Nuremberg

Charter, drawn up by America and its allies in London in the summer of 1945. Within the Roosevelt administration there had been heated debate over how to treat German war criminals.[57] Stimson was the persistent advocate of applying American legalist values of due process, in opposition to Secretary of Treasury Henry Morgenthau, who argued for summary execution of war criminals. Stimson finally won out, insisting that only through adherence to domestic liberal values could America be true to itself. Nuremberg was largely an American creation designed for German trials, but, as with the unconditional surrender, the same model was to be applied to Japan. The Tokyo Trials construed militarized Japan as a replication of Nazi Germany. As the legal scholar John Haley observes, "Little attempt was made to assess the Japanese prewar and wartime experiences on their own terms and in their own context. . . . Had such efforts been made, the prosecutors at Tokyo might have discovered that the Japanese experience bears closer resemblance to many contemporary regimes, particularly those controlled or supported by military establishments."[58]

The Americans wanted the Tokyo Trials to be a lesson in the rule of law for the Japanese people. From the start there were problems. The eleven justices came only from the victorious Allies: Australia, Canada, China, France, Britain, India, Netherlands, New Zealand, Philippines, Soviet Union, and the United States. The Tokyo Tribunal's impartiality, justice, and fairness were questionable. No one stated these misgivings more clearly than Elizabeth Gray Vining, a pacifist Quaker from Philadelphia who was brought to Japan to serve as the tutor to Crown Prince Akihito. In her memoir of this experience from 1946 to 1950, Vining recalled her visit to the trials:

> As I looked at the eleven judges, able, honorable, distinguished men . . . I could not escape the fact that they represented only the victorious nations. There was no Japanese among them. There was not even a neutral, no one from Sweden, Switzerland, Spain, Turkey, or any other nation who had stood outside the conflict. Could a court be impartial and justice be served, when the judges were also the prosecution and outcome of the trial was known from the beginning? Under ordinary circumstances would we consider a trial fair in which the judge and jury were friends and relatives of the murdered man?[59]

Indictments were brought against twenty-eight Class A war criminals. Charges fell into three categories. Conventional war crimes had to

Crown Prince Akihito strolling with his American tutor, Elizabeth Gray
Vining, in 1946. Vining later wrote popular books describing her experiences.
Bettmann / Getty Images / 515204230.

do with the laws and customs of war. But two other categories were
newly created norms not hitherto codified in international law: crimes
against peace and crimes against humanity. In a simplistic view of history, the burden of the prosecution's case was formulated as an organized conspiracy to wage aggressive war in order to take over the Asian

Defendants at the Tokyo War Crimes Tribunal, May 21, 1946. In the front row at far left is former prime minister Tōjō Hideki. Everett Collection Inc./Alamy Stock Photo/EG6M7B.

continent. In addition to the problem of the impartiality of the justices, application of newly defined war crimes ex post facto and holding individual leaders responsible for the acts of a nation added to the controversial nature of the trials. Seven men, including former prime minister Tōjō, were sentenced to death by hanging. Sixteen were sentenced to life imprisonment, one was sentenced to twenty years, and one (former foreign minister Shigemitsu Mamoru) was sentenced to seven years. As George Kennan observed after a visit to Tokyo, the trials were "profoundly misconceived from the start." The entire undertaking was "surrounded with the hocus-pocus of a judicial procedure which belies its real nature," which he characterized as "political trials . . . not law."[60]

The principles and procedures on which the judgments were made have been the subject of continuing controversy. Three of the eleven justices wrote sharply worded dissents. Justice Radhabinod Pal from India, an Indian nationalist sympathetic to the Japanese and better versed in international law than the other justices, wrote a long and vigorous dissent focused on the ex post facto nature of the charges and especially on the issue of whether the prosecution's claim of conspiracy could be sustained. Tellingly, he also spoke of the hypocrisy in overlooking the context of Western imperialism in Asia in which modern Japan had found itself. Americans could cast their expansion in terms of manifest destiny, national interest and honor, even a white man's burden, but in the Japanese case expansion was condemned as aggression pure and simple. Pal also took the opportunity to write that the firebombing of Japanese cities and the use of the atomic bomb were themselves blatant crimes against humanity.[61] Two other justices wrote dissents criticizing various aspects of the trials, especially the exemption of the emperor from prosecution.[62]

The Tokyo Trials were intended to demonstrate the rule of law in international relations and to serve as a lesson for the Japanese people. But the entire process was flawed from the start and left an ambiguous legacy. Both conservatives and progressives in Japan have found fault with the trials as victors' justice.[63] Among all the faults, the blanket immunity from prosecution that the victorious nations gave themselves seemed to the Japanese the most compelling evidence of the trials' gross injustice. The best that can be said of the trials may be that they served to advance the cause and subsequent development of international law as it relates to war crimes. The recent trials of war crimes in the Bosnian conflict, for example, owe something to the experience and lessons learned from Tokyo as well as Nuremberg and other subsequent advances.[64]

Preserving Pillars of the Old Order

While disarming the military, convicting its leaders, and embarking on revolutionary reforms, SCAP made two critical compromises with its wartime unconditional surrender demands. It decided to preserve two pillars of the old establishment: the imperial institution and the powerful civilian bureaucracy. It thus "insured that the formal democratization of Japan would take place within the conservative framework of the old regime."[65]

In contrast to Germany, where the collapse of the wartime government compelled the Occupation forces to assume direct government,

Japan had surrendered while its own government was still intact. To facilitate the work of government for Americans who lacked sufficient language specialists to handle the required tasks, SCAP chose to govern in an indirect manner, establishing itself as a supervisory organ above the existing Japanese government. The various staff sections of SCAP were organized to work through the various ministries of the Japanese government. The Occupation forces left most of the civilian bureaucracy intact to run the day-to-day business of government. SCAP thereby threw a lifeline to the powerful elite that had worked hand-in-glove with the military in prewar government. The bureaucracy survived to become the major conservative force in postwar Japanese politics. Preserving the bureaucratic elite was a fateful decision, but few in the Occupation understood its long-term consequences.

In a further momentous initiative, MacArthur asserted his determination to retain the imperial institution and to absolve the emperor of any war responsibility. Belief that the imperial institution could be used to legitimate reforms and compel obedience was an idea that had germinated during the war years—even while official policy strongly implied that it would be abolished once surrender was achieved. The way in which the emperor's call to his troops at home and abroad to lay down their arms had been met with immediate obedience gave credence to this argument.[66]

The strategy of retaining the imperial institution had developed during the war both among some American leaders and among MacArthur and his staff. Still there was no consensus in Washington. The proposal of Stimson, Grew, and the Japan hands in the State Department, which argued for retaining the imperial institution, was overruled by Truman and Byrnes and omitted from the Potsdam Declaration. The "China crowd" in the State Department was adamant in its insistence that militarism could be destroyed only by eliminating the throne. Months went by after surrender without any firm decision by the US government. In some of the Allied countries there was strong sentiment in favor of destroying the imperial institution and trying Hirohito as a war criminal. Senators Richard Russell of Georgia and J. William Fulbright of Arkansas introduced a resolution in the US Senate demanding that the emperor be tried as a war criminal.

What transpired in Tokyo, however, was quite extraordinary. Nothing could bespeak "an unnatural intimacy" better than the tacit alliance that was struck between the military men of SCAP and the emperor's advisors to work together to preserve the throne. On September 27, 1945, the emperor visited MacArthur at his residence. It was the most dramatic event of the Occupation. Dressed in a formal morning coat and striped trousers, the emperor, MacArthur later recalled, "was nervous and the stress of the past months showed plainly. . . . I offered him an American cigarette which he took with thanks. I noticed how his hands shook when I lighted it for him."[67] The general's wife, Jean, and their young son Arthur, hidden behind a thick curtain, watched the proceedings for a time. Otherwise there was no one other than the imperial interpreter, who later recalled that MacArthur did most of the talking. Nevertheless, according to the general's own account, the emperor offered to take upon himself "sole responsibility for the conduct of the war."[68] The photograph taken at this meeting, which the Occupation immediately released to the press, is perhaps the most poignant, certainly the most famous, in Japanese history: the blasé American in casual army attire, no necktie, hands on his hips, towering over the stiff and upright Son of Heaven in his formal attire. There could be no question who now ruled Japan. At the same time, it soon became clear that the Supreme Commander was standing by the embattled emperor.

In the face of opinion in Allied countries that wanted the emperor tried as a war criminal, MacArthur took a direct hand in protecting the emperor and shielding him from any responsibility for the war. He would not be subject to the war crimes trial, and any implication of him in testimony was ruled out.[69] SCAP worked behind the scenes with court officials to save the imperial institution. On January 1, 1946, Hirohito issued his so-called Declaration of Humanity, in which he stated that "the ties between Us and Our people . . . do not depend upon mere legends and myths. They are not predicated on the false conception that the Emperor is divine, and that the Japanese people are superior to other races and fated to rule the world." The declaration had been secretly worked out by members of SCAP and the Imperial Court. It was all part of the collusion that each side, for its own reasons, engaged in to preserve the imperial institution.

While the Court did its part, MacArthur tried to steamroller the opposition in Washington, warning of catastrophic consequences if the emperor were removed. In his cable he stated, "The whole of Japan can be expected, in my opinion, to resist. . . . I believe all hope of introducing

On September 27, 1945, when Hirohito paid a visit to General Douglas MacArthur at his quarters, the Occupation ordered the publication of this photograph in Japanese newspapers. World History Archive / Alamy Stock Photo / F7NHTC.

democratic methods would disappear. . . . It is quite possible that a minimum of a million troops would be required which would have to be maintained for an indefinite number of years. In addition, a complete civil service might have to be recruited and imported, possibly running into a size of several hundred thousand."[70] Such hyperbole was hardly reflective of reality in Japan. The evidence is that most Japanese at the time were preoccupied with their own livelihood and indifferent to the future of the emperor system. But to the conservative elites, its preservation was essential to their future. And for MacArthur, the emperor was needed to make the Occupation run smoothly. Such collusion almost became routine. Moreover, as the historian Yuma Totani shows, both in Washington and in the Allied advisory councils, the question of whether the emperor should be tried was left open.[71] In the meantime, SCAP and the Imperial Court worked together to ensure that the emperor was not implicated in any war crimes but rather was portrayed as having opposed the war. In a surprising convergence of interests, both the conservative elite and SCAP saw preservation of the imperial institution as serving their interests. It legitimated the continuing authority of the elite, and for SCAP it "was seen as the fundamental means by which to control the Japanese government, ensure order, circumscribe popular action and political power, and guarantee a postwar political order conducive to American interests."[72]

MacArthur's determination to keep the emperor as a constitutional monarch served to maintain political stability and to sanction and facilitate reform, but it also left a clouded and ambiguous public sense of responsibility for the war. If the sovereign himself was not even compelled to abdicate and accept responsibility for the disastrous happenings, could his subjects be expected to engage in deep self-reflection? These two omissions of the Occupation that left in place the elite bureaucracy and the emperor diluted the democratic intentions of the Americans and provided the conditions for a conservative resurgence once the Occupation ended. To anyone who thought about the uncompromising wartime goals, these decisions called into question the stubborn wartime adherence to unconditional surrender.

Imposing "the Most Liberal Constitution in History"

Americans held a very proprietary sense of constitution making because it had been embedded in the founding of the nation. Though heirs of English traditions of freedom and popular rights, the Americans believed that constitutions must be written documents, circumscribing the government, antecedent to it, and requiring ratification by the people. Constitutions could not be creations of legislatures; they must be the act of the people themselves. "When the Philadelphia convention drew up a new constitution for the nation in 1787 . . . it declared that [it] had to be ratified by the people meeting in state conventions called for that purpose only. [This] made the people themselves the actual constituent power."[73]

The Potsdam Declaration promised that a new democratic order would be achieved "in accordance with the freely expressed will of the Japanese people." MacArthur received directions from Washington prescribing that SCAP should maintain a low posture in the process of revising the Meiji Constitution, and "only as a last resort" should it issue formal instruction to the Japanese government specifying in detail the reforms to be effected.[74] Otherwise, awareness that these reforms had been imposed by the Allies "would materially reduce the possibility of their acceptance and support by the Japanese people for the future." Unfortunately, despite this expressed intention, SCAP virtually dictated the new constitution and the new political structure. By imposing democracy from above and from outside, it became involved in troubling contradictions. Epitomizing such contradictions was the Occupation's censorship regime, which employed some 8,000 censors (most all were hired Japanese) to ensure that the Occupation was not subject to criticism. Censors eavesdropped on some 800,000 phone conversations and read 330 million pieces of mail. News agencies, national and local newspapers, magazines, books, radio programs, films, and dramas were subject to censorship regime.[75] The prewar, authoritarian Japanese government had openly conducted extensive censorship and never bothered to cover its tracks, while the democratic Americans went to great lengths to conceal their censorship.[76] Censorship allowed the Americans to manipulate the restructuring of the political system while maintaining the fiction of acting "in accordance with the freely expressed will of the Japanese people." Most Japanese were not fooled for long. Many were, for the time being, pleased to have their discredited leadership forced to accede to a new progressive order.

MacArthur initially instructed Prime Minister Shidehara Kijūrō to undertake planning of the "liberalization of the constitution." Shidehara had been approved by SCAP to lead the government because, as foreign minister in the 1920s, he had been supportive of the Washington System.

But he was a staunch bureaucrat and married into the Iwasaki family, which controlled the Mitsubishi conglomerate. It quickly became clear that the conservatives he selected to consider constitutional revision were unwilling to make the changes in the Meiji Constitution that would satisfy the Americans. Losing patience and aware that the Allies would soon be organized into advisory institutions that would curtail his discretion, MacArthur directed his aide, General Courtney Whitney, to draft a model constitution for the Japanese cabinet. The model, he instructed Whitney, should preserve the emperor system in a modified democratic form and also include provision that "war and war-making would be forsworn."[77] The latter provision became the famous Article 9, the no-war clause.

In almost Alice-in-Wonderland circumstances, Whitney assembled a group of some twenty members of the Government Section of SCAP on February 4, 1946, proclaimed them a constitutional assembly, and directed them to draft a document.[78] While thin in their knowledge of Japan, the group nonetheless included a substantial number who were well schooled in law, although not constitutional law. The key person in charge of the constitution writing process was forty-year-old Charles Kades, a Harvard-trained lawyer and unabashed New Dealer who came to Japan absolutely tabula rasa. "I had no knowledge whatsoever about Japan's history or culture or myths," he later recalled. "I was blank on Japan, except of course I knew about the atrocities that had occurred during the war and I was aware of their expansion into China and Southeast Asia. But I had no knowledge other than what one would glean from a daily newspaper about Japan."[79] SCAP was rarely dismayed by its lack of knowledge of Japanese history and culture. What was most important to know was the American institutions and practices on which reforms were to be modeled.

Moving at breathtaking speed, the group drafted in six days the document that, with few changes, became the Constitution of Japan, without amendments to the present day. In drafting their own constitution in Philadelphia during the summer of 1787, the Americans had deliberated 127 days. In Tokyo drafting a constitution for another people, they needed no such deliberation. MacArthur briefly studied the draft, and in a meeting on February 13, 1946, at the foreign minister's residence, Whitney met with the Japanese committee that Shidehara had appointed to oversee revision. There, Whitney presented its thunderstruck members with the SCAP draft, which they were told they must accept or MacArthur could not guarantee the preservation of the imperial institution. Moreover, Whitney was prepared to go directly to the people with his proposal. SCAP officials made it abundantly clear that they intended to have their way, with a minimum of resistance brooked from the Japanese. The committee was stunned and asked Whitney if they could discuss the draft among themselves. The heavy-handed Whitney recalls that while he and the other Americans waited in the beautifully landscaped garden of the residence, he decided "to employ one more psychological shaft" to get his point across. He recorded that when the Japanese representatives rejoined them in the garden, the cabinet secretary Shirasu Jirō "mumbled apologies for keeping us waiting. I replied with a smile: 'Not at all, Mr. Shirasu. We have been enjoying your atomic sunshine.' And at that moment with what could not have been better timing, a big B-29 came roaring over us. The reaction upon Mr. Shirasu was indescribable, but profound. When we seated ourselves across the patio from the committee members again, I could see that Mr. Shirasu's colleagues were as upset by our proposals as he was."[80] As Yoshikuni Igarashi suggests, one may wonder if in the mind of the startled Shirasu, images of the sun, the atomic bomb, the emperor, and MacArthur suddenly conflated.[81]

If Whitney's psychological shaft, the atomic sunshine, and the roar of the B-29 were not sufficient, the threat of bypassing the cabinet to appeal directly to the Japanese people through a plebiscite and the allusion to the still-unresolved status of the emperor left these members of the conservative elite with little choice. Whitney told them that MacArthur saw this as "the last opportunity of the conservative group, considered by many to be reactionary, to remain in power. . . . The acceptance of the draft constitution is your only hope of survival."[82] Once the Japanese conservatives relented in their opposition, SCAP allowed a certain amount of negotiation and give-and-take in deciding on a Japanese translation of the democratic concepts.[83] The Japanese did what little they could to cushion the shock of the imposed constitution. When the SCAP model was translated, the Japanese were able to word passages in the Japanese text that carried nuances that made the revolutionary concepts more consonant with Japanese tradition.[84] For example, while the American text put its emphasis on constraining state power in the pursuit of democracy, the Japanese nuanced text implied the state working with the people to serve their interests.

When the text of this draft constitution was published, MacArthur issued a poker-faced statement praising the cabinet for having produced "such an exemplary document which so coincided with his own notion of what was best for the country." The English draft had echoes of the Declaration of Independence, the US Constitution, the Gettysburg Address, the Atlantic Charter, and other basic documents of the American political tradition. It made many revolutionary changes from the old Meiji Constitution. Popular sovereignty replaced imperial sovereignty, and the emperor was now "the symbol of the State and of the unity of the people." A cabinet responsible to the Diet (elected by universal suffrage), provisions for local autonomy, an independent judiciary, and a wide variety of human rights were central features.

MacArthur called it "the most liberal constitution in history."[85] And it probably was. It included many rights that do not exist in the US Constitution, most notably an explicit statement of equal rights for women as well as protection for collective bargaining, academic freedom, minimum standards of wholesome and cultural living, and other new concepts. The draft reflected the human rights movement, which was integral to the American world order and was enshrined in the 1945 UN Charter and soon after in the Universal Declaration of Human Rights championed by Eleanor Roosevelt and other liberals and adopted by the UN General Assembly in 1948. The UN Charter, enunciated just months before Americans drafted the new constitution for Japan, declared in its preamble, "We the people of the United Nations, determined to save succeeding generations from the scourge of war . . . [to] reaffirm faith in fundamental human rights . . . have resolved to combine efforts to accomplish these aims." As Akira Iriye observed, "For the first time in the history of modern international relations, human rights were codified as a universal principle."[86]

This progressive vision embodied in the UN Charter was echoed in the preamble of the constitution that SCAP drafted for Japan. The preamble—which, like the preambles of the UN Charter and the US Constitution, began "We the people"—was a ringing declaration of popular sovereignty and utopian sentiments of pacifism and internationalism. It proclaimed that Japan's security should be preserved "trusting in the justice and faith of the peace-loving peoples of the world." One can well imagine how the US Congress would react to a proposal that it cede responsibility for American security to the international community. National self-help is not a value that any nation should be expected to give up. Further, the preamble qualified Japanese sovereignty, declaring that "no nation is responsible to itself alone, but that laws of political morality are universal; and that obedience to such laws is incumbent upon all nations who would sustain their own sovereignty and justify their sovereign relationship with other nations." There was no room for national history or traditions in the provisions of this preamble and little room even for national interest.

Article 9

In the years since the promulgation of the constitution, its most controversial aspect has always been Article 9, which provided that "the Japanese people forever renounce war as a sovereign right" and declared that "land, sea, and air forces, as well as other war potential will never be maintained." Controversy has arisen over many issues. What were its origins? Did Japanese leaders have any influence in its making? Did it commit Japan to total disarmament and pacifism? Was armament for purposes of self-defense acceptable?

Article 9 is usually attributed to MacArthur, but the provision is also properly seen as reflecting Roosevelt's wartime declaration that "Japan must be disarmed and kept disarmed." MacArthur, captivated by the high idealism of the early occupation and expecting that collective security arrangements through the United Nations were being put in place, seemed prepared to leave Japan wholly disarmed. He therefore instructed General Whitney to include a provision in the constitution that "war as a sovereign right of the nation is abolished. Japan renounces it as an instrumentality for settling its disputes and even for preserving its own security."[87] The notion of placing such a provision in the constitution was familiar to MacArthur because of his prewar experience in the Philippines. In 1928 the leading nations of the world (including Japan) concluded the General Treaty for the Renunciation of War, better known as the Kellogg-Briand Pact, which condemned "recourse to war as a solution to international controversies." The 1935 Philippine Constitution, well known to MacArthur, included a proviso stating that "the Philippines renounces war as an instrument of national policy." Nevertheless, despite the currency of renouncing war as an instrument of policy, the notion of a unilateral disarmament was not intended in these earlier examples.

In his memoirs, MacArthur preferred to attribute the idea to Prime Minister Shidehara, perhaps wanting to avoid having the Japanese feel that it was imposed. If there is truth in MacArthur's account that Shidehara proposed the idea to him, it was partly because the Japanese leader was responding to cues from the Americans and also endeavoring to preserve the imperial institution, whose future was still, at the time, uncertain.[88] Shidehara later recorded that "I thought that at this time we had to take a bold step in abandoning war and establishing a peaceful Japan in order to preserve the imperial institution and protect the national polity."[89] Japanese conservatives went along with the proposal as a trade-off for keeping the imperial institution.

When the draft constitution was considered by the Diet, Ashida Hitoshi, chairman of the lower house committee reviewing the draft, made two significant amendments, perhaps wanting to leave room for Japanese self-defense.[90] He inserted two phrases with far-reaching implications. One, preceding the first sentence of Article 9, reads, "Aspiring sincerely to an international peace based on justice and order." The other, preceding the second sentence of that article, reads, "In order to accomplish the aim of the preceding paragraph." Thus, Article 9 as finally adopted reads:

> Aspiring sincerely to an international peace based on justice and order, the Japanese people forever renounce war as a sovereign right of the nation and the threat or use of force as a means of settling international disputes.
>
> In order to accomplish the aim of the preceding paragraph, land, sea, and air forces, as well as other war potential, will never be maintained. The right of belligerency of the state will not be recognized.

Kades approved these amendments with the understanding that they could be interpreted to mean that war and the threat or use of force were renounced only as a means of settling international disputes. War and resort to force were not forbidden in matters of self-defense.[91]

The article, which was foreshadowed by the unconditional surrender policy and the assertion that postwar Japan would be permanently disarmed, has been at the center of Japanese postwar political controversy. Many right-wing conservatives sought revision or reinterpretation of Article 9 to allow Japanese rearmament. Mainstream conservatives, however, would use Article 9 as a pretext for limiting their role in the cold war conflict. Progressives found it the foundation of a pacifist Japan. Within only a few years, Americans would regret their uncompromising policy and want the Japanese to remilitarize and be an activist ally in the Cold War.

Women's Rights

The aspect of reform for which SCAP was most exuberant and which was most discordant with Japanese tradition was the establishment of women's rights. The constitutional provisions for women's equal rights and the implications for the traditional family system caused Japanese conservatives the most heartburn. In prewar days, conservatives in the House of Peers had been able to forestall legislation that had passed the lower house to give women the right to vote in local elections and to serve in local government. At the same time in the 1920s, there had been a movement that also fell short to adjust the civil code to ease conservative aspects of family practice.

In the first days of the Occupation, when MacArthur handed the prime minister a list of reforms, the enfranchisement of women was the first on the list. A young American woman who was included in the deliberations of drafting the MacArthur Constitution was instrumental in inserting equal rights clauses. Twenty-two-year-old Beate Sirota, who had grown up in prewar Japan, took it upon herself to write two critical provisions. Article 14 read: "All people are equal under the law and there shall be no discrimination in political, economic or social relations because of race, creed, sex, social status or family origin." More radical was Article 24, which extended the guarantee of women's equality into the private domain of the family: "Marriage shall be based on the mutual consent of both sexes and it shall be maintained through mutual cooperation with the equal rights of husband and wife as a basis. With regard to choice of spouse, property rights, inheritance, choice of domicile, divorce and other matters pertaining to marriage and the family, laws shall be enacted from the standpoint of individual dignity and the essential equality of the sexes." These provisions went beyond even what the US Constitution today provides.

An equal rights amendment to the American Constitution, first proposed in 1922 (two years after the passage of the 19th Amendment to the Constitution in 1920, which provided for female suffrage) and introduced in Congress in 1923, has yet to gain the approval of a sufficient number of states. In light of this fact, it may not be surprising that pre-surrender planning for the Occupation in Washington did not discuss women's rights.[92]

Sirota was an anomaly among the "founding fathers" of the MacArthur Constitution. Not only was she a woman in an overwhelmingly male occupying force, but she had grown up in Japan and was fluent in Japanese. Her father had been a piano teacher at the Imperial Academy of Music in Tokyo, where she lived for ten years before going to the United States to enter Mills College in California on the eve of the war. She became an American citizen in January 1945 and at year's end returned to Tokyo as an interpreter on MacArthur's staff. Assigned by Kades to the group drafting a civil liberties section of the constitution, she took to her task with a characteristic gusto. She recalled in her memoir, *The Only Woman in the Room*, that, in addition to the two provisions that became Articles 14 and 24, she tried unsuccessfully to include many other proposed articles that would give women and children social welfare rights, such as state aid for expectant and nursing mothers and protection for disadvantaged children. Kades and others, however, thought such rights were too revolutionary.[93] When the draft constitution became public, Japanese women's groups rallied in support of it. Such groups, however, were still relatively weak and well outside the mainstream of popular views. In contrast, when the draft was reviewed in the Diet, the two articles drew a vociferous opposition from the conservatives who maintained that the unique Japanese family system would be destroyed in the face of the imposition of such individualistic values.

Ratification

MacArthur wanted a newly elected Diet to pass judgment on the constitution and other reforms. SCAP therefore ordered a general election for April 1946. As a result of the purge, most candidates for office were newcomers to elections. Most notable, women were given the franchise for the first time. More than 13 million women voted and thirty-nine were elected to the Diet. The draft approved by the cabinet was sent to the newly elected Diet, where it passed the lower house 429 to 8, with five of the eight votes cast by communists who opposed continuation of the imperial institution. In the upper house the vote was more than a two-thirds majority in favor.[94] On May 3, 1947, the emperor formally promulgated the new Constitution of Japan. Although the elected members of the Japanese people approved the constitution, to have their constitution drafted and imposed by another country was bound to prove demeaning for a proud but defeated people. As the most careful American scholars on the making of the constitution conclude: "Can Japan ever be made whole politically, without a constitution expressed in its own idiom?"[95]

A New Deal for Japan

SCAP went on from transforming the political structure to remaking the economy and society in the most far-reaching ways, which I will touch on here and elaborate later. What will emerge from this elaboration will be the culturally distinctive way in which the Japanese implemented all these reforms, including the political ones. The universalism of American institutions and values could in no way overcome the centuries of history that had made the Japanese what they were. They could in the war weariness of the time embrace these reforms, but in subsequent decades the pull of history and culture made them something quite distinct from what the Occupation intended.

There is a good deal of truth in the assertion of some observers that the Occupation was the last act of the New Deal. The recent experience of implementing the reforms of the New Deal in the United States added to the confidence that SCAP had in its ability to carry out sweeping reform measures.[96] When Roosevelt first began thinking about a postwar order, he included in the Atlantic Charter the expectation that New Deal reforms for the advancement of labor standards, employment security, and social welfare must be sought in the domestic institutions of nations, for without them, the peace and stability of the world could be affected by internal discontent.

Therefore, besides transforming the political structure, the Americans were also determined to reengineer Japanese society and reeducate the people. In their enthusiasm to remake the society, its every detail was scrutinized—the economic order, education, religion, the written language, and even the most intimate aspects of Japanese society, such as the family, parental authority, male-female relations, love, and marriage. No detail was too small to be overlooked. Holidays were changed; there was even a "postage stamp" directive, which regulated the pictures and designs that could be shown on the face of stamps. Nearly everything was turned upside down. "What has happened in Japan," a writer in *Fortune* magazine recorded in 1949, "has been the unexpected marriage of the military mind and the bureaucratic mind; the Army and the New Dealers and socialists who govern Japan, both in Washington and in Tokyo, have a natural affinity for the control of their subjects, and other differences have been submerged in the zeal of the two groups to dominate and interfere in the Japanese way of life."[97]

The influence of the New Deal and New Dealers on MacArthur's staff was huge in shaping plans to democratize the economy. New Deal historian and Roosevelt biographer Arthur Schlesinger, Jr., wrote with a coauthor, "For a time in 1946 and 1947, it was as if Franklin D. Roosevelt and the early New Dealers had been turned loose to make Japan over."[98] In the basic initial postsurrender directive of September 22, 1945, MacArthur was enjoined to undertake democratic reforms in labor, agriculture, and business and thereby bring about "a wide distribution of income and of the ownership of the means of production." The great concentration of wealth and power in the hands of the big business and landlord classes was blamed for creating the environment in which militarism could flourish. The frustration and deprivations of industrial workers and farm tenants were seen as contributing to the growth of militarism and aggression. The Occupation, therefore, set about, often in almost textbook fashion, applying the major reforms for national reconstruction that had been worked out a decade earlier in the New Deal.

Labor experts on MacArthur's staff, many of whom were members of the American trade union movement, set about instituting the theory and practice of American labor relations. Three months after the Occupation began, SCAP issued a Trade Union Law, which it sometimes referred to as the Magna Carta of Japanese labor. But the law might more appropriately be known as the "Japanese Wagner Act," as it was closely modeled on the National Labor Relations Act of 1935, authored by New York senator Robert Wagner. Like its American model, it guaranteed the right of trade union organization; set forth basic rights of workers in private industry to organize, to bargain collectively, and to strike; and prohibited unfair labor practices. Subsequent legislation during the next two years established basic working conditions, unemployment insurance, and procedures for resolution of labor disputes. Reform-minded bureaucrats who had sought protection for labor in the prewar period were a critical part of the implementation that the Occupation decreed.

Americans were surprised to find a considerable receptivity to change. The reservoir of reformist sentiment in Japan, which surely would have worked to bring about change had there been no foreign occupation, readily supported, even aided in, drafting and implementing change. This indigenous impulse was evident in the achievement of labor reform and even more so in land reform, the most successful aspect of SCAP's economic reforms. The idea of land reform caught MacArthur's imagination. Perhaps his inspiration was a Jeffersonian instinct that the small, independent yeoman farmer would be a backbone for democratic society. Or his interest may have stemmed from his father's connection with Philippine land reform at the beginning of the century. Or perhaps it was his memory of West Point lectures he had heard on the occupation policies of Julius Caesar.[99]

SCAP believed that the unequal distribution of land had contributed to the rise of militarism, offering impoverished tenant farmers the promise of new lands acquired by expansion abroad. By 1941, 46 percent of the cultivated land was tenanted, and only 30 percent of the farmers owned all the land they tilled. Absentee landlordism was widespread. SCAP pressured the Japanese government into a far-reaching program that called for a complete dispossession of absentee landlords and for retention by other owners of up to 7.5 acres farmed by the owner himself and of an additional 2.5 acres of tenanted land. It was an immense undertaking, as one of the leading students of the land reform summed up: "It involved changes in the property rights of some six million families of whom over two million had every motive for trying to obstruct its purposes. It required considerable executive ability and conscientious integrity from over 36,000 paid officials, 115,000 ill remunerated [land commission] committee members. . . . And it implied a subversion of traditional patterns of social relations which had held sway for decades or even centuries."[100] Nevertheless, by 1950 the transfer of lands was practically complete. The countryside was transformed into a society of small, independent, and—eventually—relatively prosperous and politically conservative farmers.

Less successful and more controversial was the program to break up the huge financial combines, the zaibatsu. The vast economic empires of Mitsui, Mitsubishi, Sumitomo, and Yasuda sprawled over a variety of fields to include extractive industries, manufacturing companies, trading firms, transport affiliates, and banking. SCAP set out to dismantle this economic structure by dissolving the holding companies and selling their stocks publicly to democratize the shareholding pattern. It further drew up antitrust legislation modeled after the Sherman and Clayton Antitrust Acts in American economic history to ensure that the old situation would not reemerge. This law, passed in April 1947, provided for a Fair Trade Commission to police business and to prohibit monopoly practices that would be in restraint of trade and that would prevent free and open competition. Although family control of the large zaibatsu conglomerates was ended, SCAP's ambitious plans for a sweeping deconcentration of economic power stalled amid resistance first in Japan and then in Washington as priority for Japan's economic recovery gained strength with the onset of the Cold War.

Beyond sweeping reform of the political and economic structures of Japan, the unconditional surrender policy implied an intent to reeducate the Japanese and change their way of living. The Occupation must go to the very roots of Japanese society and liberate the individual from the myriad of restraints that prevented a free expression of will and belief. It must replace the old Imperial Rescript on Education of 1890, the basis for the prewar ideology, which had set forth collectivist values of Japan as a unique family state ruled by a benevolent emperor. To radically reorient the nationalist orientation of prewar education, the Diet enacted at the Occupation's behest in 1947 the Fundamental Law of Education, which defined the purpose of education as follows: "to contribute to the peace of the world and the welfare of humanity by building a democratic and cultural state." Schools should promote "the full development of personality." In its educational reforms, SCAP mandated structural reforms that would loosen central government control and devolve responsibility to the local level, and democratize its administration with the implementation of parent-teacher associations, greater access to higher education through establishment of prefectural universities, and other American flourishes. But it placed its greatest emphasis on the instilling of new values of individualism, equality of the sexes, and international cooperation. Peace, democracy, and international cooperation were to become the themes of the new education.

Assessing the Occupation

The American Occupation undertook the most intrusive international reconstruction of another nation in modern history. The American presumption in undertaking the total reconstruction of this ancient Asian society was breathtaking. Yet Americans have looked back with pride on the Occupation and the democratization of Japan, convinced that its success was justification for the unconditional surrender policy. Historian Odd Arne Westad writes that it became the model and inspiration for all subsequent American interventions and nation-building efforts abroad.[101] But the legacy of the Occupation is a mixed one.

The unfortunate truth is that this was an American revolution in Japan. It was not a Japanese revolution. It is true that there were Japanese who joined in aspects of the reforms, and there was a degree of Japanese-American cooperation in the Occupation. But the goals, the planning, the final implementation of reform ideals were American. The Japanese themselves were deprived of a unique opportunity to reform themselves according to their own history and traditions. Imposing democracy from outside, implanting alien institutions and values, was no substitute for a Japanese revolution.

Democracy must be *achieved*. If democracy is to work, it must be owned by the people. If it is to be lasting, it must be in the lifeblood, experience, and history of a people. The superficiality of a democratic revolution in which the people were too often passive recipients of SCAP directives could not escape thoughtful critics. The playwright Yamazaki Masakazu remembered the revolution as "being given" and coming "too easily."[102] The noted movie director Kurosawa Akira wrote in his autobiography, "The freedom and democracy of the post-war era were not things I had fought for and won; they were granted to me by powers beyond my own."[103] Perhaps most poignant were the thoughts of the feminist advocate Hiratsuka Raichō. While pleased that women were to be given rights for which she had fought for decades, she nonetheless regarded the way they were won with some melancholy: "The prospect of suddenly being handed the vote by a foreign occupying force was a shock. . . . I thought of the sweeping changes that were about to take place in Japan and was overcome with complex and contradictory feelings. . . . Suddenly, along with the humiliation of defeat, the right to vote was to be handed to women on a platter, through no efforts of their own. How ironic! When I thought back to the twenty-odd year efforts of feminists that underlay this turn of events, I could not bring myself to accept the gift with good grace and unmitigated joy."[104] It was a matter of regret that the Japanese did not themselves achieve the reform of their society.

Still, one may wonder whether postwar Japan, without the Americans, would have succeeded in throwing off the culturally embedded conservative domination of government. Without the Occupation, wouldn't Japan have missed out on a democratic reform? Wouldn't the old elite have blocked fundamental changes? Americans have generally believed that their intervention was necessary to break the power of the military and to decisively tip the balance from support of the old emperor system to a peaceful democratic society.

On the other hand, it must be remembered that by the end of the war, the military and its ideology were widely discredited. There was a widespread popular revulsion from the conservative elite. So strong was popular unrest that both the military and civilian elites expressed fear of social revolution. There was an immense constituency for reform on which domestic politics might have been built had the reforms been left to the Japanese people themselves. If ever there was a time for a genuine democratic revolution, this was it. We cannot know, of course, whether a democratic revolution might have ensued. Japan was certainly capable of great reforms, but Japan has never had a revolution. Japan has never experienced a dynastic overthrow and, while borrowing much from China, never accepted the Sinic notion of a mandate of heaven that would legitimate replacing the ruling dynasty. The nearly two millennia of Japanese history are remarkable for the patterns of continuity in which the structure of government was characterized by the "slow organic nature of change." As the eminent historian John Whitney Hall observed, "In surveying the history of Japanese political institutions it would be hard to say that anything like a real revolution ever took place. There were, of course, many periods of violent warfare and bloodshed among the ruling families. And yet these did not result in the overthrow of an entire political system or of an entire ruling group. The elite of one age were generally only pushed aside by those of the next."[105]

Despite the unprecedented scale of the disaster that had befallen Japan and the deep discontent with the wartime leadership, left to themselves and given their past history and conservative traditions, the Japanese might still not have had a liberal democratic revolution. It is perhaps more likely that Japan would have had another transformation like the Meiji Restoration. Perhaps the military leaders and their allies in the bureaucracy would have been pushed aside, together with the leaders of the zaibatsu, and replaced by a rejuvenated conservative elite—bureaucrats, party politicians, business leaders—which might have carried out a sweeping reform picking up where the elitist democratic trends of the Taisho period had left off. In the 1920s, party politics blossomed and bureaucrats proposed land and labor reforms, female suffrage, and changes in the civil code. An indigenous postwar reform would surely have brought sweeping changes—an opening to Western influences, rebuilding the economy, acquiring new technology, liberalizing the education curriculum, adopting more liberal interpretations of the Meiji Constitution—all the while achieved in a conservative framework.

As we shall see, while it may have been "the most liberal constitution in history," the Japanese interpreted the constitution as well as its new institutions and values to fit their own historically embedded culture. Even with the Occupation's democratization programs, the staying power of the conservative forces was certainly formidable. While the Americans made major changes in the political economy, the conservatives proved canny in their ability to subvert the changes and find ways to restore their influence. Ultimately, they succeeded—and, ironically, they did so with American help.

From the start, the Occupation compromised its goals by retaining the imperial institution and the powerful, conservative bureaucracy. SCAP preferred the convenience of ruling within the structure of emperor and bureaucrats. As one historian observes, SCAP, together with the Japanese elites, succeeded in refurbishing the imperial system and "fashioning a new emperor system." Divesting the monarch of all direct responsibility for governance and casting him as a "symbol" uniting emperor and people made him an object of new sublimity, guaranteeing the "abstract presence of national unity in a community of feeling," and serving to underwrite respect for order and hierarchy in the postwar state.[106]

With the outbreak of the Cold War, SCAP continued a steady backtracking on its democratization goals. While completing a successful land reform it abandoned ambitious plans to break up the power possessed by the zaibatsu. Most striking was the reversal of the plan for permanent disarmament of Japan. As the Cold War began, the United States came to regret Article 9 and prodded the Japanese to rearm. SCAP found itself working closely with and helping to restore the conservative, undemocratic elite. As John Dower writes, "When the Occupation ended in 1952, the political economy was largely dominated by conservative old-guard civilians; war-crimes trials had punished a few scapegoats before being abandoned; the ideal of complete and permanent disarmament had been dismissed as the folly of a naïve interlude; Japan had been dragooned as a partner in containing the great new menace in Asia, Red China; politicians and others purged for supporting the war machine were poised to return to public life; and Hirohito was able to report the successful outcome of events to his divine ancestors."[107]

With US support, the conservatives were put back into power, and as the foremost historian of the Occupation concludes, "In the final analysis the legacy of the occupation was a new conservative hegemony in Japan."[108] Perhaps the Japanese, if left to themselves to reform their own society, could have done better. More important, they would have owned the reforms. But that was not to be.

5

The Subordination of Japan

THE ONSET OF THE Cold War forced Washington to recognize the false hopes that had been inherent in Roosevelt's ill-founded expectation that Soviet-American cooperation could be achieved in the making of a "one world system." As those hopes dimmed, the Americans made a radical change in their vision for Japan's future. Rather than the reform agenda inherent in the unconditional surrender policy, the United States shifted its purpose for Japan to meet the demands of the emerging bipolar conflict. From the late 1940s, the new strategic doctrine of containment dominated US policy toward Japan. The perceived threat of the Soviet Union overshadowed the initial idealism of the Occupation, and in a striking policy reversal the United States determined to make Japan its principal ally in Asia. With the communist victory in China and the Korean War, the Cold War engulfed Asia. As a result, the San Francisco Peace Treaty in 1951 was less about ending the Asia Pacific War and more about ensuring a new US Cold War alliance with Japan.

The consequences for Japan were huge. During the last years of the Occupation, from 1948 to 1952, the United States abandoned its enthusiasm for reform and began to build a regional security structure and to press Japan to remilitarize and serve as its key ally in Cold War Asia. In an ironic twist of stunning proportions, the United States pressed Japan to revise the American-authored Article 9 of the Constitution and prodded the Japanese to rearm. American policymakers assigned critical importance to Japan's geostrategic position and its industrial potential. Implicitly acknowledging the mistakes of the unconditional surrender policy, the Americans more and more aligned themselves with the old guard Japanese conservatives who had little commitment to liberal democratic ends. The new American vision for Japan became one of fitting it into a US-led anticommunist coalition of countries. Japan was a pawn to be played on an international chessboard. Japan was caught in the clashing intersection of two postwar orders: the liberal order that Roosevelt had envisioned and the emerging Cold War order. The first order entailed the disarming and massive reform of the Japanese nation. The second sought the rehabilitation and rearming of Japan to play a critical role in the Cold War. It was not a happy place in which to be caught.

The great majority of Japanese were dead set against the new priorities for their country, but with their sovereignty still in the hands of the Americans and with over 200,000 American troops still occupying the country, it was the US national interest that would determine Japan's future. The peace treaty in 1951 formally ended the Occupation, but a military alliance signed the same day, permitting long-term basing of American troops, was imposed on Japan as the price for ending the Occupation. This hegemonic alliance effectively circumscribed the return of sovereignty, subordinating Japan in the US-led struggle against the Soviet bloc.

The Frustration of Roosevelt's Vision

Roosevelt's goal of working with Stalin to shape a lasting postwar liberal world system was bound to fail. The high idealism with which America saw its wartime goals was illustrated by the hopes held for the United Nations expressed by Secretary of State Hull after he returned from the Moscow Foreign Ministers Conference in November 1943. In millennial terms he sketched the future for an enthusiastic Congress, assuring members that "there will no longer be need for spheres of influence, for alliances, for balance of power, or any other special arrangements through which, in the unhappy past, the nations strove to safeguard their security or to promote their interest."[1]

Believing that collective security would require enforcers, Roosevelt envisioned a great-power concert of "Four Policemen"—the USSR, Britain, the United States, and China—working together to maintain the peace. He was convinced of the need and of the possibility of working successfully with Stalin in the management of the postwar world. As John Ruggie observes, "Bipolarity was lacking from FDR's vocabulary." FDR attempted to "engage" the Soviet Union by involving it, so far as possible, in the workings of the new multilateral institutions.[2]

Roosevelt's conviction that the two powers must cooperate persisted despite the difficulty of working with the Soviet Union. Washington attempted "to construct a new world economic order without first resolving the deep political differences which divided the United States and the Soviet Union."[3] The Bretton Woods system was intended to include both capitalist and socialist countries. The Russians attended the Bretton Woods meetings but chose not to participate in the system that it established. Stalin was unwilling to allow international scrutiny of his economy or to give up its autarkic dimensions. At the Dumbarton Oaks meetings, where planning for the United Nations was undertaken in 1944, Soviet suspicions of the American-conceived organization grew. Roosevelt sought both to create a universal framework worthy of American ideals and to engage the Russians in a stable postwar security order with his notion of the "Four Policemen" that would form a concert of power that would be the basis of permanent membership in the Security Council. Six weeks before his death, Roosevelt reported to Congress on his return from Yalta that the great powers working together "ought to spell the end of the system of unilateral action, the exclusive alliances, the spheres of influence, the balance of power, and all the other expedients that have been tried for centuries—and always failed. We propose to substitute for all of these, a universal organization in which all peace-loving nations will finally have a chance to join."[4] In the remaining days of his life, however, Roosevelt acknowledged to his closest advisors his growing disillusionment with Stalin.[5]

His vision of a great power concert to manage a new liberal, democratic-capitalist international order proved unworkable. The wartime alliance and cooperation in defeating the Axis powers gave way to deep disagreements with the Soviet Union over the nature of the postwar settlement in all regions of the world. As Soviet-American relations deteriorated over disagreements in Eastern Europe and the Middle East, President Truman soon abandoned FDR's engagement of the Soviet Union. The United States began to assemble the organizations of a national security state. The National Security Act of 1947 established the institutional foundations for conducting the Cold War, merging the army, navy, and air force into a single department (the Department of Defense), and creating the Central Intelligence Agency (CIA) and the National Security Council.[6]

Growing tensions with the Soviet Union had impelled a rethinking of the Occupation's objectives, but it was the triumph of the communists in the Chinese Revolution in October 1949 and the outbreak of the Korean War the following June that brought Asia fully into the Cold War and established the bipolar world. The mistakes of the unconditional surrender policy were becoming apparent. Above all, the determination to permanently disarm Japan, enshrined in the MacArthur Constitution, now seemed ill considered and naive. Reality was setting in. The wide discretion MacArthur exercised in making policies in the first two years of the Occupation was ending. Policies regarding Japan's future would now be made in Washington, not in Occupation headquarters, and crafted to deal with the emerging Cold War.

The Cold War and Japan's Fate

The diplomat George Kennan is known for his role in Soviet-American relations and for formulation of American containment policy. His important role in rethinking American policy toward Japan is not well recognized. When it *is* acknowledged, it has often been misinterpreted. Kennan came to prominence in American politics when his authorship of an article under the pen name "Mr. X" in the July 1947 issue of *Foreign Affairs* was revealed. He wrote that the United States must adopt a "policy of firm containment designed to confront the Russians with unalterable counterforce at every point where they show signs of encroaching upon the interests of a peaceful and stable world."[7] In the same year that his X article was published, Kennan was named director of the newly established Policy Planning Staff in the State Department, intended to coordinate the many dimensions of America's vast new power and map the nation's long-term strategy.

A brilliant and thoughtful diplomat with a broad historical perspective and a keen understanding of the forces that were converging into the Cold War, Kennan had long harbored deep misgivings over the unconditional surrender policy and the idealism, legalism, and universalist pretensions in the conduct of American foreign relations. Regarding Japan, he wrote in his diary in January 1948, "Of all the failures of

United States policy in the wake of World War II, history will rate as the most grievous our failure to approach realistically the responsibilities of power over the defeated nations which we ourselves courted by the policy of unconditional surrender."[8] Kennan consistently maintained that a defeated Japan should still have an important role in the regional balance of power and that its total disarmament was from the start a mistaken policy. "It should be a cardinal point of our policy," he wrote in October 1947, "to see to it that other elements of independent power are developed on the Eurasian land mass as rapidly as possible in order to take off our shoulders some of the burden of 'bipolarity.'"[9] What he sought, as his biographer John Lewis Gaddis explains, was encouraging key potential power centers like Japan to develop as "independent forces with the strength and self-confidence necessary to defend themselves."[10]

Kennan's attention to Japan's future arose from the fact that MacArthur had declared in 1947 that the reform agenda was reaching com-

Diplomat George F. Kennan, who played an important role in shaping postwar policy toward Japan, shown here in 1951, shortly after leaving government. Everett Collection Historical / Alamy Stock Photo / CWCF1X.

pletion and that it was time to conclude a peace treaty and bring an end to the Occupation. He sought to recalibrate Occupation policy by placing it within the context of the evolving international order. Kennan was concerned that should a peace treaty be negotiated at that time, a totally disarmed Japan might soon gravitate—through subversion or intimidation or domestic radical sentiment—into the Soviet orbit. Given its educated workforce and the consequent industrial potential of its people, Japan represented a prize for whichever side might co-opt it. "Our primary goal," Kennan reasoned, was to ensure that American security "never again be threatened by the mobilization against us of the complete industrial area [in the Far East] as it was during the second world war."[11] The danger was that the Occupation, in its zeal to demilitarize Japan, would leave it an easy target for Soviet co-optation. The Policy Planning Staff concluded that in the emerging superpower conflict, "a process of political polarization is occurring with states thus far uncommitted to either side gravitating into the orbit of one or the other super powers. In these circumstances, Japan cannot possess an independent destiny. It can function only as an American or Soviet satellite."[12]

In his new position, Kennan undertook a trip to Japan in February 1948 that resulted in Washington coming to view Japan as a central part of his new strategic doctrine of containment. The sensitive Kennan was not only opposed to the course of the Occupation but also deeply repelled by the stuffiness and grandiosity of MacArthur and the self-important atmosphere that it created. He wrote privately to an associate that MacArthur's underlings and their "shrill cackling" wives behaved as if the war had been fought so that they might have "six Japanese butlers with the divisional insignia on their jackets" or so that "Miss Z might learn her skiing in the mountains of Hokkaido" at Japanese expense. He found distasteful the "American brand of philistinism" and its "monumental imperviousness to the suffering and difficulties of the [Japanese]." The Americans in Tokyo "monopolized . . . everything that smacks of comfort or elegance or luxury."[13]

Kennan recommended that the purpose of the Occupation be fundamentally revised: "No further reform legislation should be pressed. The emphasis should shift from reform to economic recovery. . . . Precedence should be given . . . to the task of bringing the Japanese into a position where they would be better able to shoulder the burdens of independence."[14] Kennan further explained:

With the Russians in occupation of North Korea, [Japan] was semi-surrounded by the military positions of the Soviet Union. Yet no provision of any sort had been made. It was simply madness to think of abandoning Japan to her own devices in the situation then prevailing. She had been totally disarmed and demilitarized. . . . In addition to this, Japan's central police establishment had been destroyed. She had no effective means of combating the communist penetration. . . . In the face of this situation the nature of the Occupational policies pursued up to that time by General MacArthur's headquarters seemed on cursory examination to be such that if they had been devised for the specific purpose of rendering Japanese society vulnerable to communist political pressures and paving the way for a communist takeover, they could scarcely have been other than what they were.

Kennan's recommendations were subsequently accepted by the National Security Council and gained presidential approval. Kennan later identified his role in revising policy toward Japan as "after the Marshall Plan, the most significant, constructive contribution I was ever able to make in government."[15]

The Reverse Course

Accordingly, MacArthur acquiesced in the changed orientation of policy and began to implement a marked shift in Occupation policy. Known wryly in Japan as "the reverse course" (*gyaku-kōsu*), it was marked by a notable retreat from the idealism and utopianism of the early Occupation. It represented a tacit acknowledgment of the mistakes of unconditional surrender policy. The entire emphasis of the Occupation shifted from reform to recovery. Along with growing concern about the Japanese left wing's strength, the Occupation aimed to stabilize and stimulate the economy. The precarious economic conditions in Japan aroused concern that the communists and socialists might succeed in winning a mass following and that Japan would be rendered susceptible to Russian political pressures. The purge procedures were revived and turned on the left wing and communists. The program for breaking up the zaibatsu concentration of economic power was curtailed. SCAP was now ready to embrace the conservative elite, including members of the wartime leadership.

In February 1949, Detroit banker Joseph Dodge was brought to Japan as a financial advisor to the Occupation for the purpose of reviving the

Japanese economy. By recommending a balanced national budget and establishing an official exchange rate, Dodge sought to curb inflation and to attract foreign investment. Dodge demonstrated that American imperial rule in Japan was not unique to MacArthur. He decreed austerity and, as one American-educated Japanese economist said, took measures that were "thrust down the throat" of the Japanese government. Ted Cohen, the labor specialist in SCAP, described the dictatorial banker as carrying out a "ruthless operation, without regard for Japanese views three and a half years and two democratic elections after the war."[16]

Later in 1949, planners in Washington also began to devote attention to providing Japan with foreign markets and sources of raw materials. With Chinese communists in power, Washington wanted to deflect Japanese trade away from China; and the favored area for Japanese economic expansion, from Washington's point of view, had become Southeast Asia. In yet more ironic evidence of the abandonment of the goals for which unconditional surrender policy had been fought, the United States decided to restore Japan to a dominant position in Southeast Asia. To promote Japanese economic recovery, Kennan remarked at a Policy Planning meeting in October 1949 that there was a "terrific problem" of how the "Japanese are going to get along unless they again reopen some sort of empire to the South." The new "empire" had to have commercial possibilities "on a scale very far greater than anything Japan knew before." Another American present at the meeting agreed, adding, "We have got to get Japan back into, I am afraid, the old Co-Prosperity Sphere."[17]

Kennan and others at State and even MacArthur himself were disposed to accept a neutral Japan in the Cold War so long as it could be ensured that the Soviets were denied Japanese industrial potential. MacArthur thought that neutralization could be ensured if the Americans made clear that a Russian attack on Japan would bring war with the United States. A Japan that was economically and politically stable would in itself be a balance against the Russians. Kennan saw no need for locking Japan into an alliance with the West or even garrisoning American forces whose continued basing on Japanese soil would cause resentment and friction. With regard to the future of Okinawa, Kennan agreed with MacArthur that its strategic value was such that the United States should indefinitely retain control of it. If that were done, it would not be necessary to have bases in Japan proper when the Occupation ended.[18] Kennan foresaw that the continued presence of American bases would polarize Japanese politics, alienate Japanese youth, and strain Japanese democracy.[19]

Kennan is sometimes remembered as the "father of the reverse course,"[20] but his purpose was to ensure that when the Occupation was over, Japan would be able to defend itself, fully recover its sovereignty, and, if it wished, choose a neutral status in the Cold War. He "wanted Japan to resume the characteristics of a significant national actor,"[21] but his vision of an economically and politically stabilized Japan that would remain neutral was soon left behind by the deepening superpower conflict. His belief that containment policy needed to be pursued in a measured way with an emphasis on diplomatic engagement and economic aid rather than militarization lost ground in the administration, and at the end of 1949 he resigned his position.[22]

The Turning Point

As the Cold War extended to East Asia, the need to build a balance of power revealed the unfortunate legacy of the unconditional surrender policy. Forrestal and other realists in the Roosevelt and Truman administrations feared that the policy would leave a vacuum, unbalance the international system, and ultimately require a counterweight to Russian influence in East Asia. Their fears were soon realized. Between the summers of 1949 and 1950 the Cold War broke out in full fury in a way that forced critical and long-lasting decisions about Japan's future.

In August 1949, President Truman received intelligence that the Soviet Union had tested a nuclear bomb. In October the communists took power in China, and four months later Stalin and Mao Zedong signed an alliance. Amid the gathering storm of superpower confrontation, Senator Joseph McCarthy from Wisconsin burst on the scene with sensational charges of internal subversion.[23] In the very midst of this domestic hysteria, Truman authorized the State Department to undertake a full-scale review of defense strategy in response to the Soviet A-bomb and the Sino-Soviet alliance. The review was finished in the spring of 1950, and the result was a top-secret report of lasting influence that culminated in a radical shift in US policy. Drafted by Paul Nitze, Kennan's successor at the Policy Planning Staff, it was known as National Security Council Document 68 (or simply NSC 68) and "laid out the rationale for U.S. strategy during much of the cold war."[24] It called for "a build-up of military strength by the United States and its allies to a point at which the combined strength will be superior . . . to the forces that can be brought to bear by the Soviet Union and its allies." The emphasis of the document was on the potential capability rather than the intention of the Soviet Union, and the rhetoric was at times breathless and apoplectic in its warning that "the issues that face us are momentous, involving the fulfillment or destruction not only of this Republic but of civilization itself." In Manichean terms, it depicted a struggle between slave and free societies. What was required was as much as a quadrupling of the defense budget, the buildup of the armed forces, and the strengthened coherence of the free world forces.

Two months later, the North Korean invasion of the South on June 25 seemed emphatic confirmation of what NSC 68 had depicted. Truman was at once resolved to intervene by committing troops to turn back communist forces. A dramatic increase in the defense budget and the readiness to respond to the challenge sprang naturally from the premises of the report, which had stressed readiness "to defeat local Soviet moves with local action."[25]

The Korean conflict inevitably drew attention to the future of Japan. Between the State Department and the Pentagon there was sharp disagreement. The commitment of American forces to hostilities on the peninsula hardened attitudes in the Defense Department, which now regarded the American position in Japan as a strategic necessity in the coming struggle.[26] Secretary of State Acheson argued for an early return of sovereignty to Japan lest the Japanese grow weary and restive under a lengthening Occupation that could provoke anti-American sentiment, bring about a radicalized politics, and undermine the US future in Japan. The Pentagon, unwilling to give up bases, feared that an end to the Occupation would permit a neutral or independent Japan. Acheson won Truman's agreement that it was time to end the Occupation and appointed the resolute and experienced Republican foreign policy strategist John Foster Dulles to resolve differences between State and Defense and negotiate a peace treaty to end the Occupation and shape a role for Japan in a security structure for the Asia Pacific region. In turning to a Republican, Truman and Acheson sought to surmount political controversy and to reach a settlement that would have bipartisan support. For this purpose, Dulles had the credentials. His grandfather had been secretary of state under President Benjamin Harrison. His uncle, Robert Lansing, had been Woodrow Wilson's secretary of state. His sister was a foreign service officer, and his brother Allen was soon to be chosen as director of the CIA.

Serving first as the Truman administration's representative to negotiate a Japanese peace treaty and then as secretary of state in the Eisenhower administration, Dulles became the architect of the new US strategy in Asia. He possessed the background to carry forward the American vision of a liberal international order to the new circumstances of the Cold War. As a student at Princeton, he had studied under Woodrow Wilson. Like Wilson, he came from a deeply religious, Presbyterian upbringing and shared his teacher's belief in American universalism and moral mission. Serving in the American delegation to the Paris Peace Conference in 1919, he helped draft treaty provisions on reparations and war guilt. Like so many of his generation, he subsequently grew disillusioned with the peace he had helped draft, recognizing the need for maintaining a balance of power if collective security was to preserve peace. "Realism" and "idealism," he wrote in 1939, were both essential, self-reinforcing to world order.[27] After Pearl Harbor, as a layman he drafted the vision statement of postwar order for the Federal Council of Churches of Christ. Known as the "Six Pillars of Peace," it bore a strong resemblance to Wilson's Fourteen Points, stressing American leadership of a new international organization for collective security.[28]

The beginning of the Korean War in June 1950 ended the standoff between State and Defense. With Dulles's mediation, the deadlock was finally broken when he assured the Pentagon that a peace treaty should give the United States "the right to maintain in Japan as much force as we wanted, anywhere, for as long as we wanted." Planning began for a peace settlement whose purpose was "to secure the adherence of the Japanese nation to the free nations of the world and to assure that it will play its full part in resisting the further expansion of communist imperialism."[29] Japanese autonomy and its place in the community of nations would have to be circumscribed. Like it or not, Japan was to be drawn into the Cold War.

The expectation in Washington was that a peace treaty ending the Occupation could be concluded on the assumption that the American bases in Japan would be maintained and Japan could now be remilitarized as an "active ally" in the superpower struggle. A CIA estimate in 1951 described the potential for a Japanese army of half a million, a supportive capacity for arms production equivalent to its World War II capacity, and a dominant economic role in Southeast Asia. General Matthew Ridgeway, who succeeded MacArthur following his dismissal by Truman, saw such a reconstituted Japanese force, "with fighting spirit and ability equivalent to that displayed by Japanese Forces in World War II," as of paramount importance in bringing stability and protection to East Asia.[30]

Yoshida's Choice

As Japan's future was being negotiated between opposite sides of the Potomac, Japan's leadership began to seek some part in the determination. Even before the deadlock between the State Department and the Pentagon was resolved, Japan's prime minister Yoshida Shigeru took a decisive step. He dispatched his trusted protégé, Ikeda Hayato, to Washington in May 1950 to express secretly Japan's readiness to accept long-term presence of US bases in Japan in return for an early end to the Occupation. Ikeda privately conveyed to administration officials that "the Japanese government herein formally expresses its desire to conclude a peace treaty with the United States as early as possible. In the case of such a peace treaty being concluded, the Japanese government thinks it will be necessary to station American forces in Japan in order to preserve the security of Japan and the Asian area. If it is difficult for the United States to make such a request, the Japanese government itself is prepared to make the offer."[31]

While acquiescing in a continuation of US bases, Yoshida privately had no intention of involving Japan in an active military role. Quite the contrary. Japan would accept its incorporation into the emerging American Cold War order but would seek to avoid a military role. His purpose was to put off the day of rearmament so that Japan could concentrate its energies on economic recovery. He was distrustful of a plan that would restore the Japanese military, and he recognized that remilitarization would be deeply divisive among the Japanese people. Therefore, he thought, with the Occupation ended, let the Americans keep their bases and thereby provide security while Japan concentrated for the time being on rebuilding its economy.

Accustomed to having their way with postwar Japan, Dulles and other American policymakers assumed that Japan would see the danger posed by the growing threat of Soviet and Chinese communist expansion and could now be readily incorporated into the US emerging Cold War strategy. Dulles had in mind a Pacific version of the North Atlantic Treaty Organization (NATO).[32] Japan, like Germany, would be integrated with its former adversaries into a multilateral alliance to contain communist expansion in Asia. The United States could provide arms and aid to create a collective security organization, among maritime nations including Australia, New Zealand, and the Philippines, under American leadership. The purpose of a "Pacific Pact" was to facilitate Japanese rearmament but to keep it under international control. Japan ought to find such an alliance a reassuring guarantee of its own security, while facilitating Japanese rearmament. Dulles reasoned that such a collective security arrangement, permitted under Article 51 of the UN Charter, would "ease reconciliation with the present . . . Constitution."[33] Dulles consulted the chief justice of the Japanese supreme court, who concurred that such an arrangement would be compatible with Article 9.[34]

In Yoshida, however, the Americans soon learned they had no pushover. It was he, more than any other postwar Japanese leader, who made decisions that fundamentally set Japan's international role in the decades after surrender. Yoshida was a formidable personality. Not since the founders of the modern state in the Meiji period had Japan seen the likes of so shrewd a political leader. He served as prime minister for most of the first decade after the war and served concurrently as foreign minister during much of this time. Brilliant and abrasive, a leading member of the prewar bureaucratic elite, Yoshida was ambassador to Italy and then to Great Britain in the 1930s. Devoted to the imperial cause in Asia, he nonetheless was a harsh critic of the military as the confrontation with the Anglo-American powers intensified. During the war, his efforts, culminating in the Yohansen appeal to the emperor (discussed above), to find an end to the conflict led to his arrest by the military police. His wartime opposition to the militarists made him acceptable to SCAP, which sanctioned his becoming prime minister in 1946. Yoshida, however, was neither a liberal nor a democrat.

He was a nationalist, as well as a realist, determined to preserve as much of the old order as possible and to restore Japan as a great power.

Yoshida had a shrewd perception of world trends and of the game of international politics. At the time that he formed his first cabinet, in May 1946, he observed to a colleague that "history provides examples of winning by diplomacy after losing in war (*sensō de makete gaikō de katta rekishi wa aru*)."[35] That is, a defeated nation, by analyzing and exploiting the shifting relations among world powers, could contain the damages incurred in defeat and could instead win the peace. Yoshida believed that disputes between victors over the postwar settlement with the defeated nation could be used to the latter's advantage. Yoshida's sense of a possible opportunity came from the recognition that Soviet-American estrangement was growing. With the Cold War taking shape, he recognized that Japan's strategic value to the Americans gave him bargaining leverage. As impoverished as Japan was, there were yet possibilities to move Japan in the direction of its own interests. He possessed the tactical insight to make the best of a desperate situation.

The Soviet-US rivalry presented both dangers and opportunities to Japan. The United States' purpose was now to draw Japan into a regional defense system and to remilitarize Japan to support the United States in the Cold War. The dangers were that Japan would be drawn into Cold War politics, expend its limited and precious resources on remilitarization, and postpone the full economic and social recovery of its people. On the other hand, Soviet-US rivalry offered certain opportunities. Yoshida knew that the Cold War made Japan strategically important to the United States. American policy toward Japan was, in short, a piece in a much larger puzzle. "The future of the world," Dulles repeatedly asserted, "depends largely on whether the Soviet Union will be able to get control over Western Germany and Japan by means short of war. . . . The world balance of power would be profoundly altered."[36] Yoshida reasoned that Japan could make minimal concessions of passive cooperation with the United States in return for an early end to the Occupation and a long-term guarantee of Japan's national security, allowing Japan to give priority to economic recovery and indefinitely defer a costly and politically divisive rearmament.

Yoshida set out to exploit the opportunities. When Dulles came to Tokyo in June 1950 to negotiate a peace treaty and the end of the Occupation, he urged Japanese rearmament and participation in a collective defense arrangement with other Pacific nations. In this and subsequent meetings, Dulles sought to undo the MacArthur Constitution and to establish a large Japanese military force. Many Japanese conservative leaders were ready to revise the constitution and undertake an all-out rearmament and join actively in the Cold War struggle. But not Yoshida. He refused to accede to American demands.[37] He established his bargaining position with Dulles by making light of Japan's security problems and intimating that Japan could protect itself through its own devices, by being democratic and peaceful, and by relying on the protection of world opinion. After all, he argued, Japan had a constitution that renounced arms, inspired by US ideals and the lessons of defeat, and the Japanese people were determined to uphold it and to adhere to a new course in world affairs. Yoshida must have privately relished the trap the Americans had created for themselves. It was, after all, in the meeting at Yoshida's house in February 1946 that General Whitney had employed his "psychological shafts" to coerce the Japanese cabinet to accept the American draft constitution with its Article 9.

Yoshida's "puckish" and bravado performance left Dulles (in the words of a colleague) "flabbergasted," embittered, and feeling "very much like Alice in Wonderland."[38] In succeeding meetings, Yoshida negotiated from this position. He skillfully argued that rearmament would impoverish Japan and create the kind of social unrest that the communists wanted. We now know that through backdoor channels he was prevailing on Japan Socialist Party leaders to whip up anti-rearmament demonstrations and campaigns during Dulles's visits to Tokyo.[39] Allusion to the prospect of a leftist government coming to power became a convenient pretext for holding to his position and dissuading the Americans from undue pressure. Yoshida further pointed out to Dulles the fears that other Asian countries had of a revived Japanese military, and he enlisted the support of MacArthur, who obligingly told Dulles that Japan should remain a nonmilitary nation and instead contribute to the free world through its industrial production.[40] The transformation of Japan into an industrial power, needless to say, was precisely what Yoshida sought.

Yoshida's manipulation of both domestic politics and US pressure was shrewd and cynical. At every step of negotiations, Yoshida invoked the strength of left wing and pacifist sentiment as a means of tempering American pressure for rearmament. Moreover, he was keenly aware of apprehension in the United States, as well as in Europe and Asia, about Japanese rearmament possibly going too far and reawakening militarism. The potential of a nationalist revival, on the one hand, and a left wing takeover, on the other, served as a brake on US demands. Above all, Yoshida's clever use of Article 9 of the American-imposed constitution served as his best shield. Yoshida took secret pleasure in reminding the Americans that it was their own enthusiasm in punishing the Japanese and remaking their political system that made it impossible to satisfy their new demands on Japan. He pointed out that Article 9, which had been written by the Americans, outlawed war potential, that the principles of peace education they had injected into postwar schools were now deeply held by the Japanese, that the MacArthur Constitution had been written to make any amendment highly difficult, and that Japanese women, to whom the Americans had insisted must be given the right to vote, were as a group overwhelmingly opposed to revision.[41] A comment Yoshida made to a young aide, Miyazawa Kiichi, is highly revealing of his method. Miyazawa, who later became prime minister and a durable political leader, records in a memoir that Yoshida told him:

> The day [for rearmament] will come naturally when our livelihood recovers. It may sound devious (*zurui*), but let the Americans handle [our security] until then. It is indeed our Heaven-bestowed good fortune that the Constitution bans arms. If the Americans complain, the Constitution gives us a perfect justification. The politicians who want to amend it are fools.[42]

Yoshida was convinced that the Cold War would require the United States to maintain its presence in Japan, which alone would be sufficient to deter a Soviet attack. He would therefore give exclusive priority to pursuing Japanese economic recovery and maintaining political stability, and would defer indefinitely the task of preparing the Japanese people for a return to the hard realities of international politics. In the protracted negotiations with Dulles, Yoshida made minimal concessions; he consented to US bases on Japanese soil and a limited rearmament. Yoshida grudgingly agreed to upgrade the National Police Reserve, which MacArthur established in July 1950 with 75,000 men, to the status of National Security Force in January 1952 with 110,00 men, which was sufficient to gain Dulles's agreement to a peace treaty and to a post-Occupation guarantee of Japanese security.

The San Francisco Peace Treaty of 1951

Three fundamental agreements fixed the essentials of the US-Japan relationship for the future: the peace treaty, the US-Japan Mutual Security Treaty, and an administrative agreement that spelled out the details of the garrisoning of American troops. The peace settlement with Japan formally brought an end to the Occupation and restored Japanese sovereignty. Dulles, the architect of the settlement, declared that "the [peace] treaty should contain no restrictions on the freedom of action of the Japanese. . . . The United States intends to restore to Japan complete and untrammeled sovereignty."[43] The reality, however, was different. In many ways, the conditions of the Occupation continued and Japanese sovereignty was compromised by the settlement.

Americans have taken some pride in regarding the San Francisco Peace Treaty as generous and lacking in revenge for the war. The security treaty, however, privately signed a few hours after the peace treaty, together with an administrative agreement concluded later, in many respects continued the military occupation. These agreements subordinated Japan in a new Cold War order that the Americans were structuring. Although President Truman asserted that the peace settlement would ensure that the former enemies would be "neither victors nor vanquished . . . but only equals in the partnership of peace,"[44] the subordination of Japan was unmistakable.

The signing of the peace treaty on September 8, 1951, was conducted in the cavernous San Francisco Opera House. Fifty-one nations formerly at war with Japan were represented at the proceedings, which attracted a vast public audience because it happened to be the first occasion on which there was coast-to-coast coverage by American television. The politics of the Cold War dominated the conference. Secretary of State Dean Acheson presided over the sometimes-tense proceedings with an iron hand, ruling Soviet objections and motions out of order. Even the address Yoshida gave to the conference was written by American diplomats. Forty-nine nations, including Japan, signed the peace treaty, while the Russians and their allies refused. Neither China nor Taiwan was invited, since the British and the Americans could not resolve their differences over diplomatic recognition. India and Burma chose not to attend, citing the absence of China. South Korea was not invited, on the insistence of Yoshida.[45] The result was a peace settlement that left

Prime Minister Yoshida Shigeru signed the US-Japan Mutual Security Treaty on September 8, 1951. John Foster Dulles (third from left), responsible for drafting the treaty, and Secretary of State Dean Acheson (third from right) look on. Bettmann/Getty Images/515411096.

out not only the Soviet bloc but most of Asia as well. The treaty did obligate Japan to provide reparations to the Asian nations it had invaded.

The Americans took pride in avoiding the mistakes of the punitive treaty ending World War I that had left a bitter legacy from which the Nazi movement drew strength. Dulles emphasized that "the lessons of Versailles should be remembered. . . . We must not make the same mistake with Japan."[46] Dulles had been at Versailles in 1919 when the Japanese had sought a racial equality clause in the League of Nations charter and was aware of how bitterly the Japanese took its rejection. "The Japanese must be made to feel that they are equals of the people of the West," Dulles repeatedly stressed.[47] He sensed that the Occupation experience had embedded in Americans a sense of superiority over the defeated Japanese. He wrote in October 1951: "We face in Japan a crucial test of whether or not it is possible for representatives of the West to deal on a basis of equality with Asiatics. . . . To meet this challenge in Japan it is peculiarly difficult because the challenge confronts soldiers who for over six years [the time of the Occupation] have looked upon the Japanese as inferiors, both because of their race and because of their defeat in battle. To alter that attitude will be tremendously difficult."[48] At about the same time he told Truman that building an equal relationship with Japan depended on "getting the colonels out of the Japanese villas."[49]

The Troubled Legacy of the Peace Treaty

In some ways, of course, it was a generous peace that avoided the burden of reparations Weimar Germany had borne. The Allies required no forthright Japanese declaration of war guilt as had been imposed on the Germans at Versailles. Still, the overall settlement left a psychologically crippling burden. Japanese guilt had already been driven home in the war crimes trials, which originated like so much else in postwar Japan in the unconditional surrender policy with its view of the war as the punishment of the guilty by the innocent and FDR's assertion that the ringleaders be brought to justice. Although noble in their purpose to demonstrate to the Japanese the rule of law, the trials were in many respects "victors' justice" and the San Francisco Peace Treaty, in its Article 11, required Japan to accept the verdict of the tribunal, leaving postwar Japan to struggle with a purely negative view of its modern history.[50] Above all, it incorporated Japan indefinitely in an American-led cold war system that the great majority of the Japanese people opposed, as their massive protests would soon demonstrate.

The peace settlement also left Okinawa, in effect, an outright colony of the United States. The long-suffering people of Okinawa, nearly 150,000 of whom (20 percent of the population) perished in the war's final horrific battle, had been sacrificed in the ketsugo strategy. With the secret encouragement of the emperor, the treaty detached the island from Japan and excluded it from democratic reforms.[51] The treaty tacitly recognized the residual sovereignty of the Ryukyus (of which Okinawa was the largest part) and the Bonin Islands, but the Pentagon was adamant that the islands not be returned because of their strategic value.

Okinawa was transformed into America's largest network of bases in Asia with a labyrinth of air, naval, logistic, and intelligence facilities. Eventually, in 1972, Okinawan sovereignty was restored, but by that time American troop assignment in Japan was so heavily concentrated on the island that it remains a source of constant protest by the Okinawans.

The treaty also left an intractable territorial dispute over four islands north of Hokkaido, which Russia seized at the end of the war. The dispute involves what the Japanese call "the Northern Territories" and the Russians call "the southern Kurile Islands." After breaking the neutrality pact and entering the war against Japan on August 8, Stalin continued warfare for several weeks after Japan's surrender on August 15, allowing him to take a large swath of territory promised to him by Roosevelt at Yalta as inducement to bring the Russian assistance to complete the unconditional surrender. FDR agreed that the Kuriles should be "handed over," but the Yalta agreement had no legal standing and Russia's refusal to sign the San Francisco Peace Treaty left Soviet-Japanese territorial issues in limbo. Although Yoshida agreed that Japan must waive claim to the Kuriles, at issue when the two countries sought to agree to bilateral peace was whether the four islands (Etorofu, Kunashiri, Shikotan, and the Habomais) were part of the Kuriles. Yoshida's successor as prime minister, Hatoyama Ichirō (1954–1956), pursued a high profile and independent foreign policy, much to Dulles's annoyance. Hatoyama set out to reach a peace agreement with Russia, and the two sides came close to an agreement in 1956 that Japan would accept return of Shikotan and the Habomais as a basis for reaching a peace treaty. Dulles, however, counseled Foreign Minister Shigemitsu to hold out for all four islands knowing that this would deadlock negotiations and prevent rapprochement with Russia. Dulles linked the dispute with the future of the Ryukyus: Shigemitsu should tell the Russians that compromising on the territorial issue might jeopardize the future willingness of the United States to return Okinawa to Japan.[52] With both Dulles's opposition and strong opposition to compromise with Russia from Japanese conservatives, the attempt to reach a peace treaty broke down. While the two sides succeeded in restoring normal diplomatic relations that year, the territorial dispute remains unsettled and no final Soviet-Japanese peace treaty has yet been signed.

The failure to invite Korean and Chinese representatives to participate in the San Francisco conference also left intractable and continuing territorial disputes over the sovereignty of adjacent islands. Although peace treaties were subsequently reached, the sovereignty of Takeshima / Tokdo remains unresolved between Korea and Japan, as does the Senkaku / Diaoyu dispute between China and Japan. Beyond these unresolved disputes, the absence from San Francisco of Japan's neighbors that had suffered so grievously from the depredations of Japanese imperialism allowed the Japanese to avoid having to confront issues of war responsibility—the "history issues"—for many decades before they burst forth in their neighbors' nationalist emotions that still fester.

The Mutual Security Treaty of 1951

Addressing the delegates to the San Francisco Conference, Acheson characterized the peace treaty as "an act of reconciliation" in which "there was nothing mean, there was nothing sordid . . . nothing hidden."[53] But in fact there were things well hidden. Deliberately kept from public scrutiny was a bilateral security pact that would continue the American military presence in Japan and an accompanying administrative agreement, the details of which were still to be worked out.[54] Acheson told Yoshida to keep the pact secret during the peace conference lest the Russians make it an issue. Several hours after the conference concluded, Yoshida, Ikeda, Acheson, Dulles, and a small number of Japanese and American officials quietly repaired to the military installation at the San Francisco Presidio to sign the security treaty. Yoshida alone signed for Japan.

The sovereignty the San Francisco Peace Treaty nominally returned to Japan was significantly compromised by the bilateral security pact signed the same day. The pact was regarded as the basis for a bilateral alliance, but Dulles himself privately told British officials that the arrangements "amounted to a voluntary continuation of the Occupation."[55] Although it came to be called a mutual security treaty, there was no mutuality. The security treaty provided that American forces would be stationed indefinitely and could be used anywhere in the Far East without consulting Japan and might even be used to put down internal disturbances at the request of the Japanese government. Neither the peace treaty nor the separate security pact gave evidence of the truly intrusive nature of the alliance on Japanese sovereignty. Those details were buried in an administrative agreement worked out behind closed doors, kept from public scrutiny until later, and never brought before the Diet for ratification.

In the negotiation of the administrative agreement, the joint chiefs were obstinate in their determination to maintain Occupation prerogatives. Even Dulles fumed that the Pentagon was determined to continue treating the Japanese as "defeated enemies and as orientals having qualities inferior to those of occidentals."[56] As finally worked out, the secret negotiations gave the US military the right to arrest Japanese nationals in areas outside the bases, and, most intrusive of Japanese sovereignty, crimes committed in Japan by the American military and their dependents would be subject to the exclusive jurisdiction of US authorities.[57] The semicolonial status imposed on Japan by the imperial powers in the nineteenth century was not nearly as intrusive of Japanese sovereignty as this "alliance."

The American Cold War Order in East Asia

Yoshida's stiff resistance to rearmament, which we have just considered in connection with the peace agreement, was instrumental in determining the architecture of the regional order that the United States created in the 1950s. As the Cold War engulfed Asia with the Chinese revolution, the Sino-Soviet alliance, and the Korean War, the Truman administration struggled to find the right structure to organize a containment policy to fit the region. Many options were considered. The future role of Japan was at the center of US thinking. As in so many ways, Eurocentric influences were important in the approach to Japan, and the example of NATO as a way of integrating postwar Germany with its previous enemies and permitting its rearmament in a collective security arrangement was highly influential. But the multifariousness of Asia, in contrast with Europe, made multilateralism difficult—just as it continues to be today. Historical, geographical, and political forces all militated against establishing a multilateral organization. The various countries in the region presented different challenges that made a common approach difficult.

For a short time, the United States considered a Pacific version of NATO. When Dulles first came to Japan in June 1950, he had in the back of his mind an organization of maritime countries, including Japan, Australia, New Zealand, and the Philippines, joined in a collective security treaty. Expecting that Yoshida would surely welcome ways to defend his country against communist expansion, Dulles believed that this multilateral design would prove appealing to Japan with its constitutional restrictions. By internationalizing Japanese forces, such an arrangement would, in effect, skirt such restrictions on an autonomous rearmament. The principal US purpose of this multilateral design was to reintegrate Japan with Asia and facilitate its rearmament as America's key ally in the region. The parallel with Germany and NATO was clearly in the American mind.

From the beginning, Yoshida's exasperating resistance to rearmament and integration with other Asian nations was the big problem. But that was not all. The British strongly objected to being left out of the arrangement and worried about the future of their remaining colonies, Hong Kong and Malaya. In Australia, New Zealand, and the Philippines, where memories of Japanese imperialism were still fresh, the governments were strongly opposed to a liberal peace treaty with Japan and to its rearming. They were also opposed to policies that would restore Japan as an economic competitor in Southeast Asia. New Zealand's foreign minister told Dulles that "Japan has been a nightmare and the . . . possibility of its resurgence [is] regarded with horror." Likewise, Sir Percy Spender, Canberra's foreign minister, said that Australia "still feared" a resurgent Japan. With all these objections in mind, especially Yoshida's stiff resistance, Dulles began to explore alternative arrangements to a Pacific pact. He pondered with Spender the possibility of separate defense relations with Pacific countries and likened them to "spokes on a wheel."[58]

With the possibility of a single blanket organization similar to NATO foreclosed by the resistance of the nations in the region, the United States decided to drop the idea of a Pacific pact and instead negotiate a series of singular agreements, which came to be known as the "hub-and-spokes" system constituting the security architecture still intact today. With the United States as the "hub" and separate bilateral agreements with Asian states as the "spokes," a network of bilateral arrangements was designed to deal with the differing circumstances of Asia's multifarious state system. First, and most important, on the day of the 1951 San Francisco Conference, the United States concluded, as we have seen, the Mutual Security Treaty alliance with Japan. At the same time, the United States also negotiated a bilateral security treaty with the Philippines and a tripartite mutual defense pact among Australia, New Zealand, and the United States. Bilateral security pacts were then signed with South Korea in 1953 and in the following year with the nationalist government on Taiwan. These two pacts, as Victor Cha describes, were fashioned to deal with "rogue allies—that is, rabidly anticommunist dictators who might start wars for reasons of domestic legitimacy that the United States wanted no part of." They were intended to control Sygman Rhee in South Korea and Chiang Kai-shek in Taiwan, who might embroil the United States in unwanted conflicts.[59] Also in 1954, key Southeast Asian countries were brought together in the Southeast Asia Treaty Organization (SEATO). Although it entailed multiple signatories, SEATO was not a multilateralized collective self-defense organization like NATO; it simply prescribed consultations in the event of outside attack.

These many treaties bound the United States to each ally but did not bind all the allies to one another, contrasting sharply with the integrated NATO structure established under American leadership in Europe. The vast power and resources of the United States were brought to bear in the creation of an Asian order loosely organized around hierarchical relations of domination and dependency.[60] The United States exercised control by providing its regional allies with security guarantees as well as the market access, aid, and technology on which the allies depended for their economic development. In return, they accepted political and military subordination in the American-centered anticommunist order in Asia. As described by one informed observer, the treaty system established by the United States in the Pacific was "piecemeal and jerry-built." It was a patchwork affair, cobbled together without creating a cohesive and integrated system.[61] Though it was a patchwork, the hub-and-spokes structure provided stability for a region that was not yet ready for a more integrated system of collective security. What was lost in the process was a multilateral framework for reintegrating Japan with Asia and legitimating its rearmament. For that, Yoshida was primarily responsible.

The Yoshida Legacy

An unfortunate result of the hub-and-spokes order was that it put off the day when Japan would come in close contact with its Asian neighbors and face up to their grievances over Japan's past depredations and their fears of Japanese rearmament. Yoshida stood in sharp contrast to his contemporary counterpart in West Germany, where Chancellor Konrad Adenauer sought to resolve the "German question" and the fear of German rearmament by integrating his country into NATO. Whereas Adenauer took the initiative in a variety of ways to reach out to former victims of Germany's wartime aggression, Yoshida made little effort to deal with issues of war guilt. While eager for economic integration with the rest of Asia for the benefits it would provide, Yoshida was not interested in disowning the past. The history issues with Japan's neighbors were left for later generations to deal with.[62]

When the Occupation came to an end in 1952, Yoshida's formative leadership of postwar Japan lasted for two more years. In this time, he continued to lay the foundation for a long-term strategy for Japan by which it would accept American bases but resist active involvement in the Cold War, allowing the nation to concentrate all its energies on economic recovery. Even as the Occupation ended, the United States maintained continuous pressure on Japan to increase its remilitarization. When Congress passed the Mutual Security Assistance (MSA) Act in October 1951, designed "to consolidate the American alliance system through the supply of weapons and equipment, participation of allied officers in training programs in the United States, and the overall coordination of military strategies,"[63] the United States offered Japan economic aid in return for a threefold expansion of its forces, increasing the size of the National Security Force from 110,00 to an army of 350,000. Yoshida knew that increasing the size of the army, besides being controversial at home, would hasten the moment when the United States pressed Japan to dispatch it for overseas conflict in the Cold War. He was instinctively hostile to participation in the arrangement, but he also knew that Japan needed aid for economic development and reconstruction. Japanese business leaders coveted the opportunity of further economic aid for reconstruction, acquisition of advanced technology, and improved industrial competitiveness. Business leaders, along with the Ministry of International Trade and Industry (MITI), also advocated building an arms export industry in Japan. The debate between the Ministry of Finance (MOF) and its allies and MITI and its allies regarding whether defense production should be the engine of postwar reconstruction was one of the most important industrial policy debates in early postwar Japan, and not one that is widely appreciated.[64] Yoshida and MOF bureaucrats were, however, leery of building a defense industry for export. A military-industrial complex could not only ensnare Japan in external military affairs but also make budgetary demands.

Yoshida once again set out to contain US pressure for military obligations and to use MSA aid for economic reconstruction and development.[65] He concentrated on diverting the bulk of MSA support into commercial purposes and, at the same time, acquiring advanced technology that could be spun off for commercial purposes, principally through licensed coproduction of US weapons. Given the pressure that Dulles and the US government brought to bear, however, Yoshida had to expand the National Security Force to preserve a satisfactory relationship with the United States. Nonetheless, Yoshida's finely honed sense of national purpose again succeeded in limiting Japan's obligations. It was to become a pattern for the future postwar decades of US-Japan relations: Japan would respond to American pressure with the minimum concessions necessary to maintain the alliance relationship and invoke the constitution to justify the minimalist approach.

The MSA agreement that Japan and the United States signed in March 1954, while acknowledging (as in the security treaty) that "Japan will itself increasingly assume responsibility for its own defense," emphasized that "Japan can only contribute to the extent permitted by its general economic conditions." It also acknowledged that "the present Agreement will be implemented by each Government in accordance with the constitutional provisions of the respective countries." At the signing ceremonies, Okazaki Katsuo, the Japanese foreign minister, explained: "There are no new and separate military duties. Overseas service and so on for Japan's internal security force will not arise."[66] Japan was able to direct substantial MSA assistance into economic development, helping to overcome the economic stagnation that set in as the Korean War ended.

In the same month that the MSA agreement was signed, the Japanese government, complying with Washington's demands, introduced legislation to reorganize and to expand the armed forces, including an air force. Even while providing the legal basis of Japan's subsequent military organization, Yoshida was able to temper US demands in significant ways. In 1954, the Japan Defense Agency was established, with responsibility for ground, maritime, and air self-defense forces, with a total of 152,000 men—substantially less than half of what the United States had demanded. Facing the strong likelihood of continued American pressure to expand its military and contribute to the Cold War struggle, Yoshida proceeded to erect new barriers against such demands. Article 9 had to be interpreted in such a way as to preempt American pressure. The government was advised by an elite bureaucratic agency, the Cabinet Legal Bureau (CLB), on legal aspects and ultimately the constitutionality of prospective legislation.[67] Yoshida personally supervised the drafting of a new CLB interpretation of Article 9 that would permit possession of only "the minimum necessary" military for self-defense in the event of an invasion. Moreover, according to this interpretation, the newly named Self-Defense Forces could not be sent abroad, nor could they participate in any collective defense arrangements. It was significant that Yoshida maintained the independence of the Japanese Self-Defense Forces from American control. In secret negotiations over the details of the Mutual Security Treaty, Yoshida refused to accede to US expectations that, in times of national emergency, American and Japanese forces would be unified and an American would command joint forces. Yoshida insisted that Japanese and American forces would only "consult" in times of emergency. At this early stage, he took steps to see that there would be a substantial distance between Japanese forces and American forces in Japan, no joint use of bases, and no interoperability.[68]

In this way, Yoshida accepted a dependency on the Americans for Japan's security needs. In the prewar period, Yoshida had been an advocate of close Anglo-Japanese relations. He now determined that Japan should associate itself with the Americans, the new hegemonic power, as closely as practicable. But this did not entail a sacrifice of the national interest to the US purpose. On the contrary, as he said perhaps half seriously, "Just as the United States was once a colony of Great Britain but is now the stronger of the two, if Japan becomes a colony of the United States, it will also eventually become the stronger!"[69]Japan could look to its long-range interest by assuming for the time being a subordinate role within the US international order. Let the Americans take charge of Japanese security, while Japan pours its efforts into economic recovery and acquires as much American aid, technology, and market access as possible.

At times, Yoshida and his associates were quite shameless in their acceptance of a dependency role. "The Japanese," the historian Iokibe Makoto (later president of the National Defense Academy) observed with irony, "were very good at being controlled."[70] Ikeda Hayato, Japan's finance minister and Yoshida's trusted associate, soon to be prime minister, explained in 1954 to an American diplomat, who was taken back by his seeming subservience, that the role of supplicant was rooted in the psychology of Japanese culture: "It has been traditional in Japanese life for the people to look for guidance, assistance, and support to some wealthy, influential patron. The United States could exploit this to our mutual advantage." He went on to explain that assumption of the role of protector and advisor need not be costly. What the Japanese desperately desire is the assurance of someone strong enough to make it meaningful. As a nation they seek the security that such assurance would afford; just as individuals covet the patronage of an employer, a political mentor, or a wealthy friend, so Japan sought a protector. Ikeda observed that perhaps the United States was making a mistake in treating Japan as a sovereign nation equal in strength and importance to itself. Perhaps, he said, it would be better if the relationship were that of teacher and student.[71] In fact, psychologists have observed such a tendency in Japanese society. One could hardly find a better political case of what eminent Japanese psychoanalyst Doi Takeo described as a tendency toward *amaeru,* or a will to dependence, except that there was a self-conscious cunning behind the willingness of Yoshida and his conservative colleagues to adopt a dependent role.[72]

As a defeated nation still occupied by a quarter million American troops, Japan had few choices of a future course. The Japanese could oppose continuation of bases on its soil and insist on neutrality in the emerging Cold War, as the progressive forces insisted. This would have prolonged the Occupation, as the Pentagon would resist any agreement that ended American bases in Japan. Or the Japanese could have agreed to rearm in an active role with the United States in the conflict with the communist bloc, as many conservative leaders favored. This would have been a costly and divisive choice. Yoshida chose a course between those two alternatives. Japan would agree to accept a long-term continuation of American bases in return for an end to the Occupation, but would not agree to an active role in the Cold War. This course would allow Japan time to rebuild its economy and allow the conservatives to restore their dominance of domestic politics at a time when democratic forces were ascendant. But it also meant a course that would lead to dependence on the United States for Japan's security needs and acceptance of American domination of its foreign policy. The two options that he rejected would have held out hope in the long run of a more independent course. As Akira Iriye writes, "It was [Yoshida] who, more than anyone else in Japan, paved the way for the country's emergence from defeat onto the world arena and who defined the nature of that emergence as being in a state of dependence on the United States."[73]

This was Yoshida's fateful choice. Although his latitude was constrained, it was not forced on him. As Iokibe writes, other conservative leaders would have made a different choice, "An anti-militaristic stance, and an economic-oriented national policy were also voluntary choices made by post-war Japan and not necessarily ideas forced upon it by the victorious allies."[74] It was Yoshida's gamble that Japan could better achieve its interests by participating in the American system than by actively resisting it. Certainly he could not foresee how his choice would stretch into decades of dependence and crippling loss of national self-respect. He could not foresee that decades of dependence on the United States would leave Japan content to ignore the infrastructure of security-related institutions that every independent nation of any size must possess.

He could foresee, however, the immediate danger of being dragged into the Soviet-American struggle and embroiled in unwanted obligations. Conservatives like Yoshida, while having a deep distaste for the Soviet Union, felt no irrepressible sympathy for the American cause in the Cold War. Most Japanese leaders were little concerned about the conflict of ideas at the heart of the Cold War. There was certainly no Japanese love lost for the Soviets, with whom they had a long and bitter rivalry, culminating in Russia's breaking its neutrality pact with Japan, entering the war in its last days, and seizing Japanese islands even after Japan had surrendered. But by the same token, Japanese conservatives were not committed to the liberal ideals of the Americans that had cost them such suffering. Likewise, in regard to relations with the new communist government in China, Yoshida told an American correspondent in 1949, "I don't care whether China is red or green."[75] Japan wanted to continue its trade with the mainland. Americans were repeatedly frustrated by what they regarded as Japan's narrow and self-centered sense of national purpose. US ambassador to Japan John Allison concluded in 1954 that Japan has "no basic convictions for or against the free world."[76] Repeatedly frustrated by the Japanese refusal to take an active role in the Cold War, the Americans reluctantly accepted that the ideals of the Western alliance and of the liberal democratic vision of world order held little persuasive power for the Japanese leadership. Dulles confessed that he was "grievously disappointed" that there was "no revival of the spirit of sacrifice and discipline" or a "great national spirit."[77] For Yoshida, the alliance gave Japan an opportunity to contract out its national defense, permitting it to concentrate on its own economic recovery—and eventually its resurgence as a new kind of power determined to make its way in the world as a great trading nation.

Subordinate Independence

When the Occupation ended, instead of recovering its sovereignty and independence, Japan was incorporated into an emerging Pax Americana. The Japanese press saw the administrative agreement as evidence of Japan's subordination. The business paper *Nihon Keizai* complained that "the will of the United States has been forcibly imposed on Japan." The *Asahi* agreed that Japanese autonomy was infringed. The Japanese press overall saw it as confirmation of an "unequal" relationship. The journalist James Reston, writing in the *New York Times*, November 19, 1951, observed that it looked like "the United States is clamping a phony independence on Japan while at the same time preserving the facilities essential to the United States military command."[78]

The Mutual Security Treaty established a highly unequal alliance—a hegemonic alliance—that has lasted to the present. In many ways it is a strange, anomalous alliance. That it joined two nations with vastly different histories and values thrown together after a brutal and merciless war fought against each other was an irony that no one could miss. For the United States, the purpose of the alliance was to ensure that Japan conformed to its global strategy. The alliance was imposed on Japan while it was still occupied by over 200,000 American troops. It was the price Japan was forced to pay for the end of the Occupation. In the classic works of international relations theory, alliances usually are designed to aggregate the power of two or more states against some commonly perceived threat; nations join together to increase their strength in the face of a mutually perceived danger. Fundamentally, it is said, "alliances must involve some measure of commitment to use force to achieve a common goal." Historically, however, alliances sometimes are motivated less by a desire to influence the balance of power than by an intention to manage and control a weaker country.[79] There can be no better example than the US-Japan alliance.

Especially in the Pentagon, there was concern that Japan might someday decide to pursue an autonomous foreign policy and independently rearm. Or, as time went on, if not an independent Japanese rearmament, a socialist government might come to power and tilt to the communist side or stake out a neutralist position such as India and Indonesia had done. In sum, the Pentagon wanted to ensure that the United States would be free to maintain bases in Japan in the post-Occupation period, that Japan would not adopt a neutral stance in the Cold War, that Japan would not fall under the influence of the Soviet bloc, that Japan would not undertake an independent rearmament, and that Japan, in short, would not become an independent state able to choose its own future. Thus, a "double containment" was inherent in the security treaty. American troops in Japan would contain both the expansion of communism in Northeast Asia and the potential desire of Japan for an independent foreign policy. The alliance was an effective instrument to maintain control of Japan.

American leaders, like those in other countries, believed that an extremist trait in Japanese character made it imperative that the United States maintain the ability to restrain Japanese behavior. As President Kennedy's undersecretary of state George Ball once put it (rather indelicately), "You never know when the Japanese will go ape."[80] Later, the top Marine Corps general in Japan told a *Washington Post* correspondent in 1990 that US troops must remain in Japan at least until the beginning of the twenty-first century in large part because "no one wants a rearmed, resurgent Japan. So we are a cap in the bottle, if you will."[81] Given such persistent distrust of Japanese national character, it was therefore imperative that the United States maintain the ability to restrain Japanese behavior as well as ensure through its bases in Japan the ability to contain communist expansion. In this way, the alliance exercised a "double containment." The alliance would control Japan's foreign policy and ensure that it supported the larger security order of bilateral treaties that the United States had shaped for East Asia. This was evident right from the start, when, to ensure Senate passage of the peace and security treaties, Yoshida was compelled to recognize Taiwan as the legitimate government of China and thus to forswear the normal relations with the mainland government that he preferred. This was a hegemonic alliance whose principal purpose was to control and manage Japan. As Iokibe bluntly sized it up: "Japan acquires security while the US acquires control. If this is indeed a security-for-control transaction, then Japan would seem to be offering up its independence as the price of its security."[82] The alliance made Japan a military satellite—some would say "a client state"—of the United States. While the Americans spoke proudly of giving their former enemy a generous peace, it might be better described as, in John Dower's apt phrase, "magnanimity under lock and key."[83]

6

For the Soul of Japan

A S THE YEARS of the Occupation wore on, Japanese of all persuasions looked forward to the day when the foreign soldiers would
be gone and Japan would regain its independence. But that day never
quite came. While the United States was intent on incorporating Japan
into its alliance system to contain communist expansion, Japan in the
1950s erupted in tumultuous opposition to American plans. Millions of
Japanese of all walks of life took to the streets, signed petitions, and
joined spontaneous groups protesting policies that subordinated Japan
to the American Cold War order and the Japanese conservative leaders
who supported this subordination. The demonstrations were by far the
largest public uprising in Japanese history. At issue was the future course
of the nation—its democratic governance and its independent foreign
policy. Japanese had welcomed the Occupation's liberation from military leadership and its reforms, but now a yawning gap opened between
the way Americans and Japanese perceived the world and Japan's role
in it. The protests represented nothing less than a struggle for the soul
of Japan.[1]

To the Americans, the struggle with the Soviet bloc was all con-
suming. As NSC 68, one of the fundamental US Cold War policy documents, stated in 1950, their foe in the Cold War was animated by a "new
fanatic faith, antithetical to our own" and was determined to impose its
"absolute authority over the rest of the world." The stakes in the struggle
were existential: "The issues that face us are momentous, involving the
fulfillment or destruction not only of this Republic but of civilization

itself."[2] Possessing such an apocalyptic and Manichean view, American leaders had little room for understanding, let alone sensitivity for, the views of a people deeply traumatized by their wartime experience.

For the Americans, the role of Japan as an essential part of this momentous conflict was critical to establishing a coalition to contain Soviet expansion. But the great majority of Japanese—politically conscious Japanese—had a distinctly different vision of their future and their place in the world. By no means did they see their interests as congruent with America's. For Japanese of all political persuasions, whether conservative or progressive, their goals were a restoration of national independence and of international respect, and noninvolvement in the superpower conflict. Japan's interest was in recovering its livelihood and above all its sovereignty, and the great majority of Japanese felt no great stake in the bipolar conflict. Japan had pursued the goals of autonomy and self-mastery since the middle of the nineteenth century, when it first lost the self-sufficiency and free security that this island nation had enjoyed from the days of its earliest history. To determine their own fate was what Japanese of all persuasions aspired to. Some conservatives believed this goal could be pursued within the alliance by achieving a more equal relationship. But most Japanese feared that the alliance would plunge Japan into the vortex of the Cold War conflict. They were weary of war. Its devastation and suffering were still fresh in memory. Their interest was in economic recovery, restoring their good name in the world, and recovering their national independence. In contrast to the Occupation's liberal democratic revolution, which lacked deep roots in the Japanese soil, the profound revulsion from militarism and war was felt in the lived experience of the Japanese people.

Trauma

In the early years of the twenty-first century, in the aftermath of the Iraq and Afghanistan conflicts, Americans are once again coming face to face with something of what war can cause to those directly involved. It was in the aftermath of the Vietnam War that the American Psychiatric Association explicitly addressed the psychological nature of combat-related mental disorders.[3] Post-traumatic stress disorder (PTSD), which has afflicted American soldiers returning home from Iraq and Afghanistan, gives us an indication of what the mass of the Japanese population experienced. One cannot begin to understand postwar Japan without pondering the trauma experienced in the lives of ordinary people. It is a psychological phenomenon that is not outlived or whose effects can be easily redressed. Trauma has two aspects: the emotional response to the terrifying experience itself, and the memory of it. PTSD is caused by anxiety and despair so intense that it disrupts normal living.

The historian Irokawa Daikichi writes with great sensitivity of the "harsh wartime experiences" of Japanese women who "without question suffered the most." In addition to "air raids, bombing, compulsory evacuations, and the dispersal of their families," they were mobilized for factory labor work with little or no compensation, all the while responsible for keeping up their households and raising the children. It is little wonder that their "indescribable sacrifices" made Japanese women in the postwar period the often quiet but most unmovable opposition to every political effort to remilitarize the country.[4]

The memory of the millions of casualties, firebombing, the atomic bombs, and defeat left the Japanese with psychic wounds that would take generations to heal. So self-absorbed were ordinary Japanese with their memories of wartime suffering that they had little consciousness of the suffering Japan had caused its Asian neighbors. The constraints of the Occupation and the American alliance insulated Japanese from their neighbors' concerns and experiences. Asian peoples, the major victims of Japanese aggression, had little part in the Occupation, sparing the Japanese of confronting responsibility for the worst excesses of their crimes. The Americans did not stress this awareness on the Japanese people in part because it was US policy to emphasize their militarist leaders' guilt. As one member of the postwar generation remembered the antiwar demonstrations of his youth in the 1950s: "It was not Pearl Harbor or Nanjing that they were referring to, but that we had the bombing of Hiroshima and Nagasaki done to us, we had the air raids done to us, we had our sons taken into the armed forces, in other words this was an anti-war and peace movement of victims."[5] Only much later did a gradual awareness grow among Japanese of the terrible human suffering their imperialist depredation had inflicted on other Asian peoples.

Postwar Progressive Politics

The decade of the 1950s was a remarkable time of awakening in Japan—a time when people, reflecting on the wartime debacle, determined to learn from the past, recover their self-determination, and create a new future. In many ways the decade following the end of the Occupation was the finest hour for the progressive forces in Japanese politics. During the 1950s the progressives—those who opposed the restoration of conservative dominance in domestic politics—succeeded in mobilizing to their cause the most articulate segments of Japanese opinion. The media, intellectuals, teachers, students, labor unions, middle-class housewives, white-collar workers, opposition parties, and certain religious groups rallied to the progressive persuasion. By one estimate, 80 percent of opinion leaders in this period were of the progressive persuasion.[6] Broadly speaking, the progressives favored neutrality in the Cold War and an end to the alliance and American bases. Theirs was a vision of Japan as a "peace state" (*heiwa kokka*) and of the Japanese as a reborn people with a mission to show the way to a new world in which disputes would be resolved without resort to arms. A mixture of pacifism, isolationism, and idealism, the popular energy that the progressives demonstrated in the 1950s was the high point of the postwar Japanese struggle to gain their sovereignty and achieve a democratic politics.

At first, it was the left-wing political parties, labor unions, and the newspapers that asserted the themes of progressive politics. But so powerful was the popular energy that it often took on spontaneous forms. It was an extraordinary time in which memories of the disastrous war, fear of being entangled in a new war, and self-conscious determination to actualize a new set of democratic values provoked an unprecedented civic activism. Initially this energy was inchoate and formless, but in the course of a succession of protests against conservative rule as well as against the US alliance and fear of Japan's position in the vortex of American Cold War policy, their ideas took shape and formed a coherent worldview and sense of national purpose. Had the progressives fully succeeded, they would have toppled conservative rule and provided a plausible basis for establishing neutrality in the Cold War. But even in falling short, they struck fear in the conservative establishment.

The Japanese people, with the traumatic experiences of war vivid in their daily lives, struggled to rebuild their cities and regain a normal livelihood. They were deeply resistant to pressures for rearmament and involvement in the Cold War. In this environment, goals of peace, democracy, and independence became intertwined. These goals related foreign policy to domestic politics and created the basis for a powerful progressive movement in the 1950s. Peace, democracy, and independence were abstract ideals, understood in varying degrees by civic activists. But all understood that these goals related directly to people's livelihood, which was impacted by the threat of entanglement in the Cold War through the security treaty and the assertion of state power by the conservative elite.

Opposition to the change in the Occupation's policy and US pressure to rearm Japan spurred the peace movement organized by opposition political parties. In 1949–1950 the Japan Socialist Party formulated its "four peace principles": (1) achievement of a comprehensive peace settlement with all former enemies, (2) opposition to a military alliance and foreign bases on Japanese soil, (3) neutrality in the Cold War, and (4) defense of Article 9 and therefore no rearmament. A high-profile group of over fifty intellectual leaders who had organized themselves as the Peace Problems Symposium (Heiwa mondai danwakai) issued a statement after the outbreak of the Korean War advocating neutrality in the global conflict as "the only true position of self-reliance and independence for Japan."[7] The statement recalled Japan's wartime suffering and stressed the unfinished work of democratic and social reform at home. Although they were called peace principles, they were as much about seeking Japanese autonomy as they were about pacifism. Independence from US domination was fundamental to the alternative vision that the peace movement was proffering. The progressives feared that integration into the Cold War configuration of international politics would create a prolonged dependency on the United States.

The most prominent of the drafters of this statement was the eminent professor of political thought at the University of Tokyo, Maruyama Masao. In the prewar period, Maruyama had been a student of Nambara Shigeru's, the postwar president of the university. A Christian who had taught political philosophy, Nambara had worked without success to bring an end to the war, and during the Occupation he worked cooperatively with Occupation officials to reform Japanese education and give it a democratic orientation. More importantly, Nambara made it a personal commitment to help the postwar generation draw lessons from their bitter experience. The victors in the war had been "reason and truth," and Japan, misled by narrow nationalism, had been on the wrong side of history. Drawing on his Christian faith, Nambara held that repentance and atonement for an unjust war could come only through devotion to peace and justice.[8]

Maruyama, although sympathetic with Christian belief,[9] was more inspired by his teacher's liberal principles. Maruyama had been in trouble with the thought police during the war and was drafted into a lowly position in the army during the last years of the war. He was stationed in Hiroshima when the bomb was dropped, surviving only because a large concrete structure stood between him and the blast. A brilliant and prolific scholar, he became the leading philosopher of Japanese democratic reform in the first postwar decades. He called for a "community of contrition," by which he meant that intellectuals like himself as well as all other Japanese needed to acknowledge responsibility for not having resisted the drift to a militarist and fascist state. Maruyama saw the challenge of absorbing democratic values as the urgent national priority. "We must again face the task of democratic revolution which the Meiji Restoration failed to complete. We must again grapple with the problem of human freedom."[10] For Maruyama, Japan's prewar state had created an "interfusion of spirituality and politics" by giving the emperor both political and religious authority, thus allowing it an "all pervasive psychological coercion" of its citizens. With the state a "moral entity," there was no place for an individual, private conscience.

The 1950s was not simply a time of "freedom from" the tyranny of the prewar state; it was now the opportunity for "freedom toward" the building of a new democratic society. Civic activism was inspired by still-fresh memories of wartime suffering and regret at not having resisted the militarism that brought on that suffering. Popular magazines filled their columns with discussions of what was required of a democratic citizenry. In his first postwar lecture, given before a public audience, Maruyama challenged the Japanese to make democracy their own. "Today, we have had freedom issued to us—forced upon us, in fact, by a foreign country. But freedom as a handout, or coerced freedom, is a fundamental contradiction in terms . . . because freedom is nothing other than the Japanese people exercising their spirit to determine matters for themselves. In other words, in order to achieve genuine freedom, we must continue a long and arduous struggle to take the freedom that has been given to us and elevate it into a freedom that exists within us."[11] Maruyama accepted the universalism of Western liberal values and the legacy of the Enlightenment, and acknowledged that "in my thinking I rely on abstractions from European culture. I consider it to be a universal legacy to human kind [*jinrui fuhen no isan*]."[12] For him, the fundamental ethical belief was that "the individual is always prior to society and stands as an 'end in himself.'"[13]

The public discourse in the popular journals and magazines of the 1950s was suffused with what was required of Japanese to become "modern individuals." Both society and the state were at fault. By valuing the group and its collectivist norms of solidarity, consensus, respect for hierarchy, and status, Japanese society had inhibited the emergence of the modern individual. The state had monopolized all values to itself, suppressing the natural urge in a modern individual for a private inner realm of personal belief. Respected intellectual leaders referred particularly to *shutaisei,* a word that connoted an individual with backbone, an autonomous individual, independent in thought, and committed to participating in the public sphere. This "modern person" would no longer be submerged in the ties and obligations of family, community, and state but instead would be free of group pressure to be self-sufficient in making judgments according to his or her conscience and to universal values. As Maruyama put it, "Only by destroying the old family structure in Japanese society and its ideology . . . can Japan democratize from the base up." It was not enough that the Occupation put in place new institutions and laws, "an internal reform in the psychological structure of Japanese society must occur."[14] Such self-criticism was very much in the air of the 1950s as the Japanese reflected on the past and their traditional values. Not surprisingly, this discourse had ready appeal to the student generation, which even in the prewar period had been receptive to liberal thought from abroad.

The popular energy in behalf of reform in the 1950s demonstrated the reformist potential that might have been mobilized at the end of the war had there been no American occupation. In the last year of the war, popular unrest on the home front was of mounting concern for Japanese leaders. The wartime suffering that came with the bad news from

the war front of lost family members and the devastation of the homeland in the carpet bombing of the last year of the war created a growing
popular unrest. The records of the time are replete with leaders' references to the unrest and disaffection of ordinary Japanese. Throughout
modern history, the conservative elite had shaped policies to prevent social disruption and to maintain the elitist ascendancy. Post–World War
I society witnessed widespread unrest among urban labor and tenant
farmers, the founding of the Japan Communist Party and social-
democratic parties, and receptivity to Marxist writings among students
and the intelligentsia. Prewar political leaders took steps to suppress
"dangerous thought," knowing that revolutionary trends were rife in
Western industrial societies and sensing that they were latent in the social tensions of their own society. The hardship of the war years threatened revival of the radical protest and raised the specter of social
revolution.

The most persuasive evidence of this elite apprehension during the
war is found in the so-called Yoshida antiwar incident (Yohansen) of
February 1945, when Yoshida Shigeru and other conservatives drafted
a document for Prince Konoe to discuss with the emperor. Konoe's appeal to the emperor to bring an end to the conflict expressed fear that
popular discontent was such that it could spark a communist uprising
that would overthrow the imperial system and the dominating role that
the conservative elite exercised in the system. The emperor chose not to
accept the advice, and for more than half a year until surrender, the
popular unrest mounted and became the source of the remarkable
popular receptivity first to the Occupation's reforms and then to the progressive politics that exploded in the decade of the 1950s.

Defeat and occupation for the first time in Japan's history left a radical legacy of popular alienation in domestic politics that offered a greater
challenge to wartime nationalist values than the Occupation's democratization program itself because it came from within—from the real-
life experiences of the Japanese people. The legacy emerged in the 1950s as
issues of remilitarization were raised by subordination in the American
Cold War order. Postwar progressive thought embraced the universalist
pretentions of the new institutions established by the Occupation. Not
only did the progressives embrace liberal values and institutions; they
were enthusiastically swept up in the mystique of a noble experiment
that the new constitution enshrined. The Japanese people's revulsion

from war was palpable in the widely held support for this new document. They would even renounce the "usual claims of sovereignty" as the new constitution's preamble abjured, "trusting in the peace-loving peoples of the world" for Japan's future survival. Progressives in the 1950s argued that it was Japan's unique mission in the postwar world to demonstrate that a modern industrial nation could exist without arming itself, and that Japan would show the way to a new world in which national sovereignty would be forsworn. Nation-states were artificial creations that would disappear, allowing the naturally harmonious impulses of the world's societies to usher in a peaceful international order.

This potential was ultimately stifled by the conservative elite and its alignment with American Cold War policies. Testifying to the conservative resurgence that the Occupation had permitted and to how far the United States had strayed from its unconditional surrender policy, SCAP "depurged" most of the former politicians and others who had been earlier purged for their wartime activities. In addition, SCAP also purged left-wing progressives, effectively weakening their embryonic movement. In the first post-Occupation election in October 1952, 42 percent of the winning candidates were men who had been purged.[15] Conservative candidates were able to outmaneuver progressive politicians in mobilizing rural support. Civic activism, though stifled, was still able to contain and limit the alignment that the postwar Japanese leadership adopted. Deference to this reformist impulse among the Japanese people caused the conservatives to adopt a strategy that positioned them between the alternative vision of the progressives and the pressure of American attempts to integrate Japan more fully into its Cold War policies.

Relentless US Pressure

Americans, having imposed a democratic revolution in Japan and convinced of its success in converting the Japanese to the values and ideals of Americans, were rarely able to understand the Japanese unwillingness to share in the challenge of defending those values and ideals in the Cold War conflict. Preoccupied with the global implications of the struggle, Americans were caught unprepared for this pushback. To the extent that they were aware of this growing resistance to the alliance, they

attributed it to the machinations of the communists and radical socialists. In some sense this was true, for the Japanese people's unease with
the alliance was for a time inchoate and formless, and left-wing groups
were the obvious source of agitation. In a short time, however, this resistance welled up in a diverse and broad-based movement of opposition to the American vision of the bilateral relationship. American
leadership, both in and out of the government, was almost uniformly
insensitive to the goals and interests of the Japanese. A succession of
events in the 1950s galvanized the Japanese into a national movement
that opposed involvement in the American alliance system and in the
bipolar conflict. In the course of this struggle, progressives formulated
central features of Japan's postwar identity as the nation that had
uniquely suffered a nuclear holocaust and its determination to translate
this experience into a unique pacifist mission in the world.

What gave form and growth to progressive thought in the 1950s was
a sharp escalation of the Cold War confrontation and the relentless
American pressure on Japan to participate actively in its alliance system.
Although Yoshida was deftly deflecting and limiting the pressure to
rearm, the Japanese public inevitably viewed the establishment of the
Self-Defense Forces and the Self-Defense Agency in 1954 as further evidence that Japan was being drawn into the Cold War. This relentless
pressure by the United States to incorporate Japan into its Cold War
strategy by promoting its rearmament came amid an intensification of
the Cold War arms race.

The United States lost its atomic monopoly in 1949 when the Soviets
carried out their first A-bomb test. The following year, Truman sanctioned the building of the thermonuclear bomb "as a matter of the
highest urgency."[16] In November 1952 at Eniwetok Island in the Pacific,
a ten-megaton thermonuclear explosion was conducted, and prepara-
tions were then made to test this actual superweapon. An armistice in
the Korean conflict was reached in the summer of 1953 but was followed
within days by the first Soviet thermonuclear test. President Eisenhower,
concerned by the mounting military budget and intent on avoiding
future local conflicts, undertook a review of military strategy, which led
to the enunciation of what became known as the doctrine of "massive
retaliation." Shortly after the negotiation of the San Francisco Peace
Treaty, Dulles, who was soon to become secretary of state in the new
Eisenhower administration, explained his view in a 1952 *Life* magazine

article titled "A Policy of Boldness." He explained that he favored *"the means to retaliate instantly against open aggression by Red Armies, so that, if it occurred anywhere, we could and we would strike back where it hurts, by means of our own choosing."*[17] This policy came to be known as "the New Look." In a January 12, 1954, speech in New York City, Dulles declared, "We need allies and collective security. Our purpose is to make these relations more effective, less costly. This can be done by placing more reliance on deterrent power and less dependence on local defensive power. . . . Local defense will always be important . . . [but] must be re-inforced by the further deterrent of massive retaliatory power."[18] Dulles's rhetoric was alarming, but he wanted the Soviets to believe that the United States would not be opposed to the use of nuclear weapons and Eisenhower placed greater emphasis on nuclear offensive capabilities.[19] Eisenhower accordingly sanctioned the reduction of the bloated US forces based in Japan from 210,000 in 1953 to 77,000 in 1957 and 48,000 in 1960 (in addition to 37,000 in Okinawa).[20]

The *Lucky Dragon* Incident

Backers of the peace movement in the early 1950s found it difficult to draw mass popular support to their cause until the occurrence of a frightening incident that alarmed the Japanese people and galvanized the postwar progressive ideology. Just before dawn on March 1, 1954, the United States detonated the first thermonuclear bomb at the Bikini Atoll in the Marshall Islands in the southern Pacific. Code-named "Bravo," it had a yield of fifteen megatons, more than 750 times more powerful than the Hiroshima bomb. It was the largest thermonuclear device the United States had ever tested. More than double the size of explosive power that scientists had predicted, the blast lit the predawn sky over Hawaii 2,500 miles away. Closer to ground zero on Kwajalein, 270 miles to the southeast, a marine corporal was startled when, as he remembered, "all of a sudden the sky lighted up, a bright orange, and remained that way for what seemed like a couple of minutes. About ten or fifteen minutes later we heard a very loud rumbling that sounded like thunder. Then the whole barracks began shaking as if there had been an earthquake. This was followed by a very high wind."[21] Eighty-five miles downwind from the test site, outside the danger zone announced by the US government, the explosion showered radioactive debris on the one-hundred-ton fishing trawler *Lucky Dragon* (*Fukuryū Maru*) with twenty-three Japanese fishermen. Members of the crew were stricken with radiation sickness as the captain headed the ship back to its port south of Tokyo. When they returned to Japan their radiation sickness quickly created near-national panic. Japanese monitoring devices reported widespread contamination of fish in the holds of many trawlers. People began to curtail their purchase of fish, and Tokyo's famous Tsukiji Fish Market shut down. The fishing industry employed a million people and provided the main diet item for all Japanese; thus, the national alarm was palpable. Historian William Tsutsui writes that "millions of Japanese (including the emperor) refused to eat fish, the tabloids proclaimed the incident yet another U.S. atomic attack on Japan."[22]

The incident quickly escalated beyond the clumsy efforts of Americans and Japanese to control. The Atomic Energy Commission and its

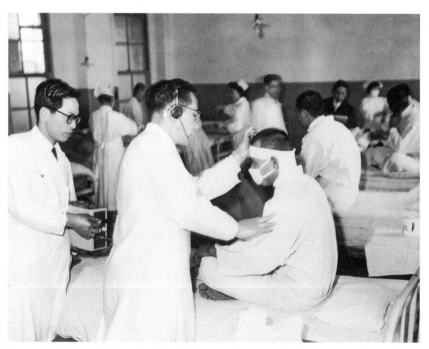

Doctors at Tokyo University Hospital examine one of the crew members of the Japanese fishing trawler *Lucky Dragon*, who were exposed to radiation during the US test of a hydrogen bomb in the Pacific on March 1, 1954.
Bettmann / Getty Images / 514954888.

chair, Lewis Strauss, intent on maintaining the secrecy of the tests, sought to put the *Lucky Dragon* under American control and have its twenty-three fishermen placed under the care of American doctors. Strauss was convinced that the *Lucky Dragon* was a disguised Soviet spy ship intent on learning the nature of the bomb tests. Japanese doctors were incensed at the attempted interference in their professional care and insisted on handling the case themselves. Strauss made matters worse by insisting that the reports of widespread contamination were "grossly exaggerated" and deploring the uncooperativeness of the Japanese doctors. In a press conference he inadvertently increased alarm not only in Japan but around the world when he described the March 1 blast as powerful enough to "take out . . . any city—even the entire New York City metropolitan area."[23] The incident continued to inflame emotions as the two governments haggled over levels of compensation. The radioman of the *Lucky Dragon* died in September, and world concern over the arms race grew.

More than any other event, it was the March 1 hydrogen bomb test that aroused the universal alarm of the Japanese people to the danger of being swept into the Cold War. One of the most widely seen expressions of the panic was the appearance in 1954 of the first Godzilla movie, featuring a monster emerging from an oceanic explosion who attacks Tokyo. In addition to its antinuclear subtext, the movie carried a strong tone of anti-American resentment. Gojira, as he was known in Japan, had lived in the Pacific Ocean for thousands of years until H-bomb testing killed off his food supply and irradiated him. Angrily he attacked Tokyo and with his atomic breath reduced the city to a pile of ashes. The images in the movie were reminiscent of the firebombed capital as well as Hiroshima and Nagasaki. The symbolic reference to US hydrogen bomb testing and the *Lucky Dragon* was obvious, and the series of Godzilla movies that followed embedded the image in national life.

Americans were insensitive, even callous, to the popular mood in Japan. The US ambassador to Tokyo John Allison privately fumed over the Japanese government's pressure to extract maximum compensation. Japan, he wrote to Washington, was hardly a dependable ally but rather "a nation which for the time being is forced by circumstances to cooperate with the United States but which intends while doing so to wring out of this relationship every possible advantage at the minimum cost."[24] Reflecting much later in his memoir, however, he regretted not making an early apology to the Japanese people for the alarm caused by the incident.[25]

Between 1946 and 1962, the United States conducted 105 nuclear tests in the Pacific.[26] Physicist Ralph Lapp, who had been a leader in the Manhattan Project, went to Japan in 1957 to interview survivors of the *Lucky Dragon* and subsequently wrote widely on the subject, testified before Congress on thermonuclear fallout, and contributed importantly in the lead-up to the Limited Nuclear Test Ban Treaty of 1963, which prohibited the testing of nuclear weapons in outer space, underwater, or in the atmosphere. Lapp captured the popular mood when he wrote, "Hiroshima and Nagasaki and their aftermath had made the Japanese deeply sensitive to radioactivity in any form. Thus the Lucky Dragon accident and the contaminated fish caused the Japanese to react instinctively. It was as though a safety valve had been suddenly shattered, allowing the pent-up steam of almost a decade to blow off. Feelings of resentment, self-pity, personal anxiety and distrust broke through the surface of Japanese reserve."[27]

The *Lucky Dragon* incident was the spark that reawakened traumatic memories of wartime suffering and social stress. Once again it was Japanese who were affected by the new weapons of war, and it is hardly surprising that the most powerful one caused near hysteria. Eighteen months after the Bravo test the Soviets detonated their first hydrogen bomb. As the Cold War arms race accelerated, the Japanese fear of being swept into its path deepened. In the Suginami Ward of Tokyo, a former professor of international law at Tokyo University, Yasui Kaoru, began a petition campaign demanding a ban on the hydrogen bomb. The Suginami appeal recalled "the tragedies of Hiroshima and Nagasaki" and declared that "now we, the Japanese people, have suffered for the third time the egregious affliction of nuclear bombs."[28] Propelled by the fear of radiation poisoning that swept through the country, the petition movement spread rapidly to virtually every locality. By August 1955 more than 30 million Japanese had signed the petition.

Like many activists, Yasui had come to regret his wartime acquiescence before state power. After being purged in the Occupation he dedicated himself to civic activism. He now saw the opportunity that Japan's unique nuclear heritage offered. Yasui said his goal was to restore the independence of Japan by forming "a broad peace movement based on strengthening close communication among the antibase movement, the ban-the-bomb movement, and all peace organizations."[29] In 1955 he chaired the first meeting of the Japan Council against Atomic and Hydrogen Bombs (Gensuikyō), which quickly grew into a national movement. Under Yasui's leadership, the movement tried to avoid divisive political issues and build on the experience of Hiroshima and Nagasaki to create a sense of mission that would help restore Japanese self-respect and independence.

He further saw this as an extraordinary opportunity for civic engagement of ordinary people. He gave special praise to the place of women in raising national consciousness for the pacifist cause, emphasizing their role in gathering signatures and their maternal concern for the children.[30] Middle-class housewives canvassing door to door were largely responsible for the success of the petition movement. For the first time, women without previous political experience or affiliation were stirred to active participation in demonstrations.[31] In his memoir Yasui recorded the reasons for the "spiritual revolution" the Japanese were undergoing and the success of the ban-the-bomb, antibase, and peace movements: "On rational reflection we take note that the Pacific War imposed incalculable suffering, especially on Asian peoples. We laid waste the countries of Asia with our muddy boots, robbed many people of their lives, and committed countless cruel sins. This is burned into our hearts as an unforgettable experience. But it was when for the first time we experienced for ourselves the series of fire bombings, urban evacuation, defeat, and occupation . . . that [the reality of modern warfare] really hit home. . . . This is why most Japanese have come to hate war from the bottom of their hearts."[32]

Hiroshima and Japanese Postwar Identity

The *Lucky Dragon* incident intensified the Japanese struggle to restore its independence from the overbearing dominance of American Cold War strategy. The antinuclear peace movement started as part of the political agendas of the communist and socialist parties, but the *Lucky Dragon* incident expanded it into a mass national movement. During the Occupation, coverage of the atomic bombing of Hiroshima and Nagasaki was strictly censored. Articles advocating the start of a world peace movement centered on Hiroshima were carefully monitored. SCAP did give its approval to Hiroshima's rebuilding as a "peace city' in the immediate postwar months, perhaps because it would imply that bombing had ended the war and brought peace.[33] Reports by Japanese scientists about radiation sickness, however, were suppressed.

For Japan, the most important result of the *Lucky Dragon* incident was its role in the formation of an identity and national mission to lead the world to abolish nuclear weapons. The incident and the resulting national petition movement brought into focus inchoate feelings present since the end of the war. Only in the last years of the Occupation was its censorship of information about Hiroshima and Nagasaki lifted to permit the Japanese people knowledge of the awful destruction wreaked by the new weapon. Hiroshima began to rebuild after the war with the aspiration of becoming a "Peace Memorial City." Tange Kenzō and other architects submitted proposals to the city for monuments that would symbolize the terrible destructive nature that war had taken on.

Even so, it was not until the panic of the *Lucky Dragon* incident that this unique experience took on special meaning. It was only then that people began to realize that it stood as a reminder of the horrors of war and as a unique experience that gave Japanese something they had not had in their history: a national identity of universal value and appeal. Where the Meiji Restoration had given Japanese an identity focused on building the power of the nation-state to restore their autonomy, now as the only victims of the atomic age they could acquire a transcendent mission to save humanity from the threat of nuclear extinction.

In a great variety of ways, the Japanese began to find meaning in expressing this new sense of identity and national purpose. In 1955, the Hiroshima Peace Memorial opened and soon became a shrine embodying the people's unique suffering. The museum was visited by millions, especially groups of schoolchildren, and annual commemoration rites were held on the anniversary of the bombing. The exhibits at that time provided no historical context on the war, but rather focused entirely on the horrors of the bomb and Japanese victimhood. School textbooks placed a new emphasis on Japan's pacifist mission as the only nation to suffer nuclear attack. Films, such as Kurosawa's 1955 *I Live in Fear*, took up the theme of nuclear fallout.

The sense of antinuclear mission provided a consensus in which the deeply divided and broad political spectrum of Japanese opinion could unite. The moral indignation at US use of the atomic bomb was sometimes explicit, particularly in left-wing, antibase opinion, and sometimes implicit. But it was usually palpable. As James Orr writes, the emperor had laid the groundwork by his statement in the August 15, 1945, surrender message when he said, "The enemy has begun to employ a new and most cruel bomb, the power of which to do damage is indeed incalculable, taking the toll of many innocent lives. Should we continue to fight, it would not only result in an ultimate collapse and disappearance of the Japanese nation, but it would also lead to the total extinction of human civilization."[34] SCAP censorship kept knowledge limited, but in 1949 John Hersey's book *Hiroshima* was translated. Originally published in 1946, it gave graphic descriptions of the suffering at ground zero. The American sociologist and student of Japan Herbert Passin, writing in 1955, described Japanese public opinion as "bordering on paranoia that they are the fated victims of American atomic policy. . . . Why are we always the victims? Are we destined to suffer from every contact we have with America? Does this not show America's contempt for us?"[35]

Conservative politicians readily picked up on the theme of victimhood and used it for their own purposes. Already, soon after surrender, conservatives began to see the possibilities of using the A-bomb experience to their advantage. The new prime minister in 1955, Hatoyama Ichirō, had said in September 1945 that "the atomic bomb is more against international law than poison gas and is a war crime."[36] In 1955, Foreign Minister Shigemitsu Mamoru, a former convicted war criminal, spoke to this effect in the Diet:

> Due to the development of weapons of mass destruction, humankind is at the crossroads of mutual existence or mutual destruction. As the only state (*yuitsu no kokka*) to have fully tasted the horrors of the atomic bomb, Japan, one should say, carries the mission of freeing the world from the nightmare of atomic war.[37]

A decade earlier, immediately after surrender, Shigemitsu had first proposed in an internal memorandum that Japan "use the atomic bombs as counterpropaganda to Allied accusations of war crimes."[38]

Japan's victimhood became a familiar theme of Liberal Democratic Party politicians intent on both co-opting the political opposition and striving to recover high ground after years of foreign criticism of Japan's militarist past. At the United Nations, Japanese diplomats have ritualistically referred to the nation's unique experience and world mission when they address the world body.

American Intrusion in Japanese Politics

Reflecting on what he called the "unnatural intimacy" that brought Japanese and Americans together in the postwar period, George Kennan wrote, "We learned a good deal about each other, good and bad, in those unhappy years. That is the nature of all intimacies."[39] Japanese learned some unpleasant truths of American Cold War policies. When the Occupation ended, Americans had grown accustomed to intruding in Japanese politics, and they had few compunctions in attempting to manipulate and even subvert the democratic institutions the Occupation had established. John Lewis Gaddis in his *History of the Cold War* describes how American leaders gradually strayed from their initial belief that international communism could be defeated without abandoning their own democratic values. It was by measuring up to its own ideals that America would prove itself worthy as an exceptional nation. As the Cold War intensified, the pressures to compromise these values quickly built up, and compromise could be readily rationalized as necessary for the greater good of victory in the global conflict.

The newly established CIA was given steadily expanding authorization to carry out covert operations deemed necessary. The authors of NSC 68 had said that Americans would have to compromise their values from time to time if they were to defend themselves in the Cold War struggle: "The integrity of our system will not be jeopardized by any measures, overt or covert, violent or non-violent, which serve the purposes of frustrating the Kremlin design, nor does the necessity for conducting ourselves so as to affirm our values in action as well as words forbid such measures, provided only they are appropriately calculated to that end." The high idealism on which the Americans had embarked on the democratization of Japan a decade earlier now was replaced by a Machiavellian approach to its world problems. A highly classified report on CIA covert operations in 1954 concluded that "we are facing an implacable enemy whose avowed objective is world domination. There are no rules in such a game. Hitherto acceptable norms of human conduct do not apply." As Eisenhower admitted, "I have come to the conclusion that some of our traditional ideas of international sportsmanship are scarcely applicable in the morass in which the world now flounders."[40] In the global contest, the military alliance with Japan was critical. The United States therefore felt no restraint in aligning its support with formerly designated Japanese war criminals, a canny and corrupt elite, using covert measures to support them, and reaching secret agreements to permit the introduction of nuclear weapons into Japan.

The *Lucky Dragon* incident stoked such intense popular resentment of the alliance that American leaders feared that the conservatives would be replaced by a left-wing government that would end the alliance. Ambassador Allison warned the Eisenhower administration that such was the Japanese people's "panic and their intense gullibility in nuclear matters" that left-wing agitation could produce a "national stampede that would sweep over any Japanese Government that attempted to halt it. In this process our own bases could be isolated or even made untenable."[41] At the height of popular hysteria over the incident, Dulles told the National Security Council that "Japan was the heart and soul of the situation in the Far East. If Japan is not on our side our whole Far Eastern position will become untenable."[42] About the same time President Eisenhower spoke to congressional leaders of his concern that if Japan should "go communist," then the United States "would be out of the Pacific and it would become a communist lake."[43]

American bases in Japan were critical to the American strategy, but to the Japanese people they were a constant reminder of their unwanted entanglement in the Cold War. In 1955 there were still 162,000 US troops stationed on hundreds of bases and installations in Japan proper. (In Okinawa there were an additional 28,000.)[44] For communities, the bases were constant irritants with noise, bars, massage parlors, and disruptions of local tranquility of one sort or another. In the first twenty-five years after the Occupation, as many as 500 Japanese were killed in automobile accidents involving US soldiers.[45] Crimes committed by US soldiers were not subject to the Japanese justice system. One particularly notorious case occurred in 1957 when an American army soldier, William Girard, shot to death a Japanese woman as she fled after scavenging for scrap at a base firing range. The Girard case drew high-profile attention to the egregious invasions of Japanese sovereignty that the security pact entailed and was further inflamed when US military and political leaders tried to keep the soldier from being tried in Japanese courts. President Eisenhower saw the absurdity of the American stance. He wrote to a friend of his irritation with Congress and the Defense Department, "We seem to be trying to make a national hero out of a man who shot a woman—in the back at something like ten to fifteen yards distance."[46] Eisenhower was able to settle the matter quietly in a way that respected the Status of Forces agreement. The Japanese courts cooperated by simply imposing a three-year suspended sentence on the GI. But the antibase movement has continued to fester for decades.

The growing power of the Japanese progressives, with their opposition to the alliance and their support of neutrality in the Cold War, steadily led the United States to support some of the most conservative leaders, including those who had been purged or designated war criminals during the Occupation. In 1955, when the fractious left-wing parties succeeded in unifying and forming the Japan Socialist Party with an agenda of neutrality in the Cold War, the US ambassador worried that Japan was "on the verge of slipping away from us."[47] Yoshida fell from power at the end of 1954, and the Americans as well as Japanese business leaders offered strong support for a successful drive to unite all conservative forces in a new party, the Liberal Democratic Party (LDP), to withstand the challenge of the socialists. (In spite of its name, it was, in fact, neither liberal nor democratic nor even, as some observers said, a full-fledged party, as it was deeply divided among warring factions.) Yoshida's successors as head of the LDP were all former purgees and distrustful of Yoshida's tacit understanding with the Americans. They favored constitutional revision, undoing other Occupation reforms, rearmament, and a more independent relationship with the Americans.

Nevertheless, among the new LDP leaders, the Americans found one with whom they were ready to work. Their close relationship with Kishi Nobusuke, who was prime minister from 1957 to 1960, demonstrated how far American policy had vectored from the wartime determination to eliminate every vestige of the old order. Kishi personified the old order. Devoted to the imperial cause, elitist and authoritarian in his habits and disposition, he epitomized the form that fascism took in Japan in the 1930s, which in contrast to European fascism was instituted from above by the alignment of bureaucrats and military leaders. His wartime career as an economic bureaucrat, working closely with the military in instituting controls over the industrial economy, made Kishi an architect of many aspects of the garrison state. He served in Tōjō's cabinet as minister of commerce and industry and signed the declaration of war on the United States. The Occupation designated him a suspected Class A war criminal and held him in Sugamo Prison for three years before releasing him in 1948. When the Occupation ended, he was elected to the Diet and was instrumental in forming the LDP.

The new US ambassador, Douglas MacArthur II, a foreign service officer and nephew of the general, struck up a close relationship with the new prime minister, persuading Washington that Kishi's intention was to strengthen Japan's security cooperation with the United States in ways Yoshida had resisted. In June 1957 Kishi was invited to Washington, where he golfed with President Eisenhower and addressed the US House of Representatives. Vice President Richard Nixon introduced him as "an honored guest" who was "not only a great leader of the free world, but also a loyal and great friend of the people of the United States." In his address, Kishi intoned his "honor of speaking in this citadel of democracy" and went on to proclaim his belief in the "lofty principles of democracy—in the liberty and dignity of the individual."[48] Kishi convinced Dulles and Eisenhower of his ambition for a more equal alliance. Kishi wanted a voice in the deployment of US forces stationed in Japan, and he wanted a fixed term for the treaty and an explicit guarantee of US protection in case of an attack on Japan.

The administration's alignment with Kishi and his younger brother Satō Eisaku[49] was so close that in response to the latter's request, the CIA, with presidential approval, began funneling substantial financial support to friendly LDP politicians.[50] Millions of dollars went first to Kishi, then to other pro-American conservatives, moderate socialists, right-wing groups, and during the Vietnam War to conservative journals.[51] After initial qualms over secretly subverting the democratic politics were overcome, the payments became routine. As one CIA official later reflected, funneling money to the LDP "was the heart of darkness and I'm not comfortable talking about it, because it worked." Subsequently, President Kennedy was informed of the payments and approved their continuation, although he agreed with his advisors that the payments be allowed to taper off. Nevertheless, the payments continued, and U. Alexis Johnson, ambassador to Japan from 1966 to 1969, confirmed that "the principle was certainly acceptable to me. We were financing a party on our side."[52] As a high-ranking American official later admitted, subverting the democratic institutions that they had established became "so established and so routine" that American leaders accepted the covert payments as a normal part of the bilateral relationship.[53] The assumption that opposition parties were receiving funding from the Soviet side helped overcome whatever compunctions Americans might have had.[54]

A still more egregious example of American intrusion in Japanese politics and subverting the democratic institutions they had established came in the midst of the mounting turmoil over American bases.[55] In March 1959, in a trial of protestors arrested for entering the Tachikawa Air Force Base outside Tokyo, the Tokyo District Court acquitted the protestors on the grounds that the Mutual Security Treaty and the stationing of American troops in Japan provided for the maintenance of war potential in Japan and were unconstitutional under Article 9. Not surprisingly, the ruling alarmed the American ambassador, but what happened next was surprising. We now know from cables made public in 2013 that the ambassador immediately urged the Japanese foreign minister to expedite an appeal directly to the Supreme Court.[56] The ambassador himself then met privately with the Chief Justice of the Supreme Court Tanaka Kotarō, who assured him that the Court would act promptly and that he would seek a unanimous ruling. In December the Supreme Court unanimously overturned the lower court and ruled that Japan retained the right of self-defense and could enter into treaties for mutual security.[57] In an extraordinary set of rulings, the Supreme Court held that American forces were not under the control of the government of Japan and therefore did not constitute illegal maintenance of war potential. As for the constitutionality of the Japanese Self-Defense Forces and other national security laws, the Court held that these were best regarded as decisions that should be determined by political rather than judicial processes. In the words of one authority, this decision not to rule on the constitutionality of the Japanese Self-Defense Forces is "the single most controversial question in Japan."[58] What most attracts our attention here, however, is the American intrusion into the independence of the Japanese judiciary—so far had the Americans strayed into the sovereignty of an "independent country."

The Anti-Treaty Demonstrations

In contrast to Yoshida's shrewd and nuanced strategy of accommodating the domestic and outside forces at work in postwar politics, Kishi had an ideological agenda and was less prone to the characteristic pragmatism of mainstream conservatives. His agenda included a more equal treaty relationship with the United States, revision of Article 9, substantial rearmament, and a more active foreign policy that would entail use of the Self-Defense Forces overseas. Kishi's determination to raise the treaty issue poured gasoline on the fiery civic activism of the peace and antinuclear movements. He reminded people of all that they detested about the wartime order. With his confrontational style, he was constantly in danger of overreaching. He affronted public opinion by stating in May 1957 that Japanese acquisition of nuclear weapons might be necessary for Japanese defense and would not be unconstitutional.[59] His attempt to pass legislation to strengthen police powers to suppress opposition to his ambition was blocked by public outcry and by members of his own party as well as the opposition parties.

He won Washington's agreement to renegotiate the US-Japan Security Treaty, or "Anpo" as it is abbreviated in Japanese, to eliminate some of its most unequal features. The Americans made a few concessions, removing the explicit right to intervene in domestic disturbances, setting a time limit of ten years before a new treaty would be negotiated, and adding a clause committing the United States to defend Japan. The public changes in the treaty were "mostly cosmetic."[60] Kishi got considerably less than he wanted, largely owing to the resistance of the Pentagon. The Defense Department wanted to maintain its free hand in the use of American bases, opposing Kishi's hope for a veto over the use of power projection from the bases, and agreeing instead to "consult from time to time" on the administration of the treaty. Significantly, however, the United States gained secret agreement to move nuclear weapons in and out of Japan. (This did not apply to Okinawa, where it was widely assumed that the Americans already stored nuclear weapons.) In a tacit agreed-on charade, both sides determined how they would keep the truth from the Japanese people. Should questions arise as to whether nuclear weapons had been introduced, the Japanese government would assert that the United States had not requested permission and therefore there must not be weapons in Japan, while the United States when queried would respond that it was not its policy to comment on the location of nuclear weapons.[61]

On February 5, 1960, Kishi submitted the new treaty to the Diet. He soon faced massive popular opposition, without parallel in Japanese history then or since. The anti-treaty movement became known as the "Anpo" demonstrations after the official Japanese title of the military security treaty. Demonstrations were initially organized by the left-wing parties with only limited public support, but as events transpired there soon became a genuinely spontaneous revolt of mass opinion against the government course. This opposition grew out of the peace, antinuclear, and antibase movements and drew further strength from distrust of Kishi.

The Cold War environment continued to stoke the Anpo movement. On May 1, an American U-2 spy plane was downed deep within Soviet territory and evoked an angry reaction from the Russians and a threat to attack any nation from which U-2 planes were flown. It was well known that these spy planes sometimes flew from American bases in Japan, but when queried by the political opposition, Japanese and American officials gave deliberately evasive responses. The *Mainichi* observed, "We begin to wonder in whose hands Japan's sovereignty actually lies. . . . In actual fact, we are still subordinate."[62] President Eisenhower eventually had to admit the U-2 was a spy plane. And the incident aroused still more intense popular anger over the presence of American bases.

Mass opposition to renewal of the treaty, which had been gathering steam, reached its peak with events in May and June 1960. More than 10 million people signed petitions opposing the security treaty, 6 million workers engaged in sympathy strikes, and on repeated occasions hundreds of thousands swarmed the streets around the Diet. The media, intellectuals, students, union members, housewives, religious groups, merchant groups, and a diverse range of other citizens joined in the Anpo protests.[63] On May 19, with opposition parties boycotting the session and barricading the Speaker of the lower house in his office, Kishi ordered 500 police into the Diet to break the barricade and allow the Speaker to be brought in to preside over the ratification vote in the half-empty chamber. Late in the night, with the opposition absent, the majority party voted approval through the lower house. Passage of the treaty would become automatic after thirty days. Kishi planned to bring President Eisenhower to Tokyo for a triumphant signing ceremony. In the month between the day it was forcibly approved and June 19, when the treaty would automatically be ratified, the public turmoil and mayhem steadily increased. When Eisenhower's press secretary James Hagerty arrived to finalize arrangements for the president's visit, he was mobbed in his car leaving the airport and had to be rescued by a US Marines

Students stage a protest rally opposing renewal of the Mutual Security Treaty in front of the Diet on June 18, 1960. Photograph by Hiroshi Hamaya, ©Keisuke Katano.

helicopter. Day after day, tens of thousands of demonstrators marched on the Diet, the prime minister's residence, and the American embassy. The governments were forced to cancel Eisenhower's visit. The treaty was officially ratified, but Kishi resigned on June 23 humiliated by the canceled visit and the political upheaval.

The Legacy of Anpo

The massive popular uprising of 1960, culminating a decade of growing resistance to Japan's subordination in the American Cold War order, was fraught with significance. On the surface it appeared to have failed. When the treaty was ratified, the turmoil subsided, the framework of Japanese political life and purpose was fixed for decades to come. The demonstrations had failed to achieve the political independence and recovery of sovereignty that demonstrators had sought. Tens of thousands of foreign soldiers would continue to be garrisoned on Japanese soil. American bases became a fixture of national life. The majority of the Japanese people would have preferred the neutralist stance that India, Indonesia, and other nonaligned countries occupied during the bilateral conflict. The Occupation and the price of ending it did not allow them this option. In short, after the Anpo demonstrations of 1960 Japanese progressives were resigned to the continuation of the security treaty and American bases. The treaty remained controversial in Japanese politics, but it was not again subject to such a massive populist challenge. Ten years later in 1970 when it came up for automatic renewal, there were demonstrations, but because renewal did not come before the Diet, the issue was not as momentous as it had been in 1960. The Anpo demonstrations had toppled Kishi, but he was replaced by mainstream conservatives of the Yoshida School and the political opposition soon began to fracture. The opportunity to break the power of the conservative elite and make a breakthrough to a more democratic politics fell short. The LDP, with its close ties to the bureaucracy and big business, kept its dominance of the system and remained in power for succeeding decades. Japanese of all persuasions realized that they would now have to live within the confines of the imposed hegemonic alliance.

Denied the ability to choose its own future by the alliance framework, Japan moved in the one direction that gave it some opportunity for achieving a measure of autonomy and national prestige, rehabilitation of its livelihood, and a certain kind of power. If Japan could not escape the political and military domination of the United States, then it would pursue economic power and the rehabilitation of the national livelihood. Kishi's successor as prime minister in 1960 was Ikeda Hayato, Yoshida's trusted disciple, who brilliantly succeeded in disarming the opposition by setting apolitical goals that all Japanese could support. Japan would limit its involvement in the superpower conflict as much as possible and pour its efforts into economic growth. Japan would return to Yoshida's strategy of avoiding all involvement in international military and strategic issues and instead pursue a narrow economic foreign policy. Japan would seek the power of a trading state, a mercantilist nation. In this way, it could pacify popular opinion at home while justifying noninvolvement in the Cold War struggle of its ally. It was an option that had a great deal of appeal since other avenues of restoring national purpose were closed off. Moreover, it was a path that would achieve domestic consensus and harmony. All could agree on the goal of building the national livelihood.

Americans saw the political turmoil in Japan through a Cold War lens. They generally regarded the demonstrations as leftist controlled and showed little understanding of the diverse forces that motivated the demonstrators. Still, the Anpo demonstrations were sobering for the Americans. The spectacle of millions of Japanese opposing the alliance and the close association that the Eisenhower administration had with Kishi, the former suspected war criminal, and his resort to high-handed tactics to achieve treaty revision that made a mockery of democratic practice was deeply embarrassing. The wartime purpose that had powered the unconditional surrender policy to remake Japan in the American image was undermined by US support for the very conservative hegemony that it had been the intention to overthrow.

In the last analysis, the most important outcome of the events of the 1950s that led up to the Anpo demonstrations was the activation of the mass of the Japanese people in politics. The Anpo demonstrations, which involved millions of Japanese people, embraced a broad and diverse set of groups and activists. The left-wing political parties, unions, and student groups initially instigated the demonstrations. But what was most significant for the future was the involvement of grassroots citizen participants. They were not, on the whole, ideologically or partisan motivated. They were not mobilized by organizations. Rather, they were spontaneously motivated by outrage over government repression, a diffuse antiwar stand, and commitment to "democracy."[64] Kishi's high-handed maneuver succeeded in turning the anti-treaty movement into a struggle to protect democratic politics. Maruyama Masao believed that the energy of "ordinary citizens" with no organizational affiliations was evidence that democracy was taking root in Japan and was becoming "indigenized." For the moment, his fear that the foreign implanted institutions were still only formalities, "something brought in from elsewhere and put on like a uniform,"[65] was quieted. It was an experience that presaged subsequent waves of civic activism in the coming decades that would gradually vitalize populist democracy and limit the elite domination of the political system. The conservative elite, long fearful of social revolution, was sobered by the mass movement and compelled to recognize the power of mass opinion. The activism of ordinary citizens was suggestive of the reformist energy that might have been mobilized earlier, after surrender, if the Japanese had been left to struggle over war issues. The eminent historian Hosaka Masayasu, who participated in the demonstrations as a student, later recalled that the anti-Kishi struggle was a belated opportunity for people to vent their judgment on wartime leadership. "The struggle,"

This massive anti-treaty demonstration was photographed by Hamaya Hiroshi and published in his 1960 book *A Record of Rage and Grief.* Photograph by Hiroshi Hamaya, ©Keisuke Katano.

he wrote, ". . . could be called the Japanese people's war criminals trial that came fifteen years late."[66]

What had begun as a resistance to involvement in the Cold War and opposition to nuclear testing ended in a struggle against the rule of a domineering conservative elite. The Occupation had given the Japanese people the institutions of democracy, but without experiencing a struggle on their own for these institutions they were not really "authentic." Only through the "arduous struggle" of the Japanese people would democracy be self-determined.[67] The popular progressive cause of the 1950s— the *Lucky Dragon* incident, the antinuclear testing movement, the antibase movement, all culminating in the anti-treaty Anpo demonstrations— represented the first great wave of civic activism of the people in the postwar period that compelled the conservative elite to respect the "popular will."

7

A Peculiar Alliance

A S THE COLD WAR YEARS UNFOLDED, Washington constructed a new international framework of military and political institutions to cope with communist power. America's initial postwar vision of a new global order based on American progressive values steadily evolved into a complex order "organized around deterrence, containment, alliances, and the bipolar balance of power."[1] The United States increasingly assumed the role of hegemon in this revised order, exercising direction and control over complex and far-flung arrangements. Alongside the international institutions designed for a democratic capitalist order, the United States established new multilateral organizations, alliances, strategic partnerships, and client states. In Europe, the most important of these new Cold War arrangements was NATO. In Asia, it was the US-Japan alliance, which incorporated Japan into the American Cold War order. Alliances were forged with other Asian states, including Australia, South Korea, and the Philippines, in a hub-and-spokes regional system, but it was the American bases in Japan, with the ability to project power in the Western Pacific and the Indian Ocean, that were essential to this regional system.

Cold War alliances were the critical mechanism through which American dominance and direction were maintained. With its power and wealth the United States was able to provide an array of public goods to attract other states to the American order. Provision of security, the creation of an open trading regime, and the opening of the American market were powerful incentives to join in alliance.

American hegemony oversaw a network of allied elites that accepted subordination in their international relations in return for the public goods provided to their states and also for the benefits the alliance gave to them to secure and enhance their own political power at home. They intertwined their fortunes with the hegemon in ways that would allow them to acquire new resources from the wealth and influence of the United States. They exploited these resources to their advantage in jockeying for power over their opponents at home. Their voluntarism in seeking this aid and subordination suited America's needs and its self-image of a benevolent protector of other peoples from the communist empire. In the view of one observer, America itself thereby became an "empire by invitation."[2] The network of allied elites further accepted the values and deferred to the culture of the American hegemon. Some authoritarian elites claimed sudden conversions to democracy, which their own behavior often belied and led observers to see their conversion as no more than lip service. Kishi, for example, claimed to have had an epiphany while serving three years in prison as a Class A war criminal, coming to see American democracy as a model for Japan. Shortly after his release, exchanging his prison clothes for a business suit, he met up with his brother Sato and mused "Strange, isn't it? We're all democrats now."[3] Whether out of constraint, convenience, or conviction, the readiness to privilege the new values in their rhetoric satisfied the American self-image of spreading the gospel of American democracy in its alliance undertakings.

To enhance the legitimacy of their position at home, the allied elites prized their visits to Washington and proudly publicized their meetings with American leaders; they joined in social events and convocations of opinion leaders in prestigious conferences. The elites in these nations deferred to policies set by Washington because the United States could provide the public goods that would support their own position at home. New international institutions established under American ascendancy—the United Nations, the World Bank, the International Monetary Fund (IMF), and others—nurtured this new transnational elite. As these new institutions thrived amid the dramatic expansion of international trade during the first postwar decades, business elites in America readily co-opted their counterparts in the allied capitals.

American "soft power" also helped provide support of these alliances. An essential element in the structure of American ascendancy in the postwar years was the diffusion of its culture through the advent of mass consumption, television and Hollywood movies, advertising, and all that was encompassed by "Americanization" in the world. The broad appeal of middle-class American culture to peoples in allied nations recovering from wartime deprivations gave intangible support to the elite deference to American primacy. In Japan, American philanthropy with the leadership of John Rockefeller III helped overcome the tense relations at the time of the Anpo demonstrations. New organizations promoting study abroad and a plethora of other programs knit together ties between intellectual and cultural elites in Japan and the United States.[4] By 2017, business ties sustained thirty-seven chapters of the Japan-America Society in the United States, and People to People programs had grown to almost 450 sister-city relationships.[5] The Japanese historian Matsuda Takeshi warned of the "perils of soft power," contending that Americans, through their cultural policies, were successfully co-opting Japanese elites and thereby contributing to "an abiding psychology of dependence on the United States."[6]

Japan's position in the hierarchical American-led order had many peculiar features that distinguished it from other states in the system. Its entry was more coerced than others. But Yoshida accepted it as inevitable and "invited" the Americans to keep their bases in Japan so as to end the Occupation and return control of domestic affairs. Once that was done, Japanese leaders, like other allied elites, looked for ways to turn subordination to their advantage. The benefits turned out to be huge. Depending wholly on American bases for its security, Japan over succeeding decades was able to acquire economic aid, technology, and market access to a greater degree than any other state.

Moreover, the conservative leadership found ways to use the alliance to their own advantage in domestic politics. They could deliver the benefits of economic aid, trade, and technology to bolster their own power. The United States sponsored Japanese admission to the United Nations and to the General Agreement on Trade and Tariffs (GATT) and to participation in the transnational elite meetings and conferences that were part of the American international order. In 1964, for example, the favor of the United States facilitated Japan's inclusion into the Organisation for Economic Co-operation and Development (OECD), its hosting of the annual meeting of the World Bank and IMF, and especially important, the hosting of the Olympic Games, which symbolized Japan's growing prestige and status in the postwar world.[7]

Visits to Washington were prized for their role in legitimizing and displaying the prestige of allied elites. From 1960 to 1982, 42 percent of all trips Japanese prime ministers made abroad were to the United States.[8] Prime Minister Ikeda's visit to the White House in 1961, his address to the House of Representatives, the luncheon in the White House, and his day sailing with President Kennedy on the Potomac received huge play in the Japanese media and demonstrated how the Washington connection could enhance leaders' stature at home. Beginning with the "Ron-Yasu relationship" between President Ronald Reagan and Prime Minister Nakasone Yasuhiro in 1982, Japanese leaders took pride in being on a first-name basis with the American president.

Sentimentalizing the Alliance

The Anpo demonstrations were a chastening experience for both the Japanese and the American elites. Both had to reflect on the damage done to the alliance by the massive demonstrations. For the American image in Asia, Anpo showed the United States as an imperial power in league with a reactionary elite, imposing its will on a resentful people. As the United States created its patchwork of anticommunist alliances in Asia, it came face to face with dilemmas that reflected deeply on its self-identity. These alliances often linked Americans with reactionary leaders and positioned the United States in opposition to nationalist revolutions supported by communists. As Gordon Wood has written, the Cold War posed an ideological challenge to American self-identity that became the source of much confused thinking. "For the first time since 1776, Americans were faced with an alternative revolutionary ideology with universalist aspirations equal to their own. . . . The fundamental threat to the meaning of our history posed by a rival revolutionary ideology blinded us to the nationalistic and other ethnocultural forces at work in the world. In such an atmosphere it became difficult for us not to believe that every revolution was in some way communist and consequently our definition of 'free' governments was stretched to extraordinary lengths to cover eventually any government that was noncommunist."[9]

During the war, Roosevelt had insisted that America would be a great power but would not behave like one. The vast expansion of American military power during the Cold War, however, posed an immense challenge to the American revolutionary heritage. Communist propaganda described the expanding American alliance and base structure in Asia as a new form of imperialism and highlighted racial discrimination in the United States as inherent in US policies. NSC 48, a series of policy directives in 1951 from the National Security Council, pointed out the challenges the Cold War presented for the United States in Asia. Its emphasis was on avoiding actions that will "expose the U.S. to charges of 'imperialism'" and on preserving "the U.S. traditional reputation as a non-imperialistic champion of freedom and independence for all nations."[10]

The Anpo demonstrations painfully epitomized the dilemmas and were a deeply disturbing embarrassment for the United States. The spectacle of millions of Japanese participating in one way or another in opposition to renewal of the alliance challenged America's self-identity as a nonimperial power. The garrisoning of tens of thousands of US soldiers in Japan and American leaders associating closely with a prime minister only recently regarded as a war criminal in opposition to the will of the evident majority of the Japanese people were profoundly troubling. The messianic sense of purpose that had powered the unconditional surrender policy and the determination to remake Japan in the American image were undermined by support for the very conservative hegemony intended to be overthrown. How could this policy be squared with American democratic self-image? To cope with this challenge and legitimize its growing military power, the United States struggled to construct an appealing image and ideology of its purpose as a global but nonimperial power. Whereas the Occupation reforms had been predicated on confidence in the universal and hence superior nature of American values and institutions, the onset of the Cold War required a softening of this claim. Americans must somehow be seen as tolerant of different cultures and supportive of their interests.

In a valuable study of the American postwar engagement with Asia, the cultural historian Christina Klein demonstrated how the expansion of US global power and the Cold War conflict fostered a redefinition of American self-identity in relation to Asia. "Cold War Orientalism," as she labels it, sought to create a sense of common purpose with noncommunist Asia. Among Americans in and outside government, she identified a "sentimental discourse" intended to soften the image of and put a benign face on American power. "Sentimental" in this sense refers to appeals to empathy and emotion in transcending differences of race and culture, forging friendships, building solidarities of community, recognizing a shared humanity, and promoting exchanges and reciprocity.[11] Rather than a nation standing alone to contain communist expansion, Americans portrayed themselves joining in "partnership" with other nations to secure peace and prosperity. Rather than define East and West as oppositional, as in Edward Said's definition of Orientalism, this sentimental discourse constructed an ideology of integration and inclusion with noncommunist Asia. At the same time, because its purpose was to legitimate the Pax Americana, Cold War Orientalism often kept the implications of Western superiority as in Said's formulation.

To undergird the global assertion of US power, it was necessary to create feelings of interconnectedness between Americans and Asians. President Eisenhower launched the People to People program in 1956 to change American attitudes at home as well as to create a favorable image abroad. Differences between peoples could be overcome, the president said, by linking Americans "in partnership with hundreds of millions of like-minded people around the globe." "Partnership" was a favored word, and Eisenhower also emphasized sympathy, the highest of sentimental values, as the defining feature of American globalism. "People are what count," he said, and a "sympathetic understanding of the aspirations, the hopes and fears, the traditions and prides of other peoples and nations" was "a compulsory requirement on us, if, as a people, we are to discharge our inescapable national responsibility to lead the world."[12]

As the Cold War heated up, liberals in America took up the task of constructing an appealing national image and ideology. Their purpose was to envision a community of interest between the United States and Asia, to build unity within the noncommunist world. An influential and representative effort was *The Vital Center* by Harvard historian Arthur Schlesinger, Jr., in which he argued that American democracy had too much stressed a selfish individualism with little appeal abroad. Instead, successfully waging the Cold War required that it be redefined in terms of "solidarity with other human beings." Above all, he wrote, if they were to win the allegiance of peoples in Asia and Africa, Americans "must reform our own racial practices—not only repeal such insulting symbols as the Oriental exclusion laws, but demonstrate a deep and effective concern with racial inequities within the United States."[13]

In defining a national identity for the United States as a global power in Asia, public intellectuals writing in mainstream periodicals like *Reader's Digest* or the liberal *Saturday Review of Literature* projected a vision of solidarity with Asians. They emphasized that success of American global power required overcoming racism at home. Asia was "alien" to Americans in the early postwar period. Immigration and naturalization laws maintained Asian exclusion and only with the McCarran-Walter Act in 1952 and the Immigration Act of 1965 was the principle of Asian exclusion ended and Asians made eligible for immigration and naturalization. Norman Cousins, editor of the *Saturday Review,* organized a series of "partnerships" to encourage connectedness with Asians. Because the partnerships were humanitarian undertakings, they had a sentimental quality that appealed to American sympathies. He launched the project known as Hiroshima Maidens to bring disfigured Japanese *hibakusha* (atomic bomb victims) to the United States for corrective surgery. Cousins wrote of the world being one family. He also built programs along with the Christian Children's Fund to encourage adoption of Asian children.

The writer who exercised the greatest influence in constructing this sentimental discourse was James Michener, whose novels and essays introduced Asia to a huge American audience. Michener was a consummate Cold War liberal who feared America would "lose" Asia to communism unless it reoriented its attitudes and understood the war of ideas at the heart of the conflict. Americans must get over the view that Asians are mysterious, remote, and "not like us." Michener's novels were written within a sentimental framework that imagined America's liberalizing race attitudes. Michener teamed with Richard Rodgers and Oscar Hammerstein in musicals to highlight mixed racial romance. *Madame Butterfly* themes of Asian American romance popularized transracial themes in novels, musicals, and movies. *South Pacific, The King and I, Sayonara,* and *Teahouse of the August Moon* were some of the best-known cultural products of the period that deliberately romanticized the ideal of racial tolerance.

An important part of the American Cold War strategy to unify the noncommunist countries of the postcolonial developing world was formulation of a strategy for capitalist development, known as "modernization theory," which gave more substance to the American wish to demonstrate community with the developing world. It was the American answer to Marxist-Leninist ideology. "Theories of modernization indeed became an ideology during the early 1960s," as John Lewis Gaddis writes. "Based upon a remarkable injection of social science into the realm of policy, these ideas claimed to provide an objective basis for diagnosing and acting to alleviate conditions that might make for Communist revolutions in the Third World."[14] It offered a social scientific ideology of Western developmental superiority. Especially, it was argued in the most representative work, W. W. Rostow's *Stages of Economic Growth* (1960), American history offered a "blueprint" for the developing world to follow. While not coercing Americanization as in the Occupation, modernization theory could make American power and "Americanization" attractive by identifying with the aspirations of postcolonial peoples. Rostow's "non-Communist manifesto" hypothesized a universal pattern of development in which all progressing nations had to advance through similar stages from tradition to modernity. Modernization theory demonstrated that Americans could join with developing countries in confronting the fundamental issues that mattered most to them. At the same time, it should be noted, it was a variant on the long-standing unilinear view that all nations must eventually converge with the American pattern.

John Kennedy brought to the Oval Office this liberal agenda of transforming the image of American global power, which he believed the Eisenhower-Dulles foreign policy had cast too much in military terms. The president turned to the academy for ideas and advisors and especially to his alma mater. In the 1950s, Harvard had become what Jeremi Suri terms a "Cold War University" with "a strong stake in formulating and defending American global strategy." The Cold War University merged the intellectual and policy worlds and honored faculty who developed applied policy knowledge. Cold War intellectuals shuttling to Washington operated simultaneously as scholars and policymakers.[15] Academic research and policy prescription often blurred.

When the Kennedy administration took over, the Harvard scholars quickly signed on. McGeorge Bundy, Arthur Schlesinger, and Henry Kissinger moved into key White House positions.[16] Intent on putting a new face on America's role in Asia, the president appointed Harvard economist John Kenneth Galbraith as ambassador to India and asked Harvard historian Edwin Reischauer to serve in Tokyo. (Significantly, Kennedy asked James Michener to serve as ambassador to South Korea, but Michener declined because his wife was Japanese and he feared that would not work well in Korea.) The appointment of Reischauer, a towering figure in the founding of Japanese studies in the United States, was typical of the hopeful era associated with Kennedy's New Frontier. Christina Klein's book does not deal with Japan in any detail and does not mention Reischauer, but, in his activities as well as in his very persona, Reischauer perfectly fits into the framework of the sentimental discourse she describes.

The Reischauer "Offensive"

Born in Tokyo to a prominent and scholarly Presbyterian missionary family, Edwin Reischauer followed his older brother, Robert, to Oberlin for college.[17] Tokyo was "home," America was a little strange, and throughout his life he sought to "fit in." Robert and he moved on to Harvard and were the first Americans to receive their doctorates in Japanese studies. Robert, who had begun a promising scholarly career, was killed in Shanghai in 1937, a collateral casualty of Sino-Japanese fighting. Edwin joined the Harvard faculty in 1939 and was almost at once swept into political analysis as the Japanese-American crisis heated up. He was invited in 1941 to spend time in a lowly State Department position and throughout the war served in various official positions.

In September 1942 he wrote a policy memorandum that is of intrinsic interest in that it foreshadows Reischauer's later concern during the Cold War that perceptions in Asia of racism in American society would disadvantage the US cause. Addressing the internment of Japanese Americans, he argued, "Up to the present the Americans of Japanese ancestry have been a sheer liability to our cause, on the one hand presenting a major problem of population relocation and military surveillance in this country and on the other hand affording the Japanese in Asia with a trump propaganda card. We should reverse this situation and make of these American citizens a major asset in our ideological war in Asia." If they were given an opportunity to serve in the military, they could be "made an asset rather than a liability."[18] In addition, he foresaw the usefulness of preserving the imperial institution after the war as a valuable way to legitimate the democratic reforms that the United States planned.

After the war, Reischauer returned to Harvard and collaborated with the China historian John Fairbank to organize a popular survey course on East Asia, from which an important text emerged, and to train scores of specialists in East Asian history who took up positions at other universities. It was in this period up to the time of his ambassadorship that he made his great contribution to the US-Japan relationship by developing the academic field of Japanese studies and educating a broad public audience on Japanese history and culture. Together with publication of his scholarly doctoral dissertation on Ennin, the Japanese pilgrim to T'ang China, he wrote a short sweeping historical account, *Japan Past and Present*, which attained a wide audience.

Gradually, however, his scholarship began to blur with policy prescription. *The United States and Japan* (1950) mixed scholarship and policy. But by 1955, when he wrote *Wanted: An Asian Policy*, he settled into a role as a policy intellectual embracing the premises of Cold War foreign policy and offering prescriptions for "winning the war of ideas." Rather than depending on a defensive military strategy that seemed to protect the status quo, the United States should undertake an ideological "offensive" that would draw on "our arsenal of ideas" and show that American ideas rather than communist ideology offered the revolutionary change Asians sought. Americans needed to identify with Asian aspirations for a better life and demonstrate to Asians how they could be achieved in a free-market, democratic framework.[19]

In the late 1950s, events in Japan drew Reischauer further into his role as a policy intellectual. In an article in *Foreign Affairs* titled "The Broken Dialogue," Reischauer interpreted the Anpo demonstrations as a breakdown of American communication with Japanese progressives. He argued that their goal of neutrality in the Cold War was a naive and "a truly frightening phenomenon" that must be challenged.[20] Bundy, the young Harvard dean who became Kennedy's national security advisor, for whom Reischauer had unqualified admiration, helped him with the article.[21] It made him a candidate for the new administration's foreign policy team. John Fairbank, his Harvard colleague (and sometime academic rival), however, told an administration official Reischauer was not "tough enough" for a major position and suggested that the ambassadorship would be appropriate.[22]

Reischauer's appointment as ambassador was intended to soften the American image. He epitomized the inclusiveness and interconnectedness with Asia that Americans sought to project to counter communist propaganda and reinforce American identity as a defender of liberal values. He had sloughed off his parents' Christian faith but retained a kind of missionary internationalism, declaring he was "a missionary for democracy." Reischauer believed that his missionary upbringing had given him values that advantaged him over virtually all other Westerners. In his autobiography he wrote that "being born in Japan freed me from the start from the racial prejudice against Japanese and other Asians then almost universal among Westerners. . . . I was a generation or two ahead of my time." In his opposition to all forms of imperialism, "I was light-years ahead of most other people."[23]

It was seemingly Camelot in Tokyo when he arrived: an eminent Harvard scholar of Japanese history, born in Japan, who had recently been joined by marriage to an aristocratic Japanese family. Significantly, it was James Michener who, shortly after Reischauer's wife Adrienne died in 1956, introduced him to Haru Matsukata, the granddaughter of the Meiji leader (*genrō*) Matsukata Masayoshi. They were married in 1957 and in an unusual gesture Reischauer put his three children up for adoption so he and Haru could together adopt them. In a sense, they became the kind of biracial family that Michener, Rodgers and Hammerstein, and others envisioned as demonstrating Americans' liberalizing views.

During his five-and-a-half-year tenure as ambassador, Reischauer asserted several themes by which he sought to co-opt and win over Japanese resistance to the security relationship. First of all, he pronounced the goals and interests of the two countries as congruent. When the ambassadorship was offered, he wondered whether his love for Japan would cloud his judgments, but he decided that "the fundamental interests and goals of the two countries were now so similar that my love for Japan need not clash with my loyalty to America."[24] His assertion that the interests and goals of the two countries coincided became litany. This was hardly accurate, as the extensive popular opposition to nuclear testing, to the bases, and to the renewal of the security treaty during the 1950s testified. Japanese goals had to do with a restoration of national independence and of international respect, and noninvolvement in the superpower conflict. Japan's interest was in recovering its livelihood and above all its sovereignty, and the great majority of Japanese felt no great stake in the bipolar conflict that preoccupied Americans. Japan had pursued the goals of autonomy and self-mastery since the middle of the nineteenth century, when it lost the self-sufficiency and free security that it had always enjoyed. To determine its own fate was what Japan aspired to. Nevertheless, even after he left the embassy, Reischauer continued to declare that the values of Japanese and Americans were the same. As he later wrote in his autobiography, "I knew that the two nations shared common basic ideals of democracy, human rights, and egalitarianism, and yearned alike for a peaceful world made up of truly independent nations bound together by as free and open world trade as possible."[25]

At a time when perhaps no two nations had a more unequal relationship—the United States having imposed its own institutions and then a hegemonic alliance on Japan—he chose to describe it at every opportunity as an "equal partnership." Such a characterization obviously flew in the face of reality. In 1962 Reischauer himself privately told Averill Harriman, then assistant secretary of state, that the purpose of American bases was not primarily for the defense of other areas in the Far East. Rather, he stressed, "the primary role of our bases in Japan, I feel, is to help insure that this country does not fall or gravitate into Communist hands or into a neutralist position."[26] While privately regarding the alliance as an instrument to control Japan, he publicly maintained it was an "equal partnership." He used the term "partnership," a favorite word in the sentimental discourse, in order to avoid using "alliance," a term that to the majority of Japanese would connote an unwanted military relationship. Reischauer wanted the Japanese to "stop thinking of the relationship . . . between the two countries as being primarily military rather than a matter of shared ideals and economic interests. . . . I even carried the matter to trivial though visible details, such as insisting on walking first through doorways whenever I was with high American military officers in the presence of Japanese."[27] The ambassador could walk through the door ahead of every general and admiral, but it did not change the reality that the American military continued to hold the upper hand in managing the alliance.

Reischauer frequently propounded what was known as "modernization theory" to counter the prevailing sympathy for Marxism among

Japanese intellectuals. At the same time he became ambassador, several American scholars who had once been his students organized an ambitious multiyear project to study Japanese modernization. Beginning at the Hakone Conference in 1960 they sought to engage Japanese scholars in viewing Japan as a model of successful modernization. Modernization theory as it was applied to Japan took on distinctive features of ideology. Rather than stressing the tragedy of Japan's modern history—the fundamental intertwining of industrialization and militarization inherent in Japan's modern revolution—it treated the Japanese experience as a successful case of capitalist and democratic development and as a model for other late developing societies. The 1930s were, in Reischauer's view, an aberration, a time when democratization was derailed, but which the Occupation had put back on track.[28] The ambassador's leadership in promoting this interpretation came to be known as the "Reischauer offensive."

A shocking incident in 1964 further added to the emotion-laden tone of his ambassadorship. As he stepped from the chancery one morning, a deranged young Japanese stabbed Reischauer in the thigh with a kitchen knife, slicing open his femoral artery. Reischauer received massive blood transfusions in a Japanese hospital. But it was later discovered that the blood was contaminated and would permanently weaken his health. As he fought for his life, he told an aide that "improving the U.S.-Japan relationship meant more . . . than life itself."[29] He sought to allay the distress and mortification of the distraught Japanese people and to turn even this unfortunate incident into an occasion of Japanese-American interconnectedness. From his hospital bed he issued a statement saying he felt "all the closer to the Japanese people because I now was of 'mixed blood.'"[30]

Reischauer's tendency to sentimentalize US-Japan relations was, ironically, embraced by the ruling conservative elite in Japan, which found it useful for their own purposes. They too avoided use of the term "alliance," preferring "ikōru pātonāshippu" (equal partnership), which would obscure the military implications of the security treaty, which was a source of wide domestic criticism.[31] It also obscured the American criticism of Japan's "free riding" on US guarantees of Japanese security. It was not until 1979 in a welcoming ceremony at the White House that a prime minister, Ōhira Masayoshi, chose publicly to refer to the United States as Japan's ally (dōmeikoku). His successor, the

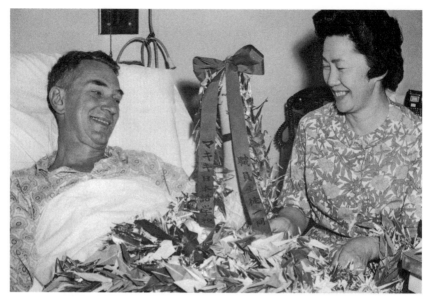

US ambassador to Japan Edwin Reischauer, wounded in a knife attack by a deranged Japanese assailant, recovering in a Japanese hospital with his wife, Haru. Bettmann/Getty Images/515034786.

hapless Suzuki Zenko, in 1981 signed a joint declaration in Washington with President Reagan that referred to the "alliance relationship" (*dōmeikankei*), but when he returned to Japan he denied that the alliance had any military implications.[32] If the Americans chose to cast the alliance in sentimental terms and gloss over the reality of American hegemony, the Japanese *elite* too would play right along.

His ambassadorship was a memorable era in US-Japan relations. For a time, at least, Reischauer changed the atmospherics of the relationship. He traveled with his wife to nearly every prefecture, preparing carefully for speeches in order to demonstrate a knowledge and appreciation for local history. But the good feelings his tireless efforts generated were soon vitiated by the growing American involvement in the Vietnam conflict. The ambassador, while privately harboring doubts, fell in line with Washington's policy. Even after leaving the ambassadorship and returning to Harvard in 1966, he continued to provide halfhearted support for the war. His biographer, George Packard, while crediting Reischauer with many successes in increasing American understanding of Japan's history, nonetheless is sharply critical of his deference to the policymakers of the Vietnam debacle, concluding that he allowed "the lure and the glamour" of his position to bend his judgment.[33]

Over time, the sentimental discourse became embedded in the bilateral relationship, masking the hard realities of US dominance and the legacies of the unconditional surrender policy, the Occupation, and a hegemonic alliance. When George Kennan, ever the realist, described the relationship as "an unnatural intimacy," he was saying that both sides, especially the Americans, have a responsibility to take account of realities and surmount the mistakes of the past: "I am not speaking here of anything sentimental. I am not speaking of love or admiration. Such things . . . have no place in the real lives of nations. I am speaking of something much deeper: a common recognition that fate—or, if you will, the mistakes of earlier generations—have thrown us in each other's path; that the effort to work things out in opposition to each other has proven worse than useless; that we have no choice but to contrive to do it together."[34]

Japan and the Vietnam Conflict

The Vietnam conflict reawakened the Japanese people's opposition to the alliance and their longing for an independent role in the world. Once again, massive popular demonstrations erupted in opposition to the alliance. The leading organization in this effort was Beheiren (short for Betonamu ni heiwa shimin rengo, or the Citizens Federation for Peace in Vietnam), founded by the young writer Oda Makoto in 1965. It was a decentralized, loosely structured movement that rejected a strategy of the old Left of tightly organized mobilization methods and instead encouraged spontaneous involvement of ordinary citizens. Many writers, including Maruyama Masao and the later Nobel Prize winner Ōe Kenzaburō, became active supporters of Beheiren.

Its dominant personality, however, was Oda, who became the popular spokesman for the postwar generation's ambivalence toward America—the attraction to American cultural and political idealism and repulsion from abuses of American power and wealth. He returned from a Fulbright year at Harvard and travels in many parts of the world in time to participate in the Anpo demonstrations. His 1961 book, a travelogue *I'll Give Anything a Look* (*Nan de mo mite yarō*), was a best seller. He was critical of the United States but also was drawn to American democracy and individual choice and responsibility. In Oda's novel *America* (1962), the young Japanese hero embraces life in America and the opportunity to escape from the stultifying conventions of Japanese society: "I want to be myself. . . . I want to live my own life my own way."[35] While admiring of American values of individualism and human rights, Oda's writings described the reality of American society as racist, self-indulgent, and insensitive to the poor societies of Asia.

The Japanese antiwar movement's intense opposition to American imperialism sought to promote a Japanese identification with Asia and a sense of pan-Asianism. Oda singled out Reischauer for a patronizing attitude toward Asia in his lecturing Japanese on their naïveté toward the issues of the Cold War. At the same time, Oda went to great lengths to make Japanese aware of their own complicity in the Vietnam War by their alliance with the United States and their economic profiting from the conflict. Japanese businesses reaped billions of dollars through direct and indirect procurement contracts with the US military. While South Korea dispatched more than 300,000 troops to fight alongside its American ally in Vietnam, the Japanese avoided direct military involvement. Beheiren focused attention on the way Japanese industry and technology supported the war and made Japanese citizens aware of this role. "We [Japanese] are all guilty of complicity in the Vietnam War," Oda wrote. "We must recognize that each of us is among the perpetrators." Yet, the Japanese, in their complicity, were also made victims of America: "Our country was a kind of 'forced aggressor' in the [Vietnam] war. Because of the security treaty, Japan had to cooperate with the American policy of aggression. In this sense Japan was a victim of its alliance with that policy, but it was also an aggressor toward the small countries in Indochina."[36]

While giving tepid public support to the war, the Japanese government allowed the United States free reign in its use of the bases, not requiring any prior consultation in the way the bases were used to prosecute the war. The US bases in Japan proper, where 45,000 soldiers and an equal number of dependents lived, were vital to the war effort, serving as staging grounds for sending troops and supplies to the war zone, as well as repair facilities and hospitals for the wounded. Thousands of soldiers each year took leave from the war zone to come to Japan for rest and relaxation. Okinawa, with its huge air and marine bases, and home to an additional 50,000 US troops, was critical. As the commander of US forces in the Pacific put it, "Without Okinawa, we couldn't continue fighting the war."[37] US bases were not so much used to defend Japan but rather to underwrite US Asian strategy.

Beheiren provided sanctuary for a number of US and South Korean soldiers who defected in Japan, and placed emphasis on a national pride in Article 9 of the constitution. It organized over 300 local chapters of antiwar protest, promoted street marches, held peace conferences, and made contact with US antiwar movements and brought their leaders to Japan. In contrast to 1960, when a revised security treaty required ratification in the Diet, ten years later renewal of the treaty was automatic unless either nation chose to end it. Prime Minister Satō, learning from his older brother's (Kishi's) mistakes, kept a low posture while supporting renewal. Nevertheless, popular demonstrations against the treaty and the war in Vietnam recalled the mass participation in 1960. In the two and a half years leading up to the renewal date of June 23, 1970, more than 18 million Japanese participated in some form of protest.[38] On June 23 alone more than 770,000 took to the streets.[39] Since renewal was a fait accompli the movement lacked the intensity and immediacy of the Anpo demonstrations ten years earlier. Beheiren did not succeed in transforming Japan's role as complicit in US Cold War strategy, but it kept alive the possibility of mass opposition to Japanese government policies and in that sense solidified the Yoshida strategy to keep tight limits on active involvement in the alliance. In addition, Beheiren also kept alive a civic activism that flourished in the 1970s' citizen concerns with pollution, the environment, and unregulated industrialism.

The Grand Strategy of the Yoshida Doctrine

While the Americans were at pains to soften their image in light of the Anpo demonstrations, the Japanese ruling conservatives were likewise adjusting their policies so as to pacify the mass opposition. The 1960 demonstrations chastened the conservative elite, especially those political nationalists in the right wing of the LDP, who had hoped to strengthen Japan's international role by building its political and military influence. The spectacle of crowds of hundreds of thousands surrounding the Diet and a fiercely divided legislature inside indicated that if conservatives continued to raise the issue of rebuilding Japan's military, they would subject the country to prolonged turmoil and probably be driven from power.

The LDP leadership concluded that to avoid divisive domestic political struggles, they must double down on Yoshida's policies of limiting the involvement in the Cold War and concentrating on economic, industrial, and scientific growth. By the time he left the prime ministership in 1954, Yoshida had established three fundamental principles that marked his tactical approach in response to American pressure to rearm and enlist in the Cold War struggle. First, Japan's economic rehabilitation must be the prime national goal. Political-economic cooperation with the United States was necessary for this purpose. Second, Japan should remain lightly armed and avoid involvement in international political-strategic issues. The Self-Defense Forces would not be deployed abroad. Japan would not participate in collective defense arrangements. Third, to gain a long-term guarantee of its own security, Japan would provide bases for the US Army, Navy, and Air Force.

After Anpo and the resignation of the disgraced Kishi, two of Yoshida's disciples serving as prime ministers, Ikeda Hayato (1960–1964) and Satō Eisaku (1964–1972), built Yoshida's policies into a more elaborate and full-blown strategy. What had been for Yoshida a short-term tactic to allow Japan time to recover from the war was developed into a grand strategy for pursuing Japanese interests in the unique circumstances of the Cold War international order. It served to manage both the domestic political divisions and the continuing US pressure for more active involvement in the bipolar conflict.

The key figure in building Yoshida's policies into a national consensus for economic growth was his understudy Ikeda Hayato, who became prime minister in 1960. Coming to power shortly after the mass demonstrations of opposition to the security treaty, Ikeda succeeded in turning the nation's attention away from the politically divisive issues to improving the nation's livelihood. Accordingly, for the next two decades the Yoshida wing of the LDP, which was acknowledged to be the party's "mainstream," shelved these divisive issues. It partially accommodated the right wing of the LDP, the political nationalists, by maintaining a stable alliance with the United States; and it propitiated the progressives of the opposition parties by steering clear of ideology, limiting rearmament, and formulating policies that would raise living standards and improve social overhead capital.

Working with economic bureaucrats, Ikeda announced a plan for doubling the national income within a decade. This plan was part of a systematic and well-coordinated effort to unify the nation and to convince most of the leaders of the ruling party that it could best consolidate and legitimate its hold on the electorate by adhering to policies of economic growth that Yoshida had initiated. Nakamura Takafusa, a leading economic historian, writes, "Ikeda was the single most important figure in Japan's rapid growth. He should be remembered as the man who pulled together a national consensus for economic growth and who strove for the realization of the goal."[40]

During the term of Ikeda's successor, Satō Eisaku, who served as prime minister from 1964 to 1972 (longer than any other individual to hold that office in Japanese history), Japan took decisive steps to ensure it would not become involved in the political and military issues of the Cold War. At the outset, Satō dealt with the thorny issue of whether to become a nuclear power. The issue surfaced when China conducted its first nuclear weapons test in October 1964. Japanese leadership faced the question of whether it should now exercise the nuclear option. Prime Minister Satō, meeting with Ambassador Reischauer in December 1964, said he felt that if the Chinese Communists had nuclear weapons the Japanese should also have them. Satō noted that nuclear weapons were "much less costly than was generally assumed and Japanese scientific and industrial level was fully up to producing them." Reischauer reported to Washington that he saw "grave dangers" and that Satō "needs more guidance and education by us than did Ikeda to keep him out of dangerous courses (such as his implied independent Japanese nuclear stand)."[41] Meeting the next month in the White House, Lyndon Johnson assured Satō that the US nuclear deterrent provided Japan with full protection.[42] For the United States, the importance of preventing a nuclear Japan was essential to the stability of the US regional order and would be regarded as a security threat to other Asian states. Japanese conservatives were reluctant to close the door to Japan's inclusion among the nuclear powers. They believed exclusion from the "nuclear club" would relegate Japan permanently to second-class status as a power.[43] However, because it would undermine the US-Japan relationship, they reluctantly concluded that it would be necessary to forgo the nuclear option.

In 1967, Satō announced the Three Non-Nuclear Principles, pledging that Japan "will not manufacture or possess nuclear weapons or allow their introduction into this country," and the Diet subsequently formalized this in a resolution. Lest the principles be regarded as unconditional, Satō clarified matters in a Diet speech in 1968, outlining the four pillars of Japan's nonnuclear policy: (1) reliance on the US umbrella, (2) the three nonnuclear principles, (3) promotion of worldwide disarmament, and (4) development of nuclear energy for peaceful purposes. Although he later received the Nobel Peace Prize for this pledge, Satō was privately cynical, referring to the Three Non-Nuclear Principles in a conference with the US ambassador as "nonsense."[44]

Even after announcing the nonnuclear principles, Japanese leaders continued to revisit the issue. In 1968, the United States and the Soviet Union proposed to the United Nations Disarmament Commission a nonproliferation agreement that was later approved by the UN General Assembly and took effect in 1970. The Nuclear Non-Proliferation Treaty (NPT) prohibited all nuclear testing and established a worldwide network of monitoring stations. The issue of ratification of the NPT held implications not only for Japan's status as a great power but also for its commercial and technological advantage. After the NPT draft was circulated, Satō commissioned a secret study of Japanese nuclear policy, which concluded that its civilian nuclear power program kept the option, but that it ought not to be exercised in light of both public and international opinion. Reluctantly, with divided hearts, the conservatives concluded that Japan would forgo the nuclear option. Nevertheless, an internal Foreign Ministry document in 1969 concluded: "For the time being, we will maintain the policy of not possessing nuclear weapons. However, regardless of joining the NPT or not, we will keep the economic and technical potential for the production of nuclear weapons, while seeing to it that Japan will not be interfered with in this regard."[45] Therefore, while Japan signed the NPT in 1970, it delayed ratification for six years while negotiating maximum leeway for its civilian nuclear power program with the International Atomic Energy Agency. Japan, by calling attention to the provision allowing withdrawal from the agreement with three months' notice should "extraordinary events" require it, signaled it would keep open the option and in the meantime press ahead with research. For the time being at least, Japan was satisfied that, as a second report commissioned by Satō put it, "the days are gone when the possession of nuclear weapons is a prerequisite for superpower status."[46]

Yet not all Japanese leaders agreed. Throughout these deliberations, Japanese conservative leaders nursed painful heartburn over the forfeiture of the prestige that possession of nuclear weapons conferred.[47] For a country whose sensitivity to status had always been keen, this factor was not easily laid aside. In December 1971, the LDP leader Miyazawa Kiichi warned other countries that Japan retained the option of rearmament, telling an interviewer:

> Recent events have been influenced by distinctions between "first-rate" and "second-rate" nations, using nuclear capabilities and atomic stockpiles as yardsticks. . . . If the major nations of the world who have nuclear capabilities try to be too assertive and push Japan around too much and too far, they may run the risk of opening up what they most want to avoid. There is already a body of opinion in Japan which feels that dependence on the US nuclear umbrella is basically incompatible with our national sovereignty. When the coming generations assume a greater role in the society, they may want to choose the lesser of two evils and opt to build their own umbrella instead of renting their neighbor's, if only to satisfy their desire to be their own masters. This may become likelier as time passes and memories of Hiroshima and Nagasaki recede.[48]

Japanese leaders were keenly sensitive to the way in which acquisition of nuclear weapons had enhanced China's status in Western eyes and to Westerners' persistent distrust of Japan's potential for return to militarist policies. In 1970 as director of the Defense Agency, Nakasone Yasuhiro, a leader of the LDP right wing, dissected in cold, analytical terms the power politics at work:

> Both the 1963 partial nuclear test ban treaty and the current nuclear non-proliferation treaty are primarily designed—even if covertly—to preempt, or rather deter, both Japan and West Germany from acquiring nuclear arms and thereby undermining the basis of US-Soviet nuclear hegemony. China opted for "going nuclear without pants." Japan, on the other hand, has remained non-nuclear, preferring to be decently dressed. Only history will be able to determine who was wiser. Whether wise or foolish, Japan should not forget . . . that nuclear arms policies tacitly are a reflection of a US-Soviet agreement regarding their respective share of the trophies of World War II.[49]

In the end, Japan gave precedence to economic and technological interests, insisting that inspection procedures of the International Atomic Energy Agency not obstruct the efficient development of the power industry or permit leaks of industrial secrets. The NPT negotiations demonstrated that in the most profound security issue of the time, Japan was increasingly defining its grand national strategy in long-term economic interests. In Korea and China, however, the suspicion persisted that Japan remained intent on developing its ability to become a nuclear power. Indeed, so far as Japan's conservative leadership is concerned, the "nuclear allergy" is overrated. Despite their emphasis on being the sole victim of nuclear weapons, Japanese leaders have since the 1950s reserved the right and have developed a full capability to develop a nuclear arsenal should circumstances dictate.[50]

In addition to the Three Non-Nuclear Principles, there were other important elaborations to the Yoshida policies. In 1970, the Mutual Security Treaty again was open to reconsideration, and with American intervention in Vietnam stirring domestic opposition, particularly the Japanese student movement, care had to be taken to defuse the kind of domestic turmoil that had roiled Japan in 1960. To preserve Japan's low posture in international politics, Satō formulated the policy of the Three Principles of Arms Exports, which provided that Japan would not allow the export of arms to countries in the Communist bloc, to countries covered by UN resolutions on arms embargoes, and to countries involved or likely to be involved in armed conflicts. This policy enshrined the position that economic bureaucrats had consistently held, namely, that Japan should resist the temptation to build a powerful military industrial complex. Subsequently, the cabinet of Prime Minister Miki Takeo (1974–1976) extended this ban on weapons exports to all countries and defined "arms" to include not only military equipment but also the parts and fittings used in this equipment.

As the grand strategy continued to take shape, Japan adopted several other self-binding policies in what we now call the Yoshida Doctrine. The Diet passed a resolution in 1969 limiting Japan's activities in outer space to peaceful and nonmilitary purposes. As a further elaboration of its strategic stance of eschewing military involvement, constraining defense expenditure to less than 1 percent of the gross national product became a practice in the 1960s, although it did not become official government policy until adoption of the National Defense Program Outline in 1976. The government explained its formulation of security policy as "an exclusively defensive defense." Troops and weapons would have no offensive capacity, nor would Japan maintain any ability to project power abroad. Thus, jets would have no capability for bombing or midair refueling. An aircraft carrier was out of the question.

As Japan became a major donor and eventually the world's leading contributor of foreign aid in the 1980s, successive policy statements emphasized that development assistance would not be given for military-related purposes or to countries with large military budgets or in situations that might aggravate international conflicts. Instead, aid, loans, and technological assistance were allocated for strategic economic purposes that would promote Japanese commercial advantage.[51]

During the Vietnam conflict, US pressure on Japan to contribute to the Cold War cause once again intensified. The Japanese leadership had two principal weapons to withstand this pressure. The first was the demonstrable popular opposition to embroilment in the conflict. The second was Article 9 of the constitution, which the government more or less interpreted to fit its strategy. The Japanese Supreme Court steadfastly resisted ruling on issues relating to the interpretation of Article 9. Instead, it was an organ in the office of the prime minister, the Cabinet Legal Bureau (CLB), which issued interpretations. This elite and influential administrative agency, shrouded in secrecy and little noticed during the Cold War, epitomized the policy autonomy bureaucrats possessed. The CLB reviewed all proposed legislation and rules for consistency with the constitution and legal precedents. Ministers and lawmakers acceded to its interpretation and the precedents its rulings created. The Supreme Court rarely overturned its rulings. In 1954, Yoshida had instructed the CLB to draw up an interpretation that Japan could possess only "the minimum necessary force" for the exercise of self-defense for the homeland. For the duration of the Cold War, the CLB bureaucrats adhered to these constraints. The CLB's interpretation of the constitution was deferred to throughout the Cold War years, and thus it became "a powerful break on major policy change."[52]

The Yoshida School prime ministers found the CLB interpretation most convenient. It gave them cover. When President Reagan took office in January 1981 and rallied US allies for a tougher stand in the Cold War, including an arms buildup, Japanese bureaucrats felt the need to shore up the Yoshida Doctrine. The issue that made Japan particularly vulnerable to pressure was the provision in the United Nations Charter authorizing all nations to engage in collective self-defense. Article 51 held that "nothing in the present Charter shall impair the inherent right of individual or collective defense." To forestall American pressure for a more forthright contribution to the Cold War effort, the CLB brought the constitutional prohibition and its public support into a more resolute stance. Shortly after the election of Reagan, the CLB in May 1981 expanded its tightly worded proscription on collective self-defense: "Since it is a sovereign state, Japan has the right of collective self-defense under international law. The Japanese government nevertheless takes the view that the exercise of the right of self-defense as authorized under Article 9 of the Constitution is confined to the minimum necessary level for the defense of the country. The government believes that the exercise of the right of collective self-defense exceeds that limit and is not, therefore, permissible under the Constitution."[53] Such minimalist interpretation of what the constitution permitted was a political rather than a legal interpretation. It was the final building block in the institutionalization of the Yoshida Doctrine's grand strategy for steering Japan through the multiple foreign and domestic challenges of the postwar period.

By the time the Cold War culminated in the Reagan years, Yoshida and his successors had a full-blown grand strategy for taking advantage of Japan's unique position in the American world order. They had a series of self-abnegating policies to avoid Japanese involvement in the political-military aspects of the Cold War. These policies might best be summed up as the "Nine Nos":

1. No overseas deployment of Japanese Self-Defense Forces
2. No participation in collective self-defense arrangements
3. No power projection capability
4. No nuclear arms
5. No arms exports
6. No sharing of defense-related technology
7. No more than 1 percent of GNP for defense expenditure
8. No military use of space
9. No foreign aid for military purpose

To the end of the Cold War, Japan adhered steadfastly to these self-abnegating policies, staying out of all international political/military affairs, leaving the protection of its national security to the United States, and acting like a merchant nation—or, as some said, like an international trading firm. It was a brilliant strategy adapted to the Cold

War system and the American world order. As the conservative intellectual Nishio Kanji said, US preoccupation with the Cold War allowed Japan to "conduct a diplomacy that exploited and totally used the U.S. Even if Japan was asked to take some responsibility, we could get away with avoiding it and simply pursue our economic interests."[54] The sharp-tongued former foreign minister Sonoda Sunao privately revealed the cynical approach the Japanese took when the United States made its constant demands for Japan to do more in behalf of its own defense. He pointed to the various policies Satō had promoted in the 1960s—the nonnuclear principles, the prohibition of exporting technology, and the 1 percent limitation on defense spending—as clever ways to shield Japan from succumbing to such pressure. With heavy sarcasm, he went on: "The Americans were always asking us to do this and to do that, take over part of their Far Eastern policies. But all their efforts were sabotaged by one Japanese Cabinet after another. That's why Satō Eisaku got the Nobel Prize. He got it for his accumulated achievements in the field of sabotage. I suppose he is the only Prime Minister ever to have got the Nobel Prize for sabotage."[55]

A foreign affairs commentator who ran for governor of Tokyo, Matsuoka Hideo, put it no less bluntly. Japan, he wrote, should continue to avoid becoming entangled in international disputes by deliberately "missing the boat" (*nori-okure*). That is, when international issues arose, Japan should always "go to the end of the line" and wait quietly, unnoticed, while all other nations stepped forward to declare their positions on controversial issues. This passive and reactive policy, he admitted, was a "diplomacy of cowardice" (*okubyō gaikō*), but it served Japan's interests of maintaining good relations with all countries and thus preserving its global access to markets and raw materials. "No matter where or what kind of dispute or war arises," he concluded, "Japan must stand aloof and uninvolved."[56] In precisely the same way, Ōkita Saburō, an economic bureaucrat who served as foreign minister in 1979–1980, said it was essential for Japanese economic interests to maintain good relations with all nations, "making a lack of principles the basic principle of our foreign policy" (*gensoku toshite mugensoku*).[57] In short, as another foreign minister put it succinctly, Japan would pursue a "value free diplomacy."[58]

Rather than translate its economic power into political and military power, Japan would, in short, stay the course as a trading state. As the colorful Ministry of International Trade and Industry vice minister

Amaya Naohiro wrote in his book *An Essay on the Merchant State* (*Chōnin kokka-ron*), Japan should remember how in its own history during the Tokugawa period the samurai had the weapons and the political power but the merchants had the wealth and ended up being the stronger class. In the same way, let the United States and the Soviet Union, like the samurai, build up their weapon systems; Japan would adhere to a merchant role. It might sometimes be humbling and even humiliating, as it was for the Tokugawa merchants, but Japan should not allow pride or principle to stand in the way of the pursuit of profit. "For a merchant to prosper in samurai society, it is necessary to have superb information-gathering ability, planning ability, intuition, diplomatic skill and at times ability to be a sycophant." The way of the merchant sometimes would require having to "grovel on bended knee before the samurai," but a merchant's wealth could be used to solve political problems. "When money can help, it is important to have the gumption to put up large sums."[59]

Indeed, in 1978 the Japanese government attempted to defuse US anger over Japan's "free ride" on defense spending by paying an increasing amount of the expenditures of maintaining the American bases in Japan. The wily Kanemaru Shin, serving as director of the Self-Defense Agency, coined the patronizing term "sympathy budget (*omoi-yari yosan*)" to show the government's "consideration" for the US forces who came all the way across the Pacific to protect Japan.[60] The sympathy budget eventually grew to an annual sum of nearly $3 billion,[61] but Americans were not always pleased by Japan's adoption of their sentimental rhetoric. During a visit to Japan in 2000, Undersecretary of State Strobe Talbot expressed indignation at the use of the term "sympathy budget," telling LDP politicians the US forces were not in Japan to receive "charity."[62] In January 2012 the US Defense Department requested that the Japanese refrain from using the term "sympathy budget" for host nation support and the Japanese foreign minister complied, asking the media to avoid the offending term.[63]

The establishment of the sympathy budget epitomized the twisted way in which this peculiar alliance had developed. Struggling to restore some semblance of autonomy from US domination, Japan had chosen to define itself as "a special state" whose constitution precluded it from participation in international politics. The Americans would be paid to defend Japan. Indeed, as Japan grew comfortable with the role of a trading state, it chose to make its influence felt by exercising its financial strength. Japan increased its contribution to international organizations, including the Asian Development Bank, the United Nations, the World Bank, and the IMF. Japan also promised to vastly increase its foreign aid. Japan's official development assistance became the principal tool of foreign policy. By the end of 1989 Japan was not only the world's greatest creditor nation but also the world's largest aid donor.

Nixon, Kissinger, and the Rough Treatment of Japan

The peculiarly twisted and contradictory nature of the alliance was never more apparent than in the rough treatment the United States accorded its ally when President Nixon, without consulting the Japanese, reversed US relations with China in 1971 and at the same time imposed a surcharge on Japanese imports to force revaluation of the yen. As Japanese high growth took off in the 1960s and the United States struggled with the burdens of its Cold War policies, the tensions and contradictions of the alliance increased. Many, if not most, foreign observers expected that Japan would soon translate this new economic power into military power. The futurologist Herman Kahn, in his widely discussed book *The Emerging Japanese Superstate* (1970), drew attention to the military implications of Japan's resurgence, concluding that the "Japanese will almost inevitably feel that Japan has the right and duty to achieve full superpower status and that this means possessing a substantial nuclear establishment."[64]

In light of Japan's emerging economic power, American leaders were frustrated by Japan's lack of support for its Vietnam policy. The growing opposition to the war in Japan often focused on the use of Okinawa and especially the increased use of B-52s stationed at Kadena Air Base for bombing missions against North Vietnam. The Japanese government, responding to the growing popular sentiment, expressed opposition to expansion of the conflict. In 1968 Secretary of State Rusk exploded with anger at the Japanese complaints in a personal message to the US ambassador in Tokyo that, since the beginning of the Cold War, "so far as I know Japan has not lost a single man in confronting those who are the major threat to Japan itself. We are in a deadly struggle in Vietnam [and] . . . it is almost more than the flesh and spirit can bear to have

Japan whining about Okinawa while we are losing several hundred killed each month in behalf of our common security in the Pacific."[65] In August 1968, the US ambassador to Japan, U. Alexis Johnson, complained to Foreign Minister Miki that "after sacrificing thousands of lives and billions of dollars in defense of areas of East Asia, an area which is at least of equal interest to Japan, we not only did not get any understanding from Japan but received criticism and harassment on essentially minor matters." It was high time Japan bore "a responsibility commensurate with its growing power. Rather than continuing to seek to be treated by the US as a minor and weak country, our relationship needed to be more firmly established on the basis of equality."[66]

The election of Richard Nixon as president in 1968 brought an administration of realists who had no time for a sentimental approach to Japan of the kind Reischauer had formulated. The year before his election, Nixon wrote in *Foreign Affairs* that it was past time for Japan to rearm. "It simply is not realistic to expect a nation moving into the first rank of major power to be totally dependent for its own security on another nation, however close the ties."[67] Nixon signaled early in his administration that he was seeking fundamental change in American Asian policy and that a new attitude toward the alliance with Japan would be part of that. The president recalled Japan's past reluctance to involve itself in world affairs and said he would not be surprised if "in five years we didn't have to restrain them." The Japanese had gone through a traumatic period since Hiroshima, he mused, but "now they are going to do something."[68] For Nixon and his principal foreign policy advisor, Henry Kissinger, the emergence of Japan as an activist power would not be an unfavorable development. They reasoned that Japan could be "the major counter-force" in Asia to China and Russia. For the United States, drained economically and psychologically by the war in Southeast Asia, prompting Asian nations, especially Japan, to share the burden of their own defense was becoming a favorite idea.[69]

In an effort to show a new sense of direction as he dealt with the Vietnam debacle, Nixon held a press conference in Guam in 1969 and asserted his determination that the primary responsibility for Asian security must be borne by Asians themselves. The Nixon Doctrine, or "Guam Doctrine" as it was sometimes called, declared that the United States would depend on its Asian allies to assume more responsibility for containing communism in the region. But the Japanese were adamant. Direct involvement in a regional security organization, said Ōhira Masayoshi, who served as foreign minister from 1962 to 1964 and 1972 to 1974, was "impossible."[70]

Nevertheless, Nixon and Kissinger set out to implement a fundamental reorientation of American Cold War strategy that had important implications for Asia and for the US-Japan alliance. They observed that Japan as well as Germany and the rest of Europe had fully recovered from the war and that the international system as a result needed to be viewed in a new way. They were convinced the painful Vietnam experience demonstrated that the international order, rather than being understood as an exclusive emphasis on the bipolar Soviet-American contest, should be viewed in a more complex and nuanced way. It was not, as NSC 68 had cast it, a zero-sum game in which the gain for the Soviets anywhere was a loss for the United States and the free world. Such a view had encouraged rigidity in the perception of American self-interest. As Kissinger wrote in 1968: "A bipolar world loses the perspective for nuance; a gain for one side appears as an absolute loss for the other. Every issue seems to involve a question of survival. The smaller countries are torn between a desire for protection and a wish to escape big-power dominance. Each of the superpowers is beset by the desire to maintain its preeminence among its allies, to increase its influence among the uncommitted, and to enhance its security vis-à-vis its opponent."[71] What had changed was the nature of power in the international system. Possession of nuclear weapons that would not be used in conflict and conventional military forces were no longer the sole measure of the strategic balance of power. There were now many dimensions of power. Economic strength had become a critically important dimension of national power.

Nixon and Kissinger saw the changing distribution of power and the emergence of a multipolar world and wanted to orient policy to this reality. Nixon explained to an audience of news executives in Kansas City in July 1971 that there were five great economic powers in the world: the United States, the Soviet Union, Western Europe, Japan, and China. "These are the five that will determine the economic future and, because economic power will be the key to other kinds of power, the future of the world in other ways in the last third of this century."[72] The following year he told *Time* magazine that "the only time in the history of the world that we have had any extended period of peace is when there has been a balance of power. It is when one nation becomes infinitely more powerful in relation to its potential competitor that the danger of war arises. . . . I think it will be a safer world and a better world if we have a stronger, healthy United States, Europe, Soviet Union, China, Japan, each balancing the other, not playing one against the other, an even balance."[73] Nixon and Kissinger embraced the new concept of "trilateralism" that acknowledged Japan was now a power in its own right and had to be given a place along with Europe. Surprisingly, they even hinted to the Japanese that they might do well to acquire nuclear weapons. For the Japanese, who had stayed out of international politics, their ally was about to push them into the deep waters, whether they could swim or not.

The Nixon administration got off to a positive start with Japan by reaching an agreement on the reversion of Okinawa to Japan. Of all the American bases scattered about the world, none matched Okinawa in terms of its strategic value as well as its sheer imposition on the local community. US military installations incorporated housing units, clubs, swimming pools, golf courses, movie theatres, dance halls, and bowling alleys. During the Vietnam conflict, a million military transport and combat flights originated in Okinawa.[74] Because of its long-term strategic importance, SCAP had detached Okinawa from Japan and excluded it from democratic reforms. At the time of the San Francisco Peace Treaty the United States had tacitly acknowledged Japanese sovereignty, but the Pentagon had strongly resisted any discussion of reversion and was even resistant to allowing Okinawan representation in the governing of the islands. Some cosmetic changes were made to provide civilian governance and some Okinawan input, but the issue festered as Okinawa remained essentially an American colony. In 1961, Kennedy's undersecretary of state, George Ball, visited Okinawa and thought it "preposterous that fifteen years after the war we should still be treating it as our colony. . . . How could we decry the colonial practices of our European allies yet persist in similar practices in Okinawa?"[75]

The Vietnam War, however, brought matters to a head, and by the eve of the Nixon administration's coming to power it was clear that the pressures for reversion from Japanese leaders and public opinion as well as mounting demonstrations within Okinawa placed the future of the alliance in jeopardy. In 1968, in the first popular election for the office of chief executive in the Ryukyus, Yara Chobyo, a strong supporter of immediate reunification with Japan, was elected. To ignore such a vote would further emphasize the imperialist character of US rule of the islands. The Pentagon reluctantly agreed to support reversion provided it was free to use the bases as before and to introduce nuclear weapons should circumstances require. Since the latter provision would contravene the Three Non-Nuclear Principles,[76] Nixon struck a secret agreement with Prime Minister Satō that, in time of emergency, the United States, upon prior consultation with Japan, would have the right of reentry and transit of nuclear weapons. Japanese records now show that Satō told Japanese officials that "if they say that they are necessary in an emergency situation, we will reply 'yes.' The three non-nuclear principles were a mistake."[77] With that secret understanding in place, Nixon agreed to reversion, which officially would take place on May 15, 1972.

Nevertheless, the fundamental contradictions of the alliance remained; and, in fact, as Japan's continuing economic growth added to the tensions inherent in the relationship, Nixon grew increasingly agitated over Japan's trade practices. Beginning in 1965 the bilateral trade balance had grown rapidly in Japan's favor, and the balance of payments deficit with Tokyo was projected to reach $3 billion by the end of Nixon's first term. US domestic politics of trade brought the issue to the surface. Part of Nixon's irritation sprang from a loss of respect for Satō, who he believed had promised to restrain textile exports to the United States as part of the Okinawa reversion agreement. Nixon needed that agreement for his own domestic political strategy of propitiating southern states. Angered by what he called "Jap betrayal," Nixon was in no mood to spare Japanese sensibilities as he and Kissinger prepared to implement their new foreign policy strategy.[78]

In the summer of 1971 the United States administered two rude shocks to its ally. The first was the centerpiece of its foreign policy revolution. The opening of relations with the People's Republic of China (PRC) after two decades of nonrecognition was carried out without consultation with or advance notice to Japan. The second shock was the announcement of the president's "new economic policies," designed to force the revaluation of the yen. When the president announced in a television address on July 15 that Kissinger had just returned from a secret visit to Beijing and that he himself would soon also visit China, the Japanese were stunned. They had been kept from developing normal relations with the PRC for two decades by US policy, and were always told they would be consulted if the United States changed its policy. But Prime Minister Satō learned of the diplomatic breakthrough that would transform the Cold War system in East Asia just three minutes prior to Nixon's announcement. The purpose was to implement the Nixon doctrine, pressure the Soviet Union to accept détente, and extricate the United States from Vietnam by establishing a new set of relations with the two communist powers. The fallout was momentous for Japan. As Ogata Sadako observed in her study of the event, "No American action left a more profound impact on Japanese foreign policy in the postwar period than the unilateral decision by President Nixon to go to Beijing to seek rapprochement. The impact went far beyond the immediate reaction of sourness. . . . It changed the meaning of the U.S.-Japan Security Treaty and forthwith the alliance itself."[79]

The Nixon opening to China was deeply wounding to the pride of the Japanese, but a second shock was intended, as Nixon said, to "stick it to Japan" for its predatory trading practices.[80] On August 15, 1971, the anniversary of Japanese surrender and one month after the announcement of his planned visit to China, Nixon announced his "New Economic Policy." Aimed primarily at the mounting Japanese trade surplus, this policy cut the dollar loose from gold, imposed an import surcharge, and forced the upward valuation of the yen. Once again, Prime Minister Satō was given only a few minutes of advance warning. In his announcement signaling America's renewed anger with Japan, Nixon chose the anniversary of Japanese surrender and invoked the 1917 Trading with the Enemy Act to imply Japanese treachery, and if anyone missed the implication, he added that the economic threat the United States faced was "far more serious than the challenge that we confronted even in the dark days of Pearl Harbor."[81]

In implementing the diplomatic revolution that opened a new relationship with China, the Americans privately spoke disparagingly of their Japanese ally. Nixon and Kissinger told the Chinese leaders the alliance gave them the ability to control Japanese rearmament and, accordingly, the Chinese ought to support the alliance. Nixon's strategy in meeting with the Chinese leaders was to play "the Japan card." He instructed Kissinger to "put them in fear" and stress "a resurgent and militaristic Japan."[82] Throughout their early meetings with the Chinese leaders, Nixon and Kissinger hinted at the latent danger of a reawakening of Japanese militarism, often implying the Japanese national character was untrustworthy. Since the PRC had always called for the end of the US-Japan alliance and urged Japanese neutralism, Kissinger told Mao and Zhou that the United States would withdraw its forces from Japan if asked, "but I don't think you should rejoice when that day happens, because some day you will regret it just as we today regret how we built up Japan economically."[83]

The strategy worked even better than anticipated, for the Chinese were indeed deeply worried about Japanese resurgence. Mao and Zhou, remembering their own struggle as young revolutionaries with Japanese militarism, were alarmed at Japan's growing industrial strength and the potential to convert it to military power. If, as the Nixon Doctrine intimated, the Americans pulled back from Asia, Japan would develop greater autonomy, acquire nuclear weapons, and replace the US influence in Taiwan. In his memoirs, Kissinger recalled that "Zhou En-lai accused us of tempting Japan into traditional nationalist paths. It took me some time to convince him that the U.S.-Japan alliance was not directed against China"[84] and that the alliance was the best way to control and restrain the unpredictable Japanese. In one of their early conversations in Beijing in 1971, Kissinger contrasted China, which "has a universal outlook but Japan has had a tribal outlook. . . . The Japanese are capable of sudden and explosive changes. They went from feudalism to emperor worship in two to three years. They went from emperor worship to democracy in three months."[85] Zhou agreed and later expressed the same concern to Nixon when he visited: "Japan's feathers have grown on its wings and it is about to take off. . . . Can the U.S. control the 'wild horse' of Japan?"[86]

Nixon and Kissinger succeeded in convincing the Chinese leadership to see the Mutual Security Treaty in a favorable light, persuading them that it served to contain "Japanese unilateralism." As Kissinger later concluded, "Mao and Zhou proved especially solicitous about American-Japanese relations. After years of condemning our security treaty with Japan, they now described it as a means of containing the Soviet Union and preventing the resurgence of Japanese militarism."[87] So persuaded were they, that the Chinese leadership began to worry that trade frictions and Kissinger's slighting of Japan might lead to a break in US-Japan relations. In fact, two years later at one of their meetings, Mao lectured Kissinger on the need to be more attentive to the Japanese, lest a loss of

trust in their American allies lead to their return to traditional nationalism. Kissinger listened while Mao told him that because of his secret
opening to China, "They are afraid of you and you should try to lessen
their fear."[88] Mao added, "When you pass through Japan, you should
perhaps talk a bit more with them. You only talked with them for one
day [on your last visit] and that is not good for their face."[89] Unlike Kissinger, Mao was not disposed to underrate the Japanese. History had
taught Mao an entirely different lesson. Japan was not to be taken lightly,
and he wanted the Americans to pay close attention to Japanese intentions. Kissinger recalled that on his subsequent visit to Beijing, Mao
"applauded my decision to spend a few days in Tokyo on my way home.
Japan [Mao continued] must not feel neglected by the United States;
Japan was inherently insecure and sensitive."[90]

The distance the administration had moved from the sentimental discourse of the "equal partnership" revealed the many peculiar aspects of
the alliance. Most obvious was that it was intended to control Japan and
ensure that it was not free to choose its own future. Some Americans
worried that the Nixon-Kissinger treatment of their ally, whatever the
irritation over its trade practices, was dangerously harsh. George Ball,
former undersecretary of state in the Kennedy and Johnson administrations, described the Japanese as prone to unpredictable and irrational
behavior. In the midst of the Nixon administration's rough treatment of
the Japanese, Ball cautioned, "You never know when the Japanese are
going to go ape." He described the Japanese as a people motivated by
"pride, nationalism, and often downright irrationality."[91]

So far as pride and nationalism were concerned, Ball was accurate
in gauging the Japanese response to their treatment. From all parts of
the political spectrum, Japanese leaders expressed anger over the Nixon
shocks. To the conservatives, the humiliation was obvious. To the
progressives, the Nixon shocks confirmed their longtime criticism of dependence on the United States and their contention that the national
interest lay in adopting an autonomous foreign policy. Overcoming
their anger and injured pride, the Japanese moved quickly to adapt to
the new circumstances, achieving normalization of relations with the
PRC and adjusting their economy to the revalued yen. The haste that
the Japanese made in normalizing relations ahead of the United States
drew Kissinger's wrath, as he exploded to an aide, "Of all the treacherous sons of bitches, the Japs take the cake."[92]

Although bruising Japanese pride, the Nixon opening to China laid the groundwork for mutual accommodation among the three powers. It led to at least tacit US-Japan-China security cooperation against the Russians. Over the next two decades a consensus on many issues became tantamount to a triple entente to contain Soviet influence in East Asia. In addition to this virtual alliance against the Russians, Japan and the United States acknowledged that Taiwan was a part of China and all three powers pledged to work for a peaceful reconciliation. Beijing accepted America's continued regional security role, including the alliances with Japan and South Korea. Japan and the United States encouraged China's economic reforms and its entry into the World Bank, the Asian Development Bank, and the IMF. China was seen to be on the path to political reforms, and the United States soft-pedaled differences with China over issues of human rights. For its part, Japan was not concerned about these issues.

While initially harsh in its treatment of an ally, the Nixon opening helped create a new and balanced triangular situation, easing Sino-Japanese enmity and leaving the United States in the position of having good relations with both nations. This implicit entente of the three powers from the mid-1970s to the end of the Cold War was an unusual period in a century of triangular relations. For more than fifteen years, until the Tiananmen Incident of 1989, the United States enjoyed close ties with both Japan and China and did not have to choose between them.

Difficulties of Communication

Together with the contradictory purposes of the two allies and the complex dynamics of their relations, still another feature of this peculiar alliance was the difficulty of communications between the elites of the two countries. The Japanese have been notoriously poor communicators in their international relations, and historically their foreign policy has suffered from this shortcoming.[93] George Kennan observed that the Japanese are "as inept at communication as the Chinese are facile."[94] Despite the long years of the alliance, genuine communication was generally absent. Brent Scowcroft, the well-respected national security advisor to the first President Bush, found Japan's decision making so opaque that it "was probably the most difficult country we had to deal with. I don't think we understood the Japanese and I don't think the Japanese understood us." He chose, therefore, to delegate to his subordinates almost all Japan-related policy.[95]

The cultural critic John Nathan is surely correct in observing that "Japanese are almost certainly not the people they appear to be when dealing with foreigners outside Japan in languages other than their own. . . . Abroad, the Japanese tend . . . to recede into a formal, tight-lipped impassivity that is actually a kind of resignation about ever making themselves understood. This unfortunate withdrawal is often interpreted as lifelessness."[96] The nuances and subtleties of Japanese expression are usually lost in this cultural mismatch.

Few American leaders have had the interest, much less the background, required to understand the intricacies of Japanese culture. "When I first came to office," Henry Kissinger later confessed, "there was no major country I understood less than Japan. . . . I did not grasp Japan's unique character."[97] In his memoirs Kissinger recalled: "Neither I nor my colleagues possessed a very subtle grasp of Japanese culture or psychology."[98] Nor did he have the time or the inclination to try. Japan seemed of limited importance in the great-power calculus. During his tenure as national security advisor and as secretary of state he gave short shrift to Japan.[99] Privately Kissinger derided the Japanese as "little Sony salesmen" or "small and petty bookkeepers" whose diplomatic documents were nothing more than trading ledgers. He detested invitations to the Japanese embassy in Washington because, he said, they always served him wiener schnitzel. Kissinger was drawn to power and its expression. He reveled in his meetings with Mao and Zhou Enlai. "Kissinger," wrote one of his close associates, "was fascinated by the Chinese, especially the urbane and sophisticated Chou En-lai. By contrast the Japanese always seemed prosaic, obtuse, unworthy of his sustained attention."[100] Journalist Don Oberdorfer, who covered Kissinger during his term as secretary of state, describes him as unsurpassed in his dismissal of Japan—what was sometimes called "Japan passing." "Kissinger," he writes, ". . . couldn't find anybody in Japan who was an equal in talking about the affairs of the world." Oberdorfer recounts Kissinger's disdain when he recalled being invited to come to Japan once before entering government. "I don't zink they understand me." He said with heavy sarcasm, "They took me down to a Japanese inn in Kyoto. *Vatever* I asked them, they sent a man to press my pants."[101] He was contemptuous of Japanese leaders not simply because they lacked the military and political power that drew his respect, but also because he found them inarticulate and not conceptual and, owing to their "anonymous style," uninteresting and unworthy of his time and attention. As he later recorded, "The typical Japanese leader is impelled by his culture to avoid explicitness in dealing with foreign counterparts—at nearly all costs. This creates an almost impenetrable cultural barrier in diplomacy." It is this unique background that presents the United States with an alliance partner, as Kissinger writes, "with intangibles of culture that America is ill-prepared to understand fully."[102]

Reflecting years after he left government, Kissinger wrote, "The Japanese in my experience are not great communicators. They tend to operate within their consensus, and when they get dropped out of the consensus and get into a dialogue with other cultures it's tough because they don't feel they have the authority to make independent decisions. So even for many of us who have Japanese friends whom we value, the problem of communication is very difficult."[103]

A good example of the difficulty of communication was Kissinger's relationship with Ōhira Masayoshi, foreign minister during Kissinger's tenure, later prime minister, and one of the most universally respected of Japanese political leaders. The soft-spoken Ōhira did not escape Kissinger's contempt. "Do you know this guy Ōhira?" he asked the journalist Don Oberdorfer, who responded: "Well, yeah, I've met him a few times." Kissinger said, "Tell me something. If he's so smart why doesn't he ever say anything?"[104] With a little reflection, Kissinger might have understood why the Japanese would be wary of him. After all, he was Nixon's national security advisor who had engineered the secret opening to China without bothering to inform the Japanese in advance. Years later, in his memoirs, Kissinger would reflect, "It is a dangerous mistake to think of Japanese leaders as unimpressive and to confuse their inarticulateness with lack of perception."[105] And he belatedly came to understand why Ōhira "was not about to reveal his thinking to an American he did not know and whose record on matters Japanese had revealed the absence of a certain delicacy."[106] In his memoirs Kissinger wrote of his belated recognition of Ōhira's character and wisdom with perhaps a faux self-deprecation. "Masayoshi Ōhira was in the classic Japanese mold, which, it is fair to say, is not automatically compatible with my more assertive temperament. It would be difficult to find two more different personalities than the subtle, indirect Japanese Foreign Minister and the analytical Secretary of State." Recalling his earlier irritation at Ōhira's laconic behavior, Kissinger, his contempt transformed by generous remarks Ōhira had made about him in his autobiography, allowed that "as time went on . . . Ōhira taught me patiently about things Japanese. He expanded my understanding of nuance. He masked his great ability in a modest bearing."[107]

Still another poignant illustration of the difficulties of communication is found in the Japanese business leader with whom Kissinger and other American political and business leaders thought they had finally achieved real personal communication: Morita Akio, cofounder of Sony. Kissinger recalled, "Morita could conduct a dialogue, and while he was a very patriotic Japanese and a firm defender of the Japanese point of view, he could communicate it in a way that was meaningful to non-Japanese. . . . He was probably the single most effective Japanese spokesman I ever met."[108] Morita's biographer, however, described Morita's interaction with foreigners as all performance. He discovered that Morita and his wife kept copious detailed notes about the personalities and idiosyncratic likes and dislikes of each of their foreign friends.[109] In fact, Morita's eldest son recalled that his father went to great lengths to give the impression of mutual understanding. "He had to act as the most international-understanding businessman in Japan. Actually, I don't think that was true, but he had to act that way. . . . He tried very hard, and he worked and he studied hard to play that role. . . . But it was never real." Morita learned to "turn off" his Japanese thinking and simulate Western behavior in order to "communicate." He once confided to a Japanese television commentator how he accommodated to Western thinking:

> *Morita:* Grammar and pronunciation aren't as important as expressing yourself in a way that matches the way Westerners think, which is very different from our thought process. You have to switch off your Japanese way of seeing things, or they will never understand what you are saying. First of all, they want to hear the conclusion right away; in English sentence structure, the conclusion comes first.
>
> *Shiroyama:* I've heard that one of our prime ministers was on his way to the United States for the first time and asked you for advice, and you suggested the critical thing was to start right out with a "yes" or "no" followed by a brief explanation—

Morita: When they ask questions or express an opinion, they want to know right away whether the other party agrees or opposes them. So in English, "yes" or "no" comes first. We Japanese prefer to save the "yes" or "no" for last. Particularly when the answer is "no," we put off saying that as long as possible, and they find that exasperating.

Shiroyama: But in Japan, as you explained, we don't come out with "yes" or "no" but prefer expressions like "I'll take this under consideration." Our feeling is that vagueness in these cases is less offensive. So when you're in America you must be clear, and when you return to Japan you must be vague—is it hard to switch back and forth?

Morita: It is more difficult than you can imagine.[110]

The impression Morita, this apparently most successful of communicators, gave to American business and political leaders that he was one of them was the result of self-consciously suppressing his Japanese thinking and adapting to American thought processes. Here was Morita, his biographer observed, "appraising Westerners from the opposite side of a cultural divide, working hard to decipher the puzzles that stood between him and successful communication, but aware of a separation." Given this effort to conceal from his American friends the distance between them and his true feelings, it was a matter of no small embarrassment when a book he coauthored in 1990 with the blustering and flamboyant nationalist Ishihara Shintarō was translated. This strident tract, *The Japan That Can Say "No,"* was clearly not intended for foreign readership. It exhorted Japanese leaders to confront foreign demands regarding their trade practices with a defiance that would demonstrate Japan's assertiveness. More than Kissinger and Morita's other American friends realized, he harbored intense nationalist feelings. As Morita's biographer observed, "It was as if a mask he had always been careful to wear in the presence of his Western friends had been momentarily torn away," and he went to great (and unsuccessful) lengths to try to suppress the translation of this tract into English.[111]

By the time he wrote his memoirs years later, Kissinger professed to have gained an understanding and appreciation of Japanese political leaders and their culturally rooted unique patterns of decision making:

The Japanese system has not been easy for Americans to comprehend. It took me a long time to grasp how decisions are made. . . . One of the features of the Japanese system is its opaqueness to outsiders. . . . A foreigner underestimates the Japanese at his peril. It is true that they are not as conceptually adept as, say, the Chinese, as articulate as most Europeans, or as boisterously open and forthcoming as Americans. [Japanese leaders] have not been selected for any of these qualities. They gather intelligence about foreigners; they do not seek to persuade them with words. They chart future actions for their society; they do not need to articulate its purposes in rhetoric. . . . It is a dangerous mistake to think of Japanese leaders as unimpressive and to confuse their inarticulateness with lack of perception.[112]

Kissinger came to see that Japan had as clear a foreign policy strategy as any other power. In fact, he recorded, "In my view Japanese decisions have been the most farsighted and intelligent of any major nation of the postwar era even while the Japanese have acted with the understated, anonymous style characteristic of their culture."[113]

The Alliance and Japan's Troubled Spirit

The hegemonic alliance was intended to control and manage a weak Japan and maintain bases there for the long term. Japan, with impaired sovereignty, became a military satellite, a subordinate state, and could be treated with the paternalism of Reischauer or with the obtuseness of Nixon and Kissinger. Under such circumstances, Japanese leaders devised their own separate, often cynical, purpose for the alliance, which was to use it to free Japan from responsibility for its own security and concentrate its full energies on economic growth. Citing Article 9, Japan developed a growing list of self-binding policies to keep it from international politics and responsibilities, and especially from involvement in American military engagements. It became a twisted and anomalous alliance of contradictory purpose.

The strategy the Japanese elites formulated was remarkably successful in allowing Japan to pursue power as a trading state. But it was also flawed because it acquiesced in the loss of an independent foreign policy. After surrender and occupation, Japan inevitably would have been dependent for a time on the United States. But to prolong this dependence indefinitely as a matter of national policy required suppression of national pride and self-respect. Both the left wing and the right wing of Japanese politics rejected the Yoshida strategy and advocated an autonomous foreign policy. Those on the left sought independence from American imperialism and a neutral stance in the Cold War. On the right, the political nationalists advocated rearmament to achieve a more equal alliance. Throughout the Cold War period of Japan's mercantilist foreign policy, a strong undercurrent of opposition to dependence persisted.

The shocking suicide of the great postwar novelist Mishima Yukio on November 25, 1970, was a dramatic act to arouse a nation to the loss of its samurai spirit. Living under a foreign-imposed constitution that required the abandonment of ancient traditions of martial valor, to be replaced by materialist and merchant values, and passively submitting to American political and military dominance was demeaning. Mishima went to Self-Defense headquarters and from the front balcony of the building harangued a battalion of cadets below, challenging them "in the name of the emperor" to restore the national soul.[114] When the cadets began to hoot and jeer, the novelist went inside and committed ritual suicide. Mishima's effort to revive the "withered soul" of Japan, while viewed at the time as an aberrant act, nonetheless remained in the minds of many Japanese "an exemplary metaphor for Japan's frustrations with its dependent foreign policy."[115]

Richard Sneider, the veteran State Department expert on Japan, captured the nature of the malaise in reporting on a conversation that he had on April 26, 1968, with Foreign Minister Miki Takeo, who complained to him of the American expectation that Japan support the US position in Vietnam:

These frustrations with the U.S. have inevitably turned more and more Japanese to brooding about the need for an "independent" Japanese foreign policy—e.g. escaping what Miki has called "excessive dependence" on the U.S. This is not new. It is a theme which has reoccurred periodically throughout the post-occupation era. . . . The hard fact is that Japan cannot escape from its economic and military dependence on the U.S. without a fundamental and costly policy change. This change, the Government and the vast majority of Japanese are unprepared to undertake. When the Japanese take a second hard look, they find that no amount of optics or whistling in the dark can override this dependence or the inherent inequality in the U.S. and Japanese position. This circumstance, however, only deepens the Japanese frustration.[116]

Yoshida's biographer, Kōsaka Masataka, admitted that the greatest challenge of the Yoshida strategy was maintaining national morale. To survive as a trading nation, Japan had to manage its crisis of spirit. All trading nations, he wrote, face this crisis because they stand for no fixed principles but simply adapt to whatever the situation requires: "This, however, tends to weaken the self-confidence and identity of the persons engaged in the operation. They gradually come to lose sight of what they really value and even who they really are."[117] Kōsaka, while recognizing that this opportunistic international behavior created "a serious identity problem for the nation," urged that Japan, in its own long-term interests, continue to adhere to the mercantilist course and "preserve an indomitable spiritual strength without having any clear-cut and explicit principles."[118]

The Yoshida Doctrine allowed Japan a kind of hothouse existence in which it took no stand and willingly deferred to dependence on the American security guarantee. As time passed, most Japanese were content to shelter under the US umbrella and enjoy the fruits of prosperity made possible by the Pax Americana. Observing "the inability of Japan to act as an independent state," a Keio University scholar wrote that "the fact that Japanese citizens . . . did not face the national problems of a modern citizenry, such as the exercise of military power and sacrifice they might have to make for the sake of the public good, would become a major liability for Japanese diplomacy afterwards."[119] The price for continued passive dependence would someday have to be paid, for it masked and concealed a restless and troubled national spirit.

8

Competing Capitalisms

B OTH THE AMERICAN WORLD order and the Occupation's plans to reform Japan were based on confidence in the universality of the
American model of development and represented an old Western idea
in a very clear and simple way. Ever since Japan had entered the modern
world in the Meiji period, it had confronted the Western worldview that
there was only one path to modernity—the Western way. It was a
product of the Enlightenment view that universal laws of nature governed human behavior and progress was determined by universal forces
of historical development rather than by particular trends of national
history. Progress, in other words, was unilinear. In the West's view, if
Japan were to modernize, it must follow the West's lead. It must look to
the cultural example of the West, which embodied "civilization." Civilized development meant not only that people would use the same machines; they would adopt the same laws and political institutions, think
and behave in similar ways, and accept the same social values.

Being the first non-Western nation to industrialize, Japan struggled
throughout the prewar period with the implications of this unilinear
view for its own civilization. A universal path of development left little
room for cultural pluralism. The Japanese in the Meiji period were the
first to ask what was the key to developing a society as advanced as
Western industrial societies. What was the key to achieving wealth and
power? What was essential to adopt from the West? What in Japanese
culture could be preserved?[1] The answers were not clear, but Japanese
had already proved adept at selective borrowing from foreign cultures

to strengthen and improve their own civilization. This had been evident in early Japanese history when institutions and practices of the great T'ang civilization in China had been adopted to order and strengthen a fledgling Japanese state. The Meiji borrowing from Western civilization in the 1870s and 1880s was more enthusiastic and extensive than any other cultural borrowing the world has seen before or since. Initially, Japanese were receptive to all manner of borrowings, but over time they adopted selectively from the best practices found in the West, taking what was useful and fitting it into their own society.[2] Along with this historical proclivity to borrow from advanced civilizations was always an innate and instinctive confidence of being able to adapt these foreign influences to fit a unique and distinctive Japanese cultural essence. As the great British historian of Japan, Sir George Sansom, observed of such periods of extraordinary receptivity to foreign culture and ideas: "The power and prestige of a foreign culture seem as if they would overwhelm and transform Japan, but always there is a hard, non-absorbent core of individual character, which resists and in its turn works upon the invading influence."[3] In the prewar period, Japanese managed to find their own path to modernity through selective borrowing while maintaining many distinctive values and practices from their own civilization.

In the post–World War II period, the Japanese were once again open and receptive to foreign influence. That experience is often compared to Meiji and called "the second opening of Japan." What especially distinguished the more recent experience was the element of coercion. Where the Meiji Japanese had voluntarily chosen to adopt selectively from Western institutional models, the postwar experience of cultural change was imposed by an occupying military power, and with the coercion was the old unilinear idea and the expectation that Japan must eventually converge with the Western pattern of development. Nevertheless, along with such coercion was also a war-weary people's receptivity to liberating aspects of the new order and enthusiasm for the private consumption of consumer culture that came with the American revolution in Japan. The ingrained inclination to adapt and to keep abreast of the times was notably focused on overcoming the relative material backwardness and especially on catching up by building a nation of science and technology. But rather than accept the unilinear view, Japan devised its own path to modernity. Over time, the Japanese once again worked on the invading influences and gradually remade them to suit their own purposes and distinctive cultural identity. They adapted the imposed economic, social, and political institutions of the American world order to fit their own history and national interest. Disregarding the unilinear view, they continued to find their own distinctive path to modernity.

The Roots of Postwar Japanese Capitalism

In charting their postwar recovery and economic growth strategies, the Japanese chose a course in direct conflict with the liberal economic doctrines that inspired the American world order. The economic philosophies of Japan and the United States clashed in their fundamental principles and became the source of persistent tension. Postwar Japan instituted policies of developmentalism and mercantilism sharply at variance with the international free trade order the United States had created. These policies of economic nationalism were instrumental in the making of "the Japanese economic miracle," but they embroiled the two nations in continuing trade friction that embittered alliance relations.

The sharply contrasting capitalist systems of the two countries were partly a reflection of the diverging cultural traditions of the two countries, but also resulted from their divergent paths to industrialization. As a late-developing economy seeking to catch up with the advanced industrial nations, Japan had given primacy since the opening of the country in the Meiji period to the role of the state in guiding its economy. Over the course of a century, through remarkable statecraft and a shrewd pragmatism focused on the national interest, Japan devised its own particular mix of policies and institutions to overcome economic backwardness and to close the gap with the advanced industrial societies. The Meiji leaders never accepted the Manchester School's liberal economic paradigm as appropriate for Japan. They set their own course for industrial development. They did not accept the views of laissez-faire, but instead argued that government intervention could speed the process of development. Ōkubo Toshimichi, the dominant leader of the 1870s, dismissed free-market views. A government role, he said, was "absolutely necessary" even if it went "against the laws of political economy." Japan, he added, was "something different (*ibutsu*)" and would advance by "different laws (*hensoku*)."[4] From whence came this confidence in the role of government in the economy? In part it came from the political economism of the late Tokugawa period when samurai reformers came to believe that their domains could strengthen themselves through government-run enterprise. It also came in part from the great influence the German Historical School of economics exercised on Japanese bureaucrats from the 1880s on.[5] The Japanese learned that they could avoid the disruptive aspects of industrialization by preserving traditional institutions and their inherent values of social cooperation. Japan embraced many aspects of German nonliberal capitalism, which had restrained the role of the market in the interest of maintaining embedded institutions of social cohesion and collectivism.[6]

The Meiji government promoted import substitution and acquisition of the newest technology, and fostered industries—including munitions, shipbuilding, shipping, railways, iron and steel, heavy engineering, and machine tools—that it saw as being in the national interest. Subsequently, in response to the exigencies of the Great Depression and the Pacific War, the Japanese defined a more elaborate set of policies to promote specific industries that would speed the growth process and increase industrial productive efficiency. Government intervention sharply increased. Bureaucrats devised policies to stimulate war-related industries. Cartels were organized and laws provided for government financing, tax benefits, and curtailment of foreign and domestic competition. The wartime experience profoundly influenced many of the central features of the postwar economy. Just as it had been the goal of establishing its economic autonomy that led Japan to gamble its future by military means in the Pacific War, so in the postwar period it became the goal by a more elaborately defined industrial policy to restore its independence.

Japanese capitalism in the postwar period can best be described as "developmental state capitalism."[7] This role of government in the modern Japanese economy did not mean that it became a command economy. Nor was it a socialist economy. Instead, it was more like what one scholar characterized as a "bridled capitalism." The economic system was not one in which market forces were given free rein. Rather, it consisted of "policies and institutions, reflecting a shared ideology of 'catching up with the West,' [which] effectively performed the role a bridle."[8] While preserving private ownership of property, the government embedded incentives in the market to promote savings and rapid acquisition of new technologies, and to provide cheap and plentiful capital for the development of critical industries.

These policies and institutions powered the nation's postwar economic growth and provided a model for all other developing economies. It was an achievement of considerable historical importance. Writing in 2011, the Nobel Prize–winning economist Michael Spence pointed to the role Japan played in pioneering the strategies pursued by other late-developing economies of the post–World War II period.

> By 1945 [Japan] was a defeated nation with an uncertain future. But it was about to become the first sustained high-growth country in the postwar period—indeed in recorded history. Its growth, and the underlying strategies and policies, became an example emulated all over Asia and eventually more broadly. Looking back, one finds it hard to overstate the importance of the example the Japan case set. Among other things, it grew at unprecedented rates armed with almost no natural resource wealth of the conventional kind, and in so doing upset much of the conventional economic thinking about the sources of wealth and growth in the developing world.[9]

What were the strategies and policies that powered the extraordinary Japanese achievement? They were not those the Americans had in mind for Japan when they imposed economic reforms in the early Occupation period. While the economic principles and practices of Japan were directly at odds with American economic liberalism, it is nevertheless true that the American-led world order provided the conditions under which Japan could achieve its remarkable growth. The expanding world trade the US-led international economic order promoted through the International Monetary Fund (IMF) and the General Agreement on Trade and Tariffs (GATT) permitted a vigorous expansion of Japanese manufactured goods and the ready purchase of abundant and cheap raw materials. Moreover, as part of its Cold War strategy, the United States kept its market wide open to Japanese exports to promote Japanese growth. American technology was made cheaply available. As one Japanese scholar observed, the international economic environment "looked as though heaven had created it for Japan's economic growth."[10]

American Economic Liberalism

The centerpiece of the liberal vision Roosevelt and American policy-makers held for the postwar order was the creation of an open world economy. The lesson the 1930s had taught was that closed economic blocs, colonial empires, protective tariffs, unfair economic competition, autarkic policies, and the resulting malfunctioning of the world economy had been a principal cause of the Great Depression and world conflict. If peace and security were to be achieved, protectionism and exclusive economic blocs must be replaced. Free trade, nondiscriminatory access to resources, and open markets would promote interdependence that in turn would ensure a peaceful world. American leadership in creating a new international economic order was "critical in salvaging international capitalism from the wreckage of the interwar depression."[11]

The vision of the postwar international economic order sprang from the values and practices of the American economic model. Americans believed that economic activity was pursued to create wealth and serve the individual consumer. Markets should be competitive to serve the interests of the consumer, and where they were not, antitrust regulation must be established. In the abstract, the norm was that markets were self-regulating, although during the New Deal this ideal was diluted. Governments might intervene where there was market failure. Exceptions to the norm existed and were found especially in matters of national defense and agriculture.

Underlying Americans' norms were, of course, their own national experience and history. In many ways it was a unique and exceptional national experience and should not have been regarded as the basis of a universal model. Endowed with free security, abundant national resources, and an egalitarian social tradition, Americans were able to afford a highly decentralized and individualist political economy. Economic development to the Americans seemed relatively easy to explain under these circumstances, and they believed that other nations should follow their course.

In the Atlantic Charter of August 1941, Roosevelt and Churchill had declared as their war aims a lowering of tariff barriers, equal access to the world's raw materials, and international collaboration to promote labor standards, employment security, and social welfare. The authoritarian economies of the Axis Powers would be reformed and integrated into a new postwar economic order. International institutions must be created by which nations would collaborate to manage economic order and prevent the return to the economic nationalism that led to World War II. The lesson was translated into the Bretton Woods System for promoting a multilateral framework for international trade and economic development and the establishment of a set of international institutions including the IMF, the World Bank, and the GATT. A liberal multilateral economic order would allow the United States to embed its ideals of the Open Door into the postwar order. The American ideal of a liberal international order was, as one political scientist described it, "vigorously prosperous democracies, enjoying security from military aggression, permitting the free movement of goods, money, and enterprise among themselves, and promoting the rapid development and integration of those nations whom liberal progress had left behind."[12] Roosevelt's secretary of treasury Henry Morgenthau declared that the new postwar economic order would mark the death of economic nationalism.[13]

Pursuit of an open world economy was more than idealism and more than abstract economic theory. As the world's dominant industrial economy, the United States sought to restructure the international system in accordance with its own economic and security interests and to create an interdependent world economy centered on the American economy. At the end of World War II, America's ideology and self-interest dictated creation of a world of economic openness. Free trade, after all, is the ideology of the strong. Because the United States had the largest and most competitive economy, a free trade order would be congenial to American interests. More than ever, the Open Door was essential. America's export-oriented industries had a powerful interest in keeping overseas markets open to American products and investment and in providing the sources of raw materials.

This American vision of a liberal international economic system guided its reform of postwar Japan's economy. Underlying and supporting Japan's international economic order must be liberal institutions that would stabilize and protect free market mechanisms. It was fundamental to Roosevelt's vision to include in the Atlantic Charter a commitment to promoting a welfare state through the kind of social protections the New Deal had sponsored. Economic democracy would provide domestic support for the international liberal order.

SCAP planners set out to accomplish "a wide distribution of income and of the ownership of the means of production." They prodded the Diet to pass a trade union act in December 1945, patterned after the National Labor Relations Act passed by the United States Congress ten years earlier. This "Magna Carta of Japanese labor" guaranteed the rights of workers to organize, to bargain collectively, and to strike. Subsequent legislation provided for acceptable working conditions, unemployment insurance, and procedures for resolution of labor disputes. Although union membership soared in the next few years, the unions functioned in ways distinct from what New Dealers envisioned. It was not uncommon for the head of a firm to take the lead in organizing the workers into a union. Identification of workers with the company for which they worked was often the result.

Far more successful was SCAP's land reform, which redistributed land on a massive scale and reduced the rate of land worked by tenant farmers from nearly 50 percent in prewar days to less than 10 percent, transforming the countryside into a society of independent farmers. For the American liberal vision, most important was the reform of Japan's giant oligopolistic financial combines known as the zaibatsu. The vast economic empires encompassed by such zaibatsu as Mitsui, Mitsubishi, Sumitomo, and Yasuda were among the largest in the world, sprawling over a variety of fields including extractive industries, manufacturing companies, trading firms, transport facilities, and banking. These combines sprang up with Japan's rapid economic growth, which had required a high concentration of capital, skilled labor, technology, and entrepreneurial risk. The giant Mitsui zaibatsu, for example, was owned by the Mitsui family and managed by a holding company that supervised seventy direct corporate affiliates that in turn controlled hundreds of other smaller affiliates.

This concentration of economic power appalled the Americans. The American industrialist Edwin Pauley, who advised the Occupation, warned that "unless the zaibatsu are broken up the Japanese have little prospect of ever being able to govern themselves as free men. As long as the Zaibatsu survive, Japan will be their Japan."[14] SCAP brought the New Deal's antitrust specialist to Japan to size up the situation. Corwin Edwards, an economist from Northwestern University who had advised FDR's attorney general on antitrust issues, concluded that the concentration of power in the hands of the zaibatsu was "beyond comparison with any other capitalistic industrial nation."[15] He recommended steps to destroy this structure of economic power in order to permit formation of an independent middle class capable of opposing a return to militarism.

SCAP accordingly embarked on an ambitious program, breaking up holding companies, requiring companies to sell off stocks to the public to diffuse ownership, and prodding the Diet to establish a Fair Trade Commission, patterned closely after American antimonopoly laws. The commission was charged with policing business and prohibiting monopoly practices that restrained trade and free and open competition. Far-reaching reform of the Japanese industrial structure would not only do away with sources of militarism and provide support for a peaceful domestic order but also serve to integrate Japan into the new open world economy the Americans were intent on creating. The Japanese welcomed the American vision of an international free trade order that would provide equal access to markets and raw materials. But Japan's plans for its domestic economic structure were often at odds with what SCAP deemed essential to the integration of Japan into the international free trade order.

A Japanese Long-Term Economic Strategy

The prospects for the Japanese economy at the end of the war were dire. But the remarkable fact now seen clearly in retrospect is that Japanese leaders formulated in the immediate postwar years a long-term plan for recovery and economic development. Especially noteworthy as the war came to an end was a group of Japan's leading economists from business, the bureaucracy, and academia who formed a committee under the auspices of the Foreign Ministry to begin developing a vision for the future of the Japanese economy. In the spring of 1946 this committee completed a document titled "The Plan for the Reconstruction of Japan's Postwar Economy," which foreshadowed a kind of grand strategy for the economy just as the Yoshida Doctrine was a grand strategy for postwar Japanese foreign policy. In fact, we may see this plan as companion to the Yoshida Doctrine. As one authority writes, "This lengthy study proved as close to a long-term blueprint for subsequent policymaking as one can find."[16] Shortly after becoming prime minister in the spring of 1946, Yoshida himself met weekly with the group to discuss its plan.

This group of leading economists was organized and chaired by Ōkita Saburō, who should be remembered as a key architect of Japan's remarkable economic growth in the postwar decades. Ōkita began his career in the Greater East Asia Ministry, the part of the wartime government charged with administering areas occupied by the Japanese. There, his special interest was in the procuring of raw materials and resources from these areas. The following anecdote reveals something of his thinking as the war entered its last months. In the spring of 1945, Ōkita visited an old friend who was an engineering professor at the Tokyo Imperial University. Knowing the war was already lost, the two men fell to talking about the lessons learned and Japan's postwar prospects. The engineer recorded in his diary that Ōkita felt not all was lost if Japan drew the proper lesson from its tragic experience, namely, that "Japan, poorly endowed with natural resources, must shape its future around precision engineering." In other words, Ōkita believed that Japan must concentrate its energies on taking imported raw materials and fashioning them into high-quality products for export:

> Ōkita made himself comfortable and we spoke for a long time. He told me this story from around 1882 which an Englishman—it might have been Bagehot—used to tell as a warning to the people of his time. A poor warrior wanted to buy a splendid suit of armor but had no money, so he cut down on the amount of food he ate and little by little saved enough to buy a fine suit of armor. A war broke out and courageously he left to fight, but because his body had become so weak from his years of semi-starvation, he could not bear the weight of his armor and was soon slain by the enemy. This was just what happened to Japan. He did not think that a defeated Japan would be allowed to rearm at all, but this would probably be a blessing in disguise. I completely agreed with what he said. I will actually be happy if rearmament is completely prohibited. An army in uniform is not the only sort of army. Scientific technology and fighting spirit under a business suit will be our underground army.[17]

The group Ōkita chaired was acutely aware of the dire straits in which the war had left Japan—resource poor, dispossessed of the empire from which it had received raw materials, and facing a punitive occupation. Yet what is striking about its report is the fundamental optimism the committee held for the economy if it were reconfigured for peaceful economic pursuits. One famous economist in the group later recalled that their meetings were held in the "burn-out South Manchurian Railway Building [in Tokyo] and in the cold, unheated place we discussed Japan's future. . . . Those meetings mobilized nearly all Japan's economic experts, who engaged in discussion with all the *élan* of patriots of the Meiji Restoration."[18]

The economists in the group had played a key role in the managed economy of wartime Japan. They possessed deep experience in state intervention in the economy, and they brought this perspective to planning the future course of the Japanese economy. During the 1930s, the conjunction of the Great Depression, the onset of war, and the rise of fascism greatly increased the imperative to bring the economy under state management. Private ownership was maintained, but the profit principle was restrained; planning and regulation were sharply increased. Japan departed decisively from orthodox liberal free market capitalism. German theories of achieving greater efficiency through "industrial rationalization" were influential. These theories limited competition though government-sponsored trusts and cartels. Strategic industries were designated for priority in resource allocation, government financing, tax benefits, and protective measures designed to curtail foreign and domestic competition. As one economist in the Ōkita group had written in 1937, "It is no longer possible to realize this goal [of a managed economy] by simply depending on entrepreneurs' initiative. Nowadays, the state has to exercise its power and directly assume its leadership in economic activities. In a semi war situation, an economy led by the state has to be coercive."[19]

The economists in the Ōkita group brought this experience to their strategic thinking about recovery in the postwar period. Their 1946 plan welcomed the removal of the military leadership and its economic priorities. The reforms the Occupation would make in democratizing the economy would be useful in reconfiguring the economy. Improved labor conditions, tenancy reforms, and dissolving the concentrated power of the zaibatsu would all be positive developments. But above all, American plans for an open international economy and creation of a free trade order would serve the interest of Japanese recovery. The report asserted that "the removal of world trade barriers and the promotion of international trade to the maximum under the leadership of United States . . . should be welcomed by Japan as promising a bright future for the nation, which depends so much on foreign trade."[20] The Ōkita group thereby stressed the transition from the autarkic pursuit of the 1931–1945 period to an active participation in international trade. Japan should shift from an inward to an outward orientation.

The value the Ōkita committee saw in an international free trade order was the access resource-poor Japan would have to raw materials and markets for industrial development. By a carefully conceived industrial policy, the Japanese economy should be structured to take advantage of the open international market. Sectoral policies to promote particular industries should be determined. Priorities should be set strategically, choosing export competitive industries for government support. The advantage Japan had was a well-educated, hardworking labor force that during the war had been highly trained to develop the military needs of the economy. This workforce could be redirected to peaceful pursuits and move steadily into more advanced products. Throughout the prewar period, although the importance of machinery and armaments was growing, cotton and silk textiles had continued to dominate the manufacturing sector. Therefore, "the nation's industries must shift gradually to the manufacture of sophisticated and high-grade commodities that will . . . be competitive with their counterparts in the rest of the world."[21] Japan should aim to develop cutting-edge products that would be in high demand in the most developed markets, especially the United States.

What is remarkable in the thinking of the economists in the Ōkita group is that they were not simply planning the recovery and restoration of the Japanese economy. They were thinking of a long-term strategy for steadily improving Japan's position through plans with a strong nationalist orientation that emphasized ways to strengthen Japan in the competition among nations. Upgrading Japan's industrial structure would allow Japan to steadily advance through the product cycle of increasingly sophisticated value-added manufacturers and to move up the hierarchy of the international division of labor. The insight and vision of these economists were remarkable. They possessed what Joseph Schumpeter called "the capacity of seeing things in a way which afterwards proves to be true."[22]

Their economic vision was quite different from the Americans' liberal vision emphasizing openness and free trade. The committee "explicitly warned against using America as a model."[23] As the report stated, "The waste of economic power that would result from allowing laissez faire play to market forces will not be permitted."[24] Looking at developments in the Soviet Union and Great Britain, and even in New Deal policies, the report asserted that the world had entered "an era of State capitalism or an age of controlled, organized capitalism."[25] Rather than looking toward a future economic vision of laissez-faire, Japan must look to centralized planning to develop large-capacity industries for an export-led growth strategy that emphasized high-value-added products— machinery, precision instruments, optical and camera goods, chemical goods, and vehicles. To rebuild the economy, planners must coordinate foreign trade and, above all, limit the influence of foreign capital and avoid being "economically colonized."[26] A recovery dependent on foreign capital would lead to a loss of independence. Economic bureaucrats would plan and guide economic development so as to protect newly developing industries, limit wasteful competition and increase market efficiency, coordinate investment and technological innovation, and limit foreign investment. While welcoming the American liberal vision for the international economy, Japanese economists had a vision for their own domestic economy that was very much at odds with economic liberalism.

To guide an export-led strategy, the committee recommended establishing administrative agencies for the specific purpose of promoting foreign trade. A planned economy with government playing a leading role in capital accumulation, promoting technological innovation, managing "strict foreign exchange control," and moving the economy into a wholly new mix of products would require a special agency. "Foreign trade will be of vital importance to the Japanese economy in the future. So there appears necessary to set up an institution for comprehensive research on foreign trade, which will undertake systematic investigation and research on various problems including trends in overseas products, provide guidance to export-oriented domestic industries, guarantee the quality of export goods and so on."[27] Moreover, to rationalize the economy and put it on a more scientific and planning basis, Japan would need to develop advanced research capability for gathering statistics and measuring national growth.[28] In these recommendations, the committee was foreseeing the creation of the Ministry of International Trade and Industry (MITI) and the Economic Planning Agency, two key new agencies established in 1949 and 1955, respectively. The economists were acutely aware of the wartime failure to take account of statistical study, and they were equally influenced by the emergence of a more scientific approach to the economy in the United States and elsewhere in the West.

Essential to this strategy was the planning of an educational system that, rather than emphasizing individualism and democracy as the Occupation reforms had mandated, fulfilled the needs of industrial development. Education must be geared to economic development. "Education in the future should aim at the training not of careerist-type utilitarians, but of those . . . who are diligent, reliable and regard their jobs as duties entrusted by heaven."[29] The committee foresaw a major restructuring of the education system to serve the specific needs of economic growth.

The members of the committee could not know it then, but they were developing a model of state capitalism that would not only become a hallmark of the Japanese economy but also one day become the model for other later developing economies in Asia and elsewhere. While the Americans were envisioning an international economy that would spell the end of economic nationalism, the Japanese were planning a set of institutions and policies of a highly nationalistic character that would take full advantage of the open, liberal global order.

Liberal theory argued that international free trade promoted interdependence among nations and therefore contributed to a peaceful world. Nations should specialize in producing goods for which they had a comparative advantage. The Japanese economists, however, regarded the liberal view of comparative advantage as static, a gift of nature that could not be transferred from one country to another, as simply a rationalization of the existing international division of labor. To the Japanese economists, comparative advantage was dynamic. It could be created by purposeful policies designed to attain a favorable position in strategic industries of international competition. The point was to optimize the industrial structure in order to maximize gains from international trade. Comparative advantage could be created by industrial policy designed to develop specific industrial sectors by erecting entry barriers, providing government subsidies, and husbanding domestic demand so as to create economies of scale. By doing so, they intended to upgrade the industrial structure. Realizing that technological innovation was a critical aspect of competitiveness, the Japanese placed great emphasis on acquiring new technology for industrial sectors considered to have strategic value for international trade. An activist policy prescribed blocking foreign access to Japanese domestic markets in those strategic sectors and building economies of scale at home as a basis for an export drive for overseas markets. This strategy was followed in the automobile, electronics, and many other industries.

The Ōkita committee's report represented a refinement of the strategy Japan had pursued since Meiji. What was different now was the lifting of the military burden and its narrow leadership from their place in the long-term strategy. Ōkita welcomed the fact that Japan would no longer be spending a large portion of its treasure on military needs. Freed from this burden, Japan could instead devote its economic planning entirely to the development of a peaceful industrial economy. The engineers and technicians who had been engaged in manufacturing war planes and war ships, gunnery, and military optics could now be put to work building a peacetime industrial economy. A modernized bureaucracy could work cooperatively with a new generation of professional entrepreneurs.

Implementing the Strategy

Already in the last years of the Occupation, almost unnoticed by the Americans, Ōkita and the other economic planners in the bureaucracy moved resolutely to implement the strategy they had formulated. They created MITI in 1949 with a charge to strengthen Japan's competitive ability in the export market, promote technological change, and enforce efficient use of resources through mergers and various kinds of collusive arrangements among the largest firms. In the same year, the Foreign Exchange and Foreign Trade Control Law gave the new ministry its first and most important tool to influence corporate decisions: the power to allocate all foreign exchange (which lasted until 1964). If they were to grow and compete, Japanese firms had to import raw materials and foreign technology. MITI used its new law to influence the growth rate of various industries and their capacity to acquire new technology. Enactment of the Foreign Capital Law in 1950, the next step in constructing the high-growth system, gave MITI the power to control foreign investment, ownership, and participation in management of business ventures in Japan. Through a combination of import barriers and severe restrictions on foreign direct investment, MITI compelled

American and other foreign firms seeking access to the Japanese market to license technology to a Japanese firm or engage in a joint venture. Transfer of technology, therefore, proceeded rapidly. Next, the Ministry of Finance (MOF) together with MITI established the Japan Development Bank in 1951 with access to a huge investment pool known as the Fiscal Investment and Loan Plan (FILP), which comprised the nation's savings in the postal savings system. The system was a favorite place for individuals to save because their accounts were tax exempt. FILP thus amassed savings four times the size of the world's largest commercial bank. It became "the single most important financial instrument for Japan's economic development" MITI used to provide low-cost capital to industries it favored for long-term growth.[30] In addition, FILP funds could be drawn on to reduce demands on the budget, allowing "spending without taxation," as well as to provide pork barrel funds for the politicians in the LDP.[31]

At the same time, MOF was ensuring the availability of capital. By insulating the domestic capital market from the international capital market, it could ration and guide the flow of capital to large firms in industries that were adopting new technology and were central to increasing productivity and exports, such as steel, shipbuilding, automobiles, electronics, and chemicals. In this way, Japan rapidly changed its export mix from light, labor-intensive industries (predominantly textiles, for which demand was stagnant) to goods for which there was a rapidly growing world demand. Government policies directed cheap and plentiful capital to the lead industries, and new laws prodded their development. Tax, monetary, and fiscal policies were all marshaled to minimize the long-term risks of adopting new technology and of boldly expanding productive capacity. The state was the guarantor. Laws to prod development of critical industries were enacted. In addition to allocating credit, the government used many other potent tools of industrial policy, including imposing high tariffs to protect domestic industries critical to the growth strategy, establishing import quotas, reforming the tax system to favor growth, and giving direct and indirect subsidies to key industries. Finally, as the Occupation ended, MITI had the US-inspired Anti-Monopoly Law revised and watered down so as to relax restrictions on cartels, interlocking directorates, mergers, and various forms of collusive behavior. In the 1950s, successors to the zaibatsu (known as *keiretsu*) emerged. Instead of being organized around holding companies, *keiretsu* brought together companies around a bank. Presidents of companies met regularly to develop common plans. Cross shareholding and interlocking directorates provided the glue to hold these conglomerates together.

An important aspect of MITI's effort to manage the economy was to increase market efficiency and eliminate wasteful "excessive competition" by reducing the number of competitors through organized cartels and supporting favored competitors through resource allocation. Market forces were kept in play, but for a limited number of competitors. Organizing the market in this way did not always work. MITI tried to limit auto makers to Toyota and Nissan, but others, most notably Honda, succeeded in spite of this discriminatory policy.

Cartels proliferated during the 1960s and permitted price controls while preventing ruinous competition. At the same time, the government severely limited imports of foreign-manufactured products through stringent quota and tariff policies, as well as through inspection procedures, product standards, and a formidable array of other nontariff barriers. One prominent economist described the sum of these policies and institutions as "the most restrictive foreign trade and foreign exchange control system ever devised by a major free nation."[32] The insulation of the Japanese economy from foreign investment and control and from political interference permitted the bureaucracy leverage over business. But in contrast to the prewar period, the bureaucracy and business generally developed common interest in working together in symbiotic relations.

In time, a pattern developed in which domestic markets were kept closed to imports, garnering high profits for Japanese companies in their home market, and allowing them to fix low prices on their exports and seize market share abroad. In one well-studied example, seven Japanese companies producing television sets colluded in regular clandestine meetings to fix their domestic pricing at high levels so they could export at well below cost into the American market, which they divided among themselves to undercut American producers and, through such predatory behavior, drive the American firms out of business.[33] Evidence points to similar practices rampant in electronics, semiconductors, and other high-demand products. The losers were Japanese consumers, who had to pay high prices in the domestic market, American firms put out of business, and workers who lost their jobs.

After joining the IMF and GATT, Japan was expected to liberalize and relax its restrictions. The pressure to liberalize was regarded with considerable trepidation as the "second coming of the black ships." New forms of voluntary cooperation were promoted by MITI and the private sector. In the 1960s a greater informal synergy of give-and-take emerged in state-business relations. Business and government worked together in a close reciprocal and interactive relationship. This cooperative relationship was forged over time through consensus on the best interests of the particular industry. Networks of communication between MITI and industry were reinforced by practices known as *amakudari* (literally, "descent from heaven"), by which bureaucrats working closely with a particular industry could often expect to land a comfortable job with a company they had been overseeing after retirement from the ministry.

These policies and institutions were effective in speeding the pace of economic growth, but they clearly were at odds with the open trade system put in place by the Americans. The MITI bureaucrat Sahashi Shigeru wrote that something similar to the wartime mobilization was needed in the new circumstances: "In order to make Japan the first class country among the first class countries, the national general mobilization is still needed today, though its format may differ from the wartime. Without the national general mobilization to consolidate the intelligence and power of the whole nation, people will assert and do whatever as they like and consequently Japan can accomplish nothing."[34] This was precisely the kind of economic nationalism the liberal trading order was designed to prevent. Under strategic leadership of the economic bureaucracy, quasi-wartime controls were implemented to close off the financial system to the rest of the world; economic strategy was devised with a military tactical sense often reflected in the terminology used. As two Japanese economists who worked for the government described it, "The banks and economic bureaucracy functioned as a general staff behind the battlefield in this second 'total war' called high economic growth."[35] MOF officials likened their tight regulatory controls over Japanese banks to "the escort of a convoy of ships by a warship."[36] The efforts of the Japanese people were won over to a consensus toward saving rather than consumption, and, as two economists who served in the bureaucracy put it, "Rapid growth became a 'war' to be won, the first total war in

Japanese history for which all of the nation's resources were mobilized voluntarily."[37]

The International Environment
and American Forbearance

The success of Japan's developmental state capitalism was ensured by many factors other than simply a strategy of government guidance; the policies and institutions formulated by the Ōkita strategy to encourage high growth succeeded not simply through the brilliant strategic planning of its bureaucrat intellectuals (although there was plenty of that) but also through uniquely favorable international conditions. More than any other country, Japan was the beneficiary of the American international order. For more than twenty-five years after the end of the war, Japan operated in extraordinary and uniquely favorable political-economic circumstances. In contrast to every other major power, Japan was spared the psychological and material costs of participating in international politics. To the end of the 1960s, Japan benefited from a special relationship with the United States under which the latter sponsored Japanese recovery and development by keeping the US market open to Japan's goods while allowing Japan to severely limit access to its own economy. The expanding world trade the United States was promoting through the IMF and GATT permitted a vigorous expansion of Japanese manufactured goods and the ready purchase of abundant and cheap raw materials. Cut off from Western industrial contacts during the war years, Japanese engineers and technicians were eager to close the technological gap. The historically honed Japanese skill in emulation was about to see its greatest successes. "The quiet visitor taking notes and photographing everything is a much derided stereotype of the Japanese businessman abroad," the anthropologist Thomas Rohlen wrote. "Yet it was precisely such seemingly enigmatic visitors who, upon returning home, applied their carefully gathered information to produce technological advancement."[38] Japan had easy access to new, inexpensive, and highly efficient Western technology, which it imported in large quantities.

> Between 1951 and 1984 . . . more than forty thousand separate contracts were signed by Japanese firms to acquire foreign technology; over that thirty-four-year period Japan paid $17 billion in royalties—a small

fraction of *annual* US R&D costs. With nylon from DuPont, nuclear power from General Electric and Westinghouse, the transistor from Bell Laboratories, and the television tubes from Corning, US technology licenses were "the technological basis for nearly all of Japan's modern industries."[39]

The other development in the international environment that aided the Ōkita strategy was the outbreak of the Cold War. It made the Americans solicitous of Japan's economic well-being so that Japan would remain on the US side in the Cold War. American forbearance, as we shall see, allowed the Japanese to implement policies and institutions that conflicted with the free trade order. In other words, even while benefiting from the free trade order, Japan was allowed to flout its principles. The Cold War also gave Japan special opportunities. The American procurement orders that poured into Japan from 1950 to 1953 as a result of the Korean War kick-started Japan's economic recovery.

Relying on American preoccupation with the Cold War to provide it with security and an open market, Japan intensified its bureaucratic controls and strengthened its mercantilist policies. Adherents to the Yoshida strategy determined to profit from the international order even while flouting its liberal norms. The conjunction of the liberal American trading order and the Cold War gave Japan the opportunity to access the American market while at the same time enjoying the American tolerance of their own illiberal institutions at home. These institutions would not have been tolerated in the liberal-democratic order the Americans originally envisioned, but the onset of the Cold War elicited American forbearance.

To strengthen its allies, the United States was willing to subordinate its short-term economic interests. It thus provided American markets, technology, and aid to its allies, singling out Japan for special treatment. As one US government official wrote in 1952:

> The most highly industrialized country in the Far East must remain outside the Soviet orbit if there is to be a free Asia, and to this end U.S. policy should be directed by whatsoever means are necessary, military or economic, to assist in the establishment of political tranquility and economic betterment in all of free Asia . . . and until it is clear that Japan can stand firmly on its own feet, the United States must of necessity lend support, even to the extent of providing an unrestricted market for such Japanese goods as American consumers find attractive.[40]

The international economic policy of the United States, the economist Marina Whitman observed, was "primarily a stepchild of our national security objectives."[41]

During the Occupation, American policymakers did not have great expectations that Japan could soon recover its industrial strengths. Even after the Korean War had helped begin recovery, John Foster Dulles told Japanese leaders they "should not expect to find a big U.S. market because the Japanese don't make the things we want. Japan must find markets elsewhere for the goods they export."[42] American officials believed Japan's future markets would be in the less developed countries of Asia. When China joined the communist side in the Cold War, Dulles insisted Japan abstain from trade with its neighbor. Later this policy was somewhat relaxed, but in the meantime American policymakers made great efforts to open up markets in Southeast Asia to aid Japan's struggling economy.

In addition, as Cold War priorities weighed on the Eisenhower administration, the president and Dulles emphasized it was necessary for the United States to make tariff concessions to "keep Japan on our side." If Japan's economic needs were not met, Eisenhower said, "they will say 'To Hell with you, we'll go Communist.' That's what this is all about. We must hold Japan for the free world or we must go to war to keep it in the free world." Members of Eisenhower's cabinet, heavily representative of business interests, expressed concern about imports from low-wage Japanese industries, but Eisenhower was insistent: "Don't let us let Japan reach a point where they want to invite the Kremlin into their country. Everything else fades in insignificance in the light of such a threat."[43]

What was gradually emerging was an informal bargain, rarely openly acknowledged by either Japan or the United States, by which maintenance of US bases in Japan was preserved in return for provision of economic advantages for Japan. In the days after the Anpo demonstrations, reflecting on US policies designed to prevent Japan's lapse into neutralism, US ambassador to Japan Douglas MacArthur II (the general's nephew) stressed the tacit bargain the United States was offering Japan: "Above all by our liberal trade policy on Japanese imports . . . [we have] accorded Japan a fair and reasonable share of our market as premise and precondition for US-Japan relationships in political and security fields . . . [which] has led to substantial expansion of Japanese exports, making possible Japan's present economic prosperity."[44] In the 1950s, therefore, Japan was able to focus its export-led growth strategy on the US market while keeping its own market closed to US exports and investment.

The Kennedy and Johnson administrations continued to give priority to Japanese economic development as a means to ensure Japan's stability. In 1964 the State Department, with the aid of the embassy in Tokyo, drafted a secret policy paper on the future of Japan that urged support of Japan's economic goals and recommended "firm Executive Branch resistance of American industry demands for curtailment of Japanese imports."[45]

Japan's ability to pursue developmentalist policies with such success in the postwar era became in great part contingent on the special circumstances of the Cold War. In Stephen Krasner's words, "Developmentalism has been tolerated by the existing international order, or more accurately slipped under the door, as a result of American security and ideological concerns which allowed, even sometimes tacitly encouraged, departures from classic liberal principles."[46] Indeed, Japan framed its postwar developmentalism with this uniquely favorable international environment in mind. Such a tacit bargain was acceptable in the 1950s when the United States was economically strong and Japan's economy was fragile. Later, in the 1980s, when Japan had become the world's largest creditor nation and the United States the world's largest debtor nation, the bargain became the source of US rancor over providing security for a country that was outcompeting it.

High Growth, 1950–1973

Japan made its way in the post–World War II world by relentlessly pursuing its own narrowly defined self-interest. Regaining its prewar level by 1954–1955, the economy then maintained an astonishing rate of growth, averaging over 10 percent for each of the next fifteen years. The high growth period from 1950 to the oil shock of 1973 saw the flowering of postwar Japanese capitalism. A strong political consensus supporting growth as the overriding national purpose served to mute political conflict. The consensus was skillfully engineered following the Anpo demonstrations by Prime Minister Ikeda and maintained by his successors. Business and government worked hand-in-glove to formulate long-term goals and policies. As a political movement, labor had little say about policy and was effectively co-opted in any case by the success of economic expansion and such features of the employment system as lifetime employment and company unions. Although double-digit annual growth increases disappeared after the oil shocks of the 1970s, the economy recovered, adjusted to the new conditions, and resumed annual growth at a healthy but more moderate pace.

As the Ōkita strategy dictated, priority was given to a fundamental transformation of the economy. Following the product cycle, Japan moved steadily up the value-added curve. By the 1960s, manufacturing output was more diversified and sophisticated, developing aggressively in a variety of high-end areas such as shipbuilding, optics, iron and steel, chemicals, machinery, automobiles, and consumer durables. MITI, for example, targeted the automobile industry for protection through quotas and tariffs, and for promotion through subsidies and tax breaks. By 1985 the Japanese automobile industry had become the world's largest. Many factors other than the protection and promotion provided by industrial policy went into the success of this industry, including the achievements of Japanese management and the culture of work of Japanese labor. Careful planning by business and government working in concert to produce goods that had strong world demand resulted in impressive export-led growth, averaging, for example, a 17 percent annual increase between 1953 and 1965.

As Japan's economic growth reached annual double digits, the distinctive features of Japanese capitalism drew worldwide attention. Particularly noteworthy was the unique pattern of labor-management relations, marked by such distinctive features as lifetime employment, seniority-based wages, company or enterprise unions, and extensive welfare provisions by the company, all of which served to ensure company loyalty. Although the Occupation had undertaken the breakup of the zaibatsu, the reform was never completed because of America's new Cold War priorities. What remained were called *keiretsu* (economic lineages). Some, like Mitsui, Mitsubishi, and Sumitomo, were conglomerates organized horizontally around banks, embracing manufacturing companies and a trading company held together by long-held ties of common interest and trust, cross shareholding, regular meetings, and so on. Others, like Toyota, were organized vertically with a large number of subcontractors and suppliers servicing the parent company. Based on

The Nissan Motor factory in Japan, at a time when export of Japanese cars became increasingly competitive in the American market, 1972. Keystone-France / Getty Images / 106498570.

long-held relationships of trust and mutual assistance, they excluded outsiders to ensure a common interest in sharing both good and diffi-cult times. They provided long-term stability, efficiency, mutual support, and reduced risk. In contrast to American companies, where profit was sought for shareholders, the Japanese company worked for the good of the stakeholder—the company's own well-being and that of its em-ployees. The upshot of these distinctive aspects of corporate culture was that the Japanese economy was impervious to foreign participation, and as high growth continued, it incited the criticism of foreign com-petitors that regarded Japan as playing by different and unfair practices.

Catch-Up and the Controversy over Japanese Capitalism

Perhaps because of its respect for hierarchy in domestic society, modern Japan has always been sensitive to its standing in the world. The ambi-tion to gain equality with and to surpass the Western powers, which in retrospect we call "the catch-up drive," became an obsession of leaders at the very outset of Japan's entrance into the international system. Japanese paid keen attention to their rank and status from the time they entered international society. Fukuzawa observed in 1875:

> [Our] sights are now being reset on the goal of elevating Japanese civilization to parity with the West, or even of surpassing it. Since Western civilization is even now in a process of transition and progress day by day, month by month, we Japanese must keep pace with it without abating our efforts. The arrival of the Americans in the 1850s has, as it were, kindled a fire in our people's hearts. Now that it is ablaze, it can never be extinguished.[47]

The obsession of the Meiji leaders became over time a national consensus, a goal repeatedly held up as one toward which all Japanese must aspire. For example, in rhetoric common to the time, Takahashi Korekiyo, who later became finance minister and prime minister, exhorted his students in an 1889 farewell address at Tokyo Agricultural College: "Gentlemen, it is your duty to advance the status of Japan, bring her to a position of equality with the civilized powers and then carry on to build a foundation from which we shall surpass them all."[48] This oft-repeated vision was supported by an optimism and a fierce determination to exert whatever effort was required to be the equal of the West.

Early Meiji reformers believed that the path of social progress was essentially unilinear, that it was uniform for all people, that as Japan advanced it would become more like the industrial societies of the West, and that Japan's progress could be measured by acquired similarities to England, France, and the United States. Such a view, however, was damaging to Japanese pride in their own civilization; and as nationalism took hold in Japan at the turn of the century, other reformers argued that it was possible to borrow selectively, to take the strong points of Western civilization and fill Japan's shortcomings while still preserving the distinctive nature (*kokusui*) of Japan's historical civilization. The government as a means to mobilize popular nationalism stressed the unique role of the imperial system and the loyalty of the people to the emperor as the essence of Japan's civilization and built its ideology on this foundation.[49]

Although the disaster of national defeat in 1945 destroyed faith in this definition of national identity, it did not extinguish Japan's pursuit of rank in international society. As the national rebuilding progressed, Japan continued to take measure of its standing. By the 1970s the century-long goal of catching up with the most advanced industrial economies was in sight. In 1972 Japan surpassed England and soon after

West Germany to become the world's second-largest economy. Japan then set its sights on overtaking America. Economic success rather than the emperor system ideology was found to be a source of pride in Japanese culture, fulfilling a deeply felt longing since Japan began its quest to catch up with the West. Catching up did not require westernization, but could be achieved by a different—a Japanese—cultural path.

Confidence mounted that Japan was overtaking the West in technological capacity. A survey conducted by the government's Economic Planning Agency in 1985 found that among Japan's 1,600 leading firms, 90 percent believed they had caught up with or surpassed the technological capacity of US firms. Japan rode the tide of an unparalleled period of expanding world trade. Japanese exports increased nearly twenty-five-fold between 1955 and 1970. Over a longer period, from 1955 to 1987, exports achieved an astonishing 114-fold increase.[50]

Japan's rise as an international investor was dramatic evidence of its economic power. Surplus savings so great that they could no longer be absorbed at home were exported to the rest of the world. Year after year during the 1980s, Japan amassed trade and current account surpluses. Japan's net external assets rose from $10.9 billion in 1981 to $383 billion a decade later. By 1990 Japan had become the largest net creditor in the world, "the greatest creditor nation the world has ever known." In 1970 the cumulative value of Japanese overseas investments was $3.6 billion, in 1980 $160 billion, and in 1991 $2.0 trillion.[51]

In Japan, the growing trade frictions with America were often dismissed as sour grapes. "Americans," observed Ōgura Kazuo, one of Japan's senior diplomats, in 1991, "simply don't want to recognize that Japan has won the economic race against the West."[52] In fact, as Cornell anthropologist Robert Smith observed, "Americans are prepared to accept almost any explanation for Japan's economic accomplishment of the past 35 years so long as it avoids acknowledging that the Japanese are superior competitors."[53] One notable exception was the sociologist Ezra Vogel, director of Harvard's East Asia Research Center, who in 1979 published his book *Japan as Number One: Lessons for America*. Arguing that Japan had outdone all other countries in its skillful organizing of a postindustrial society, Vogel concluded, "Japan is now a more effective democracy than America."[54] It was not only "number one"; it was a model for America to emulate. It was a landmark event for the Japanese, who had been striving for over a century to hear this kind of judgment.

Vogel's book at once became a runaway best seller in Japan. He had fulsome praise not only for Japan's industrial competitiveness but also for its meritocratic education, health care, pollution control, and low crime rate. The "communitarian vision" and values of social cohesiveness the Japanese prized produced a more egalitarian and harmonious society. To regain the competitiveness of its capitalism, Vogel urged the United States to create a comprehensive industrial and trade policy as Japan had done and put in place a small core of permanent high-level bureaucrats to administer the policy. The United States should promote "high levels of cooperation between companies within a given industrial sector and between the companies and the American government."[55]

Japan as Number One became the all-time nonfiction best seller in Japan by a Western author. It was not simply the foreign acknowledgment of their economic success that so pleased the Japanese; it was the belief that they had done it not by following the Western model but rather by charting their own cultural path to modernity. Vogel's argument was distinctly at odds with Americans' customary claims of the universalism of their civilization and the unilinear assumptions that all developing countries must follow the American model. As the anthropologist Amy Borovoy wisely observed, "Vogel's argument that the United States could learn from Japan in solving postindustrial social issues suggested a powerful reversal of the conventional modernization narrative in which American society was the implied endpoint—though it was a reversal that was greeted with skepticism and disbelief by many."[56] Indeed, American scholars of Japan were among the most skeptical of the notion that Japan could serve as a model for the United States and other societies. Eminent literary scholar Edward Seidensticker found it "hard to take." Political scientist Donald Hellmann observed that given the "enormous differences" between the two societies, it would require a revolution in America or perhaps, he added in an ironic quip, it would take "a Japanese occupation" of the United States to impose the reforms Vogel proposed.[57] Anticipating such objections, Vogel reminded American readers that, after all, the Japanese had throughout their modern history imported aspects of Western civilization to reform their country. Why couldn't Americans likewise borrow from superior aspects of another society? In retrospect, what was remarkable about *Japan as Number One* was that it implied doubts about the universalism of American values and institutions and prefigured Japanese conservative thinkers who would proclaim their nation's experience as a model for other late-developing societies.

The Japanese attributed their success to the unique characteristics of the Japanese people and their culture. Their historically formed institutions, with their stress on harmony and collective values, had proved more productive and competitive than those of all other countries. More than one writer drew this irresistible conclusion. The widely read economist Iida Tsuneo wrote: "Is it not possible that Japan may be quite different from other countries? Is it not possible that Japan may be quite superior to other countries?"[58] On the contrary, by 1980 the national pride in the status Japan had achieved was palpable. One of the most striking examples of the persistence of this rank consciousness is found in the quasi-official *Survey of Japanese National Character* (*Kokuminsei no kenkyū*), conducted at five-year intervals since 1953. Among the questions asked in this periodic survey is, "Compared to Westerners, do you think, in a word, the Japanese are superior? Or do you think they are inferior?" For Japan this was a natural question, given the strength of rank consciousness and the historical goal of catching up to and overtaking the West. In 1953, in response to the question, 20 percent answered the Japanese were superior. In 1983, 53 percent answered the Japanese were superior.[59]

While most Japanese were inclined to attribute their economic success to their cultural strengths, Americans and the West generally were inclined to see unfair trade practices. Japan's success became obvious in the 1970s and 1980s, and thus its institutional deviance from international norms as understood by neoclassical economic principles became a matter of controversy. Japan's unique form of capitalism became the subject of intense criticism from the West and especially from Americans. The Japanese were accused of "dumping" goods at below cost, "targeting" particular foreign markets, and "pirating" foreign intellectual property. The intense criticism was directed at Japanese economic institutions that, despite the efforts of the Occupation, had reverted to nationalist and mercantilist patterns. The criticism took on an emotional tone in the 1980s as Japan closed the technological gap and began to compete with—or outcompete—the Americans in many of the most high-end products.

Japan rode the wave of liberalism's triumph without adopting its principles. It stood on the side of the West, but its ruling elite, on the

To help laid-off workers, the Steelworkers Union sponsored a charity campaign in which people paid a dollar a shot to swing a sledgehammer at a
Japanese-made auto in Gary, Indiana. AP Photo/820910082.

whole, shared little passion for the ideals of liberalism. The superior economic performance of Japanese capitalism in the aftermath of World
War II drew worldwide attention, achieving new levels of economic
competitiveness not based on classic liberal norms but rather on distinctive Japanese organizing principles. Japan's leaders had constructed a
system of illiberal institutions that outperformed the Western capitalist
democracies. The success of Japan's unique industrial policies and its socially and culturally embedded institutions of capitalism appeared to
foretell a new era of economic and technological competition among the
great powers. Japan represented a new kind of power. As the political
economist Robert Gilpin wrote at the time:

> Western liberal societies find Japanese economic success particularly
> threatening because it is the first non-Western and nonliberal society
> to outcompete them. Whereas Western economies are based on belief
> in the superior efficiency of the free market and individualism, the
> market and the individual in Japan are not relatively autonomous but
> are deeply embedded in a powerful nonliberal culture and social
> system.[60]

As Japan's success drew international attention, its domestic institutions were scrutinized more closely. Japan's institutional divergence from international norms as understood by neoclassical principles became a matter of controversy. Formerly, adherence to the norms of a liberal open economic system meant maintaining nondiscriminatory tariffs and refraining from overt quota on imports. The growth of interdependence of national economies, however, increased the relevance of domestic social structures and economic policies to the smooth operation of a liberal international economy. The Japanese system created a clash between domestic autonomy and international norms in international negotiations. As trade friction intensified, Japan's distinctive economic institutions—industrial policy, postal savings system, *keiretsu,* antirecession cartels, public-sector procurement policies, and so on—were increasingly stigmatized in the West as illiberal, unfair, discriminatory, nontransparent, and illegitimate. To reform these practices would constitute a challenge to central features of Japanese culture, social relations, and political culture. The pressure from a liberal viewpoint abroad was intense. Some critics saw Japan as a free-rider on the international system, and others treated Japan as an "outlier."[61]

State capitalism and the role of a guided export-led growth have been repeated in other late-developing states that have profited from studying the Japanese model. Chalmers Johnson's 1982 book *MITI and the Japanese Miracle* describes Japan as a "developmental state."[62] It stood somewhere between a "command economy" (as the Soviet Union and its communist allies had been, where the state made all the decisions about the allocation of resources) and a "regulatory state" (like the United States, where the state sought to maintain a free market in the interest of the consumer). Johnson called attention to the role of the Japanese bureaucracy serving as an "economic general staff" masterminding Japan's high-speed growth. Although not aware of Ōkita's committee report, he nonetheless discerned the Japanese strategy to guide the "rationalization" of firms and industries and the structural transformation of the economy. He analyzed how MITI stimulated the movement of capital and labor out of declining industries such as coal and textiles and into promising new industries with high-growth potential—first into electronics, steel, petrochemicals, and automobiles, and later into computers, semiconductors, and biotechnology.

Johnson's analysis was pathbreaking in its insights for understanding the high-growth system and its workings. He did, however, underplay the market forces that favored Japanese growth, and he overlooked the special conditions the Cold War provided to aid Japanese success, namely, the willingness of the United States to tolerate the deep inroads of Japan's export drives into the American market so long as the Cold War was the Americans' paramount concern. Moreover, in paying tribute to the Japanese success and even recommending aspects of it to American policymakers, he did not see that the developmental state, while useful at the catch-up stage, would prove counterproductive once that stage had passed.[63]

A Japanese Assessment

In the 1980s, as the Japanese completed the century-long struggle to catch up with the advanced industrial nations, they had good cause to reflect on the meaning of their success. Much ink was spilled on the subject. Most of it was superficial, and much of it was nationalistic self-satisfaction in Japanese culture. However, one of the leading Japanese social scientists of his day, Murakami Yasusuke, a professor at the University of Tokyo, perceived the century-long process of catch-up as a model with universal application for all later developing economies. He believed that the Japanese form of capitalism, or "developmentalism," that came out of the adaptation of Japan's own civilization to the tasks of industrialization was a viable model for other later developing economies. He reacted sharply against the usual judgments the Western world had made of Japan's industrialization. The path Japan had followed as it industrialized was stigmatized as first "imitative" when it began in the Meiji period, then "deformed" when it deviated from the Anglo-American model in the prewar period, and then "illegitimate" when it succeeded in outstripping Western economies in the postwar period.

Murakami wrote a brilliant treatise in 1992 in which he took issue with the principles of economic liberalism that defined the US world order.[64] He objected to its claims of universalism, to the belief that one size fits all, and to the proposition that a single set of policy prescriptions can be applicable to all countries and all situations. He saw concepts of free trade, open economic structures, vigorous antitrust policies, and the free flow of capital, goods, and people—the concepts underlying the Bretton Woods system and GATT—as stacked in favor of the advanced industrial economies. To offer the late-developing economies a just and level playing field required recognition that they must follow a path distinct from, with different rules from, the early industrializers. Japan's distinct and successful course of industrialization was proof of this proposition.[65]

He defined "developmentalism" as a Japanese form of capitalism that had as its main objective the achievement of industrialization by government intervention in the market for the purpose of long-term promotion of industrialization. It is a transition stage between underdevelopment and classic liberalism. Policy targets priority industries, promotes technical progress, and manages competition through an activist bureaucracy. Government harnesses education to the tasks of industrialization and designs an activist social policy to minimize income disparity, thereby smoothing the transition to industrial society. Murakami further argued that what the Japanese experience had provided was a distinctive model of policies and institutions for late-developing economies to speed the process of industrialization. An active and creative bureaucracy, the Japanese experience had shown, could nurture high rates of growth by designating priority industries for development and fostering an agreed understanding of procedures among firms in those industries.

Murakami broadened his views on Japanese developmentalism to argue that, in light of the fact that Japan had demonstrated that the path to high economic growth and industrialism was compatible with different cultures and different institutions, the liberal progressive views of the West and especially the United States were no longer acceptable as a hegemonic theory.[66] Japan had demonstrated, he wrote, that countries can achieve industrialization by different cultural paths and that modernity is not the exclusive property of the West, as most Westerners had confidently presumed. The Japanese path of achieving industrialization through policy interventions made from a long-term perspective was of world historical significance because it demonstrated that the Western neoclassical path to economic growth, with its attendant liberal values, lacked universal validity. In Murakami's formulation, charges against Japan of targeting, dumping, beggar-thy-neighbor policies, economic aggression, unfair trade, adversarial trade, predatory trade, and other stigmata suddenly lost their sting. Developmental policies were a legitimate alternative to neoclassical economics.

The tensions that emerged between the norms of American capitalism and those of Japanese capitalism foreshadowed the emergence of many other late-developing societies shaped by the values of their own history. As economic power shifted from the North Atlantic to the Asia Pacific region and late-developing economies emerged with very different cultural traditions and national systems of political economy, the goal of achieving a coherent, governable international trade order became increasingly difficult. Aspects of the Japanese model were adopted in Taiwan, South Korea, Singapore, China, and elsewhere. Murakami concluded that as other late-developing economies followed Japan's path, the United States and other Western countries must recognize the need for tolerance of different cultural values as legitimate in the operation of the international economic order. Murakami argued that the leading industrial economies must adopt a rule-based international trade regime that sanctioned the practices of industrial policy by the late-developing economies.

The Crisis of Japanese Capitalism

At the end of the Cold War, there was a widespread belief that Japan had succeeded in developing a superior economic system that had not only caught up with the other advanced economies but was now prepared to lead a new international system modeled on the trading state. "The Cold War is over," Chalmers Johnson quipped, "and Japan has won."[67] Yet instead of marking the beginning of Japan's preeminence, the changed international conditions unexpectedly led to the disruption of the Japanese system. When confronting the new conditions of globalization, the Japanese economic institutions of the catch-up period proved sluggish and outdated, and the Japanese challenge faded.

The reversal of Japanese fortunes was startling. As the 1990s began, it soon became apparent that the economic boom in the latter half of the 1980s had created a bubble of alarming proportions. Following the rapid appreciation of the yen after the Plaza Accord of 1985, in which the G-5 agreed to a depreciation of the yen against the dollar to correct trade imbalances, the Japanese government, fearing economic recession, resorted to monetary stimulus by lowering interest rates and strongly encouraging banks to lend. A massive asset price inflation resulted in the tripling of stock prices and urban real estate prices. Alarmed at the heights asset inflation reached, MOF attempted to ease their price level; but once the speculative bubble burst, asset prices collapsed and economic stagnation set in. Unemployment reached postwar highs. Business failures were widespread. Banks held portfolios of nonperforming loans. Macroeconomic policy oscillated clumsily between stimulus and tax increases. Reflecting the reversal of Japanese fortunes, the trade frictions with the United States that had been so intense in the early 1990s now ebbed.

It might have been possible to blame the tide of troubles sweeping over Japan in the 1990s simply on economic policy errors, except that it became apparent the troubles had deeper sources than economic mismanagement. The transformation of the international economy in the 1990s posed an enormous challenge. The end of the Cold War removed the constraints on economic globalization the autarkic policies of communist governments had posed. National economies were increasingly linked through trade, financial flows, and foreign direct investment by multinational firms as the American government, the new World Trade Organization, and the European Union promoted further market liberalization. A new technological paradigm bringing a revolution in communications and information fueled these developments. This globalization of capitalism, as one economic historian described it, brought a host of intertwined developments:

> The digital revolution changed many dimensions of advanced capitalist societies in fundamental ways; the world economy became substantially more interdependent because trade and the cross-border flows of information, technology, and capital are larger than ever; competition grew more intense than ever because of both reduced impediments to trade and a large excess capacity in many markets of manufactured products; and to maintain or increase competitiveness, the largest firms and financial institutions merged at an accelerating pace within and across national boundaries.[68]

Japan's severe economic setbacks and the change in the international economy created a crisis for its capitalism. Its unexpected economic decline after the Cold War posed the difficult question of whether, faced with the new conditions of technological revolution and economic internationalization and the need to restore the nation's economic competitiveness, the Japanese must now abandon the distinctive institutions of Japanese capitalism that had served them so well, or whether they would be able to retain and adapt these institutions while transitioning to a more mature capitalist economy. It was not only the daunting challenges of globalization; Japan's system became "less effective when low-cost competitors from the rest of Asia followed Japan's path and started their own catch-up growth," eating into Japan's export market.[69]

As the economic malaise persisted through the 1990s and into the new century, it proved extremely difficult to change the policies and institutions put in place over many decades. The radical deterioration of Japan's economic fortunes in the 1990s gave rise to prolonged political struggles and debates over future policy. The realization dawned that persisting practices of developmentalism must bear much of the responsibility for Japan's sagging political economy. Japan's century of catch-up had been achieved, and therefore it was time to put aside the illiberal institutions and policies—governmental industrial policy, cartels and other forms of collusion, and a system dedicated to favoring producers at the expense of Japanese consumers. It would take a formidable program of political reform to shake loose the grip the bureaucracy had over special interests and their political allies. Having such power, bureaucracies do not easily surrender their power.

The danger of the developmentalist strategy, as Murakami had recognized, was that its practices would become entrenched and the system would persist beyond the catch-up stage for which it was intended. As he warned, "Once established . . . the relationship between industry and government becomes difficult to terminate; thus industrial policy continues, becoming nothing more than protectionism, and maybe even hampering the development of a competitive environment in the economy as a whole."[70] There must be sunset provisions, a way of bringing the catch-up policies and institutions to an end. "If Japan fails to end industrial policies," he wrote prophetically in 1992, "its postwar developmentalism may be judged a failure."[71] Japan had to come to grips with the issues of transforming its "catch-up" institutional structure.

Change seemed glacial over the "lost decade" of the 1990s as the economy struggled with economic stagnation and deflation. The resistance to change was powerful. The developmentalist policies and practices of Japan's modern history were inseparably woven into the fabric of its political economy. As the economist Edward Lincoln noted, "Change was difficult due to the interlocking nature of the pieces of the postwar system."[72] Over the course of a century, the guidance of a proactive bureaucracy engendered a system based on particularistic relations of cooperation and mutual trust. The institutional practices, attuned to Japanese culture and endorsed by a strong national consensus, could not readily be changed. Vested interests in government and business strongly defended the past policies and established institutions. Bureaucrats clung to their regulatory prerogatives. Small business, agriculture, and labor demanded continuation of their protection. Underlying all such resistance was an ideology of pride in the unique cultural practices of Japan's "virtuous capitalism" that had served them so well.[73] For decades, Japanese had dismissed the slash-and-burn Darwinian practices of American market-led capitalism as unacceptable in the harmonious ways of the Japanese social contract.

Still, economic hardship was a tough taskmaster, and despite hand-wringing, reforms began to take hold by the turn of the century. The economic hardship was reflected in a shocking rise in social indicators of distress: unemployment, personal debt, homelessness, divorce, crime, and suicide. For a nation that had long boasted of its social stability and personal security, such social suffering spurred the need for reform. Business leaders in the Keidanren, the nation's most powerful business lobby, pushed the government to implement deregulation.[74]

The Future of Japanese Capitalism

Slowly, ponderously, progress was made in deregulating the government supervision and transforming labor and business practices. Changes began to be made not only because Japan was now a mature economy, no longer requiring the developmentalist strategy, but also because Japanese institutions needed to accommodate the shift in the international system toward financial globalization and a radically new information technology. Business scholar Ulrike Schaede argues that despite the widespread perception of a "lost decade" of economic malaise in the post-bubble period, wholesale change was under way in corporate business practice. Hard pressed by rising competitors in South Korea, Taiwan, and China and losing their cost advantage in mass manufacturing of high-quality consumer goods, Japanese corporations adopted a strategy of "choose and focus" (*sentaku to shūchū*).[75] Companies began to slim down, focus on what they did best, and move into upstream components and niches of expertise. At the behest of reform-minded business organizations, writes Schaede, in the decade after 1998 the government "literally revised every single law pertaining to commerce."[76] New laws requiring transparency in the financial industry revealed the health of banks and companies. Japan has begun the dismantling of the developmental state practices of the past. Regulatory practices and administrative practice were phased out to the extent that one bureaucrat at the Ministry of Economy, Trade and Industry (METI—formerly MITI) lamented in 2007 that "it is no longer fun to be a METI official."[77] The comprehensive reformation of the business and regulatory / legal framework constituted, as the economic historian Mark Metzler observed, "a great shift in the system of regulation from a 'parental' style type of informal, actor-based bureaucratic regulation to a more rule-based, transaction-focused type of regulation."[78]

Still, despite this wave of reform, progress was uneven and uncertain. Some companies were bold in repositioning, innovating, and responding to market exposure, but there were many laggards. Much restructuring awaited completion. Risk and innovation, a turn to the market, only gradually replaced a system of dependency on government interventions to minimize risk. More efficient integration of women into the workforce to support a rapidly aging society and to meet a growing labor shortage are urgent and unfulfilled tasks. It will require a generation to make such fundamental changes. At the individual level, as labor rules are revised, lifetime employment practices recede, and performance pay becomes accepted, the social contract among government, companies, and employees will change. It will take a paradigm change to bring about realignment and repositioning in practice, organization, people, and cultural preference.

What will the Japanese economic system look like after a required generation of change? During the lost decade many American and some Japanese observers advised Japanese policymakers to follow the "Washington consensus." It was time for Japan to converge with the Anglo-American model of liberal capitalism. Some observers believed that if policy did not aim for the liberal model, the market mechanism, accelerating interdependence, and new international arrangements such as the World Trade Organization would force the Japanese economy to converge with liberal capitalism, lest it suffer declining competiveness.[79] They believed that globalization and increasing interdependence were fueling the rapid convergence of national systems of social and economic organization.

Still, it is by no means clear that convergence is taking place. To the contrary, as the political economist Steven Vogel argues, Japan seems to be reorganizing, not dismantling, its model. Historically embedded institutions can change only slowly. The Japanese are therefore "making incremental adjustment to refine their model building on their strengths when possible, and avoiding radical moves toward the liberal market model that would be doomed to fail in the absence of complementary institutions."[80] Japan today is a hybrid—liberal in some respects but still divergent from Anglo-American political economy. Schaede, too, is careful to insist, "Japan's answers to the new challenges will be different from those adopted by other countries, just as Japan's legal interpretations will differ from the United States even when the new laws are based on the U.S. model."[81] Japan's corporate structure is not converging with the United States but rather will be "shaped according to its own legal and corporate trajectories."[82] Moreover, as Metzler argues, "expectations of 'convergence' are regularly and predictably disappointed." That Japan will move toward a liberal and individualist model is dubious. "The implication of this external view of Japan is that more collective and social modes of operation are developmentally residual or backward. In fact, it seems more the case that times of economic constraint . . . have the effect of reconsolidating rather than loosening solidary social structures."[83] Japanese capitalism will evolve in some ways that approach a liberal model but will proceed according to a "Japanese logic" that keeps intact historically shaped values of cooperation. "We are not likely to see an end to the Japanese model but only its continuous redefinition."[84] Convergence of the Japanese political economy with the American way remains incomplete and underscores the continuing diversity of national styles of capitalism.

9

Japan's Nonconvergent Society

T HE WAY IN WHICH World War II ended, with the unconditional surrender of its enemies," historian Odd Arne Westad wrote, "proved
that America could defeat evil on a global scale. But it also proved to
most Americans that the world wanted Americanism—through its products and through its ideas. . . . Victory in World War II was therefore a
victory for the American way of life itself." America's mission in Japan
was to set its people free from age-old forms of social oppression as well
as from a false form of modernity that had distorted its way of life. Japan
would be redeemed by exposing its people to the American form of
progress.[1]

Of all the goals that prompted the unconditional surrender policy,
the most ambitious and presumptuous was the goal to reeducate the
Japanese people. It would not be sufficient simply to disarm Japan and
dissolve its empire, punish its leaders and maintain a garrison to ensure
its disarmament, and reform its political and economic structures. It was
necessary to transform its social institutions and remold its people's ways
of thinking and behaving—even believing. The social engineering that
the Occupation undertook of remolding Japanese minds, remaking
Japanese culture, and reforming Japanese behavior would instill the
values of democratic individualism that would make them a peaceful
people.

The presumptuousness of this goal of the total reconstruction of Japanese society owed much to the recent experience of the New Deal
and to the prominent role of New Dealers in the Occupation. As one

historian who traces its influence on Americans' optimism for reforming the world writes, "The New Deal was characterized by a certain
naïve cheerfulness about the efficacy of sweeping, institutional solutions to large-scale social problems."[2] The "lived experience" of meeting
the challenges of the Great Depression with an array of revolutionary
social legislation generated an enthusiasm to take the same approach
with Japan. Underlying this confidence, and fundamental to the
emerging American order, was the assumption that the progress of civilization was a unilinear path. As they progressed, nations would converge in their institutions, and America, as the most modern of all nations, was therefore a model for all others. The principles and domestic
structures in American society provided a template for the legitimate
organization of all humanity. Progress would bring about the convergence of other societies to the American model of democratic society.
Divergent societies would lack legitimacy in the American world order.

Japan's entire modern history was deemed so deviant from the
universal path of human progress as to require reconstruction of its
society, its mores, and ways of thought. "Supposedly, the Japanese were
a twentieth-century civilization," General MacArthur observed. "In
reality, they were more nearly a feudal society of the type discarded by
Western nations some four centuries ago."[3] What was needed was the
forced liberalization of this entire social structure and, above all, the liberation of the individual from the myriad of restraints that prevented
the free expression of will and belief. Changing the thought and behavior of ordinary Japanese was part and parcel of the making of a new
international order. If Japan was to fit into the new American world
order, its society and culture and their underlying values must be re-
molded so that Japanese would become democratic, peace-loving citizens
fully supportive of a new liberal world order. The American confidence
in the universal relevance of its values and institutions was fundamental to its plan to shape the world order. A peaceful world order required a compatibility of liberal domestic institutions that reflected the
American example.

At the time the Occupation was formulating its policies, the United
States was establishing one of the most important pillars of the new international order. The Universal Declaration of Human Rights, championed by Eleanor Roosevelt, embodied a set of individual rights that
should be recognized by all nations regardless of culture and history.[4] It

carried the implication that because the rights were universal they ought not to be limited by definitions of individual sovereign governments. The human rights revolution launched by the declaration drew heavily on the precedents of the American Declaration of Independence and the French Declaration of the Rights of Man and Citizen (1789).[5] Legal scholar Mary Ann Glendon describes how the notion of universality was "under siege" from the start. Voices outside the West charged that the declaration, with its emphasis on individualism, conflicted with other conceptions of community and society and undermined the cultural integrity of nations.[6] Even the American Anthropological Association expressed concern that the statement of rights was "conceived only in terms of the values prevalent in the countries of Western Europe and America."[7] Nevertheless, the UN General Assembly ratified the declaration in 1948.

In so many ways, American assumptions about the new world order were made more manifest in Japan than anywhere else. The American-drafted constitution of Japan included a long list of human rights, embodying "the most radical ideas on individual liberty found in twentieth century constitutions outside of Scandinavia."[8] Fundamentally reshaping the behavior and values of a society as ancient and complex as Japan's was implausible, but the Americans saw it as a matter of implanting values that represented the universal path of human progress. This would entail changing deeply rooted cultural values that had caused the Japanese to stray from the path that all modern nations must traverse. "Our problem," according to a 1945 instructional film for the American Occupation forces, "is in the brain inside of the Japanese head. There are seventy million of these in Japan, physically no different than any other brains in the world, actually all made from exactly the same stuff as ours. These brains, like our brains, can do good things or bad things, all depending on the kind of ideas that are put inside. . . . That same brain today remains the problem, our problem. It will cost us time, it will cost us patience. But we are determined that this fact will sink in."[9]

Americans delighted in playing the role of revolutionary, instructing the Japanese on how they should live their lives. Besides transforming the political and economic orders, they were determined to revolutionize education, religion, the written language, and even the intimate aspects of Japanese society—the family, parental authority, male-female relations, love, and marriage. It was, writes John Dower, "one of the most audacious exercises in social engineering in history."[10] Americans generally had little sense of the grandiosity of what they set out to do in postwar Japan. It took the sensitivity of George Kennan, reflecting on the "overweening ambitions and exaggerated self-glorification" that had led Americans to ask "through the formula of unconditional surrender, for a total power (and thus a total responsibility) over their affairs; we who somewhat brashly undertook to show them how to live, in this modern age, more happily, more safely, and more usefully, than they had lived before. You could hardly assume a greater responsibility than this."[11]

It was, of course, ironic that the Americans were adopting something of the autocratic manner of the prewar Japanese bureaucrats who had well-developed practices, as historian Sheldon Garon writes, for "molding Japanese minds."[12] The irony of the Occupation's method of reform is captured in the title of a *New York Times* article describing the planned changes: "Democratic Rule Ordered in Japan."[13] Japanese bureaucrats had managed Japanese society through policies shaping the thought and behavior of ordinary people in their everyday lives, giving them an identity and national purpose that served state interests. While those bureaucrats had operated within their country's own cultural traditions, the Americans were attempting to remold Japanese minds to fit an entirely different set of cultural traditions.

In retrospect, it is notable that after the implementation of Occupation reforms and the sustained influence of Western tradition in the postwar period, Japan has assimilated much but remains today a distinctly different and unique society. The first Asian country to develop a modern industrial society has not converged to a universal Western model but rather demonstrates that there are multiple cultural paths to modernity. As a matter of historical fact, Japan has been capable of reforming itself. Throughout its modern history, Japan has proved its ability to transform itself by selectively adopting institutions from societies regarded as more advanced. Leading scholars of Japanese character, from Yanagita Kunio to Maruyama Masao, have observed the Japanese tendency to move with trends and keep up with the times.[14] There are good reasons to believe that after defeat in the war, the Japanese themselves would have made major reforms in their society. They would not, of course, have been the fully liberal reforms the Americans desired, but

they would have been their own, in line with their own cultural pro-
clivities. Beginning in the Meiji period, the Japanese were intent on
acquiring Western science and technology, but also weighed social
practices in the West to determine whether they were appropriate and
valuable for Japan to adopt.[15]

The American Social Creed

Individualism was fundamental to what the Americans sought to teach
the Japanese. The core values of American society were individual dignity, individual freedom, and individual rights. These values underwrote
the democratic government and democratic capitalism that constituted
the American world order. They were what made America exceptional,
but they were no longer just for Americans; they were for all peoples.
They were, Americans thought, the essence of modern civilization and
the foundation on which a peaceful world order must be built. At the
outset of the Cold War, National Security Council Memo 68 (NSC 68)
defined the ideological basis for a massive arms buildup and struggle
whose outcome would determine "the fulfillment or the destruction not
only of the Republic but of civilization itself." What was the essence of
this civilization? NSC 68 defined it as the freedom and dignity of the
individual: "In essence the fundamental purpose is to assure the integrity and vitality of our free society, which is founded upon the dignity
and worth of the individual. . . . The free society values the individual
as an end in itself, requiring of him only that measure of self-discipline
and self-restraint which make the rights of each individual compatible
with the rights of every other individual."[16] The social engineering the
Occupation undertook to remold Japanese minds, remake Japanese culture, and reform Japanese behavior would instill the values of democratic individualism that would make the former enemies a peaceful
people.

From the beginning of the American republic, Christian belief and
the struggle against monarchical authority had embedded democratic
individualism in American identity. It found philosophical confirmation
in the writings of John Locke, who viewed the individual as preceding
society, which in turn came into being through a contract among individuals who joined in pursuing a common interest. Government was
based on the voluntary participation of individuals. The pursuit of

happiness offered the opportunity for individuals to shape their own destiny and fulfill their own God-given potential. When he wrote *Democracy in America* in 1835, Alexis de Tocqueville identified individualism as the core value of Americans: "[Americans] owe no man anything and hardly expect anything from anybody. They form the habit of thinking of themselves in isolation and imagine that their whole destiny is in their own hands. Thus, not only does democracy make men forget their ancestors, but also clouds their view of their descendants and isolates them from their contemporaries. Each man is forever thrown back on himself alone, and there is danger that he may be shut up in the solitude of his own soul."[17]

Daniel Walker Howe describes the two great intellectual traditions that shaped the American sense of self. "Protestantism taught that the natural self was corrupt and in need of redemption; the Enlightenment taught that human beings were capable of self-direction and self-definition."[18] Seemingly antithetical, these traditions came through education and self-discipline to a kind of distinctive synthesis that resulted in a balanced sense of self. While leaving the individual free, the framers of the American Constitution provided an institutional structure that would limit the passions and interests that resulted. This did not mean self-indulgence, but it did mean that Americans valued opportunities for choice of personal identity. "It is the age of the first person singular," Ralph Waldo Emerson wrote in his journal before publishing his 1841 essay *Self Reliance,* which became a classic assertion of the values of individualism and nonconformity to which Americans aspired.[19] An admirer of Emerson, Walt Whitman wrote in *Leaves of Grass,* "One's-self must never give way—that is the final substance—that out of all else is sure. . . . One's-self I sing, a simple separate person."[20] For Americans, the dignity of the individual is fundamental to his or her identity. As Robert Bellah and his associates wrote in their study of individualism in American life, "Anything that would violate our right to think for ourselves, judge for ourselves, make our own decisions, live our lives as we see fit, is not only morally wrong, it is sacrilegious. Our highest and noblest aspirations, not only for ourselves, but for those we care about, for our society and for the world, are closely linked to our individualism."[21]

Countless critics of American democracy have observed how some of the dangers Tocqueville perceived have grown more apparent in the years since he wrote his classic study. They were faults that the Japanese, with their collectivist values, inevitably perceived as well. Individualism in twentieth-century America tended to escape the constraints that religion and republican traditions had implied and to stress rather expanding claims of individual rights and individual autonomy. In *The Irony of American History*, Reinhold Niebuhr observes that Americans have lost the underlying religious principles of their Puritan ancestors. "The Christian ideal of the equality of all men before God and of equality as a regulative principle of justice is made into a simple historical possibility. . . . The Christian idea of the significance of each individual in God's sight becomes, in bourgeois civilization, the concept of the discrete individual who makes himself the final end of his own existence. The Christian idea of providence is rejected for the heady notion that man is the master of his fate and the captain of his soul."[22] The limitless faith in human rights was the opportunity to become the kind of person one wanted to be without any regard for the claims of society. As the psychiatrist Robert Coles wrote, the self became "the only or main form of reality."[23]

The Japanese Experience

When the Occupation began, nothing divided Americans and Japanese traditions more profoundly than the way they viewed the social role of the individual. The Occupation's reforms challenged fundamental social values that history had bred in the Japanese people over centuries. As the anthropologist Robert Smith observed, "[Americans] are taught that there is no task more important than nourishing and developing our individuality. Our sense of self stops with the skin. . . . Among us social conformity is disvalued. . . . [We] are likely to find the Japanese to be excessively group oriented, far too willing to submerge the self in the collectivity, and possessed of weak and permeable ego boundaries. They seem willing even eager to forego the rewards of growth as individual human beings and to eschew the very behavior that will lead to self-realization."[24]

All of Japan's institutions, from the historical paradigm of village life and family practice to the modern corporation, instilled a sense of interdependence. Japanese take for granted that human relationships are reciprocal and complementary in character, and everyone is made aware from the earliest stages of life that the human being is the product of interrelationships with others. Rather than producing character traits of individual achievement, self-responsibility, and independence, history has ingrained the importance of interdependence and of acceptance of social deference. Notions of the autonomous self and of society as a compact of individuals voluntarily coming together were foreign to their national experience. As Smith observed, for the Japanese, "the self is not an inherent entity that must be discovered; it is thought to develop through time. . . . We must seek the Japanese 'self' in the 'social.' The self is something which has a development; it is not initially there, at birth, but arises in the process of social experience and activity, that is, develops in the given individual as result of his relations to that process as a whole and to other individuals within that process. . . . The self is developed in the context of social interaction."[25] Americans find it difficult to fathom and appreciate the degree to which Japanese society is marked by an interconnectedness, a web of obligations and expectations that envelops the individual. In an apt and memorable metaphor, Maruyama Masao described Japanese society as akin to "an octopus pot (takotsubo)."[26]

The extended family was the fundamental Japanese social institution. Many ties held these traditional, large lineage groups together, but most important was the economic interdependence of its members. It was taken for granted that members of this basic unit of social organization would sacrifice personal desires for the well-being of the group from which they drew their identity. The family provided training in collectivist values and hierarchy, respect for age, male superiority, sacrifice for the overall good, and the importance of finding one's proper place in the group. The family was the model for all institutions in society. The state itself was described in prewar ideology as the family writ large.

Yet, the Japanese did have a liberal legacy from the Meiji period, which was suppressed as the government after 1890 undertook the nationalist mobilization of the masses for the march to industry and empire. In the Meiji period when Japan looked to the West for keys to building a modern nation, Fukuzawa Yukichi (1835–1901), the great apostle of modernization, introduced the concept of individualism. For him, individualism was the source of the West's strength in science and practical learning. Conversely, he regarded subordination of the individual to the will and interests of the family group as the source of

Japan's backwardness. Shedding the values of the family system and replacing them with individual responsibility and initiative were essential if Japan was to transform itself into a great nation. New Japanese words had to be coined to express the concepts of liberty, rights, individualism, and democracy.

While Fukuzawa's concern was with the nation's political destiny, the first writers of the modern Japanese novel explored the spiritual implications of an autonomous self. The introduction of Christianity by missionaries in the Meiji period was often the vehicle for drawing attention to the individual's unique and independent existence apart from the welter of social relationships. The modern novel in Japan took on a strong confessional predilection, allowing the writer to retreat from social life and turn to the inner self. The Christian insistence on individual salvation and relationship to God prodded this "discovery of the self," the theme of early novels. The new values, however, were both attractive and tortuous to live by in Japanese society. How difficult it was for even these talented and creative young writers in the Meiji period to live according to the new concept can be seen in the mental turmoil and spiritual angst prevalent among them. The search for selfhood led toward writing about firsthand, directly perceived experience and pursuing individual liberation. Writers often retreated into a spiritual exploration of their inner world, a quietist and separatist journey that often had more in common with traditional Japanese religious experience in the Buddhist sense of finding fulfillment in release from worldly bonds.[27]

No Japanese explained the essence of the Western concept of individualism better than novelist Natsume Sōseki, whose 1914 essay "My Individualism" is a classic of the literature.[28] Sōseki offered a balanced understanding of individualism. A young Japanese should pursue interests in life that match his or her own personality but at the same time avoid the unbridled assertion of one's own interests without respect for the interests of others. "My ideas on the subject have come down to this: first, that you will be unhappy for life," he told students, "unless you press on to the point where you discover work that suits you perfectly and enables you to develop your individuality; second, that if society is going to allow you such regard for your own individuality, it only makes sense for you to recognize the individuality of others and show a similar regard for their inclinations."[29]

Already by the time Sōseki wrote, however, the influence of a nationalist orthodoxy promulgated by government and instinctively supported by popular sentiment found individualism colliding with the collectivist values that were so comfortable and familiar in Japanese society. "Many people," Sōseki wrote, "seem to think of individualism as something opposed to—even destructive of—nationalism. . . . Many go so far as to assert that our nation will perish unless this terrible 'individualism' is stamped out. What utter nonsense! . . . A nationalistic morality comes out a very poor second when compared with an individualistic morality."[30]

The introduction of the Western concept of individualism by intellectuals in the Meiji period could not, however, dent the influence of centuries of cultural experience. Cooperation, deference to authority, conformity with the needs of the community, subordination of individual interest to the consensus, maintenance of harmonious relations—all these collectivist values gave the government a broad basis on which to build an ideology that likened the nation to a harmonious family. Through education and mass media, the Meiji government built its national ideology around the concept of the family state (*kazoku kokka*) and took every opportunity to inculcate as the paramount value the importance of loyalty to the state over personal and private interest. As a typical social studies textbook put it, "Our country is based on the family system. The whole country is one great family, and the Imperial House is the Head Family. It is with the feeling of filial love and respect for parents that we Japanese people express our reverence toward the Throne of unbroken imperial line."[31]

Japan's premodern values inclined people in this direction, but the state shaped and molded them into a modern nationalist orthodoxy, propagating collectivist values of a unique social harmony, selfless devotion to state and society, and obedience to superiors. In the 1930s world trends seemed to demonstrate the weakness of Western liberal principles. As the Ministry of Education's major ideological manifesto, *Shinmin no michi* (The way of the subject), issued in August 1941, put it, "An old order that has been placing world humanity under individualism, liberalism, and materialism for several hundred years is now crumbling. A new order is now in the making amid unprecedented world changes."[32]

Japan's Religious Tradition

In its goal to change Japanese thought and behavior, the Occupation set out to overcome a Japanese religious tradition that has been one of the distinguishing features of its civilization. "There was not, in the Japanese tradition," Robert Bellah observed, "a strong philosophical or religious orthodoxy such as existed in China, the Islamic world, or the West."[33] Foreign religions have long been introduced into Japan but rarely possessed the power to establish abstract norms and transcendental values to which the Japanese state should be subject. Buddhism never attained a dominance or an institutional foundation equivalent to the papacy in Rome, from which it could propound norms for the political world. In the Japanese religious tradition, as Nakamura Hajime pointed out, the native creed that came to be called Shinto (literally, "the way of the gods") is remarkable for its emphasis on the "fluid and arresting character of observed events [which] regards the phenomenal world itself as Absolute and rejects the recognition of anything existing over and above the phenomenal world."[34] Transcendental and universalist norms were weak.[35] As Maruyama Masao wrote, "Japanese tradition has no 'axis' analogous to Christianity in the West or Confucianism in China. It is a 'tradition without structure,' that lacks a great organizing heritage of thought comparable to Christianity or Islam. What is lacking is an 'absolute being or a "Way" that logically and normatively orders the world in its own characteristic manner.'"[36] The point these scholars make is that Japanese religion has tended to be this-worldly in orientation, characterized by ritual and sacramental practice. Lacking was "a transcendental reference point, outside the world so to speak, that made it possible to criticize and in principle to revise the fundamental social and political premises of existing societies."[37]

To help mobilize loyalty to the nation, the Meiji leaders turned to their ancient sacred hierarchical order to provide a nationalist ideology. Their religious traditions made possible the fusion of deity and ruler, the emperor as a living god (*kami*). To build support for the modern state, they drew on a variety of traditional values and concepts and with great skill wove them into a tapestry of nationalist ideology surrounding the imperial throne. Practices of the Shinto folk religion, including veneration of ancestors, feudal values of loyalty, and respect for hierarchy, were appropriated to create the basis for a mass worship of the emperor.

Scholars have called this "the invention of tradition," by which elites manipulated cultural symbols and practices. For centuries ordinary Japanese had worshipped at tens of thousands of shrines devoted to the concerns of local inhabitants—healthy children, good crops, and prosperous communities. Communal spirits or deities (*kami*) were worshipped according to simple rituals to elicit their protective powers. These local observances were the product of popular practices since prehistoric times. At the national level, since the earliest times the Japanese imperial line had based its claims to sovereignty on Shinto myths that proclaimed the imperial family's descent from the sun goddess Amaterasu. The Meiji government therefore reworked the deeply rooted traditions of the imperial cult to enfold it with local customs. The Shinto folk religion became State Shinto, a modern ideology of extraordinary power and appeal. A hierarchy of thousands of shrines, focused on worship of the emperor and Shinto deities, were under government oversight. Shinto priests were civil servants. Imperial shrines were funded by the Imperial Household, and national shrines by the government. At the pinnacle of the State Shinto system were the Great Shrine of Ise, home of the ancestral Sun Goddess, and the Yasukuni Shrine in Tokyo, which commemorated all those who died in war.

The Occupation not only wanted to break the bond between Shinto and the state that had promoted Japanese nationalist ideology; it also wanted to establish religious freedom. The Potsdam Declaration had promised freedom of religion, and SCAP inserted provisions in the constitution that went beyond anything the US Constitution provides by separating the state from any religious activity. Article 20 holds both that "freedom of religion is guaranteed to all" and that "no religious organization shall receive any privileges from the State, nor exercise any political authority." Article 89 forbids use of public monies for any religious institution.

Fundamental to the remaking of Japan into an American-style democracy was the belief that it must be accompanied by a spiritual revolution. The Americans had always believed that democracy was, as MacArthur put it, "a thing largely of the spirit" and must have "a spiritual core" of Christian principles.[38] It was no surprise, then, that MacArthur frequently urged American churches and the Vatican to send missionaries to fill the spiritual vacuum. Japan seemed like a spiritual wasteland and was replete with contradictory practices. Although the

Occupation was asserting a policy of freedom of religion, abolishing State Shinto, and insisting that there be no connection between religion and the state, MacArthur gave official preference to Christian missions. He wrote to American Protestant and Catholic leaders in the early days of the Occupation, urging them to send missionaries as soon as possible because "we are on the verge of a great moral revolution." Missionaries were the first professional group admitted to occupied Japan, more than a year and a half before businessmen were permitted entry.[39] In the first three years of the Occupation, more than 2,000 American missionaries arrived. Moreover, they were extended postal, medical, transportation, supply, and education privileges—in short, "most of the privileges of the conquering American military forces."[40] SCAP was oblivious to the contradiction inherent in this patronage given missionaries at a time when it was directing the Japanese government to end support of Shinto shrines and inserting the principle of separation of religion and state in the new constitution.

Imperial Court officials, seeking to protect the emperor from war crimes charges, seemed to pander to MacArthur's prejudices. The Court gave missionaries access to the palace and to the imperial family. Japanese Christians, such as Kagawa Toyohiko, were invited to give lectures to Hirohito on the Christian dogma. In his first meeting with the emperor on September 27, 1945, MacArthur recalled that "the Emperor privately declared his willingness to make Christianity the national religion of Japan."[41] Such pandering came to an end with the conclusion of the Occupation.

Nevertheless, despite SCAP's support for proselytization, Christianity made only small inroads among the Japanese. MacArthur eventually concluded that "pride of race . . . would prevent Japanese from becoming Christian" and gave up making public advocacy of Christian missions.[42] At the time of the San Francisco Peace Treaty, John Foster Dulles still worried that the Japanese suffering from a vast "spiritual vacuum" would be susceptible to the appeals of communism. He believed that the Japanese were "fundamentally non-religious" and therefore did not possess "the requisite religious and spiritual qualities to withstand Communism over the long haul."[43] Nambara Shigeru, president of the University of Tokyo and a Christian, observed in 1949 that "the time has come for [the people of Japan] to make their serious encounter with this world religion which recognizes and upholds man as *persona* or a being whose value is intrinsic and universal." But elsewhere he admitted that such an encounter "is basically a task that will last several centuries into the future."[44]

The postwar novelist Endō Shūsaku, who became a Christian at a young age through the influence of his mother, explored through his many widely read novels the possibilities of Christianity in Japan. He described his quest for an indigenization of Christianity as replacing an "ill-fitting suit" imported from the West: "God must be found on the streets of Shinjuku or Shibuya, too—districts which seem so far removed from Him. . . . It will be one of my tasks to find God in such typical scenes. . . . If I succeed in doing that, my 'Western suit' will no longer be Western, but will have become my own suit."[45] Christianity of course was not the only foreign-born religion in Japan. However, from the start of the modern period, Christianity became associated with the West as an aspect of its imperialist domination in Asia. In contrast with Korea, for example, where the Christian church often sided with Korean nationalism in its struggle for independence from the Japanese colonial yoke, Christianity in Japan was most often seen as a threat to nationalism.

In a 2008 poll by the *Yomiuri* newspaper, 72 percent of Japanese responded that they did not believe in a religion.[46] This result is similar to those of any number of polls taken in Japan. But it does not mean that Japanese are not a spiritually inclined people. In fact, 70 percent of Japanese consider themselves spiritual.[47] The word for religion, *shūkyō*, connotes for the Japanese a Western concept of religion as an organized and exclusive belief system that has "universalizing dimensions that are taught through the transmission of doctrines, texts, sermons, and the words of founders and teachers."[48] The Japanese generally do not consider as *shūkyō* such common spiritual practices as visits to shrines and temples, participation in their festivals, funeral rites, veneration of ancestors at a household altar, and annual visits to family graves. Therefore, when surveys ask Japanese if they believe in a particular religion (*shūkyō*), the overwhelming number of Japanese say no.

Only 1 percent of Japanese are members of a church, but at the same time, more than 10 percent of Japanese feel a certain empathy (*shitashimi*) for Christianity, and among young Japanese the percentage is several times higher.[49] Half of all Japanese weddings are held in a Christian or quasi-Christian form. In general, Christianity has had a much greater influence on education and social reform movements than what the limited number of converts would suggest. It has often been said to be most prevalent among the intellectual elite. The present empress graduated from a Catholic school and was known to be a Christian.[50] Interestingly, Yoshida Shigeru asked on his deathbed to be baptized, and he was buried as Joseph Thomas More with funeral rites held in a Catholic cathedral in Tokyo.[51]

The role of Shinto in postwar Japan has aroused some considerable controversy, because while the constitution proscribes any relation of the state to the shrines, there has been support and nostalgia for restoring a limited relationship. The controversy has been most visible with regard to the Yasukuni Shrine, founded in the early Meiji period to honor the spirits of the war dead enshrined there. Many postwar prime ministers have insisted on visiting the shrine; but because it seems to celebrate battles fought by the prewar military and because of a 1978 ceremony to enshrine convicted war criminals, it inflames the nationalist reactions of Korea and China. Japanese conservatives have argued, however, that other countries honor their war dead; even at Arlington Cemetery Confederate soldiers who might have supported slavery are honored.[52] Prime ministers routinely visit the Ise Shrine, which commemorates the mythical founding of the Japanese state, without controversy. As a consequence, though issues of state and religion remain conflicted today, the prevailing spirituality is still distinctly Japanese.

Japan's Meritocracy

Revolutionizing Japanese education was a colossal undertaking in thought reform. One notable skeptic was Sir George Sansom, the British diplomat and authority on Japanese history. As a member of the Far Eastern Commission, an allied advisory group, Sansom had been dubious of the wisdom of occupying Japan. He wrote in his diary of the Americans leading education reform: "I do not think they realize how deeply rooted and how strong is the Japanese intellectual tradition: they seem to think that Japan can be supplied with a new system of education as a tailor might furnish a new suit." The education system in the United States, he added somewhat patronizingly but perhaps not without cause, "is not of such a quality as to encourage one in feeling that it provides a good model for any other country."[53]

In pre-surrender planning, the Americans concluded that in addition to its nationalist indoctrination and highly centralized structure, Japanese education needed a vast reform because it had promoted elitism by separating students on the basis of testing ability into a multitrack system in which the brightest were advanced to leadership of the bureaucracy and big business. The Americans thought that "universal education based on advancement by merit, while admirable in many respects, served the interests of the state, not the people. Japan's highly centralized and selective school system transformed 'the best brains of the nation' into an elite loyal to the state and big business but discouraged individual initiative and original thinking."[54]

The Occupation began by purging wartime teachers and eliminating the social studies and ethics texts that had been in use. Japan had 40,000 schools, 400,000 teachers, and 18 million pupils.[55] More than a quarter of the teachers were forced into retirement for their wartime activities.[56] A fundamental reorientation of Japanese education then grew out of the recommendations of the twenty-seven-person United States Education Mission, led by the president of the University of Illinois, George Stoddard. The group arrived in Japan in March 1946 for a brief tour of study. At the first meeting of the mission, Abe Yoshishige, the minister of education, cautioned the Americans that while they were "in a position to do anything it pleases with Japan," it would not be wise "to impose upon us simply what is characteristic of America or of Europe. . . . There are some young idealists among the Americans . . . who tend to use Japan as a kind of a laboratory in a rash attempt to experiment on some abstract ideals of their own, ideals which have not yet been realized even in their own country." He expressed hope that the members of the mission would come to "realize that democratic education cannot be carried out in our country in exactly the same way as it is in yours."[57]

The Education Mission, which included many distinguished American educators, seemed to agree, and MacArthur instructed the Education Ministry to appoint a panel of Japanese academic leaders to work with the mission. Chaired by the president of the University of Tokyo, Nambara Shigeru, this panel did much to shape and extend the recommendations of the Education Mission. It was an example of the liberal reformism that existed in some parts of Japanese leadership, and in many areas of Occupation reform, the Japanese participated and were influential in the outcome. Nambara, who was often at odds with Prime

Minister Yoshida and the conservative elite, worked well with the Americans because he accepted much of their belief in the need to democratize the educational system. In fact, the Japanese educators themselves seemed to have been responsible for a large portion of the reforms, demonstrating again the indigenous potential for reform.[58] Both the Japanese panel and the US Education Mission joined in recommending a vast decentralization of the powerful Ministry of Education. The rigid control that it had exercised was to be replaced by popularly elected boards of education at the local level, which would assume power over staff, curriculum, and textbook choice. The overall structure of the education system was to be transformed so that it closely approximated the American system. In the old system, after six years of compulsory education, children were sorted into a multitrack system in which, depending primarily on their abilities, they were directed either into a line of commercial and technical training or into a middle school of five years that prepared them for higher academic training. With the support of Nambara, SCAP ordered a single-track system along American lines of six years of elementary schooling, followed by three years of junior high school and three years of senior high school for all children. The Americans together with Nambara's panel of Japanese liberal educators argued that it was more democratic to mingle students of varying abilities rather than to sort them into a multitrack system that had encouraged elitism.

Coeducation was established in schools at all levels. The new textbooks emphasized the principles of family reform to be embodied in the new legal code. "That men and women should be truly equal," said one government-approved textbook, "that marriage should be guaranteed economic security, that marriage should be free—these are foundations of a healthy and undistorted system of monogamous marriage."[59]

Similar Americanization was recommended for the system of higher education, which had been differentiated among higher technical schools, normal schools, and the imperial universities. The Education Mission recommended that institutions of higher learning be transformed into four-year universities, arguing that the normal and technical schools did not give sufficient time to broad social and humanistic studies. Moreover, each prefecture should have its own university in a pattern reminiscent of the American state university system. In place of the old diversity of higher education, higher schools, normal schools, and technical institutes were turned into universities, increasing their number from 49 in 1942 to 245 in 1955. The result of all this structural reformation was not only a homogenization of education but also an explosion in the number of students in higher education. In the two decades after the Occupation, the number of students attending institutions of higher learning more than tripled, and Japan was second only to the United States in the percentage of the population enrolled in higher education.[60]

Of even more basic concern than the structure of the system to the educational reformists was the inculcation of new values. Under SCAP's guidance, the Diet rescinded the Imperial Rescript on Education of 1890, which had set forth the basic nationalist orientation of Japan's prewar education. In 1947, the Fundamental Law of Education was passed, which defined the purpose of the education system as contributing to "the peace of the world and the welfare of humanity by building a democratic and cultural state." Schools were to promote "the full development of personality"; and peace, democracy, and international cooperation were to become the themes of the new education.[61]

The work of writing textbooks heretofore rigidly determined by the Ministry of Education was turned over to private enterprise. Locally elected school committees, which now had charge of textbook choice, had, in many cases, a wide variety from which to choose. History was no longer to teach the glorious reign of former emperors or the exploits of the Japanese military. Instead, it should be written in an objective way, offering a critical knowledge of the development of Japanese institutions. However, because teachers soon organized into a powerful union dominated by left-wing leaders, most history texts emphasized class divisions, economic exploitation, and "the struggle of the people" for freedom from the oppression and despotism of the ruling classes.

The democratization of Japanese education instituted by the Americans and Japanese reformers ran into strong headwinds when the Occupation ended. The Ministry of Education began to roll back the administrative reforms and regain its influence. The locally elected school boards were replaced with boards appointed by the government, and choice of textbooks came under a Ministry system of review and approval. The American model of high school education, which sought to foster individual expression, independent thinking, and diverse talents, was subordinated to the goals of the state. Education was harnessed to the goals of economic growth and the needs of big business. Working with business interests, the Ministry formulated a comprehensive program to transform the purpose of education and produce human capital required for industrial society. Shortly after Prime Minister Ikeda announced his National Income Doubling Plan in 1960, the Education Ministry issued a white paper indicating "the goals of education must be tied to developing human talent to support the long-term planning which will lead to a doubling of the national income."[62] Testing became a ubiquitous aspect for entrance into all levels of education. Mastery of detailed information for these tests required rote memory work, and the intense competition for entrance into the best schools tended to promote qualities of diligence and sacrifice. The school system became a meritocracy offering "equal educational opportunity, making it frankly competitive and then uses the order of ability or merit produced to stratify individuals according to the many grades of work in society."[63] In the American ideal of meritocracy, equal opportunity made upward mobility dependent on "one's own wits, cultivated skills, and resourcefulness, the promise of being 'self-made.'"[64] The Japanese ideal held very different assumptions. Rather than cultivating individual creativity, the educational system focused on producing economically useful talent. Rather than fostering individual expression and diversity, the main function of higher education was to rate students according to their ability and diligence, represented by their mastery of detailed knowledge over the long process of educational competition. Consequently, entrance examinations, which had been important in the prewar period, became far more important in the mass education world of postwar Japan. Preparation for these highly competitive university entrance examinations meant getting into the best high schools—and soon the hierarchy of prestige extended to all levels of education, as did the pattern of competitive examination. Many children at every level of schooling attended private schools, known as *juku*, after regular school hours. These cram schools were designed to prepare students for entrance exams to the best schools.

As the democratic reforms were watered down by the bureaucracy-business alliance, Japanese liberals were appalled at the overheated examination system, the stress on academic hierarchy, and the emergence of "an ideology dominated by the one-dimensional glorification of academic competence (*nōryokushugi*)," which had turned schools into

Preparing for entrance exams despite an injured arm, a Japanese schoolboy sits in a class at a *juku* (cram school) in 1982. His headband says "struggle to pass." Kaku Kurita / Getty Images / 50591034.

"arenas for the most vicious forms of competition related to social selection and advancement."[65] Both the Americans and their Japanese counterparts had hoped to establish a schooling in which there would be "freedom of inquiry rather than exclusive memorization of factual material."[66] Instead, over the next two decades the education system became overwhelmingly focused on careerism and qualification for a job. At the expense of the creativity and spirit of individualism and spontaneous inquiry, the system fostered a different set of virtues—"diligence, sacrifice, mastery of detailed information, endurance over many preparatory years, willingness to postpone gratification, and competitive spirit— . . . motivated largely by a rather selfish individual desire to get ahead."[67] This change in focus was, of course, not only a reflection of individual ambition; it was also essential to the national goal of economic growth and catching up. Thus, it produced generations of disciplined workers socialized to perform in "a rigorous hierarchical, and finely tuned organizational environment."[68]

By the 1980s, when Japan had largely caught up with the advanced industrial nations, it became clear that the education system would need to be overhauled. No longer able to import knowledge and technology from abroad, Japanese would need creative thinkers capable of producing new ideas. In 1984, Prime Minister Nakasone appointed an advisory council on education to make recommendations. Nakasone and his advisors believed that during the long years of catching up with the West, the school system had become so highly centralized and rigid, so intent on rote memory work and test scores, so focused on meeting company hiring policies and a mass-produced supply of workers for Japanese industry that it stifled qualities of creativity and diversity that Japan would need in the future. Many people in business were also coming to the conclusion that standardization and regulation of education had become a dead weight inhibiting the development of a more diverse and creative workforce that the economy would need in the twenty-first century.

In 1987, the education council recommended changes to liberalize and loosen up the rigid system, introduce great latitude into curriculum, and establish a wider range of criteria for judging achievement than simple test scores. It advocated the encouragement of greater individuality and imagination so that Japan could provide the ideas and creativity required to increase its economic growth. What the council wanted to achieve sounded a bit like the Occupation reformers except that the council's reforms were designed, as its critics said, simply to build the nation's economic strength.

Nakasone and his advisors also wanted the schools to take the lead in the "internationalization" of Japan. They wanted to open schools to international influences, remove obstacles to hiring foreign teachers and enrolling foreign students, improve foreign language instruction, and

Japanese prime minister Nakasone Yasuhiro and his wife entertain President Ronald Reagan and the First Lady at their private retreat. While Nakasone pours sake, Reagan fumbles with his chopsticks. Dirck Halstead / Getty Images / 50538732.

enhance Japanese understanding of other cultures. The desired product of a reformed education was a newly self-confident Japanese, at home in the world, not clinging to other Japanese when abroad but rather communicating easily with foreigners and understanding their mores.

The recommendations were swept up in criticism first from the left, which saw in them signs of the revival of nationalism, and then from the right by the "notoriously conservative" Ministry of Education, which was resistant to any effort to loosen its control of the education system. Although the recommendations were initially frustrated, they nevertheless "set the trajectory and policy agenda for the future."[69] In the years since the Nakasone initiative, the ministry has implemented many of the recommendations, which have been directed at "internationalizing" the education system in ways that would serve the national interest. The goal of replacing the rigidly uniform and entrance-exam-based education with a more relaxed approach focused on promoting individuality and creativity was not easily achieved. Measures to teach a more diverse and international curriculum that would prepare students for a more global environment, to hire more foreign teachers, to enhance English-language ability, and to attract an international student body were all promoted as a response to globalization. Results were often disappointing, and a breakdown in classroom discipline, youth alienation, and growing student disinterest in study abroad raised questions of how well the reforms had been planned.[70]

The apparent failure of the reforms introducing a more Western emphasis on promoting individuality gave the nationalist prime minister Abe Shinzo an opportunity in 2006 to push through a longtime conservative goal of revising the Occupation's Fundamental Law of Education by replacing the emphasis on individual creativity and independence with the goals that conservatives had always said were absent in postwar education: love of country, service to the nation, and goals of the state. The underlying theme in the revision was on the purpose of education in maintaining "a spirit of community." Later we will see this "spirit" working itself out in a distinctive Japanese communitarian democracy.

The Ambivalence of Japanese Women

The Occupation took great pride in its reforms to benefit Japanese women, including enfranchisement and full participation in politics, equality before the law, and equal rights in marriage. Equal rights for women were part of the universal pattern of domestic societies that were held to be essential in the American world order. The first article of the founding Charter of the United Nations, signed in June 1945, declared that the organization's purpose was to achieve international cooperation in promoting human rights without distinction to race, sex, language, or religion. Likewise, the UN Declaration of Human Rights, adopted in December 1948, affirmed in gender-neutral language that "all human beings are born free and equal in dignity and rights . . . without distinction of any kind, such as race, colour, sex, language, religion . . . birth or other status." Americans held that equality of the sexes was the path that all modern nations would follow, and since the United States was farthest along this path, Japan would converge with this pattern.

At a time when American leadership in the United Nations was asserting principles of gender equality, it was inevitable that the Americans would seek to elevate the status of Japanese women, which they regarded as a glaring example of a backward and deformed social structure that contributed to militarism. An article in the *Saturday Evening Post* titled "The Unhappiest Women in the World," published in July 1944, described Japanese women as "either the servant or pretty toy of men" who demanded "unquestioning obedience." Even the empress was a "frightened, timid, little" being who was "unable to break through the wall of her own shyness and sense of inferiority." "The Japanese woman has very few pleasures" whatever her class, while "the only pleasure to which [she] . . . can look forward is the satisfaction of becoming a mother-in-law" whose abuse of her daughter-in-law is "another case of the legalized sadism of the Japanese."[71] The reforms that SCAP made to "liberate" Japanese women came to be a symbol for Americans of the Occupation's success in democratizing Japan. Having been emancipated, Japanese women could now acquire the equality, individuality, and spontaneity of American women and so contribute to a democratic and peaceful Japan. As *Life* magazine of February 18, 1946, observed, "If they can shake off their status as dolls and chattels, Japanese women may become an effective brake on militarism."[72]

Freeing the individual meant attacking the most fundamental institution in Japanese society, the institution that was the model for most others in Japanese society—namely, the family. The Civil Code of 1898 embodied many of the ideals of the old family system. Still in force after half a century, it was based on a manner of family organization that gave authority to the extended family, to the head of the house, and to male dominance. The extended family or "house" was considered far more important than the individuals who made it up. The traditional household, or *ie*, was not simply a nuclear family of husband, wife, and children but an extended family that included several generations. Typically, the core of this extended family group was composed of grandparents, their eldest son (who was their heir), his wife, and unmarried children. Other sons, when they married, formed branch families that were still part of the larger unit, while daughters left the family at the time of their marriage, entering the household of their husband. Many ties held these large lineage groups together, including economic interdependence, family traditions, property, and reverence for ancestors. Continuity of the family was a moral duty: rather than let a family die out, a childless couple would adopt an heir. The family taught female subordination. Thus, for example, the husband's primary obligations for support were to his parents and his children and only thirdly to his wife. The 1898 civil code vested great power in the head of the family, who had the legal right to determine the place of residence of all members of the extended family, to remove a member from the family register, and to require his approval for the marriage of any member.

The ideology of femininity in the Meiji period was summed up in the slogan "good wife and wise mother" (ryōsai kembo), which was widely promoted by government leaders and accepted by Japanese women. Women would contribute to the nation through efficient management of the household, responsible upbringing of children, frugality, and hard work. This was a Japanese version of contemporary Western ideals of female domesticity. In the 1920s middle-class women's groups responded to government encouragement that they take the lead in public causes that appeared to lie within the special domain of women, such as campaigns to increase household savings, improve welfare and health measures for mothers and children, and other civic-minded causes. Later, in the militarist era, even liberal feminists began to collaborate with the state as women's groups grew to play a prominent role in wartime mobilization causes. Women were encouraged to "give birth and multiply" (umeyo fuyaseyo) in order to provide greater military and industrial manpower.

In the first weeks of the Occupation, MacArthur gave the prime minister a list of five required reforms, of which the first was "emancipation of the women of Japan through their enfranchisement." In the spring of 1946 in the first postwar election, thirty-nine women were elected to the Diet. The constitution and the civil code elaborated further women's rights. The self-congratulatory mood of SCAP was nowhere more evident than in the satisfaction taken over reform of the role of Japanese women. "Of all the reforms wrought by MacArthur," observed his chief aide, Courtney Whitney, "none had such heartwarming results as that which changed the status of women. Almost overnight more than forty million people who had been virtual serfs achieved freedom and equal rights. Not since Lincoln had such a revolutionary change of status been accomplished on such a mass scale."[73]

It is interesting that in the planning for the Occupation in Washington, little attention was given to women's rights.[74] What is notable is that the Occupation's reforms went beyond anything Washington had in mind. It was the initiative of Beate Sirota, the young American assigned to draft provisions in the constitution, who introduced "one of the world's most radical experiments with women's rights."[75] Particularly critical in this respect was Article 24, which "by extending a guarantee of women's equality beyond the public sphere into the private domain of the family, it goes well beyond what most constitutions of the world provide," including the US Constitution.[76] An equal rights amendment for women that Congress approved in 1972 has yet to be ratified. Article 24, which Sirota also authored, stated that "marriage shall be based only on the mutual consent of both sexes and it shall maintain through mutual cooperation with the equal rights of husband and wife as a basis. Laws shall be enacted considering choice of spouse, property rights, inheritance, choice of domicile, divorce, and other matters pertaining to marriage and the family from the standpoint of individual dignity and the essential equality of the sexes." Accordingly, SCAP approved a new civil code on January 1, 1948, which among other things included the legal abolition of the "house" and the elevation of the legal status of women.[77] The authority of the extended family and of its house head came to an end. Instead, it gave legal recognition to the small nuclear family of husband, wife, and unmarried children. In place of the old system of primogeniture, the new code prescribed equal inheritance by all children, irrespective of sex. Parental consent to a marriage was no longer required over the age of twenty. Whereas previously a wife had to obtain her husband's permission to exercise property rights, this provision was now deleted. Under the old civil code, infidelity was grounds for judicial divorce only if committed by the wife; but under the new code, adultery by either partner became legal grounds.

SCAP's radical changes were legally prescribed but generally not observed in actual practice, at least in the first decades after the war. Owing to the persistence of traditional attitudes, women often refused to accept their inheritance from their parents, and most women acquiesced in divorces sought by their husbands. Family court records show that more than twice as many women as men refused their share of a parent's estate. Relatively few divorces were judicial. In 1900 virtually all divorces were by consent; in 1980 the figure was still almost 90 percent. As one anthropologist observed at this time, "In this statistic lies one more bit of evidence of the glacial character of fundamental change in the conjugal relationship. Divorce by consent, it is well known, makes it notoriously easy for a husband or his family to *force* a woman to agree to an action that she does not seek. . . . The high percentage of divorces by consent may be taken as a handy index of female powerlessness in Japanese society."[78]

When the occupiers left, Japanese bureaucrats went to great lengths to maintain the family's role in providing social welfare. To keep welfare costs low, bureaucrats were proactive in developing policies that kept the family responsible for supporting the needy and the aged and working to prevent a Western concept of an individual's "right" to receive state welfare. The Economic Planning Agency in 1977 explained that "we do not expect our country to become a Western-style individualistic society"; therefore, Japan would need to rely on "families and local communities." The "three-generation family" was deemed Japan's "hidden asset" in welfare

And in fact, most elderly Japanese are still taken care of by the younger generation—typically by daughters-in-law.[79] With burdens of social care borne by the family, the housewife became a "welfare surrogate."[80]

The reforms that SCAP made to "liberate" Japanese women came to be a symbol for Americans of the Occupation's success in democratizing Japan. Over the years, however, Japanese women have seemed ambivalent about the role the Americans supposed they should take. As the Princeton anthropologist Amy Borovoy observed, Americans were puzzled that Japanese did not seem to be converging to the American model. They have seemed ambivalent about absolute gender equality. They have not participated as actively in electoral politics as expected, and they have not actively pursued equal rights. Japan did not seem to be converging with the American pursuit of gender equality. Americans were taken aback by the persistence of Japanese women's "traditional orientation." A 1984 *National Geographic* article featured the modern economy's coexistence with women's traditional ethic of deference to men. As Borovoy writes, "The problem that Japanese women posed to the wider American audience was the nature of modernity itself, and the tacit expectation that sooner or later all nations would converge on a similar endpoint: the valuation of absolute gender equality, autonomy, and self-determination. To most Americans Japanese women did not seem fully modern."[81] The high expectations that the Occupation held have fallen short, and the reasons need to be explored.

Japanese women did not seem to take up the opportunity that their enfranchisement offered. Despite SCAP's initial enthusiasm, the election of thirty-nine women to the lower house of the Diet in 1946 (accounting for 8.4 percent of the legislators) was for decades the high-water mark of women in electoral politics. This first election seemed to foretell a major role for women in postwar politics, but the number serving in the Diet declined markedly and did not reach such levels until decades later. In the lower house election of August 2010, a record fifty-four women were elected, or 11 percent of the total, exceeding 10 percent for the first time. Nevertheless, by 2016 Japan was 156th in global ranking of female representation in lower chambers of parliament.[82] Women have not made a strong concerted effort to change public policy in favor of their needs. Ueno Chizuko, an outspoken feminist, often expresses her disappointment that young women are not more politically active in their own behalf and that they are not more committed to working for a "gender equal society."[83] In a survey taken in 2009, Japan was ninety-fifth among world nations in a ranking of women in electoral politics. Japanese politics remains very much a man's world for a variety of reasons. Whatever the Occupation's reforms, the political system has not been welcoming of women's participation in its actual operations. "Both the bureaucracy and the LDP have been dominated by men and by conservative norms that value the role women have traditionally played in the family over and above their potential to contribute through paid employment. Given this power structure, women's groups have had only limited opportunity to challenge public policies that push them to give up work and stay at home with their children."[84]

The reasons are debated, but in general, women did not find politics attractive. The Keio University sociologist Iwao Sumiko wrote in her book *The Japanese Woman* that money politics and the tight factional politicking were distasteful to women and, in any case, not easy to break in on. "The majority of Japanese, women more so than men, see politics as a remote, alien realm, a world of power mongering, influence peddling, and corruption—in short, a filthy occupation that has no relation to their lives and values. . . . Japanese women have exercised influence and power mainly in their personal or local spheres, through providing services that assure them a measure of control of economic resources and community or emotional attachments, totally outside of the formal apparatuses of national politics."[85]

Indeed, Sheldon Garon has argued that focusing as Americans do on women's limited role in electoral politics misses the activism that women undertake in community tasks. In fact, women's associations concerned with the problems of everyday living often work with the government to achieve frugal and efficient households, assist local schools, and contribute to programs for community well-being and improvement. In this way, women are much more engaged with the state than are men in postwar Japan.[86] SCAP looked askance on the way in which women's associations worked closely with the government on community tasks, wanting them to be "emancipated" and autonomous from government ties, but eventually gave in to what seemed natural to the Japanese.

In political issues that impacted the well-being of the family, women did play an important, if oftentimes unnoticed, role. For example, women played a central role in the peace movement that blossomed at the mass level in the 1950s, and they have continued to play a central role in accounting for the strength of pacifism in Japan. Often this role is overlooked because no particular woman has been identified as a leader, but it was middle-class housewives meeting in small neighborhood groups and circulating petitions that launched the movement. In the great demonstrations of the 1950s, especially in their violence and outright activism, the face of the protests seemed to be students; but in the lasting effects of the opposition to incorporation in the Cold War, it was the role of women that was more significant. Through the postwar decades, much more than most historians have recognized, it was the quiet persistence of women who defended Article 9 and resisted remilitarization and involvement in foreign entanglements. Women were mobilized less by abstractions of peace and democracy than by the concrete issues of life and especially motherhood.[87] Women remembered acutely the wartime suffering—husbands and sons going off to battle and often never returning, the wartime deprivation, and firebombing of the cities. The *Lucky Dragon* incident of March 1, 1954, was a critical event in this regard because it awakened concern for the safety of food and the environment as well as memories of what the horrors of war had done to family life. Housewives were responsible for the massive petition drives that galvanized the antinuclear and antibase peace movements that led up to the anti-treaty demonstrations of 1960.

In general, Japanese women have lagged far behind the women of most other countries in the pursuit of gender equality. In 2014, the World

Economic Forum, host of the annual Davos meetings, ranked Japan 104th among 142 countries in a measure of gender equality.[88] Although far more women were in the labor force in the postwar period and most women held down a job at some time in their lives, relatively few pursued a lifetime career outside the home. Women's compensation was less than 60 percent of men's, and they generally did not qualify for the age-seniority system that tied pay to length of service. Women's work was usually regarded as temporary, in that they would leave when they married, bore their first child, or reached age thirty. Even if they later returned to the same firm, they would start at the beginning as far as actual accrual of time was concerned. Women's work was generally a means of supplementing the family income, and, in this sense, "work is not an alternative to homemaking; it is an extension of the home role."[89] Women in the workforce is described as following an "M curve." As Schoppa defines it, "Japanese women work in high numbers in their twenties before they marry and have children, work at much lower rates in their thirties as their family responsibilities grow, and then return to higher rates in their forties and fifties when their children are older. Japanese M-curve patterns stands [sic] in stark contrast to workforce participation patterns in other advanced industrialized nations."[90]

The United Nations adopted in 1979 the Convention on the Elimination of All Forms of Discrimination against Women, sometimes described as an International Bill of Rights for Women. In response to such international pressures, the Diet passed in 1985 the Equal Employment Opportunities Act. "It *encourages* employers to refrain from discriminating on the basis of gender in all stages of the employment process, including recruitment, hiring, training, compensation and promotion policies, and retirement. No explicit penalties are imposed on employers who do not conform."[91] Most firms have responded to this legislation by offering women the choice between two tracks when they apply. One track has a set of job classifications designed mostly for men, with better pay, promotions, and benefits in return for complete dedication to the job; the other track is designed for women, who are expected to quit when they marry. The first track is unappealing to most women because it is so demanding in time and endurance and conflicts with hopes and customs of family life.

Many anthropologists have found middle-class, internationalist Japanese women deeply ambivalent about the role of the American woman as a model for their own lifestyle.[92] On the one hand, they are attracted to the role of women in American society. The possibility of self-fulfillment, freedom, romance, gender equality, and expressivity stands in contrast to the confining reality of Japanese life. On the other hand, in her study, Amy Borovoy found that Japanese women are often troubled by the trade-off that the American model requires. "The absorption of American values and ideas turned out to be a complicated and partial process."[93] Although the American-authored constitution and civil code attempted "to redefine the nature of family, describing marriage as a private relationship based on the mutual decision of the two parties and placing the spousal relationship at the center of family life," that ideology has not been fully accepted. Despite the evidence of increased "love marriages," the reality has been more often a modified version of the traditional *ryōsai kembo* role of good wife and wise mother with marriage based on separate but compatible spheres, women managing the home, emphasizing the role of motherhood, and providing nurturance while the husband supported the family as the wage earner.[94]

From a frequently offered conservative perspective in Japan, adherence to the American-imposed values in the constitution and civil code led to the weakening of the family, a decline in the birthrate, and a rise in divorce. While the divorce rate in Japan has grown to one in three marriages, it is not as high as the rate in the United States, where half of marriages end in divorce. The conservative argument is that for most Japanese, the family, rather than the individual, was the fundamental unit of society. They preferred to see the roles of husbands and wives as complementary and mutually dependent. The wife ordinarily had a great deal of power and autonomy in managing the household and raising the children and was often the caretaker of the elderly parents. Frequently, the middle-class husband turned over his entire paycheck to his wife, who was responsible for budgeting, saving, and managing the finances in the domestic realm. As Iwao Sumiko wrote of this conservative perspective: "Most Japanese women, while admiring American women for persistently demanding equality with men, cannot help but deeply sympathize with the American women they observe who are waging what looks like a losing battle to live up to the lofty ideal of the woman who is active professionally and culturally and still manages to be a good mother, wife, and community member."[95]

For an extended time during the postwar period, government policy, especially tax policy, as well as the benefits package of large corporations, encouraged women to stay at home, but the demands of the market are beginning to change policy. With the growing labor shortage, initiatives to encourage female participation in the labor force are increasingly favored. The erosion of lifetime employment likewise makes the one-wage family less viable. Borovoy concludes "that the domestic ideal, particularly the role of the mother, apparently continues to be compelling to many young Japanese women. . . . Forsaking the idealization of motherhood and state support for the family, even though it may be accompanied by an opening of broader opportunities for women, will be experienced as great loss."[96]

While many women are content with the *ryōsai kembo* ideal, others are quietly opting out. Some have called it a "quiet revolution." Others have called it "a gender revolution" or "a quiet rebellion."[97] Women are marrying later (or not at all) and having fewer children. The divorce rate particularly among older couples has noticeably increased. More significantly, the lengthening of the life cycle added decades to one's life. In 1935, the average lifespan of Japanese women was 49.6 years; fifty years later it was over 80 years. Changes in the industrial sector made jobs in an expanding service sector available to women.[98] Moreover, increasing affluence and the availability of new conveniences gave women more free time. One interesting indication was found in the regular surveys of attitudes. In response to one such survey that asked respondents whether they would prefer to have been born as a member of the opposite sex, between 1958 and 2008 the percentage of women replying that they are content to have been born female rose from 27 to 72 percent. For men who are content to have been born male, the percentage was steady at about 90 percent.[99] The results probably reflect new labor-saving technology and the growing middle-class prosperity by the 1980s, but not necessarily a lasting sense of satisfaction with gender relations in Japanese society.

The causes of Japan's declining fertility rate, now one of the lowest in the industrialized world, are complex. The desire to increase family well-being also limited the size of families. Abortion and family planning were widely discussed. In 1948 the Diet passed the Eugenics Law, which made abortion available to women for "economic reasons," but this provision was not enforced and it was widely recognized that abortion was easily available to all. The fertility rate began a steep decline during the 1950s. Even so, through the late 1970s the population replacement rate of 2.08 was still achieved, but after 1980 it continued to fall and by 2004 it had reached 1.29. The rate for Tokyo fell below 1.00.[100] The government's reluctance to provide state support for professionalized care made "caregivers' exhaustion" a topic in public discourse.[101] The implications for Japan's future were of course huge, and there is a voluminous writing on the causes for declining fertility. So significant a change is obviously the source of deep underlying changes in attitudes and aspirations and mounting concerns about the growing labor shortage and the burdens of supporting a rapidly aging society.

Japan's Conservative Society

Japan remains a resolutely conservative society, and, in this sense, its postwar intimacy with the United States, with its instinctive liberal traditions, is indeed unnatural. Japan is notorious for a continuing reluctance to accept immigrants, political refugees, foreign workers, and even foreign investment. At a time when millions of political refugees have sought shelter, they have found the world's third-largest economy virtually closed. In 2014, Japan gave political asylum to eleven refugees.[102] Even with a population in steep decline, discussion of admitting foreigners to solve the crisis of a shortage of workers has drawn little enthusiasm. Inward foreign direct investment is one-tenth the level of OECD countries.[103] Americans, even those who have devoted their lives to explaining Japanese culture, have been exasperated by the introversion and ethnocentrism of its society. Edward Seidensticker, in his final column for the *Yomiuri* newspaper in 1962, concluded that the Japanese "are not like other people. They are infinitely more clannish, insular, parochial, and one owes it to one's self-respect to preserve a feeling of outrage at its insularity."[104] Even Reischauer, with his extraordinary devotion to the Japanese people, wrote in the last years of his life that they "must overcome their sense of separateness and, to put it bluntly, show a greater readiness to join the human race."[105]

Living in a world order so dominated by liberal values, the Japanese were deeply conscious of their own contrasting conservative traditions. More than any other people, the Japanese struggled with the cultural hegemony Western Enlightenment values and institutions have exercised from the opening of the country in the Meiji period to the postwar Occupation. The claims of this progressive view were deeply divisive in modern Japanese life. Japanese liberals, Christians, socialists, Marxists, and pacifists have been attracted to progressive values, believing that as Japan advanced it must increasingly converge with the universal values represented in the West. While their claims did not occupy the mainstream of Japanese political life, they were unsettling. American values served as a negative identity to criticize their own traditions. Such claims, however, were anathema to nationalists, who looked for arguments that would support Japan's unique values and traditions. Many Japanese throughout the modern period were inwardly divided over these issues. What was the nature of social progress? Was it compatible with diverse social structures? Or did the functional necessities of industrial society inevitably overcome the diversity of social and cultural forms? Were Western liberal values the universal path that all modernizing nations must follow? For the Japanese, as the first non-Western peoples to pass through the industrial revolution, the issues were profoundly troubling.

For young Japanese wanting to escape the web of obligation and stultifying tightness of human relations, the freedom of American society offered a haven. Here the alienated Japanese youth could find the liberal values that freed them for individual creativity. In contemporary Japan, the novelist Murakami Haruki epitomizes the attachment to American society as an escape from "the social claustrophobia" with its "group-mindedness, the submission of individual desires to collective, familial duties" in his home country. As Ian Buruma observed in an insightful interview of Murakami in 1996, the novelist's writings so popular among Japanese youth were, at that time, marked by an "almost complete absence of references to Japanese culture."[106] Murakami, the most celebrated writer of the recent past, was wholly absorbed as a youth with American culture because "it was a way to be free—if not socially, then at least spiritually." Nevertheless, it was frequent that young Japanese drawn to such ideals later abandoned them and returned to the familiar cultural ways.

It is true that the American lifestyle exercised great influence on the goals of this consumer-driven culture. In the prewar period, American consumer goods, especially automobiles, movies, baseball, jazz, beauty parlors, and many other cultural icons, were objects of Japanese consumerism, and it is surprising how, despite the efforts of the government to censor and suppress these pursuits, they persisted even during the war years. As one authority writes: "Given the persistent popularity of modern and Western—particularly American—culture even in the face of wartime censorship, it is no surprise that in the immediate postwar years, consumers embraced this culture without restraint."[107]

Characteristic of the mass middle-class consciousness in the high-growth period was a desire for consumer durables, a university education for the children, and home ownership. The result was a mass-consumption market, a homogeneous lifestyle, and a scramble to keep up with the purchases of one's neighbors: sewing machines, televisions, refrigerators, washing machines, vacuum cleaners, automobiles, air conditioners, and so on. In this headlong race for a modern lifestyle, the Americans were the model. As Jordan Sand writes, "From the time of the Occupation, the United States became overwhelmingly the dominant model for emulation, partly because of the presence of Americans on Japanese soil and the heavy hand of American administration in shaping postwar Japanese society, but perhaps even more because of the impact of the affluent lifestyle of American families as seen in popular media."[108] Nevertheless, the influence of the material lifestyle did not carry over into fundamental changes in Japanese cultural style.

Despite the most direct and sustained influence that America exercised in Japan through the Occupation reforms, the hegemonic alliance, and the decades of cultural dominance and interaction, Japanese social, political, and economic institutions have maintained their own distinct traditions. Japan has adopted some aspects of the liberal value system and its institutions, but it has implemented them in their own peculiar ways. Japanese society has not converged with classic liberal ways as was earlier expected. One of Japan's leading conservative thinkers, Murakami Yasusuke, coauthored an ambitious study in 1979 of Japan's social evolution that sought to show Japan had successfully achieved modernity by relying on a distinctive combination of traditional household (*ie*) and village (*mura*) principles. The purpose of the study, he wrote, was to demonstrate the multilinear evolution of modern societies:

"Modernization" used to be viewed as an essentially "unilineal" process of convergence toward an ideal final state presumably epitomized by the historical experiences of the Western industrial societies. This process of convergence was supposed to wipe out indigenous culture. Considering the Japanese as well as many other recent non-Western experiences, however, "modernization" might be re-defined more broadly as a process of interaction, conflict, and adaptation between industrial technology and preindustrial indigenous culture. This will imply that modernization as a whole may well be "multi-lineal," reflecting, to some extent, each society's cultural heritage.[109]

Perhaps some would argue that the nonconvergent behavior of Japan was a matter of a time lag; they may contend that given the famously conservative nature of Japanese society it would require a much longer time but eventually Japan would finally converge with a universal model of social structure. In the early twenty-first century, however, the evidence to support such a contention is not yet persuasive.

10

Democracy in Japan

THE PRINCIPAL MOTIVATION for the unconditional surrender policy was the conviction that transforming the domestic polities of the enemy powers was essential to the American goal of creating a new international order. Simply defeating Japan and forcing it back to its original borders would not be enough to preserve the peace. External constraints on Japan or a negotiated accommodation or a favorable balance of power would not be sufficient. A lasting peace in Asia required the reconstruction of Japan's internal regime. Democratizing Japan would ensure a peaceful Japan. A fundamental tenet of America's dominant foreign policy ideology in the twentieth century (and since) was the liberal credo that democratic nations never or very rarely go to war with each other.

The roots of this fundamental tenet can be traced to the American Revolution and the Founders, who, "inspired by the philosophes, hoped that their revolution would commence a reformation of the world, that it would usher in a new era of peace and free trade that would eventually replace the customary system of great-power war and mercantilism."[1] Especially it was Thomas Paine, the passionate English American pamphleteer, who proclaimed in his writings America's "power to begin the world over again" by spreading democratic influences. Paine was a prophet for what political scientists now call the democratic peace theory. Several years before Immanuel Kant's essay "Perpetual Peace" (1795), typically cited as the locus classicus of the origins of democratic peace theory, Paine wrote at length of the peaceful nature of democracies and of how an international order made up of democracies constituted the hope for changing the world.[2] In "The Rights of Man" (1791) he proclaimed: "Monarchical sovereignty, the enemy of mankind, and the source of misery is abolished; and sovereignty is restored to its natural and original place, the nation. . . . Were this the case throughout Europe, the cause of war would be taken away."[3] Paine became a supporter of interventions in behalf of democratic revolutions. "If universal peace, civilization, and commerce are ever to be the happy lot of man, it cannot be accomplished but by a revolution in the system of governments."[4] In short, the spread of democracies would transform the international system.

By the summer of 1945, two world wars had provided American liberals, Michael Howard wrote, "sufficient evidence about the belligerent nature of undemocratic societies—the militarism of both Wilhelmine and Nazi Germany and Imperial Japan" to make the universalization of democratic institutions necessary. "The object of the new world order was to make possible the extension of democratic governments. Peace and democracy were interdependent."[5] Paine's revolutionary democratic liberalism was echoed not only in the messianic interventionism of Wilson and Roosevelt; we find it succinctly expressed by none other than Douglas MacArthur, who explained in *Life* magazine in 1947 why changing Japan's domestic institutions was necessary: "War's genesis lies in the despotic lust for power—frequently its rallying media for intense nationalism renders it the last refuge of the despot whose power is threatened from within. Never has it originated in the voluntary action of a free people; never will a free people voluntarily associate itself with the proposition that the road to peace and well-being and happiness lies through the crucible of war. . . . Peace will be retarded and the imminence of war advanced so long as despotism governs men's lives."[6] Democratization would ensure Japan's peaceful nature and thus help transform the international system.

Self-Determination

When did Japan have its democratic revolution? When did Japan become a democracy? It is hard to find a landmark date at which Japan became a democracy. The most common judgment would be that Japan became a democracy with the promulgation of the MacArthur Constitution, which established democratic institutions and the principle of popular sovereignty. But democracy cannot be simply decreed, because it is more than formal institutions. It entails wide acceptance of norms of freedom, rights, and the rule of law. It also entails processes. As Charles Tilly wrote: "A regime is democratic to the degree that political relations between the state and its citizens feature broad, equal, protected, and mutually binding consultation."[7]

Values grow out of the history and traditions, the culture, of a people. Democracy must be fought for, achieved, won. The Japanese people have never on their own achieved a democratic revolution. The Meiji Constitution of 1889 was drafted by the oligarchs and given to the people as a gift from a beneficent sovereign. The Occupation's imposition of democratic institutions was in the same tradition of bestowing rights on the people rather than having them won from below in a popular struggle. As a consequence, democracy was not in the lifeblood of the people. Nambara Shigeru, the postwar president of the University of Tokyo, justifiably feared that Japan would soon return to its traditional conservative values because, "unlike America, political democracy in Japan has not acquired true life."[8] In his first lecture at the university in December 1945, Maruyama Masao observed: "Today, we have had 'freedom' issued to us—forced upon us, in fact, by a foreign country. But freedom as a handout, or coerced freedom, is a fundamental contradiction. . . . To achieve genuine freedom, we must continue a long and arduous struggle to take the freedom that has been given to us and elevate it into a freedom that exists within us."[9] As the movie director Kurosawa Akira wrote in his autobiography, "The freedom and democracy of the postwar era were not things I had fought for and won; they were granted to me by powers beyond my own."[10]

The Americans left a mixed legacy insofar as democratization was concerned. The Potsdam Declaration said the Occupation would continue until the Japanese government removed "all obstacles to the revival and strengthening of democratic tendencies among the Japanese people. Freedom of speech, of religion, and of thought, as well as respect for the fundamental human rights shall be established." In planning the Occupation, Americans were uncertain about how the democratization of Japan would be achieved. On the one hand, the Potsdam Declaration said the ultimate form of government would be achieved "in accordance with the freely expressed will of the Japanese people." On the other hand, it was clear from the unconditional surrender policy that Japan must have a democratic form of government if it was to become a peaceful nation, no longer be a threat to regional security, and be aligned with the new international order. MacArthur's instructions from Washington were that only as a last resort should SCAP order changes, because "the knowledge that they have been imposed by the Allies would materially reduce the possibilities of their acceptance and support by the Japanese people in the future."[11] MacArthur, however, lost patience with the foot-dragging of the Japanese conservatives and ordered his staff to draft a "model constitution" acceptable to the Occupation. As one authority sums up, "MacArthur had decided to turn tutor."[12] Although the Japanese were able to make minimal changes to the SCAP draft, it remains true that "no modern nation ever has rested on a more alien constitution."[13] Left to their own efforts, the Japanese would surely have fashioned a constitution more reflective of their own history and values. Instead, they were handed a draft document rooted in basic ideals from the Anglo-American legal tradition. From the time of its promulgation, its origin has been a bone of contention in Japanese politics between conservatives assailing its foreign authorship and progressives defending its liberal principles. Nevertheless, in the way it has been flexibly interpreted and implemented over time by conservative politicians and the courts, it has proved to be a "living document." While Germany's 1949 constitution has been amended more than fifty times, Japan's is "the oldest unamended constitution in the world."[14]

Most narratives of Japan's postwar history have implicitly accepted a belief that outside intervention was necessary to break the power of the imperial system. Historians, however, are uncovering evidence that at the grassroots level by the end of the war there was an extraordinary openness to political change and reform. At the local level, despite the hardship and struggle for survival, there was a readiness throughout Japan to engage in politics, critique the past, experiment with self-expression, and envision a new future. It was this popular energy for reform and for a government responsive to the public will that burst forth in the 1950s, culminating in the Anpo demonstrations. Even as MacArthur decided to intervene in the constitution drafting and "tutor" the Japanese, public opinion polls showed that over 50 percent of Japanese favored electing a special committee or convention to revise the old constitution.[15] Such a convention, however, could not be controlled by SCAP. MacArthur was impatient to move ahead with reforms and wanted a popularly elected Diet to pass on the Occupation's reforms. He also wanted to preempt the interference of the Allies who were likely to try the emperor, but MacArthur thought the emperor needed to be kept to legitimize the reform process.

In drafting the constitution, SCAP not only overruled popular self-determination but subsequently, at the end of the Occupation, left administration of the constitutional structure to the conservative elite, whose sympathies were decidedly not with democratization. Tsuji Kiyoaki, the distinguished postwar scholar of government, believed that an opportunity for a popular democratic revolution in Japan was lost when the Occupation restored the power of the bureaucracy.[16] The popular energy for achieving a new form of government was powerful in the wake of the disaster that had befallen the nation. That the Occupation bestowed the constitution from above, as it were, was indeed a lost opportunity.[17] The unconditional surrender policy, the resulting occupation of Japan, and the sweeping reforms imposed deprived the Japanese people of struggling over their own future.

Nearly a century before the American Occupation, John Stuart Mill wrote a classic essay on "interventions," in which he opposed foreign interventions designed to extend democratic values to another people. "The virtues needful for maintaining freedom," Mill wrote in 1859, must be cultivated by the people themselves. "It is during an arduous struggle to become free by their own efforts that these virtues have the best chance of springing up. Men become attached to that which they have long fought for and made sacrifices for, they learn to appreciate that on which their thoughts have been much engaged."[18] As I have remarked earlier in these pages, we cannot know how things would have turned out if the Japanese people had been left to their own devices to reform their political economy after the disastrous war. Mill argued that "a state is self-determining even if its citizens struggle and fail to establish free institutions, but it has been deprived of self-determination if such institutions are established by an intrusive neighbor. The members of a political community must seek their own freedom, just as an individual must cultivate his own virtue. They cannot be set free, as he cannot be made virtuous, by any external force. Indeed, political freedom depends upon the existence of individual virtue, and this the armies of another state are most unlikely to produce."[19]

It was the nature of the American order that Americans would hold the world in tutelage. Americans would use their power and influence to tutor the world to adopt their democratic values and institutions. The American experience would be universalized. In that sense, US relations with Japan reflect the very essence of the American world order. MacArthur expressed this view quite succinctly when he wrote that the source of his reforms in the Occupation "lies deeply rooted in the lessons and experiences of American history. . . . I have merely sought to draw therefrom the political, economic, and social concepts which throughout our own past have worked and provided the American people with a spiritual and material strength never before equaled in human history. There is no need to experiment with new and yet untried, or already tried and discredited concepts, when success itself stands as the eloquent and convincing advocate of our own."[20] The general was dismissive of the possibility that a different history or different culture would suggest a different set of constitutional principles. "Nor," he wrote, "is there factual basis for the fallacious argument occasionally heard that those high principles upon which rest our own strength and progress are ill-fitted to serve the well-being of others, as history will clearly show that the entire human race, irrespective of geographical delimitations or cultural tradition, is capable of absorbing, cherishing and defending liberty, tolerance and justice, and will find maximum strength and progress when so blessed."[21] In terms of what Mill described as "self-determination," the Japanese were doubly handicapped in the aspiration for democracy. The Japanese were given democratic institutions, but then control of those institutions was turned over to conservative elites who had little enthusiasm for democratic principles.

The Prewar Roots

The prewar Japanese political system was not a democracy, because it did not provide for popular sovereignty. Nevertheless, there were democratic elements in the system, and from the time of the Meiji Restoration there was a rich history of debate over liberal concepts of government introduced from the West on which postwar Japan could build. The establishment of the Meiji Constitution of 1889 and the opening of a national assembly with an elective lower house were adopted because they were regarded as essential elements of modernity, but having accepted that necessity, the Meiji leaders were determined to control the processes of government. As in 1946, the Meiji Constitution was drafted behind the scenes and presented from above. Drafted by the oligarchs, the Meiji Constitution was a "gift" from the emperor, who was described in the preamble as "sacred and inviolable," the descendant of a dynasty "which has reigned in an unbroken line of descent for ages past," and in whom resided all sovereignty. At the same time, to control the processes of government, a modern bureaucracy was established. The bureaucrats, recruited through an astonishingly rigorous training and examination system, thought of themselves as "servants of the emperor." Their pervasive influence reached from the cabinet level, where they drafted virtually all laws enacted by the Diet, to the grassroots level of everyday life, where the police and other local officials managed a wide-ranging oversight of citizen activities. Although a powerful conservative force, the bureaucracy could often be progressive and reformist if it would serve the nation's need for social solidarity and strength. Proposals for female suffrage in local elections and for labor and tenancy reforms emanated from bureaucratic leadership in the post–World War I period.

A vigorous two-party politics developed in the Diet. Largely conservative in character, the parties grew in influence by striking deals with the oligarchs and bureaucrats. A complex web of elites from business, the military, and the parties, together with the bureaucratic elites, dominated the system. Bureaucrats and party leaders worked closely together in advancing reforms that were often inspired by liberal trends in the Western world. The rise of democratic political philosophies in the Taishō period (1912–1926) seemed to augur a more open and progressive system. In 1918, the leader of the majority political party was appointed as prime minister. Universal male suffrage passed the Diet in 1925. Optimists foresaw an emerging democracy, although Yoshino Sakuzō, the intellectual leader of this trend, defined Taishō democracy in elitist terms as "government for the people."

Expectations for the continuing development of democratic practice proved illusory. In the 1930s, with the rise of a Japanese form of fascism, the influence of the parties was eclipsed and constitutional prerogatives of imperial sovereignty were used to suppress the earlier liberal trends. The coincident crises of foreign affairs and domestic economic hardship brought the bureaucrat elites together with military elites in common cause to manage the national crises. Both saw the need for tight control of the economy and for centralization of power and worked together to oversee strategic industries, while leaving private ownership and a large measure of private management intact. Authoritarian leaders set out to create a new mass political party that would embrace all groups in the Diet and serve as the nucleus of a new authoritarian political structure. While nascent democratic trends were suppressed in the turmoil and crises of the war years, the experience of pluralist, albeit elitist, politics in the 1920s bequeathed a legacy of indigenous democratic potential for the postwar period.

The Postwar Political System

In light of the intentions of the Americans to transform the postwar political system, what is most notable is the continuity from the prewar days of the elitist nature of the system and the dominant role of the bureaucracy. The resilience of this conservative elite was never clearer than in the days after World War II when it clung to power even though it was discredited by the catastrophic defeat and America, the occupying power, initially sought to weaken, if not displace, it. The elitist nature of the prewar political system and the dominant role of the bureaucracy carried over into the postwar period and handicapped the development of democratic principles the Occupation sought to instill. In the prewar days the bureaucracy had been one among multiple elites competing for power and influence in the political system. During the Occupation, the other elites—the military, the parties, and the zaibatsu—were primary targets of the purge. The seasoned and experienced bureaucrats were left largely unscathed and in a dominant position because the Occupation needed them to govern the country.

It soon became clear that the new political system was not operating in the way the reforms had intended. Although the MacArthur Constitution provided universal suffrage and popular sovereignty, and made the Diet "the highest organ of state power," the political system operated in a way that was at odds with this democratic structure.[22] The Occupation's decision to leave the deeply rooted and powerful bureaucratic elite in place set the stage for the evolution of a postwar conservative system that was often unaccountable to the electorate. Although Japan now had all the formal institutions of democracy, when the bureaucrat elites returned to power, they implemented the institutions in ways that were in keeping with their own traditions. In her study of the MacArthur Constitution, the sociolinguist scholar Kyoko Inoue shows how Japanese bureaucrats toned down the liberal content of the constitution when they translated the SCAP draft into the official Japanese text. Rather than the Anglo-American notion of popular sovereignty by which the people are prior to the government—that is, they come together to form government—the tone of the translated Japanese text conveyed a sense of "communitarian democracy." They used syntax, she writes, that suggested "the people and the government jointly take responsibility in creating democratic government, and jointly commit themselves to securing the fundamental rights and liberties of the people. The people and the government are to work together to implement and maintain the new political and social order."[23]

Historically rooted values of respect for hierarchy and status and for the sanctity of authority held by its central governing institutions underwrote steady support for a strong state. Together with these values, the bureaucracy held extraordinary legitimacy. That is, membership in the bureaucracy was achieved through success in a rigorous and competitive educational system. This meritocratic recruitment ensured new talent and gave the bureaucracy the reputation of being "the best and the brightest." They struck a benign posture of ruling in behalf of the people. The impact of opinion outside government contributed to the structuring of debates among the elite, but the bureaucrats set Japanese policy. The bureaucracy initiated and drafted virtually all important legislation, as it had in the prewar period, and possessed extraordinary administrative prerogatives in interpreting and implementing laws. Arrogantly, but with some justification, a former vice minister on one occasion characterized the Diet as no more than an "extension of the bureaucracy."[24]

The postwar Liberal Party, led by Yoshida Shigeru, brought veteran bureaucrats into the party and fashioned a close working relationship between party and bureaucracy. As the Occupation ended, conservative forces worked to consolidate their power. Progressive forces were ascendant in the 1950s, and for a time it appeared that the Socialist Party might soon come to power. In the face of this challenge, the conservative parties, encouraged by business leaders as well as the Americans, merged in 1955 to form the Liberal Democratic Party (which, despite its name, was neither liberal nor democratic nor, some might add, a party because of its many factions). The LDP succeeded in dominating the fractious progressive parties.

In the 1960s the political system functioned through close reciprocal relations among three entities—the LDP, the bureaucracy, and the combined forces of big business and agriculture. This "ruling triad" worked so smoothly that outsiders sometimes called it "Japan, Incorporated." Party leadership was made up of former bureaucrats who naturally worked in harmony with their former colleagues as well as hand in glove with big business. Agricultural interests were rewarded with subsidies, price supports, and the pork barrel. Business gained legislative rewards in the form of cheap capital, a protected domestic market, and a wide array of high-growth policies.

When the progressive forces fractured into several parties and became a perpetual opposition, the LDP settled into a comfortable one-party rule that lasted more than half a century. Mastering the practices of clientelism, the LDP used the highly centralized fiscal system to buy the support of farmers, business, construction workers, and other constituencies to establish perpetual domination of the political system. Opposition parties found it difficult to establish a strong base and to recruit viable candidates. Japan became a one-party dominant state.[25] Without an alternation of parties in power, a healthy democratic politics was handicapped. Real competition for power occurred among factions within the LDP. Although for a time former bureaucrats dominated the party leadership, eventually the LDP produced professional politicians who rose through its ranks, serving special interest groups and mastering the use of the pork barrel to secure their positions. Bureaucratic influence slowly came to be shared with the professional politicians.

The Japanese political system went through a steady evolution during the postwar period. In the 1970s the LDP was challenged by pressures generated by a burgeoning middle-class society demanding attention to the quality of life in the cities. As the number of independent urban voters grew, they signaled their concerns by voting for smaller parties, including the Communist Party. The LDP's iron grip on power began to slip. Faced with a discontented electorate, the conservatives did what Japanese conservatives have been so adept at: they began to co-opt the opposition and its proposals. Japanese conservatism is characteristically nonideological and opportunist, intent on maintaining power rather than ideological principle as its ultimate objective. The LDP, once largely dependent on the support of farmers, merchants, and the self-employed, reached out to urban white- and blue-collar workers for support. It became a catchall party seeking to respond to the interests of the broad masses. The more politically active middle class made the politicians more responsive to the electorate, but LDP Diet members still worked closely with special interest groups and the bureaucrats with jurisdiction over the resources needed to respond to the special interests. Meeting the needs of a more diverse constituency, the LDP expanded its clientelist base, won over independent voters, and rebuilt its control of the Diet. As its one-party rule persisted with only brief interruptions, in 1993–1994 and 2009–2012, the LDP became "the most successful party in the history of competitive democracies."[26]

In the wide latitude in which elites exercised power, Japan functioned as an elitist democracy.[27] The continuity of elite power from the prewar period continues even today. A web of interpersonal connections, often invisible to foreign eyes, defines relations among members of the elite. Marriage politics, for example, plays an important role in cementing ties binding elite families. There is remarkable continuity among the families that dominate LDP leadership. Critics of Japanese democracy in the postwar period argued that the elites dominated and distorted the formal institutions and that it "has been brokered, in ways that respect the form but frequently kill the spirit of democracy."[28] Aside from its extraordinary longevity, the absence of alternation of parties in power, and its close relations with an elite and unaccountable bureaucracy, LDP rule was characterized by several distinctive institutions, especially the widespread practice of *amakudari* (literally "descent from heaven"), by which bureaucrats were reemployed in business and public corporations after retiring from government. This practice served to cement ties between bureaucratic and business elites. Despite efforts to reform this practice, especially in the aftermath of the Fukushima nuclear disaster in 2011 (which called attention to the close ties between bureaucratic regulatory agencies and electric power companies), continuation of *amakudari* was evident in an October 2015 report that seventy-one senior central government officials and forty-five senior prefectural bureaucrats had retired into positions in electric power companies.[29]

In addition to *amakudari*, another extra-institutional practice of LDP rule at odds with liberal democratic ideals was the prevalence of factions (*habatsu*). For much of its life, the LDP was something less than a unified party and more like a coalition of factions. Owing to the reality of long-term one-party rule, factions within the LDP competed for power and influence. The LDP was riven by five or six factions, organized not to promote particular policies or principles but rather to cluster around an individual Diet member in the interests of gaining presidency of the party and hence the prime ministership with the attendant power to appoint cabinet members as well as to fill many other offices. They operated with considerable autonomy, caucusing frequently to strategize tactics for intraparty competition for power. A prime minister would typically distribute cabinet positions and other posts among the factions whose support he would need in governing. The composition of a government cabinet would be a complex balancing of LDP factions based on their relative strength and personal relations. The practice often resulted in rather weak prime ministers who were, in effect, first among equals. Collective leadership was exercised through complex interpersonal relations and factional bargaining whose dynamic was often not clear to outsiders. There were some notable exceptions, but for the most part the prime minister was "among the weakest democratic leaders in the world."[30] Decision making emerged out of protracted consultation and consensus building among factions and their interaction with special interests and bureaucrats. Both the public and foreign leaders were often at a loss to understand this opaque decision-making process. Electoral reforms passed in 1994 that were designed to weaken factions and the role of money and increase the focus on policy issues in elections had some effect in achieving these goals, but institutional practices were not easily abandoned.

Still another extra-institutional practice that hindered a healthy democratic development was the *koenkai* (support groups). Politicians in other democracies have support groups but nothing to compare to the *koenkai*, which are mass-membership groups attached to a particular person and not representing an ideology or policy or party.[31] Politicians formed groups to support their candidacy and favored them with pork barrel rewards and subsidies for highways, bridges, and public works of all kinds. The support groups were social as well as political organizations, enjoying the company of citizens in their region. Prime Minister Tanaka Kakuei's *koenkai* in his district on the Japan Sea Coast was legendary. It had a membership of nearly 100,000, which mobilized support through its own newsletter, social meetings, outings to hot springs with Tanaka, attendance at baseball games, sumo contests, cooking classes, tea ceremony classes, and so on. In return, Tanaka's well-oiled machine showered his district with every conceivable pork barrel subsidy, from a bullet train connecting to the capital to efficient snow removal. Money became the mother of politics and helped ensure an increasingly "canny and corrupt" conservative leadership.[32]

The growth of the *koenkai* in the 1970s made possible the institution of "hereditary politicians" (*nisei giin*), which extended the elite domination of the system. When a politician retired, these support groups were readily transferred to a son or another relative who loyally carried on the particularistic and personal practices of interest politics. As a consequence, seats in the Diet passed within families from generation to generation with remarkable frequency. Typically, hereditary politicians made up as much as 40 percent of the Diet seats.

Nevertheless, from this unfavorable climate, it appeared that early in the new century a genuine two-party politics might finally be emerging. The Democratic Party of Japan (DPJ) formed in 1998 when a number of opposition groups joined together. Coming to power in 2009, it sought to assert control over the bureaucracy and strike a more independent role in the US alliance. Not surprisingly, both the bureaucrats and the Americans were unhappy with the new administration and resisted cooperating with it. The DPJ proved so inexperienced and inept in its management of domestic and foreign policy that it was swept out of power in the 2012 elections. After a three-year interval, the LDP returned to power with a rejuvenated dominance of the political system.

Japan's Distinctive Civil Society

One important way democratization developed in the postwar period was through citizen activism. The actions of ordinary citizens reflected a new willingness to join groups actively engaged in political and social issues. This is sometimes defined as civil society—groups that spontaneously arise in the public sphere, independent of government, to pursue political and social objectives. Tocqueville believed that a useful check on American individualism was the propensity to join groups that had the larger interests of the community in mind. Recently, the willingness of Americans to engage in such community groups has waned in the view of many commentators. If a present danger for a healthy American democracy is atomistic individualism, the obstacle in Japan is, in contrast, the propensity of the state to co-opt and manage local associations with a consequent jeopardy to free society—or, as it is now commonly called, civil society. From an American perspective, civil society is an autonomous public realm outside government in which individuals freely interact and organize in voluntary associations. In Japan there is something distinctive about the way state and society interact. In the prewar period, the Japanese government attempted to manage Japanese society and maintain a sense of community by shaping the thought and behavior of citizens in their everyday lives and encouraging them to work cooperatively with government-sponsored programs. Government intervened to reorganize and regulate a variety of agricultural, trade, and social organizations, providing them with subsidies and other benefits, and organizing them into hierarchical organizations that surrendered autonomy and supported government policy.

When the American Occupation began, the Americans wanted Japanese to be independent of the state, conscious of their rights and individual freedoms. The goal was a democratic civil society. Once the Occupation was over, the Japanese bureaucracy soon restored many of its methods of molding Japanese behavior, mobilizing citizens in their everyday lives to work cooperatively in maintaining social programs to serve the community. The return to their old methods was not always easy, as now there was more pushback, more independent behavior from a citizenry that still remembered their wartime suffering brought on by the state.

In the postwar period a more assertive civil society emerged. Popular discontent with conservative policies was often frustrated by a government that proved less than accountable. This popular frustration with policies of the elite was expressed in waves of civic activism. It was the beginning of a protracted democratization that gradually took hold over the succeeding decades. "Popular struggle," Tilly argues, "affects whether and how democratization comes to pass."[33] It involves domestic confrontation and popular contention in order to check autonomous power centers "in a way that augments the influence of ordinary people over public politics."[34] This popular confrontation was the "arduous struggle" that John Stuart Mill identified as the essence of democratic development. It was what Japanese had been deprived of in the Occupation. The peace movement and the Anpo demonstrations, although initially instigated by progressive groups, evoked spontaneous grassroots protest groups in the 1950s when "workers defending class interests marched alongside farmers fighting expansion of military bases; teachers concerned about state control of education joined housewives involved in the movement to ban nuclear weapons; religious groups joined citizens trying to protect their participatory interest against revision of the constitution."[35]

A new wave of civic activism emerged in the late 1960s and early 1970s with the rise of an environmental and consumer protest over the costs of rapid economic growth. The movement was organized around local issues of livelihood and well-being: clean water, clean air, and parks. Women often played the leading role in these local issue movements. Between 1,500 and 3,000 citizen groups organized during this period to seek pollution control by the early 1970s, but they were generally quite small and lacked legal status, tax-exemption, postal privileges, and nonprofit status to support their activities. The citizens' movement struck fear in the elite coalition because it generated a popular excitement comparable to the civil rights movement in the United States and threatened the leadership with a loss of control over social change. The government moved to co-opt the citizens' groups by adopting their language and welfare goals and forging links with them.

In the 1990s there appeared to be what observers called a "volunteers boom" or "volunteers revolution," initiating another marker of an emerging civil society. In January 1995, the massive Hanshin earthquake in Kobe killed over 6,000 people and devastated the city. The government was caught flatfooted. Prime Minister Murayama Tomiichi was slow to react. The Self-Defense Forces were eventually sent in, but on arrival were caught in a massive traffic jam, partly because thousands of volunteers had rushed in to help the victims. This outpouring of volunteers drew attention to what seemed to be a popular trend that was then quietly encouraged and guided by the government, particularly by the Ministry of Health and Welfare bureaucrats. They drafted the 1998 Nonprofit Organization (NPO) Law to facilitate citizen participation in activities that "benefit society" and "contribute to the advancement of public welfare." It promoted volunteerism and the incorporation of certain types of nonprofit groups serving the needs of the elderly, youth, environment, crime prevention, and consumer protection, primarily at the local level. Overtly political and contentious groups were left out. Instead, the bureaucracy steered civic activism down paths that would contribute to community solidarity and allow bureaucratic guidance. By 2004, the number of NPOs had grown to over 15,000.[36] Housewives and retirees tended to be the primary source of volunteerism. Still, the bulk of NPOs remained small, were relatively underfunded and underprofessionalized, and often lacked legal recognition.

The greatest challenge yet to the resilience of the bureaucracy and its ability to manage and mold social problems was offered by the triple disaster of the 9.0 magnitude Great Tohoku earthquake of March 11, 2011, the ensuing tsunami, and the Fukushima Daiichi nuclear reactor meltdown. The earthquake and tsunami left 20,000 people dead and created a nuclear disaster ranking with Chernobyl. It brought forth a torrent of criticism of the bureaucracy, the ruling elite, and prodigies of civic activism. Blame was heaped on the political class and its "cozy relationship" with the supposed nuclear regulators who had failed to provide the oversight needed to prevent or prepare for a crisis. The "nuclear village" was a metaphor widely used in the Japanese media to describe the energy policy community in which bureaucrats, politicians, and business leaders colluded in promoting nuclear power and propagated a myth of nuclear power as a safe source of energy. The extent of the disaster produced a national soul-searching that went in many directions. Citizen groups blamed the tragedy on collusion and ineptitude of policymakers but also reflected on the complacency of long-term one-party rule and a mind-set of deferring to officialdom and other shortcomings of democracy in Japan. The Nobel laureate Ōe Kenzaburō saw the disaster as a reflection of Japan's postwar mentality and said it offered an opportunity to open a new chapter in Japanese democracy.[37] In fact, the disaster did not transform the political system as some thought such a massive tragedy might. But it did evoke a new level of "public spiritedness by volunteers" and stirred unprecedented cooperation among local government entities that seemed to presage a more engaged citizenry. "The rhetoric of crisis," Richard Samuels concludes in his study of the effects of the triple crisis, "infused democratic politics, empowered new actors, stimulated long-awaited if piecemeal reforms, aroused considerable protest, and may have pushed the policy process in the direction of transparency."[38]

Although the conservatives were skillful in propitiating these waves of discontent by flexible policies that often co-opted the opposition, nevertheless over time the ruling elite in the bureaucracy and the LDP were compelled to take greater account of mass opinion. The experience of these waves of civic activism left a legacy of spontaneous group activities, but the postwar state often began subsidizing and, in other ways, intertwining many of these organizations with the state. There is considerable evidence of citizen groups springing up, but there is also evidence that government (the bureaucracy) has attempted to co-opt these groups, to channel their activities into areas that are not contentious and political and that will serve community interests, maintain social order, and contribute to the common welfare. There is also evidence that citizen groups often welcome a working relationship with government, which can give them legitimacy, financial subsidies, and other benefits. Patricia Maclachlan concludes that the historical legacy in Japan has given the Japanese complementary spheres: "The state helps nurture civil society, while civil society helps perform state functions for the sake of the community. Japan, in other words, has a strong state and a vibrant civil society all at the same time."[39] One may interpret the role of bureaucracy as "co-opting" public discontent, or one may see this process as establishing what Tilly calls "trust networks" between the state and citizens. At the local level, citizens have cooperated with government for projects that enhance community welfare. From this perspective one may interpret this as a distinctive Japanese communitarian democracy.

Postwar civil society in Japan presents a distinctive character. It has demonstrated a vibrant history of spontaneous and autonomous organizations springing up to protest government's unresponsiveness to social problems. But it has also demonstrated a willingness of civic groups to cooperate with government to meet social needs and the intertwining of civic groups with the state. Nongovernmental organizations and independent volunteers continue to emerge, and the government continues to find ways to enmesh them in the workings of the state.

Civil society groups express their opposition to raising the consumption tax
and to Japan's participation in the Trans-Pacific Partnership trade agreement,
April 25, 2012. Jeremy Sutton-Hibbert / Getty Images / 143365820.

The Spirit of Japanese Law

The rule of law is an essential foundation of a democracy. The gulf separating the workings of Japanese and American political systems is nowhere clearer than in their contrasting views of law. As one authority writes, "In no other industrial society is legal regulation as extensive or coercive as in the United States or as confined and weak as in Japan. . . . Both societies represent extremes of a kind. . . . Underlying the contrasts between the two societies are profound differences in concepts of law and morality and the interrelationships between the two, as well as the role of law in protecting the citizen from the state."[40]

Americans' commitment to the rule of law has always been strong. Tocqueville noted in 1835, "If they prize freedom much, they generally value legality still more; they are less afraid of Tyranny than arbitrary power."[41] Moreover, in the American view, morality and law are closely related. Americans take the attitude that moral conduct is "a matter of rule following, and moral relationships consist of duties and rights determined by rules."[42] Norms of respect for individual freedom, human rights, majority rule, and the rule of law are essential aspects of democracy. A commitment to justiciable rights and an independent judiciary to uphold these rights are fundamental. Moreover, Americans assume that consciousness of individual rights is a prerequisite to a modern democracy.

The Japanese approach to law is markedly different. The dominant conservative view is that "their legal system functions on the basis of harmony, consensus, and compromise rather than legally binding rights and duties."[43] It rests on patterns of governance deeply rooted in their own history. The Japanese approach to law was shaped by the three important institutional legacies of their history: feudalism, the village, and the extended family. The first taught respect for hierarchy, knowing one's proper place in society, and deference to political authority. Centuries of feudal experience left Japan with traditions of legitimacy for those who governed as benevolent rulers and who determined administrative regulations and criminal penalties. The second, the village, which was largely self-governing and centered on patterns of rice cultivation, required collectivist values of consensus, harmony, and respect for the welfare of the community, consensus, and cooperation. The third, the extended family, reinforced values of interdependence, deference to age, and respect for tradition of ancestors. These three legacies did not give rise to transcendent norms or values. As the sociologist Robert Bellah observed, "It [was] the particular system or collectivity of which one is a member which counts, whether it be family, *han* [feudal domain] or Japan as a whole. Commitment to these tends to take precedence over universalistic commitments, such as commitment to truth and justice."[44]

Critics further stressed that the way in which the Japanese historically have prized collectivist values not surprisingly influenced the postwar democracy. Democracy is generally equated with majority rule, but when consensus is preferred, the decision-making process will be affected. As one American anthropologist observed, "At the small group level there is a definite reluctance to call a vote if the outcome might be divisive (which in most cases means not unanimous). Voting makes public the fact of dissensions and creates winners and losers. In small groups, fraternal organizations, and many other intermediate scale entities, the Japanese preference is to avoid majority rule. One wonders, as a result, about the social foundations of democracy in Japan.

Qualities of group maintenance take precedence over expeditious use of rules."[45]

It would be wrong, however, to overlook a long tradition of dissent and conflict in Japanese history. In the premodern period, peasant uprisings protesting government negligence and misdoings came in great waves. Such protests were often expressions of the breaking of a moral compact between ruler and ruled by which a beneficent ruler should look after the needs of the people. In the modern period, the post–World War I rice riots throughout Japan and later tenancy disputes and labor strikes continued the occasions of popular protest.[46] The notion of a moral compact at the heart of government was strong and stood in contrast to Western notions of popular rights and the rule of law.

For most of Japanese history, rule by law, rather than rule of law, was reality. Law was an instrument of government control. Needless to say, there was no concept of the rights of the individual. When the notion was first discussed after the opening of relations with the West in the Meiji period, a new vocabulary had to be coined to express the concepts of rights, freedom, and individual dignity and the idea of a private sphere of human activity into which the state could not intrude. These concepts were revolutionary. When the Meiji Constitution of 1889 was written, various rights were allowed only where the state permitted them. There was nothing absolute, innate, or inalienable about them. The contrast with American legal culture, therefore, is stark.

Law in Post-Occupation Japan

When the Americans sought to establish the rule of law in postwar Japan, they knew they were challenging long-held customs and practices. It was not that the Japanese lacked a legal tradition. In the Meiji period, continental European law had been imported to give the modern state a framework and to satisfy the demands of the Western powers, which refused to give up their extraterritorial privileges until modern laws were established. Heavily influenced by German jurisprudence, this form of law was neither liberal nor democratic. The 1947 constitution was largely the work of American lawyers who were intent on establishing the rule of law as they knew it. The cabinet and the bureaucratic organs of administration were to be accountable to the parliament. The constitution cataloged a long list of human rights to be protected by an American-style judiciary with the power to ensure their enforcement. This independent judiciary would not only protect individual rights; it was also given the power to check the legislature by reviewing its acts to ensure they were commensurate with the provisions of the constitution.

Japanese progressives in the early period feared that the weakness of the rule of law would inhibit the development of democratic institutions. Japan, wrote Kawashima Takeyoshi, Japan's leading legal scholar after the war, suffered from a "weak legal consciousness" that encouraged individual submission to the will of the group and the social pressure of superiors. Rather than rely so heavily on laws, the Japanese rely more on informal means of maintaining social order, especially consensual governance. This inhibited the development of individual rights. Progressives drew hope from the fact that it was not only traditional values accounting for the weak legal consciousness but also the role of the state, which had promoted the extrajudicial dispute-resolution process. If state suppression of rights consciousness could be overcome, the rule of law would develop. The state had stressed conciliation to settle disputes as a means to maintain social order. The relative lack of lawyers, the reluctance to resort to litigation to resolve disputes, a politically cautious judiciary, and the reliance on informal and personal relations between business and government all seemed to most observers that, yes, the Japanese were moved by different cultural values. As a result of this absence of assertion of individual rights, Japanese democracy, the critics said, could not develop fully.

Kawashima and other Japanese progressives put their hopes in the belief that as Japan modernized, its legal culture would change and Japan would become more like and "converge" with Western concepts of the rule of law. But this has not happened. Despite the Occupation's imposition of codes and institutions drawn from the Anglo-American legal tradition, the Japanese implemented these codes and institutions in ways largely unforeseen by the Americans. Japan has depended much less on detailed enforcement aspects of law to maintain order than the United States. Instead, Japanese legislation has been comparatively weak in its reliance on the power to coerce and compel obedience to the law. Maintenance of social order in Japan is left more to informal mechanisms and to the bureaucracy, which is able to manipulate these informal mechanisms.[47] The Japanese state uses law to lay down norms of behavior, but it does not use its very considerable authority to pre-scribe remedies or enforcement powers. Much is left to informal mech-anisms of dispute resolution. As a result, the rule of law has been lim-ited by traditional values that discourage litigation and assertion of individual rights. The Japanese state is especially reluctant to prescribe intervention in behalf of the individual. The individual is not the ulti-mate source of concern; the well-being of the community takes prece-dence. In Japan, the state is less coercive. As Higuchi Yoichi, a constitu-tional law scholar at the University of Tokyo, bluntly puts it, "Society is the tyrant."[48]

Norma Field describes the force of peer and social pressure Japanese individuals confront when they assert their rights. Going against pre-vailing social norms "to take an unpopular stance (such as objecting to an updated version of folk custom) is bad enough, but to assert it as a right . . . makes things much worse. People greet such arguments with suspicion. . . . The recognition of rights compels a community to coun-tenance uncustomary behavior. . . . To assert a difference of view in the form of a right is at the very least to create awkwardness."[49] Assertions of individual self-interest tend to be regarded as selfish and destructive of community and stability. Recognition of constitutional rights in Japan is relatively low in the American view.

Conservatives take pride in Japan's values as achieving a unique so-cial harmony. They point to the low levels of litigation, judges, lawyers, prosecutors, and police per capita in comparison with the United States and other Western countries. They also point to lower crime rates. They credit a culturally embedded willingness to compromise and to respect the claims of the group rather than the selfish interests of the individual, and they trace this to the long years of village life in which reliance on the group was a condition of survival. Writing in 1980, one of postwar Japan's leading bureaucrats, Amaya Naohiro, celebrated the collectivist values he perceived in Japan:

> Japan's history is much different from that of the United States. Japan did not establish the atomistic individual as the basic unit of society and rarely had individuals who "spun off" from society and lived by them-selves. Today, as in the old days, the basic unit of Japanese society is not "atomistic" individuals, but "molecule-like" groups. These groups con-sist of "villages" and "families." One may consider "families" as mono-mers and "villages" as polymers. Individuals live as an organic element of their groups within this group structure.

The fundamental ethic which supports a group has been "harmony." Such American values as individual freedom, equality, equal opportunity, and an open-door policy can be considered "foreign proteins" introduced into the traditional body of Japanese society.[50]

Conservative Japanese, as Amaya's views reflected, characteristically identified law and litigation with Western individualism, an unwelcome influence challenging Japan's traditional respect for consensus and harmony. Amaya and others point out that Western legal concepts were foreign intrusions. They were first introduced in the late nineteenth century to satisfy the demands of the Western imperial powers, and then again by the American Occupation. But he and many others contend that such importations went against a Japanese national character naturally inclined to a more harmonious society.

And yet, the work of legal scholars has demonstrated convincingly that what often seemed to be a cultural proclivity for conciliation was also the result of the bureaucracy's manipulation of the legal framework in order to contain litigation and prevent the development of a rights consciousness that would weaken the role of the bureaucracy as the managers of social change.[51] It was not culture so much as institutional barriers that have limited litigation. For example, in the late 1960s when the headlong economic growth brought with it alarming levels of industrial pollution, public protest led to a series of court cases that caught the government off guard. But once bureaucrats addressed the problems, they did so in ways that sought to deflect the problems decisively from formal litigation to informal mediation. The government quickly instituted strict pollution controls on industry, established an administrative program of compensation for victims, and established a bureaucratically staffed system to mediate and resolve disputes. Rather than allow the public outcry to broaden into a massive series of formal litigation, the government skillfully contained the fallout and successfully defused the threat of sustained protest by mediation and selective compensation of the aggrieved.

The conservative elite, especially the bureaucracy, has sought to manipulate and structure the legal framework to prevent easy resort to litigation and thus preserve their role as social managers. The government has consciously sought to contain the amount of litigation in Japanese society by limiting the size and growth of the necessary institutions. The relative lack of litigation in Japan can best be accounted for by seeing the institutional arrangements that have discouraged lawsuits and encouraged dispute resolution through mediation. The relatively limited number of judges and lawyers is startling when compared with the number in America. Looked at over a long period of time, the number of judges has failed to keep pace with the growth of the population, with industrialization, and with the complexity of modern life. As a consequence, the caseload and overcrowding in the courts make resort to the courts a protracted and frustrating process. The most striking example of an institutional barrier to litigation—especially from the American perspective—is the small number of lawyers. This is the result of conscious government policy to limit the size of the profession. For example, in 1975, 74 percent of Americans taking the bar examination successfully passed, whereas in Japan only 1.7 percent passed. The number of legal actors in Japan is astonishingly small when compared with that of other industrial democracies. In the 1990s Japan had fewer prosecutors (fewer than 2,200), fewer judges (about 2,600), and fewer practicing attorneys (about 15,000) per capita than in other comparable countries.[52]

The nature of its judiciary tells us a great deal about the character of postwar Japanese society. The judicial system in postwar Japan is notable for its cautious and conservative approach. It has not been the activist judiciary the Occupation envisioned; rather, it has hewed consistently to protecting its sense of the community's well-being. Rather than staking a role of protecting abstract and universal precepts of the rights of individuals, it has been devoted to preserving a "sense of society." At the beginning of the twenty-first century, consensus, caution, consistency, and community continue to be the hallmark of the legal system and its actors.

Nevertheless, with the advent of globalization, business, political, and legal circles have begun to believe that Japan has increasing need for legal services and more and better-qualified lawyers. A major reform effort announced in 2001 is attempting to modify the characteristics of the Japanese legal system. The government appointed a Justice System Reform Council, which made important recommendations, including reforms to increase the number of lawyers to meet the growing demand for legal services. To bring new and better-trained entrants into the legal profession, the council recommended sweeping reform of legal education and the establishment of new graduate-level law schools. The business leaders, who had hitherto criticized America as a country with too many lawyers and too much litigation they said hampered US competitiveness, were the most notable of the reform advocates.

Another important set of reforms recommended by the council sought to increase popular participation in the legal system. Most noteworthy was the introduction of lay participation in the judging of criminal cases in order to increase popular trust in the justice system. In its fundamental philosophy the council said it was seeking to strengthen popular sovereignty: "[These] various reforms assume as a basic premise the people's transformation from governed objects to governing subjects and at the same time seek to promote such transformation. This is a transformation in which the people will break out of viewing the government as the ruler (the authority) and instead will take heavy responsibility for governance themselves, and in which the government will convert itself into one that responds to such people."[53] This was a remarkable statement of democratic intentions that contrasted with the traditional professional aloofness of the Japanese legal profession on which elitist politics depended. The lay jury system was inaugurated in 2009 but surprisingly was greeted with lukewarm support in public opinion polls. Many people were reluctant to serve in the lay juries, citing lack of ability and confidence to make legal judgments. Some said they would prefer judges continue to make decisions. A large percentage of people chosen to serve either declined or did not appear for jury duty.[54] Whether legal reforms as well as political and social changes outside the legal system lead to "a greater reliance on universalistic rules, more individual rights assertion, more litigation, and less reliance on social norms as the glue that orders social relations" remains to be seen.[55]

Assessing Japanese Democracy

Japan has never had a democratic revolution of its own making. Democratization has been a slow and evolutionary process and has developed in a variety of ways. This is always the case, even where there has been a revolutionary upheaval. America's own democracy has taken over 200 years to try to fulfill its fundamental principles of equality of all its citizens. But in Japan's case, democratization continues to be a particularly protracted process. The "intervention" of the Occupation denied Japan the possibility of a democratic revolution.[56] Nevertheless, Japan today is a democracy. Because democratic institutions were not self-determined and were the product of the alien Anglo-American tradition, the Japanese have undergone a protracted and arduous struggle to Japanize these institutions. Reflecting on the propensity of the United States to intervene in foreign countries to impose its form of government, the political scientist Michael Doyle writes, "There is no universal form of free government. Authentic freedom is the right and capacity to discover and make your own version of self-determined governance for you and your fellow citizens."[57] Democratization, as a consequence, developed slowly and piecemeal during the postwar years as Japan struggled to adapt the new institutions to its own national life.

With the rise of China, Japanese foreign policy has made much of its commitment to democracy and human rights as a way of differentiating its ideals from the authoritarian regime in the People's Republic. While not so openly assertive and high profile in its defense of human rights as the Americans or Europeans, Japan nevertheless has made these values an important principle in its recent diplomacy with other Asian nations.[58] Nevertheless, in domestic society, various political and social forms of discrimination against Koreans, Okinawans, and other minorities remain a challenge to be overcome. Whatever the public diplomacy, commitment to the long list of rights in the constitution is outweighed by communitarian norms deeply rooted in Japanese history.

The postwar period has witnessed a continuing struggle to accommodate the imposed institutions of democratic government to the historical values of the Japanese people. Those values that have weighted social solidarity, however, have been modified by political and social change, giving legitimacy to a vision of democracy with Japan's own cultural nuances. The sociolinguist Kyoko Inoue shows the way in which Japanese have shaped democracy to their historically rooted culture. Tracing changes in high school textbooks during the postwar period, she demonstrates a growing acceptance of the fundamental notions of democratic government, albeit in a distinctly Japanese form. Textbooks at first explained democratic values in a way that blurred respect for hierarchy and individualism, but more recently they have been clearer in explaining the concepts of democracy and human rights. As Inoue writes, the explanations of individual dignity and human rights in textbooks show a clear change over time while still maintaining a distinctly Japanese approach:

At the end of the twentieth century, what has emerged in Japanese textbooks is a sense of communitarian democracy emphasizing social rights. They teach that the central idea of democracy is respect for individuals and protection of their fundamental human rights, and they clearly stress equality, not hierarchy. . . . But they do not encourage people to protect their rights against the government. Rather, they indicate that cooperation between the government and people is the key to bringing a just and fair society for all people. . . . The Japanese seem to be creating their own communitarian version of democracy. While rights should be observed because all people are worthy of respect . . . people are not encouraged to assert their rights against strong communitarian sentiments.[59]

Inoue's conclusion is very much in accord with the view of legal scholar John Haley, who argues that the spirit of Japanese law reflects the customs and norms of the community. He notes that the Supreme Court interprets its role as protecting "the informal rules and norms evolved through time and accepted by tacit assent and community adherence."[60] Despite the changes, Japanese encouragement of an active defense of individual rights against government interference is still weak relative to that of the United States and other liberal democracies.

11

Japan in the Twilight of the American Century

HENRY LUCE wrote his famous essay "The American Century" in 1941, shortly before the bombing of Pearl Harbor. In his essay, the magazine publisher urged his countrymen to lay aside the "moral and practical bankruptcy" of isolationism and take the opportunity provided by American power to rehabilitate the world. The "American century," he said, "must be a sharing with all people of our Bill of Rights, our Declaration of Independence, our Constitution, our magnificent industrial products, our technical skills. . . . It now becomes our time to be the powerhouse from which the ideals spread throughout the world and do their mysterious work of lifting the life of mankind from the level of the beasts to what the Psalmist called a little lower than the angels." For Luce, the son of missionary parents in China, America was to be "a good Samaritan" in redeeming the world. The values and institutions that came out of the American experience were for all peoples, and America must be active and forceful in leading the world to realize them. Americans must "accept wholeheartedly our duty and our opportunity as the most powerful and vital nation in the world and in consequence to exert upon the world the full impact of our influence, for such purposes as we see fit and by such means as we see fit."[1] Luce was a Republican, mistrusted by liberals and no friend of Franklin Roosevelt, but they too shared his view.[2]

When war came, there was nothing inevitable in the way that the United States would choose to fight the war. Nor was it foreordained that to defeat Japan the United States would require the right to occupy and remake it. As the American historian David Kennedy wisely observed, "America *chose*—I emphasize the word deliberately—to fight a certain kind of war. In doing so, it succeeded to a degree unmatched by virtually all other combatants in that or any other war, in fighting on its own terms."[3] The goal chosen would not be, as in other wars, a negotiated peace. Neither would we be satisfied to drive the enemy back to its own borders. Nor would we simply seek to establish supremacy in the region. Diplomacy and compromises were ruled out. This war would be fought to achieve victory on our own distinctive terms. The goal was to achieve a revolution in international affairs and a new American world order of the kind that Thomas Paine had dreamed and Woodrow Wilson had attempted. Americans overwhelmingly embraced the view that it was our destiny to shape the future of the world. Confidence in the moral imperative of this crusading international role legitimated the use of maximum military might. The stupendous potential of its industrial economy and technological superiority allowed the United States to succeed in its grandiose goal and, in fact, to succeed in defining an "American century" in world history.[4]

The peculiar character of American belligerency had a profound impact on Japan. Japan would not be left as a defeated or diminished power, still independent. It would not be left to reform itself after defeat. It must *be* reformed to conform with the revolution in international affairs. An understanding of postwar Japan, I have argued, must begin with the American policy of unconditional surrender and its ultimate purpose of establishing a new international order. Major landmarks of postwar Japan—the utter devastation of its cities, its identity as the unique victim of the atomic age, the constitution and other Occupation reforms, the hegemonic alliance, the long-term presence of foreign troops and bases, the mercantilist foreign policy, and the struggles to reconcile imposed social and political structures with Japan's historical values—all had their origins in the uncompromising goals of the victors.

Japan's subordination in the new world order shaped its politics and social movements for more than half a century, but the day when such subordination would end was bound to come in one way or another.

Early in the twenty-first century, the extraordinary postwar period of American domination of Japan is passing. In the post–Cold War years, the components of world order have changed in such sweeping ways as have rarely been seen in modern history. The collapse of the Soviet system and its ideological underpinnings, globalization and a new technological paradigm, the rise of Asia and an assertive China—all have wrought a fundamental change in Japanese domestic politics and a revolution in its foreign policy. Japan is regaining its voice. The political will and spirit first silenced by the trauma of defeat and then suppressed by the strategic priorities of a mercantilist foreign policy are resurfacing. "Japan is back," the nationalist prime minister Abe Shinzō proclaimed in a policy speech in 2013. Replacing the self-binding policies of its passive mercantilist strategy with a proactive foreign policy, Japan has adopted a new activist role in international politics not seen since 1945. The Japanese public is wary of taking on greater foreign policy obligations, but the volatility of the Northeast Asia region is steadily weakening its resistance.

Not only is Japan regaining its self-assertion and an independent voice in world affairs; the American world order itself is undergoing fundamental change in ways that challenge American primacy in the Asia Pacific region and make a new relationship with Japan critical to the US capacity for leadership. The US-Japan alliance is experiencing the biggest change in its long history, acquiring a reciprocity and common purpose that it has never had. At the same time, however, China's growing power and a new nationalist orientation in the Trump administration have raised deep uncertainty over America's continued commitment to the liberal international order it created and has led for seven decades. As a consequence, the trajectory of the international order is reaching a critical inflection point.

Post–Cold War American Triumphalism

For Americans, the fall of the Berlin Wall in 1989 and the demise of the Soviet Union in 1991 brought forth a wave of celebration reminiscent of that in 1945. The bipolar world was gone. America was the sole superpower. So decisive a victory in the Cold War vindicated confidence in the universalism of American values and institutions. The titanic struggle between the Western and communist worlds ended in the massive implosion of the Soviet system and seemed to promise a lasting liberal hegemony. Basking in the decisive outcome, Americans foresaw an inevitable global democratic revolution. Having defeated its authoritarian, fascist, and communist rivals in the three great power struggles of the twentieth century—the two world wars and the Cold War—the United States, along with its allies, as one prominent American intellectual put it, had arrived at "the end point of mankind's ideological evolution and universalization of Western liberal democracy." There were at last no ideological competitors. Francis Fukuyama wrote that "the triumph of the West, of the Western ideal, is evident . . . in the total exhaustion of viable alternatives to Western liberalism."[5] Anthony Lake, President Clinton's national security advisor, in 1993 proclaimed a change of grand strategy from containment to "a strategy of enlargement—enlargement of the world's free community of market democracies."[6] Every country must now be inspired to converge with the American model.

Other events also put wind in American sails. On the heels of the Cold War triumph, the United States organized a thirty-four-nation coalition to end Saddam Hussein's invasion of Kuwait, which ended in a sweeping victory over Iraqi forces in the Gulf War of 1991. At about the same time, the fading of the Japanese challenge and its economic model, as well as the collapse of the socialist model, contrasted with the strong performance of the American economy in the 1990s and conferred legitimacy on American capitalism as a model of universal applicability. Americans proclaimed a "Washington consensus" on a liberal, market-driven capitalism as the most efficient way to promote growth under the new conditions of globalization.

Lest any would-be challenger fail to recognize the triumph of American ideology, a Defense Department policy paper drafted in March 1992 asserted that America's military power would ensure that no rival was allowed to emerge anywhere.[7] A "revolution in military affairs" promised American mastery of digital warfare and precision weaponry that would achieve "asymmetrical technological advantages" over any adversary. What some writers termed "a unipolar moment" at the end of the Cold War would be transformed into a lasting unipolar era. A resurgent Germany or Japan, a united Europe, a revanchist Russia, or an emergent China—none would be allowed to challenge the American superpower

in the future. The Pentagon's goal was to maintain "full-spectrum dominance" in all regions of the world and "to operate in all domains—
space, sea, land, air, and information."[8] Confident of American hyperpower, President George W. Bush in his second inaugural address proclaimed America's commitment "to seek and support the growth of
democratic movements and institutions in every nation and culture,
with the ultimate goal of ending tyranny in our world." It was, Jeremi
Suri observed, "the most universalistic foreign policy mission in the nation's history."[9]

The apparent unipolar world that Americans envisioned at the end
of the Cold War proved illusory. The hubris that it evoked soon led to
overreach in costly US failures to topple regimes and promote democracy in Afghanistan, Egypt, Iraq, Libya, Syria, and Yemen. The failures
called into question a foreign policy encouraging indiscriminate interventions to spread democracy and nation building abroad. Wars in Iraq
and Afghanistan became the longest and costliest in American history,
making Americans wonder whether the United States could afford to
be the world's policeman or its tutor. It is noteworthy that even Henry
Luce in his ambitious essay had written that the purpose of the American
Century was "not to police the whole world nor to impose democratic
institutions on all mankind."[10] Washington assumed that post–Cold
War Russia would move inexorably toward economic and political liberalism and be integrated into a single world system under American
leadership. But Russian leaders, reacting to the enlargement of NATO
into its former sphere and finding liberal politics threatening, soon began
to contest the American world order. China, too, adopted a revisionist
role in resisting the liberal order.

Amid celebration of the end of the Cold War, Americans ignored how
the fundamentals of the world system had changed since 1945. New
powers were rising, especially in Asia, and the international institutions
that Americans had created needed reforms to meet new conditions and
reflect the changing distribution of power. In retrospect it is clear that
the United States, lacking imaginative leadership, lost the extraordinary
opportunity offered by its unipolar moment to restructure the global
system that had emerged from World War II to better reflect the changes
that occurred from 1945 to 1990. The self-indulgence meant that America ignored the changes that had taken place in the world since the
1970s. As Odd Arne Westad observed, "Most Americans still believed

that they could only be safe if the world looked significantly more like their own country and if the world's governments abided by the will of the United States. . . . The United States squandered many chances to prepare for a new century in which its relative power will be reduced. Lessons from the Cold War indicate that its main aim should have been to tie others into the kinds of principles for international behavior that the United States would like to see long term, especially as its own power diminishes."[11]

American triumphalism drew sour reactions from Japanese conservatives who felt once again the sting of Western liberal domination. For the whole of its modern history, since the Meiji Restoration, Japan had been compelled to live in international systems made primarily by the Anglo-American powers and reflecting their liberal beliefs. Japan adapted to this reality within a powerful conservative tradition that was embedded in its national life. For this reason, American celebration of the collapse of communism was not altogether pleasant. Flushed with victory, convinced of the impregnability of their values, the Americans were seen by many Japanese conservatives as self-righteous and intolerant of other cultures. Again and again throughout the twentieth century Japan was confronted with American insistence on the universalism of its values. It was the essence of the principles of international liberalism that President Wilson enunciated at Versailles in 1919. It was the essence of the demands that President Roosevelt insisted on in the summer of 1941 if the crippling trade embargo were to be lifted. It was the essence of the unconditional surrender terms and the reforms imposed during the postwar occupation of Japan. It was the essence of American criticism of Japanese economic institutions during the trade frictions of the 1970s and 1980s and then of Americans' impatient advice that post-bubble Japan reform its economic and political institutions to accord with the neoliberal "Washington consensus" of free market fundamentalism.

The Tokyo University social scientist Murakami Yasusuke expressed distaste at the renewed claims of universalism. He was dismayed by the persistence of American self-righteousness and intolerance of cultural diversity. Reflecting on Japan's modern experience, he described American universalism as amounting to a "homogenization" of culture and as an "ideology of bloodshed" because it justified interventionism and sought to erase rather than "understand" the traditions of other cultures.[12] Throughout their modern history Japanese had often been inclined to see themselves and their culture through the spectacles of Western Enlightenment thought and to be left uncomfortable and uncertain in their uniqueness.

The outspoken Finance Ministry bureaucrat Sakakibara Eisuke likewise rejected liberal celebration over the end of the Cold War. The capacity of the West, especially the United States, to use its industrial and military strength to overpower other civilizations in the nineteenth and twentieth centuries had created a false confidence in the incontestable superiority of Western liberalism as the universal path of human civilization. But the emergence of Asia would demonstrate that the future of world order must be compatible with a multiplicity of cultural values. In the emerging post–Cold War order, he wrote, the values of the Asian historical experience will be required because that experience demonstrates that "diverse civilizations can coexist peacefully if tolerance and moderation are practiced."[13] While satisfied that international communism had collapsed, still in their heart of hearts, Japanese conservatives retained a distaste for the dogmatic assertions of international liberalism and its justification for interventionism and unilateralism.

The Turning Point in Japanese Foreign Policy

When the unanticipated and abrupt ending of the Cold War shook the world, no country was less prepared for the new era of international politics than Japan. For forty years the Japanese had anchored their foreign policy and domestic system in the unique conditions of the bilateral order. The Yoshida strategy was designed to succeed in the Cold War system and brought extraordinary success, but it was immediately outmoded when the conflict ended. With the end of superpower rivalry, the United States was no longer willing to provide automatic guarantees of Japanese security and demanded that Japan shoulder greater responsibility for its own security and for international order. Japan had neglected, in fact deliberately averted its attention from, developing an infrastructure to take responsibility for defense of its security. Self-binding policies ensured that Japan could stay out of political and military involvement, interpreting Article 9 to mean that there would be (what I have called the "Nine Nos") no overseas deployment of the Japan Self-Defense Forces, no participation in collective defense, no power-projection capability, no possession of nuclear arms, no arms exports, no sharing of defense-related technology, no spending of more than 1 percent of GNP for defense expenditure, no military use of space, and no foreign aid for military purposes. Japan existed as a trading state and depended on the United States to provide its security. This grand strategy left Japan ill prepared for the post–Cold War era. Exclusive concentration on economic growth left the nation without political-strategic institutions, crisis management practice, intelligence gathering, or strategic planning. Incredibly, the Japanese had no plan or legislation that would allow the government to deal with national emergencies. Japan, supposedly a sovereign country, had in effect no plans for ensuring its national security. Dependence had become the foundation of the nation's foreign policy.

Throughout Japan's modern history, the recurrent pattern of Japanese geopolitics has been one of adapting its domestic system to meet the conditions of its international environment. Beginning with the Meiji Restoration, Japanese leaders had repeatedly accommodated its policies and institutions to changes in the prevailing external realities. The historically formed character of the conservative elite was always noted for its realism and pragmatism, its readiness to adapt to meet the needs of national power.[14] As the new post–Cold War reality sank in, Japan behaved in its classic fashion. Once again Japan's conservative elite would change its foreign policy and revise the domestic infrastructure in response to the changing external order. Step by step, fitfully, Japan began undoing its Cold War strategy and constructing a new one to fit the still emerging post–Cold War order in its region and in the world. Moving away from an exclusive emphasis on economics and becoming engaged in political-military strategic affairs, successive prime ministers steadily loosened Japan's self-binding policies.

Adopting a more orthodox role in the international politics of a conflict-prone world required an institutional revolution and the formation of a security infrastructure that was wholly lacking in the years of the Yoshida strategy. If Japan was to become an actor in international politics after more than a half century of shunning this role, it would need organizations responsible for strategic and military planning. Developing a foreign policy with greater symmetry between the economic and political dimensions of its international role would challenge the institutional and informal practices sanctified by decades of success in purely economic matters. The Finance Ministry's domination of the budget-making process must be modified in ways that would give military-strategic criteria greater influence. The prime minister's capacity to provide bold leadership in foreign policy, to formulate a strategic vision, and to implement security policy must be greatly enhanced to deal with fluid and rapidly changing international circumstances. The constitution must be amended or reinterpreted to define the role of the military, to make collective self-defense legal, and to clarify the national purpose.

A series of crises in their external relations forced Japan's leaders to acknowledge that the strategies effective in the Cold War were no longer viable and that Japan must adapt to new circumstances. The first great international crisis of the post–Cold War period revealed how shockingly unprepared Japan was for the new era. In the Persian Gulf War of 1990–1991, in which the United States assembled a UN-sanctioned coalition of nations to counter Saddam Hussein's aggression against Kuwait, the Japanese government, citing Article 9, sought to take refuge from demands that it contribute personnel support to the coalition. Despite the fact that it was a great economic power utterly dependent on the stability of the Middle East for its energy needs, the Japanese government insisted that its constitution prohibited deployment of the Self-Defense Forces to participate in such a collective security undertaking. The Americans, no longer restrained by the priorities of the Cold War, were outraged by Japan's "free-riding." The House of Representatives passed a resolution threatening to begin withdrawing troops from Japan.

Under intense US pressure, the Japanese government ultimately made a $13 billion contribution to support the coalition.[15] Although a sizable sum, it was belittled abroad as "checkbook diplomacy" and an inadequate way to meet Japan's responsibilities to uphold international order. The storm of international criticism that greeted its grudging support of the UN-sanctioned coalition stunned Japan. Much more than is generally appreciated outside Japan, the Japanese were deeply humiliated by the international criticism. The experience began a growing criticism within Japan of the Yoshida Doctrine as a viable strategy for the future. Former prime minister Nakasone led a chorus of national self-criticism when he said that such "prevarication" (*gomakashi*) of the Yoshida Doctrine no longer held credibility and demonstrated the need for a new national strategy.[16] Inoki Masamichi, the widely respected former head of the National Defense Academy, said it was time to stop resorting to the "devious" (*zurui*) excuse of the constitution for evading Japan's responsibilities to the international community.[17]

Such criticism initiated a national debate. No one was a stouter defender of the Yoshida strategy than Miyazawa Kiichi, who became prime minister in 1991 in the immediate aftermath of the Gulf War crisis. "We must clearly state," Miyazawa had declared before taking office, "that we cannot change the Japanese Constitution at this time. Even if other countries say that having such a constitution is outrageous (*keshikaran*) we must maintain the position that we decided on this and it's not for others to interfere."[18] Miyazawa is particularly interesting because, unlike other conservative leaders who often were cynical in their use of the Yoshida strategy and its Article 9 defense, he was a true believer.[19] As a young man, he had been an aide to Yoshida and a close associate of Ikeda. Subsequently serving as foreign minister and minister of finance before becoming prime minister, he tenaciously defended a passive role for Japan by holding that the constitution made Japan a "special state" (*tokushu kokka*), which precluded it from normal participation in international politics. In creating a peace state, he wrote in 1984, "the Japanese people (*minzoku*) have gambled their future (*unmei*) in a great experiment, the first of its kind in human history."[20] Miyazawa, as it turned out, was the last of the Yoshida school prime ministers.

The Persian Gulf crisis proved to be a turning point in postwar Japanese history. It posed the changed conditions of the international order as a challenge to the Yoshida Doctrine in such clear terms that Japan's Cold War grand strategy began to crumble as the nation's leaders groped for ways to accommodate the new realities. Japan must become, said Ozawa Ichirō, a dominant new political personality, "a normal country" (*futsū no kuni*).[21] The immediate outcome of this humiliating disarray was the passage in 1992 of legislation permitting participation in UN peacekeeping operations, but only under restrictions that limited the Self-Defense Forces' involvement to logistical and humanitarian support and providing aid in civil administration. They would not be deployed near combat zones or in situations requiring the use of force. It was, however, the first time the Self-Defense Forces were allowed to deploy abroad and the first break from the Yoshida Doctrine.

A new direction and sense of national purpose, however, did not come readily. The development of a new proactive foreign policy came slowly and incrementally over the next two decades. Typically, each step required American pressure. The Yoshida strategy, which was deeply embedded in Japan's postwar institutions and sanctioned by its extraordinary successes in building Japan's international economic power, had great staying power and was not easily overturned. Sections of the bureaucracy, the opposition parties, remnants of the Yoshida school conservatives, the Komeito Party (which was the LDP's coalition partner), and much of the voting public resisted each incremental step. The economic bureaucrats had long dominated the budgets of the Self-Defense Forces, and the elite bureaucrats in the Cabinet Legal Bureau had maintained firm control of the narrow interpretation of the constitution's Article 9 because the Supreme Court in the Sunakawa case of 1959 had declined to rule on it as a matter that should be determined by the executive and legislative branches.

The United States nevertheless kept relentless pressure on Japan. After the September 11, 2001, terrorist attacks in the United States and the organizing of Operation Enduring Freedom to take down the Taliban in Afghanistan, the deputy secretary of state summoned the Japanese ambassador in Washington to say that the United States expected Japan to "show the flag." Similarly, when the invasion of Iraq began, the United States asked the Japanese for "boots on the ground." In both cases the debates in Japan were protracted. The fundamental issue was always whether the constitution allowed collective self-defense. Recalling the humiliation of the Gulf Crisis, the government drafted special legislation to allow noncombat, logistical support of US and other coalition forces in the Afghanistan and Iraq campaigns. With successive international crises involving the United States and its allies, Japan's more active engagement continued to evolve. Japanese adaptation to the post–Cold War conditions might have continued at a slow, incremental pace were it not for the emergence of a newly assertive China and a more threatening regional environment. In addition to the external environment, fundamental change in domestic politics also fueled a more rapid tempo of change.

Political Nationalism: The New LDP Mainstream

The postwar political system in Japan, which had been shaped by the Cold War order, began to change with the dissolution of that order. There had long been three fundamental centers of political power in the Diet: first, the LDP's conservative mainstream, which adhered to the Yoshida doctrine; second, the Japan Socialist Party (JSP), which supported the 1947 constitution and advocated neutrality in the Cold War; and third, the political nationalists who composed the right wing of the LDP and who wanted to revise the constitution, rearm, and assert a more independent role in the world. The end of the Cold War undermined the first two. It undercut the LDP mainstream's Yoshida school because the Americans were less willing to provide the benefits of the alliance that were necessary to Japanese security. The international criticism of Japan's role in the Gulf War, together with the end of Japan's economic success from the bursting of the bubble, soon brought to a close the Yoshida strategy of the LDP mainstream. By the turn of the century, as one close observer wrote, "the once proud conservative mainstream, which had ruled the LDP for the better part of its existence, has all but disappeared."[22]

The end of the Cold War also decisively undermined the JSP's policies. In 1994 the Socialist prime minister Murayama Tomiichi, as part of his party's arrangement of a coalition government with the LDP, accepted the new reality and repudiated virtually the entire agenda of the JSP. He disowned his party's longtime opposition to the Self-Defense Forces, the American alliance, the US bases in Japan, and all other major aspects of its previous foreign policy positions stretching back to the Anpo demonstrations in the 1950s. Having abandoned its essential progressive stance, the JSP almost at once lost its identity, credibility, and popular support. With two of its three centers of power gone, the long-standing paradigm of Japanese domestic politics, known as the 1955 System, disappeared. Of the three, only the right wing of the LDP, the political nationalists with their commitment to revise the constitution and overturn all that remained of the American-imposed order, was left intact. It soon became the new mainstream of the LDP.

The political nationalists in the right wing of the LDP had sought revision of the constitution from the time of the party's founding in 1955. Arguing that the constitution was forced on Japan and that it did not reflect the history, traditions, and values of the nation, they had made revision a plank in the party's founding document.[23] When he became prime minister two years later, Kishi Nobusuke, a leader of the political nationalists, made revision a centerpiece of his agenda, but after the Anpo struggle toppled him, the Yoshida school mainstream returned to leadership and the political nationalists' agenda was shelved. But it remained latent and was kept alive by a steady stream of popular writers in the mass media, such as the prominent critic Etō Jun, who emphasized the constitution's illegitimacy and demeaning nature.[24] The shocking ritual suicide of the famous novelist Mishima Yukio in 1970 after deriding Self-Defense cadets for lacking the traditional Japanese warrior spirit was the most notable of many events that also kept the issue of the constitution alive. In addition to their goal of revising the MacArthur Constitution, the political nationalists produced a stream of writings attacking the judgments of the Tokyo War Crimes Trials and the liberal values in the imposed Fundamental Law of Education, and advocating rearmament and a more independent role in international politics. Always latent, the troubled spirit of postwar Japan, a legacy of the Occupation, was set to surface when the paradigm of domestic politics changed.

More than two decades passed after the Anpo turmoil before the political nationalists regained the prime ministership from the LDP mainstream. In 1982 the veteran nationalist Nakasone Yasuhiro came to power determined to overturn the Yoshida school's strategy of self-binding restraints on involvement in international politics. Recognizing that he lacked the necessary majorities in the Diet, he chose not to attempt revision of the constitution. Nakasone wrote on the eve of taking power, "I would still like to see a new constitution of our own making. But I would not want to rip Japanese society apart over this question."[25] Instead, with the slogan "settling postwar accounts" (sengo sōkessan), he tried to reform education and create a new sense of national pride and identity by returning Japan to an active role in international political and strategic affairs and preparing Japan for international leadership. Many of his goals, however, were stymied by the opposition of the bureaucrats, opposition parties, and popular attachment to the pacifist constitution. It took a major change in the external environment and the changes it brought to politics to create conditions favorable to the political nationalists.

The opportune time for the political nationalists arrived in 2012 with the LDP's landslide victory in the general election and Abe Shinzō's return as prime minister. After a brief first term (2006–2007) as prime minister, marked by mishaps and bad judgment, Abe was followed in the next five years by a succession of five weak prime ministers, and from 2009 to 2012 the LDP lost its hold on government to the

DPJ. The DPJ proved hapless and incapable of keeping public confidence in its ability to govern. When Abe and the LDP were returned to power in 2012 after such political disarray, the public was ready for a strong prime minister and in succeeding elections over the next several years gave him a series of electoral victories. Abe was a political blue blood with deep family roots in the world of elite politics. His father had been foreign minister, and his grandfather and great uncle had been prime ministers. The memory of his maternal grandfather Kishi's tumultuous three-year term shaped his philosophy of political nationalism.

Abe rose to power as the leader of a conservative reaction to Japan's long subordination in the American order. In his book *Toward a New Country* (*Atarashii kuni e*), which he published at the outset of his second term in 2012, he declared his intention to end the legacy of the Occupation and recover Japanese autonomy. For too long the Japanese people had enjoyed prosperity without "the clear awareness that the lives and treasure of the Japanese people and the territory of Japan must be protected by the Japanese government's own hands."[26] Abe was the darling of dozens of new conservative groups that denounced the imposed constitution, the liberal social values, the hegemonic alliance, and, above all, the victors' version of history, which concentrated blame for the Asia Pacific War on Japan.

The post–Cold War era was the seed time of right-wing nationalist organizations. Dozens of new groups and newly revitalized groups, often joined by interlocking memberships, sprang up among politicians at the national and local levels. Abe was closely associated with many of the groups. One Diet group with seventy-five members that he chaired, Sosei Nippon (Japan Rebirth), dedicated to replacing the postwar order with a new structure founded on Japan's traditional values, provided key support in his election as president of the LDP in 2012.[27] The group that drew the most attention in the media for its size and influence was Nippon kaigi (the Japan Council or Conference), founded in 1997. As of 2016 it claimed 38,000 members, headquarters in all 47 prefectures, 240 local branches, 1,700 local assembly members, and 281 Diet members, with Prime Minister Abe and Deputy Prime Minister Asō Tarō as special advisors. Its goals were constitutional revision, patriotic education, building a strong national defense to engage in an active international role, and establishing a positive view of Japan's history to replace the verdicts of the War Crimes Trials.[28] The large numbers of Diet members belonging to these groups was indicative of a new generation of politicians in the LDP and their reaction to the rise of an assertive China and a nationalist South Korea and their persistent demands for apology and remorse for Japan's wartime atrocities.[29] There was a notable turnover in LDP Diet membership that replaced an older postwar generation with younger politicians who were no longer inclined to adopt a low posture in the face of criticism from Japan's neighbors.[30] For them, China was no longer seen as a victim of Japan's militarism but rather as a rising rival and challenge to Japan's future. They were ready for a proactive Japan, exercising its influence in the world. Membership in one or another of these interlocking groups provided new networks of intra-LDP organization at the expense of factional influence.[31]

Many other nationalist groups supported Abe and the political nationalists. Several newly revived Shinto organizations sought the ending of the Occupation's Shinto Directive and the constitution's separation of religion and state. The goals of these groups were to replace the secular order with a restored Shinto influence in public life, most notably seeking the nationalization of the Yasukuni Shrine, but also including policies of moral education and revising textbook accounts critical of Japan's modern history, especially accounts of the Nanjing massacre and of the comfort women forced into sexual slavery during the war. The Shinto seiji renmei (The League Promoting Ties between Politics and Shinto), which is the political arm of the Jinja honchō (Association of Shinto Shrines), represented 80,000 shrines. Its membership included 240 members of the Diet and 16 of the 19 ministers of Abe's 2012 cabinet. There were also new groups with specific purposes of protecting the traditions of the Imperial Household, claiming to expose propaganda about Nanjing and comfort women, promoting moral education, and encouraging Diet members' visits to Yasukuni. The dozens of right-wing groups among the LDP leadership that supported these changes lacked any deep ideological substance. In contrast to the Nakasone administration's impressive mobilization of intellectual task forces to provide substance and intellectual depth to Nakasone's agenda, the groups surrounding Abe provided no such underpinning. Being more advocacy groups among politicians, the right-wing groups represented a point of view but with little philosophy to support it. Above all, they provided no strategic vision of the future.[32]

A group of Japanese Diet members visiting the Yasukuni Shrine, the controversial war memorial to Japanese war dead, August 15, 2017. Kyodo News / Getty Images / 831492738.

Abe repeatedly stated that his goal was "an end to the postwar structure (*rejimu*)" and the "recovery of independence (*dokuritsu no kaifuku*)." The groups with which he was associated were resentful of the view of their history imposed by the Tokyo War Crimes Trials, which they regarded as victors' justice, one sided, and biased. The Greater East Asian War, as many called it, should not be so readily attributed to Japanese militarism alone. It was the West's original intrusion into Asia that led Japan to arm and expand to defend itself. Many conservatives acknowledged that the Japanese military committed aggression against its Asian neighbors, but they bristled at their neighbors' interference in how the Japanese taught their own history. They pointed out that the Chinese had not come to an honest assessment of the crimes committed as a result of Maoist policies and that the Koreans had not been willing to acknowledge the positive contributions of Japanese colonial rule. They rejected descriptions of the Nanjing massacre and of coerced sexual slavery as inaccurate and exaggerated. As for the war with the United

States, the attack on Pearl Harbor was a desperate act by a Japan driven into a corner by US ultimatums. The war's ending in their view was a cruel bombing of a country that was already seeking a mediated settlement.

Revision of the 1947 constitution is essential to their view of ending the postwar structure. In 2012 the LDP issued the party's draft of a revised constitution that replaced the universalism and the principles of American liberal democracy in the existing constitution with a Japanese communitarian vision of democracy that significantly strengthened the role of the state. From the first sentence of the preamble—which replaces the existing "We, the Japanese people . . ." with "Japan is a nation with a long history and unique culture, with a *tennō* [Emperor] who is a symbol of the unity of the people . . ."—the draft stresses pride in the uniqueness of the nation and the people's commitment to defend it.[33] In place of universal concepts of human rights, the draft provides for rights based on Japan's own history, traditions, and culture. It replaces emphasis on individualism with the provision that the family is "the natural and basic unity of society." Revisions to Article 9 include deleting the prohibition of maintaining "land, air and sea forces" and renunciation of the "right to belligerency" and inserting a new declaration that nothing would "prevent the exercise of the right to self-defense."

Japan's struggle to define itself in ways that fill its need for a prideful past and that are accepted by the outside world is ongoing. The American intervention in postwar Japan was so extreme that a conservative reaction should not be surprising. Perhaps more surprising is that it has been so long in coming. Nor should it surprise us that the Japanese should want to write their own constitution, that the Japanese would find the procedures and simplistic verdicts of the War Crimes Trials unfair, or that the Japanese should want to regain more autonomy from the overbearing American nature of the alliance. At issue for Japan is to find a credible balance between correcting the "self-flagellating" views of the past and coming to terms with its historical faults. The belief that the War Crimes Trials were not conducted in a fair and dispassionate way is certainly true, but that is not dispositive of Japan's horrendous wartime atrocities. The contention that Western imperial powers had encroached on Japanese sovereignty and treated its rise with racial prejudice is true, but it does not condone Japanese contempt for the national aspirations of its neighbors. The fact that the Greater East Asian War, as some conservatives still call it, contributed to the end of Western imperialism in Asia is true, but does not gainsay the Japanese ambition to establish its own imperial order. The Allies' targeting of civilian populations in the ending of the war cannot be denied, but neither can the irresponsible decision of Japan's leaders to continue fighting at the terrible cost to their own people be disavowed. The conservatives' attempt to revise victors' history must be accomplished in a balanced and dispassionate way if it is to stand the test of time and provide an enduring consensus for the Japanese in the future. Thus far, a consensus with such balance has not been achieved.

China's Challenge to American Primacy

The end of the Cold War seemed to mark the culminating victory of a liberal world order governed by the framework of rules and institutions established in the American century, but permanent victories in international relations are rare. The American celebration of the Soviet collapse soon passed as new, unanticipated challenges to the American world order emerged in the form of terrorist attacks on the homeland, the upheaval in the Middle East, adversaries' missile testing and nuclear proliferation, new forms of asymmetrical cyberwarfare, and the Great Recession of 2008. Countries sought to undermine and delegitimize the liberal order. A revanchist Russia annexed Crimea in 2014, unmoved by condemnations of its flouting international law. Secretary of State John Kerry, indignant at the noncompliance with the rules of the international order, condemned it as outdated behavior. "You just don't in the 21st century behave in 19th century fashion by invading another country on completely trumped up pretext."[34] But neither his logic nor economic sanctions served to deter Vladimir Putin's continuing challenges to international rules. Nor did international law dissuade China from establishing new island outposts in the South China Sea in violation of sovereignty rights of other Asian states. Post–World War II international institutions—the UN, the World Bank, the IMF, and NATO— seemed less credible in their appointed tasks. The foundations of the existing order were further weakened by costly US failures to spread democracy and attempt nation building in the Middle East. In a stunning challenge to the existing order, the election of Donald Trump as president

in 2016 with an "America first" agenda augured a weakening commitment by the United States itself to the liberal international order.

A fundamental challenge to the character of the American world
order as it had existed since World War II lay in the far-reaching changes
in the international distribution of power. With its preoccupation with
armed rivalries and military conflict, the Cold War had masked the shift
in the center of the global economy from the North Atlantic to the Asia
Pacific region. The post–Cold War years revealed that a vast shift in
the international distribution of power was under way. In the twenty-
five years after the end of the Cold War, US transpacific trade grew to
twice transatlantic trade. Asia, which had been a colonial backwater
when the Cold War began, had quietly transformed itself into a region
of dynamic economic growth that dramatically improved living standards, health, and literacy. South Korea, Taiwan, Hong Kong, Singapore,
and Thailand, drawing on lessons from Japan's experience, entered on
rapid economic development, and then others, most notably China and
India, followed. Asia was recovering the position it had held prior to the
Industrial Revolution, when the per capita incomes of many Asian
countries had been at or above the world average. Throughout the
modern period, the industrial West had dominated Asia, shaping the
regional order and determining the rules, norms, and institutions that
governed it. Asia had been, in effect, a subsystem of the Western international system.

The complexity of the new Asian state system surpasses that of the
historical European state system. Across its vast geography appeared a
striking number of states of a wide range of territorial size, population,
and stages of economic development. There are as well sizable power
asymmetries and a diversity of cultures, religions, ethnicities, and histories. Both integrative and divisive forces are at work. Economic growth,
intraregional flows of trade and investment, and vastly improved communications integrate the region as never before. But regional identity
and common aspiration struggle against rising nationalisms, strategic
rivalries, and resulting arms races. These complex and contradictory
new forces in the region make for uncertainty about the nature of the
future order in Asia.

As it becomes the new center of gravity in world politics, Asia is in a
kind of interregnum, lacking a consensus of the rules and norms required for a settled and legitimate regional structure. American power

is still preeminent, but Asian leaders are resistant to American universalism as dogmatic, legalistic, and disrespectful of cultural diversity. Pursuing catch-up strategies with developmentalist policies, they often reject free market capitalism and instead advocate state-led economic growth. Their cultural underpinnings value the welfare of the community more than individual rights and freedoms. In this new era, the United States will not have the preponderance of power to impose order in the way that it did in the post–World War II era. During this interregnum, the United States serves as a kind of "regent" keeping order. For a time, Asian leaders hoped that the challenges of the new power and diversity in the region could be accommodated through the development of new multilateral institutions to manage economic issues and resolve political and security issues. Various proposals for a "Pacific Community" have been offered in connection with new Asian multilateral institutions—the Association of Southeast Asian Nations (ASEAN), Asia Pacific Economic Cooperation (APEC), ASEAN Regional Forum (ARF), and others—but they have often proved fragile and lacking effective power.

These multilateral efforts to create a new regional structure are overshadowed by the rapid expansion of Chinese economic and military power and the prospect that China would eventually seek regional hegemony. America's dominance, which has relied on the forward deployment of its military, the reach of its Seventh Fleet, its hub-and-spokes alliance system, access to its markets, and technological and financial assistance, provided stability and security for more than seventy years. China has emerged as a revisionist power to challenge American primacy in the region and eventually beyond. During the Clinton administration, the United States believed that a policy of "constructive engagement" would allow the United States to manage China's rise, encourage a reformist middle class, and bring China into the American order as a "responsible stakeholder." A rising power, however, with a worldview shaped by historical traditions of regional hegemony, finds little satisfaction in accepting a regional order that it had no part in establishing and defining. The issue for Chinese leaders is that the institutions and rules of the system are rooted in principles of democratic capitalism they view as designed to promote liberal reforms and ultimately threaten their domestic order. An increasingly ambitious and authoritarian China, defining its core interests in ways that challenge the maritime commons and the Seventh Fleet's long-term preeminence, steadily weakened the hopes of liberal reforms and of making China a "responsible stakeholder" in the American-led order.

The gathering contest for supremacy between China and the United States in the twenty-first century is bound to recall the US-Japan contest a century earlier. Like prewar Japan, a rising and ambitious China seeks a regional order that fits its own preferences and interests, but it does so without many of the vulnerabilities of Japan. The contest for supremacy inevitably raises the problem of great power transitions, which in the past have been settled by warfare. Both American and Chinese leaders are aware of the dangers, and the two nations are locked in a codependency that serves to moderate the contest. China's rise has been facilitated by the liberal international economic order and by American trade, technology, and investment, while America has grown dependent on Chinese credit and the well-being of the Chinese economy, which is essential in maintaining global economic stability. The extent and density of interdependence between two great-power rivals is without parallel in the modern era.[35]

Given such codependency, American strategy has pursued both engagement and balancing to manage China's rise and to keep China within the American world order. During the George W. Bush administration, the United States began allocating more resources to the Pacific to enhance the force structure of the United States and its allies and partners. The goal was to maintain the superior position of the United States by building up its Cold War hub-and-spokes alliance system, strengthening the defense relationships among the spokes, and also adding new relationships with India and other Asian countries.[36] Ostensibly, the purpose was not to contain China's rise but rather to dissuade it from trying to challenge American preponderance. During the Obama administration, Secretary of State Hillary Clinton gave a public name to its new strategic emphasis, announcing a "pivot" to Asia.[37] The "pivot" claimed to give new US attention to Asia and to adjust to the region's new power. The Obama administration committed itself to a rebalance of naval and air power from 50/50 in the Atlantic and Pacific to 60 percent in the Pacific by 2020. It put great effort into the complex negotiations for the Trans-Pacific Partnership (TPP), an ambitious multilateral trade agreement designed to bind the United States, Japan, and ten other Pacific nations while fixing standards for market access, environmental protection, finance-sector reform, energy policies, and health and education cooperation. It was expected to counter China's growing regional influence while urging China to sign on to this agreement and accept its standards. The ultimate goal of Obama's "pivot" strategy was to manage the greatly increased power of China and the decline of American power in relative terms by enmeshing China in the existing international system, convincing China that it could thrive and have its interests well served in the American-led system.

President Xi Jinping, who came to power in 2012, laid aside Deng Xiaoping's low-profile stance and economic development priorities. Instead, he adopted an assertive posture of restoring China's place in the sun. In 2013 he launched the Belt and Road Initiative (BRI), a grand strategy to shape Eurasia and establish Chinese preponderance according to China's own interests and worldview. This highly ambitious vision, though still amorphous, proposes "a vast network of transportation, energy, and telecommunication infrastructures, linking Europe and Africa to Asia and accompanied by strengthened monetary cooperation and increased people-to-people exchanges."[38] The BRI constitutes a frontal challenge to the broad principles underlying the American-led regional order, which have sought to preserve free trade patterns, promote democratic politics, and maintain a stable balance of power in which no other country would become so strong as to dominate the region.

The prospect that China might dominate the Eurasian continent represents the greatest foreign policy challenge that the United States and Japan face both separately and together. In the early Cold War period, Japan weighted its policies toward engagement with China, influenced heavily by economic interests, but China's rapid rise brought Japan to an assertive balancing posture in coordination with Washington. In 2010 China displaced Japan as the world's second-largest economy. Annual double-digit increases in China's military spending—together with its determination to build a bluewater navy and assert its territorial claims in the East and South China Sea, which threaten Japanese maritime interests, especially rival claims to the Senkaku Islands (which the Chinese call Diaoyu)—inflamed nationalist reactions in Japan. China made Japan a primary target of its patriotic education, emphasizing Japan's past aggression and atrocities as the most damaging part of China's "century of humiliation." Raising history issues with Japanese leaders plays prominently in Chinese domestic politics. An older generation of Japanese leaders included advocates of friendly Sino-Japanese relations, but with the change of generations, impatient younger LDP lawmakers openly demanded an end to deference on history issues. Many other issues, including Japanese sympathetic ties with Taiwan and China's opposition to Japan's aspiration to join the UN Security Council as a permanent member, stoked the rivalry, which plays out in a competition for regional leadership. While the United States and Japan, both separately and together, are likely to continue strengthening their balancing effort, they will also continue to engage China because their economies depend so heavily on trade and investment there.

Abe's Revolution in National Security Policy

At the beginning of his second term as prime minister in 2012, Abe gave a policy speech in Washington hyping his new diplomacy and announcing that "Japan is back."[39] With a strong electoral mandate after voters lost confidence in the foundering DPJ, Abe captured the public imagination by announcing three arrows to be unleashed to revive the economic dynamism of an earlier time: loose monetary policy, fiscal stimulus, and structural reform. The results were slow in coming, but he was given credit for strong leadership. Together with his economic initiatives, Abe moved steadily and self-confidently to realize his goal of replacing a dependent foreign policy with an activist international role. In his first year in office, he established Japan's first-ever National Security Council (NSC), staffed with its own secretariat, to overcome the notoriously balkanized policymaking process. Intent on strengthening his role in making foreign policy, he wrested power from the bureaucrats and consolidated it in the prime minister's office, where he had the needed advice and intelligence to determine strategy and manage crises. At Abe's direction, the NSC soon promulgated the first-ever comprehensive National Security Strategy (NSS). Because it depended on the United States for the last seventy years, Tokyo had never had a comprehensive plan for pursuing its security interests. Emphasizing the changing balance of power, globalization, new technology, and a range of emergent threats from cybersecurity to maritime security, the NSS recommended tighter alliance relations and security partnerships. Next, to encourage sharing of intelligence with the United States, Abe pushed through controversial legislation to provide greater protection of state secrets.[40]

Most significant—the centerpiece of his foreign policy revolution—Abe broke through the postwar deadlock on collective self-defense (CSD) in a series of calculated steps. He set out to overturn the long-standing interpretation of Article 9, which permitted the Self-Defense Forces only the minimum level of defense capability to act if Japan were attacked directly. Again, wresting power from the bureaucrats, he asserted political control over the Cabinet Legal Bureau, which had maintained minimalist interpretations of Article 9, and appointed a commission to review and advise him on the legal interpretation of Article 9. The handpicked commission predictably recommended a new and broader interpretation that would allow for CSD in a variety of scenarios. On July 1, 2014, the cabinet approved this interpretation. Subsequently, legislation to implement the new interpretation of CSD passed the Diet.

A firewall in place for a half century had been breached. This revolution in policy was carried out "from above" in the face of the opposition of most voters. Abe accomplished this by sidestepping the difficulties of formal constitutional revision and, instead, achieving a reinterpretation of Article 9 through a cabinet decision. Such a bold demarche was made possible by the 1959 Supreme Court decision in which the court declined to interpret Article 9, ruling it to be a "political matter" that must be left to the Diet. Legal scholars in Japanese universities overwhelmingly opposed reinterpreting the constitution without following prescribed procedures for amending the constitution, which required passage by a two-thirds majority in both houses of the Diet and a simple majority in a national referendum. The cabinet's decision to reinterpret Article 9 sparked large-scale street demonstrations of opposition, and an older generation of postwar progressives watched wistfully as the constraints of Article 9, so important to their national identity, were swept away. Public opinion polls showed strong opposition to a foreign policy that might entangle Japan in foreign conflicts. Nevertheless, given the unprecedented weakness of opposition parties, Abe was free to move ahead.

The assertion of political control over the interpretation of Article 9 opened the way for further loosening of the constraints on an activist security policy by Abe and his successors. Certain broad constraints on the exercise of CSD were included in the legislation,[41] but, as Christopher Hughes argues in his exhaustive study, these constraints are vague and subject to flexible executive interpretation. With this new constitutional interpretation, "Japan has embarked on a genuinely radical trajectory in security policy. . . . It does indeed mark a sharp break with the antimilitaristic principles of the past . . . and necessitates consideration of Japan as a far more serious military player in international security."[42]

Foreign policy has always been a sector in which the prime minister has the most freedom of action, not having to satisfy a factional constituency.[43] Moreover, a skilled prime minister can also act independently of public opinion on foreign policy when other issues weigh more heavily with voters. As Samuels and Schoff have observed, "The connection of public opinion to policymaking is particularly tenuous with respect to national security."[44] Abe is a notable example of a prime minister whose foreign policy initiatives have often been unpopular without preventing his electoral success. By skillfully emphasizing popular economic and welfare issues at election time and downplaying his controversial foreign policies, he has circumvented public opinion and achieved his foreign policy revolution "from above."

The Changing Character of the Alliance

Abe's revolution in security policy led to the most profound change that the US-Japan alliance has experienced since its inception at the end of the Occupation. For the first time, the United States and Japan had a common purpose in their alliance. What had been a hegemonic alliance imposed on Japan as the price for ending the Occupation has become a more reciprocal alliance. Originally it had been an instrument intended to control and manage a weak Japan and to maintain US bases there for the long term. It was to control Japanese foreign policy and keep Japan from neutrality in the Cold War or from independent rearmament, ensuring that Japan would not be an independent state able to choose its own future. Thus, Japan became a military satellite, a subordinate state, and could be treated with the paternalism of Reischauer or the obtuseness of Nixon and Kissinger.

Under such circumstances, Japanese leaders devised their own separate, often cynical purpose for the alliance, which was to use it to free

Japan from responsibility for its security and concentrate its full energies on economic growth. Iokibe Makoto, the Japanese authority on the alliance, observed, "The Japanese were very good at being controlled."[45] Japan became a trading state, uninvolved in international politics, standing for no clear political principles. To keep Japan from involvement in American military engagements, Yoshida and his successors developed a list of self-binding policies (the "Nine Nos"). Between the US forces based in Japan and the Japanese Self-Defense Forces, there was limited communication and planning, no interoperability, and no joint command. For nearly forty years this twisted and anomalous alliance of contradictory purpose was maintained.

The changed conditions in the post–Cold War era made Japan receptive to a new alliance relationship. The emergence of a more powerful and assertive China and the juggernaut of North Korea's growing nuclear and missile capabilities were central to the changed attitudes. In the face of such growing threats, Abe and his advisors were now less worried about being dragged into American conflicts elsewhere in the world and more concerned about ensuring American commitment to support Japan's security concerns. With the new policies permitting CSD, the alliance is taking on the character of "classic" alliances, in which states aggregate their power against a commonly perceived threat. Revised US-Japan Defense Guidelines agreed on in 2015 spelled out a detailed blueprint for greater integration, interoperability, coordination of strategy, and geographical scope of cooperation. With consciousness of shared interests, the alliance can become more cohesive; with agreement on expectations and defined obligations to act in specified contingencies, the alliance can become more operational. For the Americans, a more proactive and cooperative Japan is critical to the maintenance of a regional balance of power. For the Japanese, keeping the Americans deeply engaged in the region through burden sharing is essential to coping with the rise of their neighboring colossus and dealing with North Korea.

All of Japan's self-binding policies ("the Nine Nos") are being rolled back—except for the ban on possession of nuclear arms, which is nevertheless under constant review. Some of these rollbacks preceded Abe, but they were tentative and constrained, as was the deployment abroad of the Self-Defense Forces. Cooperation with the United States in ballistic missile defense beginning in 2003 quietly transgressed the prohibition on militarization of space. Abe's resolve ended the long-standing ban on arms exports, in place since 1976, giving new energy to the domestic arms industry. He revised the foreign aid (official development assistance) charter to permit support abroad for military-related projects. In a Diet speech in March 2017, he brushed aside the formal policy of limiting defense expenditure to 1 percent of GNP. There was no thought in his administration for maintaining that limitation. Picking up on this assertion, the LDP's Research Committee on Security recommended that Japan take as a point of reference NATO's 2 percent of GDP benchmark for defense expenditure. For half a century bureaucrats in the powerful Ministry of Finance (MOF) rode herd on the politicians to maintain the 1 percent limit, but Abe had installed Asō Tarō, his vice prime minister, to serve concurrently as minister of finance to oversee the usually veiled processes of the MOF bureaucrats.[46] Annual increases in defense spending allowed Abe to eye plans for new capacity to project military power, including cruise missiles capable of hitting foreign bases and conversion of the Izumo helicopter carrier into an aircraft carrier that could accommodate new F-35B jets.

As the regional environment has grown more volatile, the Japanese public has grown more appreciative of the alliance. Cooperation between the Self-Defense Forces and the US military in responding to the March 2011 Fukushima disaster was important in the increasing popular support. In 2015 Abe became the first Japanese prime minister to address a joint session of Congress, using the occasion to pledge still closer bilateral ties. The following year he hosted Obama in Hiroshima and soon after visited Pearl Harbor, symbolically seeking to lay to rest the bitter memories of the past.

Abe became more pragmatic when forced to choose between his ideological predilections and more flexible and realist positions on many issues.[47] In spite of his goals of ending the legacies of the American Occupation, including the constitution, the education system, the historical judgments of the War Crimes Trials, and the hegemonic alliance, he has given precedence to working as closely as possible with the Americans in strengthening the alliance and softening the emphasis on his nationalist themes. Seeing the need to strengthen security ties with South Korea and to assist American efforts to mediate Japan–Republic of Korea differences, facilitate trilateral security cooperation, and propitiate American concern over his conservative views, Abe

Barack Obama, the first sitting US president to visit Hiroshima, hugs atomic bomb survivor Mori Shigeaki at the Peace Memorial Park, May 27, 2016. Prime Minister Abe Shinzō (far left) looks on. Aflo Co. Ltd. / Alamy Stock Photo / G2EKH9.

moderated his earlier ideological assertions. The softening of his nationalist stance in his widely noted statement on the seventieth anniversary of the end of the war on August 15, 2015, and in his subsequent agreement reached with South Korean president Park Geun-hye making further concessions from his previous hardline stands on the comfort women issue angered many in the right wing. But as an *Asahi* journalist noted in commenting on Abe's "pragmatism," those supporters had nowhere else to go and had to fall in line with Abe, whose conservative bona fides remained intact.[48]

Because Japan had become a status quo power with a substantial stake in the existing rules-based order, Abe appropriated liberal rhetoric. In his public statements supporting the TPP trade agreement, he repeatedly referred to Japan's support of "universal values," which to some observers did not ring true to his longtime support for replacing liberal American values with Japanese values in education. In explaining why Japan was joining the negotiations for the TPP in an upper house session in May 2015, he said, "Creating new rules with our ally and with other countries that share universal values such as freedom, democracy, basic human rights, and the rule of law and deepening mutually dependent economic relationships with these countries has strategic significance for our country's security as well as for the stability of the region."[49] Abe's espousal of a liberal regional order was part of his desire to forge a closer alliance relationship with the United States. As he said in a New York speech before the Trump administration's withdrawal from the multilateral trade agreement, "It is my belief that Japan and the United States should lead the Indo-Pacific Century to make it one that cherishes freedom, democracy, human rights, and a rule-based order, with the TPP as its backbone."[50] More subtly, Abe was crafting a national identity that would identify Japan as a regional democratic leader over authoritarian China. Like the political nationalist Nakasone, who modified his nationalist ideology after becoming prime minister, Abe too became more pragmatic when forced to choose between his ideological predilections and a realist national security policy.[51] Such a transition put him squarely in the long tradition of modern Japanese conservatism—pragmatic, nonideological, and realist.[52]

The Changing Order

Abe has great ambition for his new policies. He had high hopes for ending the territorial dispute with Russia over the Kurile Islands, but has been stymied by Vladimir Putin's intransigence. The initiative to which he is most committed is building a matrix of cooperative security and economic relations among Asian countries, perhaps even an Asia Pacific version of NATO. Abe has actively promoted strategic relationships with the ASEAN countries, Australia, and India as a counterbalance to Chinese ambitions for regional hegemony. India and key ASEAN countries are likely to emerge as the drivers of regional economic growth in future decades. By 2030, India is forecast to pull ahead of Japan and become the world's third-largest economy.[53] Either way, Japan and India are destined to be Asia's second- and third-largest economies for the foreseeable future.

India and Japan are free of the history problems that confound Japan's relations with its neighbors. Abe has long felt an affinity with

India, growing out of India's wartime sympathy with Japan's struggle against Western colonialism and especially the dissent of the Indian jurist Radhabinod Pal, who was the only one of the eleven justices on the Tokyo War Crimes Tribunal to reach a not-guilty verdict for Japan's wartime leaders. Pal roundly criticized the former Western imperial powers for their hypocrisy in condemning Japanese imperialism, and he added that Hiroshima and Nagasaki constituted war crimes. For his support, a monument honoring Pal was erected at the Yasukuni Shrine in 2005. On his first visit to India as prime minister, Abe made a point of visiting Pal's son. India, like Japan, is alarmed at the prospect of Chinese regional hegemony. Both have border disputes with China. Both are resentful of China's opposition to their being permanent members of the UN Security Council.

One of Abe's signature foreign policy initiatives is his vision of an Indo-Pacific security framework for the twenty-first century. He originated the concept during his first administration in an address to the Indian Parliament in 2007, which he titled "Confluence of the Two Seas," envisaging a "broader" or "expanded Asia" constituting both Pacific and Indian Oceans. Keeping the sea lanes of the Pacific and Indian Oceans free and open would be a common interest binding together the region's maritime democracies. He returned to this theme at the outset of his second term in 2012, in an essay making explicit his concern over China's naval and territorial encroachments on the maritime commons:

> The South China Sea seems set to become a "Lake Beijing" . . . a sea deep enough for the People's Liberation Army's navy to base their nuclear-powered attack submarines, capable of launching missiles with nuclear warheads. Soon, the PLA Navy's newly built aircraft carrier will be a common sight—more than sufficient to scare China's neighbors. That is why Japan must not yield to the Chinese government's daily exercise in coercion around the Senkaku Islands. . . . Japan's top foreign policy priority must be to expand the country's strategic horizons. Japan is a mature maritime democracy and its choice of close partners should reflect that fact. I envisage a strategy whereby Australia, India, Japan and the US state of Hawaii form a diamond to safeguard the maritime commons stretching from the Indian Ocean region to the western Pacific.[54]

Abe developed a personal chemistry with Narendra Modi, who took office as India's prime minister in 2014. Based on their economic and geopolitical needs, they agreed on a "special strategic and global partnership," which soon resulted in a string of deals underscoring India's position as Japan's largest aid recipient. One high-profile deal was Japan's highly concessional $17 billion loan and the technology to build India's first bullet train to connect Mumbai and Ahmedabad, in Modi's home state of Gujarat. The far more significant deal was a civil nuclear deal signed in November 2016 allowing Japanese companies to export atomic technology. To reach this agreement, Abe overcame considerable opposition at home because India is not a signatory to the Nuclear Non-Proliferation Treaty. In the meantime, Abe succeeded in having Donald Trump sign on to his pet concept during the president's visit to Japan in November 2017, in which they announced agreement on pursuing an "Indo-Pacific security strategy." To counter China's BRI, Modi and Abe have proposed the Asia-Africa Growth Corridor envisioning development cooperation, infrastructure building, and economic partnership. The purpose is to build a network of maritime facilities stretching from East Asia to the Middle East and Africa that will meet Africa's development needs. Like the much more visible BRI, the Asia-Africa Growth Corridor is in its early stages but offers a potential point of collaboration for the United States and others to join in funding.

The military dimensions of the Japan-India relations are still limited. Japan has joined the bilateral US-India naval exercises, known as the Malabar series, designed to develop coordination and interoperability among the navies. Beijing has expressed displeasure over this development, which it correctly sees as aimed at its military vessels entering the Indian Ocean. In January 2018, high-ranking naval officers from Japan, the United States, Australia, and India met in New Delhi to affirm their commitment to maintaining "free and open waters in the region."[55] Such military linkages could grow substantially in the future should India feel comfortable in enhancing such cooperation. The Indo-Pacific framework highlights Abe's activism, his focus on Asian leadership, and his desire to ease Japan's dependence on the bilateral relationship with the United States. The Japan-India relationship is still at an early stage—both countries do far more trade with China than with each other—but their complementary interests carry potential for future development.

Japan's immediate priority is to strengthen its alignment with the United States, but in the longer term Japan will increasingly move toward a more national foreign policy, one that offers greater autonomy and room to adjust to its perception of the shifting balance of power in the region. Japan will also closely weigh the reliability of American assurances and the future direction of US policy in Asia. Perception of the enduring credibility of American policy in protecting Japan's interest will play a critical part in Japan's calculations. Washington's more limited means have raised doubts about US staying power. One senior Japanese military officer put the situation this way using a common metaphor: "We have been at our parents' knee (*oya no sune ni kajiru*), but US shins have become thin."[56] The Trump administration's "America first" rhetoric, abrupt withdrawal from the TPP, and other unsettling references to alliances and multilateralism inevitably deepened latent Japanese concerns over American commitment to continuing to carry the burden of security in the western Pacific.

North Korea's expanding nuclear and missile technology, which may include the ability to threaten the US homeland, is causing Japan to question whether the United States would place an American city at jeopardy to come to Japan's aid. Should North Korea succeed in achieving full-scale nuclear capability, the credibility of the US nuclear umbrella for its allies in South Korea and Japan will be seriously diminished. In such circumstances, the incentives for Tokyo to acquire its own nuclear weapons will greatly increase. From its earliest history, Japan's security has been linked to the peninsula, and Japan could not long tolerate a nuclear Korea.

Absent the stability of the American order, the future will appear dangerously uncertain to the Japanese. In such circumstances of transition in the international order, Japan has historically experienced rapid swings in geopolitical positions. The pacifist and antimilitarist identity that postwar generations have long embraced could quickly give way to a very different orientation. The postwar scholar Maruyama Masao once observed that a pragmatic tendency to conform to the environment is a key aspect of Japanese political psychology. Foreigners, he observed, are often baffled by two contradictory tendencies in Japanese politics: the difficulty of making change and the rapidity with which change takes place. Maruyama's explanation is that a characteristic reluctance to break with the past is offset by the readiness to accommodate the realities of the time, which, he wrote, is the hallmark of the pragmatic and nondoctrinaire nature of Japanese conservatism, in contrast to the stubborn and principled conservatism in Europe. Therefore, in Japanese politics, he adds, it is difficult to break with the past, but once change is under way it spreads rapidly.[57] With the growing uncertainty of regional conditions, we should not be surprised if the prolonged resistance of the Japanese public to revision of the constitution and even possession of nuclear weapons changes quickly.

The Twilight of the American Century

The American Century, with the United States possessing the power and the will to rehabilitate the world as Henry Luce envisioned it in 1941, is coming to an end; and along with it, the extraordinary period of American domination of Japan is passing. In 1945 the United States had nearly half of the world's economy, but in 2018 the US share is estimated to be less than 25 percent. The United States was once the world's greatest creditor nation, but its massive debt to foreigners, especially to China and Japan, has become "one of the principal problems in global finance."[58] For the last seventy years the American military has dominated the Pacific, but in 2018 that dominance is challenged in the western Pacific by Chinese military power.

The rise of China and other countries is part of a growing diffusion of power reducing American influence and ability to shape the region's future. Rather than the hegemony that America exercised in the heyday of the American Century, leadership will be more complex and require greater reliance on allies. Asia is now a multipolar region with several powerful actors and a larger group of lesser but strong secondary players. The region is not only the center of gravity in world economic dynamism but also the new center of gravity in global politics. All the world's principal military powers and several of the key middle powers are in Asia. These countries, in rough descending order of military power, are the United States, China, Russia, India, Japan, South Korea, Pakistan, and North Korea. Six of these eight powers possess nuclear weapons, and the other two are near nuclear.[59] While for the foreseeable future America will remain a superpower with extraordinary dynamism for innovation and strengths, including military dominance, there is no escaping the fact that power in the world is diffusing. American primacy will be less pronounced. America will be constrained by the increasing leveling of the playing field and a multipolar world. To meet the changing conditions, a successful foreign policy must be commensurate with the power available to it, have a clear set of priorities, and have a strategy attuned to the new realities.

Contesting China's goal of a regional hegemony will require an American commitment to engaging a coalition of Asian countries in a regional balance of power. Such engagement must be fundamentally different from American regional dominance of the postwar period. Asian countries will insist on greater respect for their views and increasingly resist having norms imposed from outside. America will lose some of the ideological hegemony that has been a hallmark of the postwar world order. We can no longer hold the region in tutelage by claiming a single universal truth from our national experience. The long-standing belief in a unilinear path of development by which all nations will converge with our pattern of modernity will be put to rest. As newly rising Asian countries emerge, they will bring with their nationalist pride diverse values and concepts of order and will not readily conform to our notions of universal liberal values. That is not to say that with time our ideals of democracy and the rule of law will not make their influence felt on these emerging societies. Because of its deep crisis, US democratic politics no longer inspires support for American values in the way it once did; and more important, commensurate with their growing power, the emerging powers will expect to modify or transform the framework of rules and institutions established in the postwar era. From their divergent cultural histories they will bring with them new conceptions of order, legitimacy, the relationship of state and society, and the rules that should govern commerce and diplomacy, telecommunications, and internet standards. They will seek a greater say in determining the rules and institutions that govern international economic and political affairs. Many countries will seek to establish state control not only over markets but also over the flow of ideas and information. The multifariousness of Asia should teach us that the most notable characteristic of the emerging world order will likely be its diversity, not its uniformity.

America can learn from its experience with Japan that modernity does not mean convergence with American values. Just as the sharp contrasts that emerged between the norms of American and Japanese capitalism over Japan's developmentalist phase revealed, by the same token the emergence of many other late-developing economies shaped by the values of their own history and developmentalist strategies will make the problems of achieving a coherent, governable international trade order increasingly difficult. Just as postwar Japan, despite our heavy-handed tutelage, did not converge with the American political economy and society, so too the rest of Asia will be a region of multiple modernities.

Over the long postwar period, Japan and the United States have in some ways come closer in their ideals. Japan's developmental capitalism took a distinctly different path from American free market capitalism, but having achieved its catch-up goal it has adopted more aspects of liberal economics. Japanese democracy, similarly, has progressed through its own stages as democratic norms have gained greater influence, albeit in a distinctly Japanese way. Also, Japanese society has found greater openness to new forms of Japanese-style individualism. In short, slowly and in stages, Japan has changed in ways that seem to narrow the degree of difference between American and Japanese society—even as America itself changes. Japan, however, remains Japan. Whether greater convergence will take place in the future is still unclear.

The reality of a dynamic region of newly risen powers will require of us a new strategy and approach to Asia. The challenge is to structure a regional equilibrium that incorporates the new powers and that fashions out of a multiplicity of cultures a common set of rules that achieves a legitimate order. No country will be able to achieve this alone. No country will have the power to establish the order that we had in the postwar period. If America is to lead in meeting this challenge, we must use our military power to sustain a credible and coherent balance of power while working closely and cooperatively with Asian nations to help them become strong enough to withstand a regional hegemony.

Such cooperation will require that we approach the region with greater self-awareness. In a region of such divergent national experiences we must temper our leadership style with a recognition that the goals we work for will take time. The foundations of an Asian regional order must respect cultural diversity and recognize that there are multiple cultural paths to modern civilization.[60] Recognition that we live in a nonconvergent world does not mean that Americans should abandon hope for a regional order that enshrines our values of human rights, freedom, and democratic capitalism. That must still be our goal, but we cannot expect that the new powers of Asia will readily converge to our ways. New institutions and their norms cannot be imposed. They must be cultivated.[61] Progress toward the kind of order we seek will likely be achieved only in stages. With Japan's political economy and society changing slowly over time, while not converging, we now share more in common than we once did, and thus we can hope that in time a new and stable order that reflects our liberal values can be forged. In the meantime, we must accept that governance of a new regional order must be compatible with a diversity of values and a peace maintained through a viable balance of power. Attaining a cooperative order with legitimacy will require a patient, long-term strategy that begins with an understanding of the emerging reality that Asia will be a region of multiple modernities. If America is to lead in this changing order, its strategies must come to terms with an interdependent but nonconvergent world.[62]

Notes

Introduction

1. George F. Kennan, *The Cloud of Danger: Current Realities of American Foreign Policy* (Boston: Little, Brown, 1977), 109.
2. David Ekbladh, *The Great American Mission: Modernization and the Construction of an American World Order* (Princeton, NJ: Princeton, 2010), 20.
3. Reinhold Niebuhr, *The Irony of American History* (Chicago: University of Chicago Press, 2008), 71.
4. Michael W. Doyle, *The Question of Intervention: John Stuart Mill and the Responsibility to Protect* (New Haven, CT: Yale University Press, 2015), 4, 154 defines "intervention" as "'dictatorial interference' or 'forcible intrusion in domestic affairs' by deployment of military forces to coercively intervene between the domestic authority of a foreign state and some or all of its population." Michael McFaul, *Advancing Democracy Abroad* (Lanham, MD: Rowman & Littlefield, 2010), 205–208 lists thirty "major US interventions" from the Philippines in 1898 to Iraq in 2003.
5. Kennan, *The Cloud of Danger*, 109.
6. *Asahi Shimbun*, December 6, 2016. Please note that this book follows the Japanese practice of placing family names before given names.

1. Two Rising Powers

1. As Judith Shklar put it in her notable analysis of the Tokyo Trials, "What does appear clear, though, is that the events which led up to the war were long in the making and involved complex clashes of interest and traditions that to think of the war as the product of a simple conspiracy is absurd." Judith N. Shklar, *Legalism* (Cambridge, MA: Harvard University Press, 1964), 188.

2. Akira Iriye, *Pacific Estrangement: Japanese and American Expansion, 1897–1911* (Cambridge, MA: Harvard University Press, 1972), viii.

3. Ibid., 26.

4. See the thoughtful essay by Ernest R. May and Zhou Hong, "A Power Transition and Its Effects," in *Power and Restraint: A Shared Vision for the U.S.-China Relationship,* ed. Richard Rosecrance and Gu Guoliang (New York: Public Affairs Press, 2009), 3–22.

5. Kenneth B. Pyle, "International Order and the Rise of Asia: History and Theory," in *Strategic Asia 2011–12: Asia Responds to Its Rising Powers—China and India,* ed. Ashley J. Tellis, Travis Tanner, and Jessica Keough (Seattle: National Bureau of Asian Research, 2011), 35–64.

6. Samuel Flagg Bemis's phrase. See Ernest R. May, *American Imperialism: A Speculative Essay* (New York: Atheneum, 1968), 4. See also Ernest R. May, *Imperial Democracy: The Emergence of America as a World Power* (New York: Harcourt, Brace & World, 1961). In the former work, May discusses the many interpretations that historians have offered. For a recent interpretation, see Kristin L. Hoganson, *Fighting for American Manhood: How Gender Politics Provoked the Spanish-American and Philippine-American Wars* (New Haven, CT: Yale University Press, 1998).

7. Charles S. Maier, *Among Empires: America's Ascendancy and Its Predecessors* (Cambridge, MA: Harvard University Press, 2006), 1.

8. Ibid., 2.

9. Quoted in Henry Kissinger, *World Order* (New York: Penguin Press, 2014), 236.

10. Walter Nugent, *Habits of Empire: A History of American Expansion* (New York: Vintage, 2009), xiv.

11. Maier, *Among Empires,* 4.

12. Herman Melville, chapter 36 of *White-Jacket: or The World in a Man of War,* quoted in Karen Orren and Stephen Skowronek, *The Search for American Political Development* (New York: Cambridge University Press, 2004), 33.

13. Quoted in Godfrey Hodgson, *The Myth of American Exceptionalism* (New Haven, CT: Yale University Press, 2009), 1.

14. Second annual message to Congress, 1862.

15. Reinhold Niebuhr, *The Irony of American History* (Chicago: University of Chicago Press, 2008), 4.

16. Quoted in Hodgson, *The Myth of American Exceptionalism,* 27.

17. Gordon Wood, *The Idea of America: Reflections on the Birth of the United States* (London: Penguin, 2011), 320–322.

18. American historians have contested the assertion that the frontier was closed in 1890.

19. John Mack Faragher, *Rereading Frederick Jackson Turner: "The Significance of the Frontier in American History" and Other Essays* (New York: Henry Holt, 1994), 32.

20. Ibid., 59.

21. Woodrow Wilson, "Democracy and Efficiency," *The Atlantic*, March 1901.

22. Woodrow Wilson, "The Ideals of America," *The Atlantic*, December 1902.

23. Wilson had supported decisions to take Hawaii, Guam, and the Philippines and even occasionally referred to himself as an "imperialist." John Milton Cooper writes that "breaking with fellow Democrats, he publicly argued that America should take Hawaii, Guam, and the Philippines as colonies in order to prevent Germany or Russia from taking them. . . . When the Democrats charged the Republicans with 'imperialism' during the 1900 presidential campaign, Wilson supported McKinley's foreign policy. . . . In an essay in *The Atlantic*, he maintained that possession of the Philippines 'put *us* in the very presence of the forces that will make the politics of the twentieth century radically unlike the politics of the nineteenth' and that Americans must help 'undeveloped peoples still in the childhood of their natural growth[,] . . . inducting them into the rudiments of justice and freedom.'" John Milton Cooper, Jr., *Woodrow Wilson: A Biography* (New York: Knopf, 2009), 75–76. Thomas Knock also quotes Wilson as later saying it was his preference not to take the Philippines. Thomas J. Knock, *To End All Wars: Woodrow Wilson and the Quest for a New World Order* (New York: Oxford University Press, 1992), 10.

24. Niall Ferguson, *Civilization: The West and the Rest* (New York: Penguin Press, 2011), 218.

25. *Congressional Record*, 56th Congress, 1st session, 1899–1900, 33, part 1: 704–712. See also John Braeman, *Albert J. Beveridge: American Nationalist* (Chicago: University of Chicago Press, 1971), 44–45.

26. Walter LaFeber, ed., *John Quincy Adams and American Continental Empire: Letters, Papers and Speeches* (Chicago: Quadrangle Books, 1965), 45. See also the remarks by Ernest R. May, "'Who Are We?' Two Centuries of American Foreign Relations," *Foreign Affairs* 73, no. 2 (March-April 1994): 134–138.

27. Richard Hofstadter, *The Age of Reform: From Bryan to F.D.R.* (New York: Knopf, 1956), 277n5.

28. Shimizu Yuichirō, *Kindai Nihon no kanryō: Ishin kanryō kara gakureki erito e* (Tokyo: Chūkōshinshō, 2013), chaps. 1–2.

29. R. R. Palmer and Joel Colton, *A History of the Modern World*, 8th ed. (New York: Knopf, 1995), 582.

30. Quoted in Marius B. Jansen, "Modernization and Foreign Policy in Meiji," in *Political Development in Modern Japan*, ed. Robert E. Ward (Princeton, NJ: Princeton University Press, 1968), 175.

31. Mark Metzler, *Lever of Empire: The International Gold Standard and the Crisis of Liberalism in Prewar Japan* (Berkeley: University of California Press, 2006), 259.

32. Quoted in Fareed Zakaria, *From Wealth to Power: The Unusual Origins of America's World Role* (Princeton, NJ: Princeton University Press, 1998), 172.

33. Aaron Friedberg, *A Contest for Supremacy: China, America, and the Struggle for Mastery in Asia* (New York: Norton, 2011).

34. For security dilemmas, see Robert Jervis, "Cooperation under the Security Dilemma," *World Politics* 30, no. 2 (January 1978): 167–214; John J. Mearsheimer, *The Tragedy of Great Power Politics* (New York: Norton, 2001), 35–36. Also see Robert Gilpin, *War and Change in World Politics* (Cambridge: Cambridge University Press, 1981), 94.

35. Walter LaFeber, *The Clash: A History of U.S.-Japanese Relations* (New York: Norton, 1997), 90.

36. Sadao Asada, *Culture Shock and Japanese-American Relations: Historical Essays* (Columbia: University of Missouri Press, 2007), 67.

37. David C. Evans and Mark R. Peattie, *Kaigun: Strategy, Tactics, and Technology in the Imperial Japanese Navy, 1887–1941* (Annapolis, MD: Naval Institute Press, 1997), 148.

38. Asada, *Culture Shock,* 69.

39. Ibid., 70.

40. R. J. C. Butow, "A Notable Passage to China: Myth and Memory in FDR's Family History," *Prologue* 31, no. 3 (Fall 1999): 175.

41. John King Fairbank, *The United States and China,* 4th ed. (Cambridge, MA: Harvard University Press, 1979), 324. See also Warren I. Cohen, *America's Response to China: An Interpretive History of Sino-American Relations* (New York: John Wiley, 1971), 149.

42. LaFeber, *The Clash,* 66.

43. George F. Kennan, *The Kennan Diaries,* ed. Frank Costigliola (New York: Norton, 2014), 542–543.

44. David Kennedy, *Freedom from Fear: The American People in Depression and War, 1929–1945* (New York: Oxford University Press, 1999), 501–502.

45. See the superb treatment of Japanese perceptions of China from the Tokugawa period to the Asia Pacific War in Matsumoto Sannosuke, *Kindai Nihon no Chugoku ninshiki* (Tokyo: Ibunsha, 2011).

46. "Tōyō no seiryaku hatashite ikan," *Jiji shimpō,* December 1, 1882.

47. Frederick R. Dickinson, *War and National Reinvention: Japan in the Great War, 1914–1919* (Cambridge, MA: Harvard University Press, 1999), 56.

48. Quoted in Charles E. Neu, *The Troubled Encounter: The United States and Japan* (New York: Wiley, 1975), 99.

49. G. John Ikenberry, *After Victory: Institutions, Strategic Restraint, and the Rebuilding of Order after War* (Princeton, NJ: Princeton University Press, 2001), 124.

50. Wilson's ideals stemmed from the late eighteenth-century writings of Immanuel Kant, whose ideal of a "perpetual peace" could be achieved if "a league of peace" made up of nations with stable representative institutions was established. "The reason is this," Kant wrote. "If the consent of the citizens is required in order to decide that war should be declared, . . . nothing is more natural than that they would be very cautious in . . . decreeing for themselves all the calamities of war." See Jeremi Suri, *Liber-*

ty's Surest Guardian: American Nation-Building from the Founders to Obama (New York: Free Press, 2011), 30.

51. Henry Kissinger, *Diplomacy* (New York: Simon & Schuster, 1994), 44, 54.

52. Quoted in Akira Iriye, "The Failure of Economic Expansion: 1918–1931," in *Japan in Crisis: Essays on Taisho Democracy*, ed. Bernard Silberman and H. D. Harootunian (Princeton, NJ: Princeton University Press, 1974), 242.

53. See, for example, Konoe Fumimaro, "EiBei hon'i no heiwashugi o haisu," *Nihon oyobi Nihonjin*, December 15, 1918. Konoe argued that the world was divided between the "have countries" (*moteru kuni*) and the "have-not countries" (*motazaru kuni*) and that Japan as one of the latter was prevented access to the resources and territories that the former countries monopolized. This essay is reprinted in Kitaoka Shinichi, *Sengo Nihon gaikō ronshū* (Tokyo: Chūōkoronsha, 1995), 47–52.

54. George F. Kennan, *American Diplomacy*, expanded ed. (Chicago: University of Chicago Press, 1984), 39.

55. LaFeber, *The Clash*, 126.

56. Robert Gordon Kaufman, *Arms Control during the Pre-nuclear: The United States and Naval Limitation between the Two World Wars* (New York: Columbia University Press, 1990), 15–16.

57. Quoted in Kissinger, *Diplomacy*, 373–374.

58. Iriye, *Pacific Estrangement*, 153–154.

59. Margaret MacMillan, *Paris 1919: Six Months That Changed the World* (New York: Random House, 2003), 306–307.

60. N. Gordon Levin, Jr., *Woodrow Wilson and World Politics: America's Response to War and Revolution* (New York: Oxford University Press, 1968), 114.

61. Naoko Shimazu, *Japan, Race and Equality: The Racial Equality Proposal of 1919* (London: Routledge, 1998).

62. Shimazu Naoko, "The Japanese Attempt to Secure Racial Equality in 1919," *Japan Forum* 1 (April 1989): 93–94.

63. Quoted in Eri Hotta, *Pan-Asianism and Japan's War 1931–1945* (New York: Palgrave Macmillan, 2007), 157.

64. Asada, *Culture Shock*, 66–67.

65. Quoted in Greg Robinson, *By Order of the President: FDR and the Internment of Japanese Americans* (Cambridge, MA: Harvard University Press, 2001), 38.

66. Quoted in Ogata Sadako, "The Role of Liberal Nongovernmental Organizations in Japan," in *Pearl Harbor as History: Japanese-American Relations, 1931–1941* (New York: Columbia University Press, 1973), 468.

67. See Donald Scott Carmichael, ed., *F. D. R. Columnist: The Uncollected Columns of Franklin D. Roosevelt* (Chicago: Pellegrini & Cudahy, 1947), 56–60. See also, "Franklin D. Roosevelt Editorials for the Macon Georgia *Telegraph*," GeorgiaInfo, http://georgiainfo.galileo.usg.edu/topics/history/article

/progressive-era-world-war-ii-1901-1945/franklin-d.-roosevelts-editorials -for-the-macon-telegraph. The column was dated April 30, 1925.

68. Randall L. Schweller, "Managing the Rise of Great Powers: History and Theory," in *Engaging China,* ed. Alastair Iain Johnston and Robert Ross (New York: Routledge, 1999), 15.

69. See Ronarudo Dōa, *"Kō shiō" to ieru Nihon* (Tokyo: Asahi shimbunsha, 1993), 169.

70. Metzler, *Lever of Empire,* xiv.

71. Sadao Asada, "Japanese Admirals and the Politics of Naval Limitation: Kato Tomosaburo vs Kato Kanji," in *Naval Warfare in the Twentieth Century 1900–1945: Essays in Honor of Arthur Marder,* ed. Gerald Jordan (London: Croon Helm, 1977), 158.

72. Mark Peattie, *Ishiwara Kanji and Japan's Confrontation with the West* (Princeton, NJ: Princeton University Press, 1975), 32, 52.

73. LaFeber, *The Clash,* 169–172.

74. In a 1947 article in *Foreign Affairs,* Stimson wrote regretfully that "we lacked the courage to enforce the authoritative decision of the international world. We agreed with the Kellogg Pact that aggressive war must end. We renounced it and condemned those who might use it. But it was a moral condemnation only. We thus did not reach the second half of the question—what will you do to an aggressor when you catch him? If we *had* reached it, we would easily have found the right answer, but that answer escaped us for it implied a duty to catch the criminal and such a choice meant war. . . . Our offense was thus that of the man who passed by on the other side." Henry L. Stimson and McGeorge Bundy, *On Active Service in Peace and War* (New York: Harper & Brothers, 1947), 262.

75. Sadako Ogata, *Defiance in Manchuria: The Making of Japanese Foreign Policy, 1931–1932* (Berkeley: University of California Press, 1964), 179.

76. Louise Young, *Japan's Total Empire: Manchuria and the Culture of Wartime Imperialism* (Berkeley: University of California Press, 1998), 9, 428.

77. See Janis Mimura, *Planning for Empire: Reform Bureaucrats and the Japanese Wartime State* (Ithaca, NY: Cornell University Press, 2011).

78. See Tetsuo Najita and H. D. Harootunian, "Japanese Revolt against the West," in *The Cambridge History of Japan,* vol. 6, *The Twentieth Century,* ed. Peter Duus (Cambridge: Cambridge University Press, 1988), 748; Bernard Bernier, "National Communion: Watsuji Tetsurō's Conception of Ethics, Power, and the Japanese Imperial State," *Philosophy East and West* 56, no. 1 (January 2006): 84–105.

79. James B. Crowley, *Japan's Quest for Autonomy: National Security and Foreign Policy* (Princeton, NJ: Princeton University Press), 196.

80. Japanese leaders also entered into the Tripartite Pact to ensure that Germany recognized that seizure of French and Dutch colonies in Asia would be Japan's and not Germany's prerogative. See Jeremy A. Yellen, "Into

the Tiger's Den: Japan and the Tripartite Pact, 1940," *Journal of Contemporary History* 51, no. 3 (2016): 555–576.

81. Hata Ikuhiko, "Continental Expansion, 1905–1945," in *Cambridge History of Japan*, 6:312.

82. Harold L. Ickes, *The Secret Diary of Harold L. Ickes: III, The Lowering Clouds 1939–1941* (New York, 1954), 588, quoted in Scott D. Sagan, "The Origins of the Pacific War," in *The Origin and Prevention of Major Wars*, ed. Robert I. Rotberg and Theodore K. Rabb (Cambridge: Cambridge University Press, 1989), 335.

83. Ibid., 336.

84. Robert L. Beisner, *Dean Acheson: A Life in the Cold War* (New York: Oxford University Press, 2006), 15.

85. Roosevelt was "guilty," George Kennan later reflected, "of great mistakes, the greatest of which in my opinion, was the provocation of the unnecessary war with Japan." Kennan, *The Kennan Diaries*, 542.

86. Christopher Thorne, *Allies of a Kind: The United States, Britain, and the War against Japan, 1941–1945* (New York: Oxford University Press, 1978), 83.

87. Sadao Asada, *From Mahan to Pearl Harbor: The Imperial Japanese Navy and the United States* (Annapolis, MD: Naval Institute Press, 2006), 283.

88. Eri Hotta, *Japan 1941: Countdown to Infamy* (New York: Knopf, 2014), 267.

89. Waldo Heinrichs, *Diplomacy and Force: America's Road to War, 1931–1941* (Chicago: Imprint Publications, 1996), 197.

90. Foreign Minister Tōgō, at the decisive imperial conference of December 1, 1941, concluded (in Robert Butow's words) that "if the government accepted the latest American proposal, the international status of the Empire would drop even below what it had been prior to the Manchurian Incident. Acceptance would endanger the existence of the state. As Tōgō spoke in this vein, his remarks tended to suggest, though never quite openly, that a negotiated settlement would mean forsaking the opportunity to conquer China, to dominate Eastern Asia, to secure the fruits of an Axis victory in Europe, to invade the Soviet Union, and to obtain raw materials at will and in unlimited quantities." Robert J. C. Butow, *Tojo and the Coming of the War* (Stanford, CA: Stanford University Press, 1961), 361.

91. Akira Iriye, *Origins of the Second World War* (New York: Longman, 1987), 164–165.

92. Asada, *From Mahan to Pearl Harbor*, 259.

93. Dean Acheson, *Present at the Creation: My Years in the State Department* (New York: Norton, 1969), 36.

94. Kennedy, *Freedom from Fear*, 809.

95. Hotta, *Japan 1941*, 286.

96. Gilpin, *War and Change*, 51–52.

97. Henry A. Kissinger, *A World Restored: Metternich, Castlereigh, and the Problems of Peace, 1812–1822* (Boston: Houghton Mifflin, 1957), 146.

98. Scott D. Sagan writes aptly that "if one examines the decisions made in Tokyo in 1941 more closely, one finds not a thoughtless rush to national suicide, but rather a prolonged, agonizing debate between two repugnant alternatives." See his "The Origins of the Pacific War," in *The Origin and Prevention of Major Wars,* ed. Robert I. Rotberg and Theodore K. Rabb (Cambridge: Cambridge University Press, 1989), 324.

2. Unconditional Surrender Policy

1. Christopher D. O'Sullivan, *Sumner Welles, Postwar Planning, and the Quest for a New World Order, 1937–1943* (New York: Columbia University Press, 2008), chap. 3.

2. Robert Dallek, *Franklin D. Roosevelt and American Foreign Policy, 1932–1945* (New York: Oxford University Press, 1979), 282.

3. Ibid., 284.

4. Ruhl J. Bartlett, ed., *The Record of American Diplomacy,* 3rd ed. (New York: Knopf, 1954), 623–625.

5. Emily S. Rosenberg, *A Date Which Will Live: Pearl Harbor in American Memory* (Durham, NC: Duke University Press, 2003), 11.

6. Samuel I. Rosenman, ed., *The Public Papers and Addresses of Franklin D. Roosevelt, 1941: The Call to Battle Stations* (New York: Harper & Brothers, 1950), 514–516.

7. Ibid.

8. Samuel I. Rosenman, ed., *The Public Papers and Addresses of Franklin D. Roosevelt, 1942: Humanity on the Defensive* (New York: Harper & Brothers, 1950), 41–42.

9. Edward J. Drea, *In the Service of the Emperor: Essays on the Imperial Japanese Army* (Lincoln: University of Nebraska Press,1998), 194; also Edward J. Drea, *Japan's Imperial Army: Its Rise and Fall, 1853–1945* (Lawrence: University Press of Kansas, 2009), 222.

10. Carl von Clausewitz, *On War,* ed. and trans. Michael Howard and Peter Paret (Princeton, NJ: Princeton University Press, 1976), 605.

11. Ibid., 87.

12. Anne Armstrong, *Unconditional Surrender: The Impact of the Casablanca Policy upon World War II* (New Brunswick, NJ: Rutgers, 1961), 229.

13. The literature on Roosevelt's unconditional surrender policy is very large. Two works that are particularly valuable for understanding its background as it relates to Japan are Iokibe Makoto, *Beikoku no Nihon senryō seisaku,* 2 vols. (Tokyo: Chūō kōronsha, 1985); and Dale M. Hellegers, *We, the Japanese People: World War II and the Origins of the Japanese Constitution,* 2 vols. (Stanford, CA: Stanford University Press, 2001).

14. Rosenman, *The Public Papers and Addresses of Franklin D. Roosevelt, 1941,* 523–524.

15. Ibid., 30.

16. Sadao Asada, *From Mahan to Pearl Harbor: The Imperial Japanese Navy and the United States* (Annapolis, MD: Naval Institute Press, 2006), 285.

17. Raymond Aron, *The Century of Total War* (Garden City, NY: Doubleday, 1954), 26; emphasis in original. See also Leon V. Sigal, *Fighting to a Finish: The Politics of War Termination in the United States and Japan* (Ithaca, NY: Cornell University Press, 1988), 153.

18. *Postwar Foreign Policy Preparation, 1939–1945* (Washington, DC: Department of State, 1950), 127. See Hellegers, *We, the Japanese People*, 1:138–139. For a remarkably detailed account of postwar planning, see Iokibe Makoto, *Beikoku no Nihon senryō seisaku* (Tokyo: Chūō kōronsha, 1985), vol. 1, chap. 2.

19. Dallek, *Franklin D. Roosevelt and American Foreign Policy*, 373–376.

20. Nigel Hamilton, *Commander in Chief: FDR's Battle with Churchill, 1943* (Boston: Houghton Mifflin Harcourt, 2016), 29.

21. Frank Freidel, *Franklin D. Roosevelt: A Rendezvous with Destiny* (Boston: Little, Brown, 1990), 463.

22. See Dallek, *Franklin D. Roosevelt and American Foreign Policy*, 374–376. See also Freidel, *Franklin D. Roosevelt*, 463. There are a variety of accounts of Churchill's reaction to the announcement. He himself changed his own account. There is no doubt, however, that he had been apprised of FDR's policy and gave his approval, although he clearly had considerable reservations and at times sought to persuade the president to change his view.

23. Samuel I. Rosenman, ed., *The Public Papers and Addresses of Franklin D. Roosevelt, 1943: The Tide Turns* (New York: Harper & Brothers, 1950), 59–60. See also Sigal, *Fighting to a Finish*, 91.

24. Rosenman, *The Public Papers and Addresses of Franklin D. Roosevelt, 1943*, 72.

25. Michael Howard, *Grand Strategy, August 1942–September 1943* (British Official History of the Second World War) (London: Her Majesty's Stationery Office, 1972), 284. Dale Hellegers, in her meticulous study of the issue, concluded that "there is substantial evidence that no one, Allied or Axis, really understood the larger implications of unconditional surrender—or some of the practical ways in which it might affect military issues." Hellegers, *We, the Japanese People*, 1:xi.

26. Rosenman, *The Public Papers and Addresses of Franklin D. Roosevelt, 1943*, 33.

27. Rosenman, *The Public Papers and Addresses of Franklin D. Roosevelt, 1942*, 418.

28. Rosenman, *The Public Papers and Addresses of Franklin D. Roosevelt, 1943*, 33.

29. For example, see Winston S. Churchill, *Triumph and Tragedy* (Boston: Houghton Mifflin, 1953), 642.

30. Gideon Rose, *How Wars End: Why We Always Fight the Last Battle* (New York: Simon & Schuster, 2011), 105. Also see Robert Sherwood, *Roosevelt and Hopkins: An Intimate History*, 2 vols. (New York: Bantam Books, 1948), 2:554–555. David Holloway stresses Stalin's ultimate goal of Japan's complete and utter defeat and its removal as a great power. Still, Stalin did not

want that defeat to happen before Russia could enter the conflict and claim its spoils. See David Holloway, "Jockeying for Position in the Postwar World: Soviet Entry into the War with Japan in August 1945," in *The End of the Pacific War: Reappraisals,* ed. Tsuyoshi Hasegawa (Stanford, CA: Stanford University Press, 2007), 163–164.

31. James M. McPherson, "Lincoln and the Strategy of Unconditional Surrender," in *Lincoln, the War President: The Gettysburg Lectures,* ed. Gabor S. Boritt (New York: Oxford University Press, 1992), 41; Armstrong, *Unconditional Surrender,* 13–14, 252–253. See also Sigal, *Fighting to a Finish,* 89; Herbert Feis, *Churchill, Roosevelt, Stalin: The War They Waged and the Peace They Sought* (Princeton, NJ: Princeton University Press, 1957), 111–113.

32. John Lewis Gaddis, *The Long Peace: Inquiries into the History of the Cold War* (New York: Oxford University Press, 1987), 236–237.

33. Raymond G. O'Connor, *Diplomacy for Victory: FDR and Unconditional Surrender* (New York: Norton, 1971), chap. 1.

34. Quoted in Jeremi Suri, *Liberty's Surest Guardian: American Nation-Building from the Founders to Obama* (New York: Free Press, 2011), 15.

35. Quoted in John W. Dower, *War without Mercy: Race and Power in the Pacific War* (New York: Pantheon, 1986), 33.

36. Greg Robinson, *By Order of the President: FDR and the Internment of Japanese Americans* (Cambridge, MA: Harvard University Press, 2001), 6. See also Greg Robinson, *A Tragedy of Democracy: Japanese Confinement in North America* (New York: Columbia University Press, 2009), 6, 49, 305n2.

37. Gerhard Weinberg, *A World at Arms: A Global History of World War II* (Cambridge: Cambridge University Press, 1994), 438.

38. Rose, *How Wars End,* 79.

39. Sherwood, *Roosevelt and Hopkins,* 2:302.

40. Ibid. The First Lady seconded her husband's decision in a statement addressed to American women. Eleanor Roosevelt wrote in June 1944 that it was necessary to avoid the mistakes of the last war. "I think the mothers of this country . . . will not be so foolish as to ask for a negotiated peace which is what we have had before." Quoted in John Lewis Gaddis, *The United States and the Origins of the Cold War, 1941–1947* (New York: Columbia University Press, 1972), 9.

41. See the observation by Ernest R. May, *"Lessons" of the Past: The Use and Misuse of History in American Foreign Policy* (London: Oxford University Press, 1973), 18. FDR's remark to Stimson is found on page 18.

42. FDR press conference, July 29, 1944. See Samuel I. Rosenman, ed., *The Public Papers and Addresses of Franklin D. Roosevelt, 1944–45: Victory and the Threshold of Peace* (New York: Harper & Brothers, 1950), 210.

43. Ibid., 339.

44. Akira Iriye, *The New Cambridge History of American Foreign Relations: The Globalizing of America, 1913–1945* (Cambridge: Cambridge University Press, 2013), 199–200.

45. Sherwood observes that maintaining his "freedom of action" was one of FDR's favorite phrases. Sherwood, *Roosevelt and Hopkins*, 507. David Kennedy writes that FDR typically wanted to "defer tough political bargaining until the war's end. When the unconditional surrender was announced it was the policy of a militarily unprepared nation with little scope for maneuver. It would survive into an era when America wielded unimaginable power and when the supple Roosevelt was no longer alive to temper its application. By then the unconditional-surrender doctrine would have taken on a life of its own with consequences not visible in January 1943." David Kennedy, *Freedom from Fear: The American People in Depression and War, 1929–1945* (New York: Oxford University Press, 1999), 588.

46. Warren F. Kimball, *The Juggler: Franklin Roosevelt as Wartime Statesman* (Princeton, NJ: Princeton University Press, 1991), 17.

47. Ibid., 76.

48. Henry Kissinger, *World Order* (New York: Penguin Press, 2014), 257.

49. Dallek, *Franklin D. Roosevelt and American Foreign Policy*, 438.

50. Mark Mazower, *Governing the World: The History of an Idea* (New York: Penguin Press, 2012), 198–199.

51. Address to Congress, March 1, 1945; Rosenman, *The Public Papers and Addresses of Franklin D. Roosevelt, 1944–45*, 586, 584.

52. Sean L. Malloy, *Atomic Tragedy: Henry L. Stimson and the Decision to Use the Bomb against Japan* (Ithaca, NY: Cornell University Press, 2008), 100.

53. Hellegers, *We, the Japanese People*, 1:255–256n1.

54. Ibid., 33.

55. Brian L. Villa, "The U.S. Army, Unconditional Surrender, and the Potsdam Proclamation," *Journal of American History* 63, no. 1 (June 1976): 66–92, especially 71. See also Charles F. Brower, "Sophisticated Strategist: General George A. Lincoln and the Defeat of Japan," *Diplomatic History* 15, no. 3 (Summer 1991): 317–337.

56. Hellegers, *We, the Japanese People*, 1:5.

57. Makoto Iokibe, "American Policy towards Japan's 'Unconditional Surrender,'" *Japanese Journal of American Studies*, no. 1 (1981): 40.

58. Hanson Baldwin writes of Roosevelt's "personalized foreign policy": "Had the President been able to lean upon a younger and more vigorous Secretary of State and a stronger State Department he might have depended less upon intuition and snap judgment and more upon careful research and group study. . . . His great wartime power, the record of victory, the high esteem in which he was held by the world, and the weakness of the State Department all combined to reinforce the President's tendency to depend upon himself. Had the nation then had a National Security Council, or organization for reconciling and present military-political views, had it had a strong well-integrated State Department, this personalized foreign policy might have been tempered by riper judgments and

more carefully thought out decisions." Hanson W. Baldwin, *Great Mistakes of the War* (London: Alvin Redman, 1949), 5–8.

59. *The Memoirs of Cordell Hull* (New York: MacMillan, 1948), 2:1379.

60. Hellegers, *We, the Japanese People,* 1:87–88; also Robert J. C. Butow, *Japan's Decision to Surrender* (Stanford, CA: Stanford University Press, 1954), 40–41; Yukiko Koshiro, *Imperial Eclipse: Japan's Strategic Thinking about Continental Asia before August 1945* (Ithaca, NY: Cornell University Press, 2013), 163–169.

61. For elaboration of the confused pattern of the State Department's role in policymaking, see Hugh Borton, *American Presurrender Planning for Postwar Japan,* Occasional Papers of the East Asian Institute (New York: East Asian Institute, Columbia University, 1967).

62. Robert L. Beisner, *Dean Acheson: A Life in the Cold War* (New York: Oxford University Press, 2006), 16.

63. Acheson, *Present at the Creation,* 38.

64. Kai Bird, *The Chairman, John J. McCloy: The Making of the American Establishment* (New York: Simon & Schuster, 1992), 245.

65. Hugh Borton, *Spanning Japan's Modern Century: The Memoirs of Hugh Borton* (Lanham, MD: Lexington, 2002), 97–98. See also Borton, *American Presurrender Planning,* 12–13.

66. Wm. Roger Louis, *Imperialism at Bay, 1941–1945: The United States and the Decolonization of the British Empire* (New York: Oxford University Press, 1977), 200.

67. Churchill rejected Roosevelt's persistent suggestions for concessions to Indian nationalist leaders, writing him, "Anything like a serious difference between you and me would break my heart, and would surely deeply injure both our countries at the height of this terrible struggle [against the Axis powers]." Winston S. Churchill, *The Hinge of Fate* (Boston: Houghton Mifflin, 1950), 221. See also Kenneth B. Pyle, "America and the Quest for India's Freedom: A Study of American Policies and Attitudes towards India's Desire for Independence, 1918–1947 (thesis, copy in Widener Library, Harvard College, 1958).

68. Winston S. Churchill, *Closing the Ring* (Boston: Houghton Mifflin, 1951), 328.

69. Dallek, *Franklin D. Roosevelt and American Foreign Policy,* 389.

70. R. J. C. Butow, "A Notable Passage to China: Myth and Memory in FDR's Family History," *Prologue* 31, no. 3 (Fall 1999): 158–177.

71. Dallek, *Franklin D. Roosevelt and American Foreign Policy,* 389–391.

72. Louis, *Imperialism at Bay,* 280. The Chinese record is the one quoted here.

73. Feis, *Churchill, Roosevelt, Stalin,* 246–247.

74. John Hunter Boyle, *Modern Japan: The American Nexus* (Fort Worth, TX: Harcourt, Brace, Jovanovich, 1993), 211.

75. Sadao Asada, *From Mahan to Pearl Harbor: The Imperial Japanese Navy and the United States* (Annapolis, MD: Naval Institute Press, 2006), 217.

76. Ibid., 277.

77. Kennedy, *Freedom from Fear,* 526.

78. "Never before had such a comparatively large area been conquered in such a short time." Paul Kennedy, *Strategy and Diplomacy: 1870–1945* (London: George Allen & Unwin, 1983), 185–186.

79. Akira Iriye, *Power and Culture: The Japanese-American War, 1941–1945* (Cambridge, MA: Harvard University Press, 1981), 64.

80. Hata Ikuhiko, "Continental Expansion, 1905–1945," in *The Cambridge History of Japan,* vol. 6, *The Twentieth Century,* ed. Peter Duus (Cambridge: Cambridge University Press, 1981), 302.

81. Asada, *From Mahan to Pearl Harbor,* 287.

82. Drea, *In the Service of the Emperor,* 194; also Drea, *Japan's Imperial Army,* 222.

83. Nobutaka Ike, *Japan's Decision for War: Records of the 1941 Policy Conferences* (Stanford, CA: Stanford University Press, 1961), xxv–xxvi.

84. As Dower writes, they "gave virtually no serious thought to how the conflict might be terminated. Somehow, before too long, they hoped, the Allies would tire of the struggle and agree to a compromise settlement which left the Co-Prosperity Sphere essentially intact." Dower, *War without Mercy,* 293.

85. Butow, *Japan's Decision,* 39–40.

86. Iriye, *Power and Culture,* 163.

87. See Daikichi Irokawa, *The Age of Hirohito: In Search of Modern Japan* (New York: Free Press, 1995), 29. A slightly different translation appears on page 92.

88. Michael Doyle, *The Question of Intervention: John Stuart Mill and the Responsibility to Protect* (New Haven, CT: Yale University Press, 2015), 154.

89. Butow, *Japan's Decision,* 136.

90. Howard, *Grand Strategy,* 285.

91. Koshiro, *Imperial Eclipse,* 163–169, 178–182, discusses Japanese reluctance to give up Korea in offering concessions to Russia in the summer of 1945 to maintain Soviet neutrality and seek Soviet mediation of peace.

92. Michael Walzer, *Just and Unjust Wars: A Moral Argument with Historical Illustrations* (New York: Basic Books, 1977), 113. For reflections on application of just war theory, see John Rawls, "Fifty Years after Hiroshima," *Dissent,* Summer 1995.

93. Walzer, *Just and Unjust Wars,* 267–268.

94. Gaddis, *The Long Peace,* 236.

95. May, *"Lessons" of the Past,* 18.

96. Gaddis, *The Long Peace,* 237.

97. Stanley Hoffmann, "An American Social Science: International Relations," *Daedalus* 16, no. 3 (Summer 1977): 44.

98. Hans J. Morgenthau, *In Defense of the National Interest: A Critical Examination of American Foreign Policy* (New York: Knopf, 1951), 93–97.

99. George F. Kennan, *American Diplomacy,* expanded ed. (Chicago: University of Chicago Press, 1984), 100–101.

100. Morgenthau, *In Defense of the National Interest,* 13.

101. Ibid., 29.

102. Sigal, *Fighting to a Finish,* 93.

103. Hanson W. Baldwin, *Great Mistakes of the War* (London: Alvin Redman, 1950), 13.

104. Paul Kecskemeti, *Strategic Surrender: The Politics of Victory and Defeat* (Stanford, CA: Stanford University Press, 1958), 206–207.

3. The Decision to Use the Atomic Bomb

1. As McGeorge Bundy, President Kennedy's foreign policy advisor, wrote, "No single decision ever made by any American president has aroused more discussion and debate." McGeorge Bundy, *Danger and Survival: Choices about the Bomb in the First Fifty Years* (New York: Vintage, 1990), 54.

2. Associated Press story carried in the *Seattle Times,* February 24, 1999.

3. John Keegan, *The Battle for History: Re-fighting World War II* (New York: Vintage Books, 1996), 28. For discussion of the historiography of the decision to use the atomic bomb, see Tsuyoshi Hasegawa, ed., *The End of the Pacific War: Reappraisals* (Stanford, CA: Stanford University Press, 2007); and also Michael Kort, *The Columbia Guide to Hiroshima and the Bomb* (New York: Columbia University Press, 2007). For my views of the historiographical issues, see Kenneth B. Pyle, "Hiroshima and the Historians: History as Relative Truth," *Pacific Northwest Quarterly* (Summer 2013): 123–132, reprinted and slightly revised in *Asia-Pacific Review* 22, no. 2 (November 2015): 14–27.

4. See Pew Research Center, "70 Years after Hiroshima, Opinions Have Shifted on Use of the Atomic Bomb," July 31, 2015, which showed declining support in both the United States and Japan for America's bombing of Hiroshima and Nagasaki.

5. John W. Dower, "The Bombed: Hiroshima and Nagasaki in Japanese Memory" in *Hiroshima in History and Memory,* ed. Michael J. Hogan (Cambridge: Cambridge University Press, 1996), 119.

6. John Whittier Treat, *Writing Ground Zero: Japanese Literature and the Atomic Bomb* (Chicago: University of Chicago Press, 1995), 362–368.

7. As Reinhold Niebuhr wrote in 1952, America "finds itself the custodian of the ultimate weapon which perfectly embodies and symbolizes the moral ambiguity of physical warfare. . . . Thus the moral predicament in which all human striving is involved has been raised to a final pitch for a culture and for a nation which thought it an easy matter to distinguish between justice and injustice and believed itself to be peculiarly innocent." *The Irony of American History,* rev. ed. (Chicago: Chicago University Press, 2008), 39.

8. *New York Times,* February 1, 2003.

9. Ben-Ami Shillony, "Auschwitz and Hiroshima: What Can the Jews and the Japanese Do for World Peace?," *International House of Japan Bulletin* 27, no. 1 (2007): 2.

10. Robert Jay Lifton and Gregg Mitchell, *Hiroshima in America: A Half Century of Denial* (New York: Avon Books, 1995), 222.

11. See Edward T. Lilienthal and Tom Englehardt, eds., *History Wars: The Enola Gay and Other Battles for the American Past* (New York: Henry Holt, 1996).

12. *Seattle Times,* April 7, 1995.

13. *Wall Street Journal,* April 7, 2009.

14. *NHK News,* May 21, 2016.

15. *Reuters,* May 28, 2016.

16. The letter is reprinted in Kort, *Columbia Guide,* 172. Shortly before he died, Einstein told Linus Pauling, "I made one great mistake in my life . . . when I signed the letter to President Roosevelt recommending that atomic bombs be made; but there was some justification—the danger that the Germans would make them." Quoted in Theodore McNelly, *The Origins of Japan's Democratic Constitution* (Lanham, MD: University Press of America, 2000), 130–131.

17. Historians date the exact time somewhat differently, but it was in the autumn of 1941.

18. Sean L. Malloy, *Atomic Tragedy: Henry L. Stimson and the Decision to Use the Bomb against Japan* (Ithaca, NY: Cornell University Press, 2008), 56. The physicist Arthur Compton, a key figure in the Manhattan Project, records that "so acute was our concern about the Germans' progress that when the Allies landed on Normandy beaches on 6 June 1944, certain of the American officers were equipped with Geiger counters." Arthur Holly Compton, *Atomic Quest: A Personal Narrative* (New York: Oxford University Press, 1956), 222–223.

19. Richard Rhodes, *The Making of the Atomic Bomb* (New York: Simon & Schuster, 1986), 426.

20. Oppenheimer was a member of a number of front organizations, had many relatives, friends, and colleagues who were Communist Party members, and was under FBI surveillance. See Kai Bird and Martin J. Sherwin, *American Prometheus: The Triumph and Tragedy of J. Robert Oppenheimer* (New York: Vintage Books, 2006), 135, 231.

21. As Bundy writes, "Roosevelt's reservation of policy responsibility to himself, powerfully reinforced by the intense secrecy on which he insisted to the end of his life, did indeed create a situation in which there were no arrangements for the orderly and timely consideration of questions that went beyond making the bomb as fast as possible. One of the consequences of this situation was that important questions were put off or neglected, and many sorts of advice not sought." *Danger and Survival,* 47.

22. Dean Rusk, who later served as secretary of state, reflected in his memoirs that "we made a mistake with the Manhattan Project from its inception.

We should have built in a political task force to consider the ramifications of using the bomb. . . . Such a task force might not have affected the outcome, either at Hiroshima or the arms race that followed, but at least we would have boxed the compass of all possibilities." Dean Rusk, *As I Saw It* (New York: Norton 1990), 122.

23. Kort, *Columbia Guide,* 175.

24. Martin J. Sherwin, *A World Destroyed: The Atomic Bomb and the Grand Alliance* (New York: Vintage, 1977), 123.

25. Leslie R. Groves, *Now It Can Be Told: The Story of the Manhattan Project* (New York: Harper & Brothers, 1962), 184. See also Kort, *Columbia Guide,* 46–47.

26. Sherwin, *A World Destroyed,* 209–210. Sherwin also writes that initially it was thought that the bomb would be used against the Japanese fleet so that if it failed to detonate it would fall into the water and be difficult to retrieve. Conant, Bush, and Groves thought as early as May 1943 that it would be better to target Japan than Germany, lest a dud fall into German hands and aid their effort. Roosevelt showed no interest in determining targets, deferring such planning to the future. Other possible reasons that the bomb was used on Japan rather than on Germany were the expectation that the war in Europe would end before the bomb was ready, it was safer to assemble it in the Pacific than in England, and delivery in a US-dominated theater of war would emphasize US primacy in the Anglo-American effort. See also Malloy, *Atomic Tragedy,* 57–58.

27. Barton J. Bernstein, review of *Racing the Enemy: Stalin, Truman, and the Surrender of Japan,* by Tsuyoshi Hasegawa, *H-Diplo Roundtable Reviews* 7, no. 2 (2006):.15, http://www.h-net.org/~diplo/roundtables/PDF/Bernstein-HasegawaRoundtable.pdf.

28. John Lewis Gaddis, *George F. Kennan: An American Life* (New York: Penguin Press, 2011), 167–168.

29. Paul Kennedy, *Engineers of Victory: The Problem Solvers Who Turned the Tide in the Second World War* (New York: Random House, 2013), 349.

30. On September 1, 1939, Roosevelt made an "urgent appeal to every Government which may be engaged in hostilities publicly to affirm its determination that its armed forces shall in no event, and under no circumstances, undertake the bombardment from the air of civilian populations or of unfortified cities." Bundy, *Danger and Survival,* 63. Roosevelt said, "Ruthless bombing from the air . . . which has resulted in the maiming and in the death of thousands of defenseless men, women, and children, has sickened the hearts of every civilized man and woman, and has profoundly shocked the conscience of humanity." John W. Dower, *Cultures of War: Pearl Harbor / Hiroshima / 9–11 / Iraq* (New York: Norton, 2010), 220.

31. There is no clear account of the number dead, but as the historian Richard Frank writes, "A figure of 90,000 to 100,000 came to be accepted, but even these immense totals are sometimes challenged as too low." Richard

Frank, *Downfall: The End of the Imperial Japanese Empire* (New York: Random House, 1999), 17–18.

32. Dower, *Cultures of War,* 185.

33. LeMay further said, "Killing Japanese didn't bother me very much at that time. . . . All war is immoral, and if you let that bother you, you're not a good soldier." Richard Rhodes, *Dark Sun: The Making of the Hydrogen Bomb* (New York: Simon & Schuster, 1995), 21–22.

34. Bernstein, review of *Racing the Enemy,* 15.

35. Dale M. Hellegers, *We, the Japanese People: World War II and the Origins of the Japanese Constitution,* 2 vols. (Stanford, CA: Stanford University Press, 2001), 1:87.

36. Malloy, *Atomic Tragedy,* 119.

37. Perhaps the president had on one occasion mentioned the atomic bomb to Truman in general terms when the two met briefly on August 18, 1944, to discuss the upcoming presidential campaign. See Robert H. Ferrell, *The Dying President: Franklin D. Roosevelt, 1944–1945* (Columbia: University of Missouri Press, 1998), 3–4.

38. The memorandum discussed with the president in its entirety is in Henry L. Stimson and McGeorge Bundy, *On Active Service in Peace and War* (New York: Harper & Brothers, 1947), 635–636.

39. Also included were George Harrison, William Clayton, and Ralph Bard. Malloy, *Atomic Tragedy,* 210n54.

40. Kent E. Calder, *Embattled Garrisons: Comparative Base Politics and American Globalism* (Princeton, NJ: Princeton University Press, 2008), 283.

41. Quoted in Barton Bernstein, "Understanding the Atomic Bomb and the Japanese Surrender," in Hogan, *Hiroshima in History and Memory,* 78.

42. Sherwin, *A World Destroyed,* 208. Also see Appendix L for text of notes from the Interim Committee meeting, 295–304.

43. Michael Howard, *War and the Liberal Conscience* (London: Temple Smith, 1978), 131.

44. Ibid., 95.

45. Quoted in Michael Walzer, *Just and Unjust Wars: A Moral Argument with Historical Illustrations* (New York: Basic Books, 1977), 263.

46. Stimson and Bundy, *On Active Service in Peace and War,* 629.

47. Henry L. Stimson, "The Decision to Use the Atomic Bomb," *Harper's* 194 (February 1947).

48. Winston Churchill, *Triumph and Tragedy* (Boston: Houghton Mifflin, 1953), 639.

49. Bernstein, review of *Racing the Enemy,* 15–16.

50. Bundy, *Danger and Survival,* 60.

51. Malloy, *Atomic Tragedy,* 98.

52. Makoto Iokibe, ed., *The Diplomatic History of Postwar Japan* (London: Routledge, 2011), 21.

53. Brian Villa, "The U.S. Army, Unconditional Surrender, and the Potsdam Proclamation," *Journal of American History* 63, no. 1 (1976): 66–92.

54. The journalist Robert Sherrod is quoted in Townsend Hoopes and Douglas Brinkley, *Driven Patriot: The Life and Times of James Forrestal* (New York: Vintage, 1993), 197.

55. Walter Millis, ed., *The Forrestal Diaries* (New York: Viking, 1951), 52–53. Also see Hoopes and Brinkley, *Driven Patriot,* 209.

56. Millis, *Forrestal Diaries,* 53.

57. Kai Bird, *The Chairman, John J. McCloy: The Making of the American Establishment* (New York: Simon & Schuster, 1992), 245.

58. Ibid., 246.

59. James Reston, *Deadline: A Memoir* (New York: Random House, 1991), 501–502.

60. Ernest R. May, "The Development of Political-Military Consultation in the United States," *Political Science Quarterly* 70, no. 2 (June 1955): 174.

61. Gideon Rose, *How Wars End: Why We Always Fight the Last Battle* (New York: Simon & Schuster, 2010), 104.

62. A June 1945 poll asked: "Japan may offer to surrender and call her soldiers home provided we agree to not send an army of occupation to her home islands. Do you think we should accept such a peace offer if we get the chance, or fight on until we have completely beaten her on the Japanese homeland?" Eighty-four percent favored fighting on, while 9 percent said they would accept the offer. Ibid., 108.

63. Malloy, *Atomic Tragedy,* 101.

64. Hellegers, *We, the Japanese People,* 103–104.

65. Malloy, *Atomic Tragedy,* 140–141.

66. Roger Buckley, *Occupation Diplomacy: Britain, the United States and Japan, 1945–1952* (Cambridge: Cambridge University Press, 1982), 10–12. See also Hugh Borton, *Spanning Japan's Modern Century: The Memoirs of Hugh Borton* (Lanham, MD: Lexington, 2002), 96–97; Hellegers, *We, the Japanese People,* 34.

67. Waldo H. Heinrichs, Jr., *American Ambassador: Joseph C. Grew and the Development of the United States Diplomatic Tradition* (New York: Oxford University Press, 1966), 364–365.

68. Nakamura Masanori, *The Japanese Monarchy: Ambassador Joseph Grew and the Making of the "Symbol Emperor System," 1931–1991* (Armonk, NY: M. E. Sharpe, 1992), 66–67.

69. Heinrichs, *American Ambassador,* 374.

70. Herbert Bix, "Japan's Delayed Surrender: A Reinterpretation," in Hogan, *Hiroshima in History and Memory,* 81–82.

71. James Chace, *Acheson: The Secretary of State Who Created the American World* (New York: Simon & Schuster, 1998), 106.

72. Leon V. Sigal, *Fighting to a Finish: The Politics of War Termination in the United States and Japan* (Ithaca, NY: Cornell University Press, 1988), 127.

73. "According to Eric Larrabee, one proof of FDR's political genius was to make World War II seem to the American people like a logical extension of the domestic New Deal crusade—that is, opposition to the power of entrenched interests at home and opposition to vicious tyrannies abroad 'were made to appear as but two articles of the same democratic, humanitarian faith.' . . . FDR's success in this endeavor had the curious effect in 1945 of making hard-line ideologues out of liberal New Dealers when it came to issues like compromise with evil dictators for the purpose of saving American lives or guarding against the destruction of all hope in the defeated enemy countries. It was notable that Forrestal and the other advocates of flexibility were not New Dealers, but pragmatic bankers, lawyers, and diplomats. They were thinking beyond the war to the need for structure and stability in the postwar world. The New Dealers, by and large, considered it immoral and politically dangerous to tamper with FDR's legacy of 'unconditional surrender' and found it difficult to think beyond the winning of a total military victory for the forces of decency. As Forrestal put it in 1946: 'We regarded the war, broadly speaking, as a ball game' to be finished 'as quickly as possible,' but with 'little thought as to the relationships between nations which would exist after Germany and Japan were destroyed.'" Hoopes and Brinkley, *Driven Patriot,* 209.

74. John W. Dower, *Embracing Defeat: Japan in the Wake of World War II* (New York: Norton, 1999), 299. See John D. Chappell, *Before the Bomb: How America Approached the End of the Pacific War* (Lexington: University of Kentucky Press, 1997), chapter 8 for a survey of public attitudes toward unconditional surrender policy.

75. See the exploration of the ambiguity in public discussion of this issue in Hal Brands, "Rhetoric, Public Opinion, and Policy in the American Debate over the Japanese Emperor during World War II," *Rhetoric and Public Affairs* 8, no. 3 (Fall 2005): 431–457.

76. Chace, *Acheson,* 107.

77. The memo in its entirety is in Stimson and Bundy, *On Active Service in Peace and War,* 620–624.

78. Wilson D. Miscamble, *The Most Controversial Decision: Truman, the Atomic Bombs, and the Defeat of Japan* (Cambridge: Cambridge University, 2011), 60.

79. David Holloway, "Jockeying for Position in the Postwar World: Soviet Entry into the War with Japan in August 1945," in *The End of the Pacific War: Reappraisals,* ed. Tsuyoshi Hasegawa (Stanford, CA: Stanford University Press, 2007), 171–172.

80. Tsuyoshi Hasegawa, *Racing the Enemy: Stalin, Truman, and the Surrender of Japan* (Cambridge, MA: Harvard University Press, 2005), 154–155.

81. Churchill, *Triumph and Tragedy,* 642.

82. The Potsdam Declaration is sometimes referred to as the Potsdam Proclamation.

83. Miscamble, *The Most Controversial Decision*, 101. See also Sigal, *Fighting to a Finish*, 128; Malloy, *Atomic Tragedy*, 130–131, 215n37.

84. Barton J. Bernstein, "Writing, Righting, or Wronging the Historical Record: President Truman's Letter on His Atomic-Bomb Decision," *Diplomatic History* 16, no. 1 (Winter 1992): 163–173.

85. Alvin D. Coox, "The Pacific War," in *The Cambridge History of Japan*, vol. 6, *The Twentieth Century*, ed. Peter Duus (Cambridge: Cambridge University Press, 1988), 364.

86. John W. Dower, *Japan in War and Peace: Selected Essays* (New York: New Press, 1993), 103.

87. John W. Dower, *Empire and Aftermath: Yoshida Shigeru and the Japanese Experience, 1878–1954* (Cambridge, MA: Harvard University, 1978), 265. Also see chapter 4 of Dower, *Japan in War and Peace*; Jeremy A. Yellen, "The Specter of Revolution: Reconsidering Japan's Decision to Surrender," *International History Review* 35, no. 1 (2012): 1–22.

88. Bix, "Japan's Delayed Surrender," 107n.

89. As Akira Iriye has concluded, after the Yalta Conference at the beginning of 1945 it was evident to Japan's supreme war council that Russia might eventually join in the war against Japan and that Allied forces were advancing on Iwo Jima and Okinawa. "February 1945, therefore, should have been the point when the Japanese leaders clearly recognized the futility of their approach and began to explore alternative ways of speedily terminating the war." *Power and Culture: The Japanese-American War, 1941–1945* (Cambridge, MA: Harvard University Press, 1981), 235. As Butow writes in his authoritative account, "If the ruling elite had known, in the spring of 1945, that the Soviet government had promised in February, to enter the war in the Pacific within two to three months after the German defeat in Europe, [they] might have turned directly to the United States or Great Britain in spite of the current belief that such a step could only result in unconditional surrender." Robert J. C. Butow, *Japan's Decision to Surrender* (Stanford, CA: Stanford University Press, 1954), 90. Had there been a venue where talks were conducted between the belligerents, such knowledge might well have swayed Japanese decision making.

90. Jon Tetsuro Suzuki, *Decoding Clausewitz: A New Approach to On War* (Lawrence: University Press of Kansas, 2008), 179–180.

91. See Malloy, *Atomic Tragedy*, 193n26.

92. See Richard Frank, "Ketsu Go: Japanese Political and Military Strategy in 1945," in *The End of the Pacific War: Reappraisals*, ed. Tsuyoshi Hasegawa (Stanford, CA: Stanford University Press, 2007), 69–71.

93. Hasegawa, *Racing the Enemy*, 110.

94. See Yukiko Koshiro, *Imperial Eclipse: Japan's Strategic Thinking about Continental Asia before August 1945* (Ithaca, NY: Cornell University Press, 2013); also see Yukiko Koshiro, "Eurasian Eclipse: Japan's End Game in World War II," *American Historical Review* 109, no. 2 (April 2004): 417–444.

95. Michael Barnhart observes, "The Americans of the summer of 1945 may have given little thought to the future of East Asia, beyond Japan's elimination from it, but Japanese leaders, no less than Chinese or Soviet ones, thought about little else." See *History: Reviews of New Books* 43, no. 2 (April 2015): 75.

96. Japanese scientists examined the devastation at Hiroshima and reported to Tokyo that it had been a nuclear bomb. It is a little-known story, but the Japanese had been working on their own atomic bomb project, a poorly coordinated and underfunded effort. The Japanese had several leading scientists of international stature who had been working in nuclear physics since the early 1930s, but they believed during the war that they could not achieve a bomb in the immediate future. Not the least of their problems was that they could not find uranium in Japan or in any of its occupied territories. They therefore sought it from Germany. In May 1945 a German U-Boat destined for Japan with 560 kilograms of uranium oxide surrendered to the United States in the Atlantic on learning of the end of the war in Europe. John Dower writes that "this essentially commercial transaction . . . seems to be the only point of contact between the Japanese and Germans involving . . . potential development of an atomic bomb. There appears to have been no contact whatsoever between the scientists of the two countries, and development of nuclear weaponry was never discussed at the official level." Dower, *Japan in War and Peace*, 80.

97. See Andrew Barshay, *The Gods Left First: The Captivity and Repatriation of Japanese POWs in Northeast Asia, 1945–1956* (Berkeley: University of California Press, 2013).

98. Michael D. Gordin, *Five Days in August: How World War II Became a Nuclear War* (Princeton, NJ: Princeton University Press, 2007), 98–100.

99. Secretary of Commerce Henry Wallace recorded this in his diary. See Henry A. Wallace, *The Price of Vision: The Diary of Henry A. Wallace, 1942–1946* (Boston: Houghton Mifflin, 1973), 474.

100. Bix, "Japan's Delayed Surrender," 110.

101. See the thoughtful essay by Edward J. Drea, "Chasing a Decisive Victory," in *In the Service of the Emperor: Essays on the Imperial Japanese Army*, ed. Edward J. Drea (Lincoln: University of Nebraska Press, 1998).

102. The emperor also wanted to avoid a battle in the homeland and believed that "the conditions" in the Potsdam Declaration, together with the subsequent clarifying exchange of notes with Truman, ensured the chances of the imperial institution surviving the "unconditional surrender." See Suzuki Tamon, *"Shūsen" no seijishi, 1943–1945* (Tokyo: Tokyo daigaku shuppankai, 2011), 175–186.

103. Sean L. Malloy, "'A Very Pleasant Way to Die': Radiation Effects and the Decision to Use the Atomic Bomb against Japan," *Diplomatic History* 26, no. 3 (June 2011): 544. See also Malloy, *Atomic Tragedy*, 53.

104. Commentary by Barton J. Bernstein, roundtable on *Racing the Enemy: Stalin, Truman, and the Surrender of Japan,* by Tsuyoshi Hasegawa, *H-Diplo Roundtable Reviews* 7, no. 2 (2006): 16, 14, accessed March 2, 2011, http://www.h-net.org/~diplo/index.html.

105. Frank, *Downfall,* 214–215.

106. Quoted in Richard Wightman Fox, *Reinhold Niebuhr: A Biography* (San Francisco: Harper & Row, 1987), 224.

107. Ibid., 225.

108. Raymond Aron, *The Imperial Republic: The United States and the World, 1945–1973* (Englewood Cliffs, NJ: Prentice-Hall, 1974), 23.

109. Hans J. Morgenthau, *In Defense of the National Interest: A Critical Examination of American Foreign Policy* (New York: Knopf, 1951), 96.

110. David M. Kennedy, *Freedom from Fear: The American People in Depression and War, 1929–1945* (New York: Oxford, 1999), 855–856.

111. Contemplating the trade-offs between a negotiated peace and unconditional surrender cannot leave one with an easy resolution. It is perilous to try to reconstruct the past. John Dower's observation suggests the ambivalence with which one might be left: "One can thus argue that compromising the demand for unconditional surrender in a way that even die-hard militarists could have accepted in 1945 might have opened the door to a negotiated capitulation before the bombs and Soviet Union descended upon Japan simultaneously—and that this, measured in terms of Cold War Realpolitik, would have served the United States just as well. But MacArthur would have been a conspicuously diminished figure in this case; the grassroots participation his early radical reforms made possible would likewise have been diminished; and the grand ideals of 'demilitarization and democratization' that many Japanese continued to cherish after the reversal of policy would never have found such unequivocal expression and institutionalized protections. Postwar Japan would have been a different place." Dower, *Cultures of War,* 241. Still, it must be acknowledged that even having the grand ideals and institutions that MacArthur bestowed, in the end the conservative hegemony was restored, Japan was remilitarized, and the Japanese were deprived of the self-determination to achieve reforms on their own and were left in a long-lasting dependency on the Americans.

4. An American Revolution in Japan

1. Gideon Rose, *How Wars End: Why We Always Fight the Last Battle* (New York: Simon & Schuster, 2010), 122.

2. Ibid.

3. David M. Kennedy, *Freedom from Fear: The American People in Depression and War, 1929–1945* (New York: Oxford University Press, 1999), 856.

4. Warren F. Kimball, *The Juggler: Franklin Roosevelt as Wartime Statesman* (Princeton, NJ: Princeton University Press, 1991), 145–146.

5. Niall Ferguson, *Colossus: The Price of America's Empire* (New York: Penguin, 2004), 67.

6. Wm. Roger Louis, *Imperialism at Bay 1941–1945: The United States and the Decolonization of the British Empire* (Oxford: Clarendon Press, 1977), 351.

7. Akira Iriye, *Power and Culture: The Japanese-American War, 1941–1945* (Cambridge, MA: Harvard University Press, 1981), 130.

8. Robert Dallek, *The American Style of Foreign Policy: Cultural Politics and Foreign Affairs* (New York: Knopf, 1983), 152–153.

9. Robert Dallek, *Franklin D. Roosevelt and American Foreign Policy, 1932–1945* (New York: Oxford University Press, 1979), 429. For a careful study of one trusteeship, see Stephen C. Murray, *The Battle over Peleliu: Islander, Japanese, and American Memories of War* (Tuscaloosa: University of Alabama Press, 2016), chap. 6.

10. Iriye, *Power and Culture*, 129.

11. Ferguson, *Colossus*, 68.

12. Catherine Lutz, ed., *The Bases of Empire: The Global Struggle against U.S. Military Posts* (Washington Square, NY: New York University Press, 2009), 10.

13. Reinhold Niebuhr, *The Irony of American History* (New York: Scribner, 1952), 3.

14. Robert Dallek, *The American Style of Foreign Policy: Cultural Politics and Foreign Affairs* (New York: Knopf, 1983), 153.

15. Theodore Cohen, *Remaking Japan: The American Occupation as New Deal* (New York: Free Press, 1987), 6.

16. Sean Malloy, *Atomic Tragedy: Henry L. Stimson and the Decision to Use the Atomic Bomb* (Ithaca, NY: Cornell University Press, 2008), 101.

17. Sir George Sansom, the British representative in Tokyo and later the dean of Western historians of Japan, supported modifications in the Meiji Constitution to establish civilian control of the military and to increase the power of the Diet, but he believed that other reforms should be left to the Japanese themselves. See Roger Buckley, *Occupation Diplomacy: Britain, the United States and Japan, 1945–1952* (Cambridge: Cambridge University Press, 1982), 10–12; see also Hugh Borton, *Spanning Japan's Modern Century: The Memoirs of Hugh Borton* (Lanham, MD: Lexington, 2002), 96–97. Sansom cautioned Americans against planning wholesale reform of a society that was deeply conservative. He opposed any thought of the Allies assuming the governing functions in Japan but said that they should work through the existing government, depending on sanctions to enforce reforms. Dale M. Hellegers, *We, the Japanese People: World War II and the Origins of the Japanese Constitution*, 2 vols. (Stanford, CA: Stanford University Press, 2001), 1:341n58.

18. For the Occupation's relationship to international law, see Nisuke Ando, *Surrender, Occupation, and Private Property in International Law: An Evaluation of US Practice in Japan* (London: Oxford, 1991). See also Pitman B. Potter, "Legal Bases and Character of Military Occupation in Germany and Japan," *American Journal of International Law* 43 (1949): 323–325. Also

Yoram Dinstein, *The International Law of Belligerent Occupation* (Cambridge: Cambridge University Press, 2009); and Eyal Benvenisti, *The International Law of Occupation* (Princeton, NJ: Princeton University Press, 1993). Dinstein terms the US Occupation of Japan as "brazenly inconsistent with the Hague Regulations" (33).

19. Benvenisti, *International Law,* 7. See also Ando, *Surrender,* chap. 4.

20. Michael W. Doyle, *The Question of Intervention: John Stuart Mill and the Responsibility to Protect* (New Haven, CT: Yale University Press, 2015), 150–151.

21. John W. Dower, *Cultures of War: Pearl Harbor / Hiroshima / 9–11 / Iraq* (New York: Norton, 2010), 364.

22. David H. Price, *Anthropological Intelligence: The Deployment and Neglect of American Anthropology in the Second World War* (Durham, NC: Duke University Press, 2008), 172.

23. Ibid., 177.

24. See, for example, Douglas Lummis, "Ruth Benedict's Obituary for Japanese Culture," in *Reading Benedict / Reading Mead: Feminism, Race, and Imperial Visions,* ed. Dolores Janiewski and Lois W. Banner (Baltimore: Johns Hopkins University Press, 2004), 126–140.

25. Pauline Kent, "Japanese Perceptions of *The Chrysanthemum and the Sword,*" *Dialectical Anthropology* 24 (1999): 181–192.

26. Takeo Doi, *The Anatomy of Dependence* (Tokyo: Kodansha, 1973), 13. Other Japanese intellectuals at the time were more critical than Doi. See Adam Bronson, *One Hundred Million Philosophers: Science of Thought and the Culture of Democracy in Postwar Japan* (Honolulu: University of Hawai'i Press, 2016), 91–98.

27. Clifford Geertz, *The Interpretation of Cultures* (New York: Basic Books, 1977), 44.

28. Judith Schachter Modell, *Ruth Benedict: Patterns of a Life* (Philadelphia: University of Pennsylvania Press, 1983), 279.

29. Ruth Benedict, *The Chrysanthemum and the Sword* (Cambridge, MA: Houghton Mifflin, 1946), 1.

30. Clifford Geertz, *Works and Lives: The Anthropologist as Author* (Stanford, CA: Stanford University Press, 1988), 120.

31. Takami Kuwayama, *Native Anthropology: The Japanese Challenge to Western Academic Hegemony* (Melbourne: Trans Pacific Press, 2004), 88.

32. Benedict, *Chrysanthemum,* 253–254. See also Jennifer Robertson, ed., *A Companion to the Anthropology of Japan* (Malden, MA: Blackwell Publishing, 2005), 6.

33. Benedict, *Chrysanthemum,* 43.

34. Ibid., 45.

35. Kuwayama, *Native Anthropology,* 104.

36. Benedict, *Chrysanthemum,* 98.

37. Ibid., 222–224.

38. In this guilt-shame dichotomy, critics of Benedict perceive a strong undertone of cultural superiority: "Shame appears as less developed, less autonomous, less evolved than guilt. Shame is felt always in relation to the Other, unlike guilt with its sturdy, consistent standards of morality (guilt is confessable). Shame is more primitive. Shame allows the most heinous deeds. . . . In understanding Japanese shame, Americans could understand well the superiority of their guilt culture; through their immense labor of reconstruction demanded by the postwar Occupation, the occupiers could help Japan comprehend the shame of its shame culture, ensuring its future sublation as an Americanized ally with imported democratic values, mass cultural pleasures and the proprieties of guilt." Marilyn Ivy, "Benedict's Shame," *Cabinet Magazine*, no. 31 (Fall 2008), 3, http://cabinetmagazine.org/issues/31/ivy.php.

39. Benedict, *Chrysanthemum*, 294.

40. Modell, *Ruth Benedict*, 285.

41. Benedict, *Chrysanthemum*, 295–296.

42. Ivy, "Benedict's Shame," 3.

43. Louis Hartz, *The Liberal Tradition in America: An Interpretation of American Political Thought Since the Revolution* (New York: Harcourt Brace, 1953); Gordon S. Wood, *The Idea of America: Reflections on the Birth of the United States* (New York: Penguin, 2011).

44. Michael Schaller, *Douglas MacArthur: The Far Eastern General* (New York: Oxford University Press, 1989).

45. Ibid., 8. See also Douglas MacArthur, *Reminiscences* (New York: McGraw-Hill, 1964), 32.

46. Jeremi Suri, *Liberty's Surest Guardian: American Nation-Building from the Founders to Obama* (New York: Free Press, 2011).

47. John Milton Cooper, Jr., *Woodrow Wilson: A Biography* (New York: Knopf, 2009), 75–76.

48. Woodrow Wilson, "The Ideals of America," *The Atlantic*, December 1902.

49. Quoted in John W. Dower, *Embracing Defeat: Japan in the Wake of World War II* (New York: Norton, 1999), 550.

50. MacArthur, *Reminiscences*, 281–282.

51. Douglas MacArthur, "A Fourth of July Message," *Life Magazine*, July 7, 1947.

52. Quoted in Richard H. Rovere and Arthur Schlesinger, Jr., *General MacArthur and President Truman: The Struggle for Control of American Foreign Policy*, 2nd ed. (New Brunswick, NJ: Transaction Publishers, 1992), 93.

53. Michael Howard, *War and the Liberal Conscience* (London: Temple Smith, 1978), 31. See also Gordon S. Wood, *Revolutionary Characters: What Made the Founders Different* (New York: Penguin Books, 2006), 166–169.

54. MacArthur, *Reminiscences*, 275.

55. Richard B. Finn, *Winners in Peace: MacArthur, Yoshida, and Postwar Japan* (Berkeley: University of California Press, 1992), 83.

56. John Gunther, *The Riddle of MacArthur: Japan, Korea, and the Far East* (New York: Harper, 1951), 149.

57. See Gary Jonathan Bass, *Stay the Hand of Vengeance: The Politics of War Crimes Tribunals* (Princeton, NJ: Princeton University Press, 2000), 147–205.

58. John O. Haley, review of *The Tokyo International Military Tribunal: A Reappraisal,* by Neil Boister and Robert Cryer, and *The Tokyo War Crimes Trial: The Pursuit of Justice in the Wake of World War II,* by Yuma Totani, *Journal of Japanese Studies* 35, no. 2 (Summer 2009): 445–451.

59. Elizabeth Gray Vining, *Windows for the Crown Prince* (Philadelphia: Lippincot, Williams, and Wilkins, 1952), 169.

60. Dower, *Embracing Defeat,* 453.

61. Ibid., 471–473.

62. B. V. A. Röling and Antonio Cassese, *The Tokyo Trial and Beyond: Reflections of a Peace Monger* (Cambridge, UK: Polity Press, 1993).

63. See the summary exploration of Japanese scholarship on the controversial nature of the war crimes trials in Higurashi Yoshinobu, "Tōkyō saiban," in *Rekishi mondai handobukku,* ed. Tōgō Kazuhiko and Hatano Sumio (Tokyo: Iwanami, 2015), 26–35.

64. See the discussion in Yuma Totani, *The Tokyo War Crimes Trial: The Pursuit of Justice in the Wake of World War II* (Cambridge, MA: Harvard University Asia Center, 2008), which offers a somewhat positive interpretation by arguing that it contributed to the development of an international justice system.

65. Herbert Bix quoted in Takemae Eiji, *The Allied Occupation of Japan* (New York: Continuum, 2003), 473.

66. MacArthur's own thinking was influenced by one of his aides in the Pacific, Brigadier General Bonner Fellers, who accompanied him to Tokyo. Several days after MacArthur's first meeting with the emperor, Fellers wrote a memorandum for MacArthur in which he said, "If the Emperor were tried for war crimes the governmental structure would collapse and a general rising would be inevitable. The people will uncomplainingly stand any other humiliation. Although they are disarmed, there would be chaos and bloodshed. It would necessitate a large expeditionary force with many thousands of public officials. The period of occupation would be prolonged and we would have alienated the Japanese." Nakamura Masanori, *The Japanese Monarchy: Ambassador Joseph Grew and the Making of the "Symbol Emperor System," 1931–1991* (Armonk, NY: M. E. Sharpe, 1992), 89–90.

67. MacArthur, *Reminiscences,* 288.

68. Ibid.

69. When General Tōjō inadvertently referred to the emperor in a way that seemed to implicate him, SCAP saw to it that he changed his testimony.

70. U.S. Department of State, *Foreign Relations of the United States, 1946* (Washington, DC: Government Printing Office, 1971), 8:395–396.

71. Yuma Totani, *The Tokyo War Crimes Trial*, 43–62.

72. William Marotti, *Money, Trains, and Guillotines: Art and Revolution in 1960s Japan* (Durham, NC: Duke University Press, 2013), 40–42.

73. Wood, *The Idea of America*, 173–178.

74. Hellegers, *We, the Japanese People*, 1:242; Ray A. Moore and Donald L. Robinson, *Partners for Democracy: Crafting the New Japanese State under MacArthur* (New York: Oxford University Press, 2002), 86.

75. Dower, *Embracing Defeat*, 407; Monica Braw, *The Atomic Bomb Suppressed: American Censorship in Occupied Japan* (Armonk, NY: M. E. Sharpe, 1991), 59; Takemae Eiji, *Allied Occupation*, 386–387. See also Katō Tetusrō, "Beikoku no senryō seisaku—kenetsu to senden," in *Rekishi mondai handobukku*, ed. Tōgō Kazuhiko and Hatano Sumio (Tokyo: Iwanami, 2015), 161–171.

76. Jay Rubin, "From Wholesomeness to Decadence: The Censorship of Literature under the Allied Occupation," *Journal of Japanese Studies* 11, no. 1 (Winter 1985): 97.

77. Moore and Robinson, *Partners for Democracy*, 94–95.

78. Summary notes of Whitney's meeting with the Government Section group record that Whitney intended to convince Japanese leaders "that the only possibility of retaining the Emperor and the remnants of their own power is by acceptance and approval of a Constitution that will force a decisive swing to the left. General Whitney hopes to reach this decision by persuasive argument; if this is not possible, General MacArthur has empowered him to use not merely the threat of force, but force itself." See Takayanagi Kenzō, Ohtomo Ichirō, and Tanaka Hideo, eds., *Nihonkoku kempō seitei no katei* (Tokyo: Yuhikaku, 1972), 1:100–106.

79. Dower, *Embracing Defeat*, 223.

80. Courtney Whitney, *MacArthur: His Rendezvous with History* (New York: Knopf, 1956), 250–251.

81. Yoshikuni Igarashi, *Bodies of Memory: Narratives of War in Postwar Japanese Culture, 1945–1970* (Princeton, NJ: Princeton University Press, 2000), 34–35.

82. Moore and Robinson, *Partners for Democracy*, 109.

83. Although there were Japanese liberals who proposed draft constitutions that the Americans took notice of, the fact remains that this was overwhelmingly a product of foreign authorship. It would have been difficult for an informed Japanese people to believe that this was anything but a SCAP-inspired document since the language was awkward and filled with concepts that were unmistakably alien. As two authorities write, "Whitney and his staff intimidated Japanese officials in secret negotiations, forcing them to accept most of the SCAP draft as a Japanese product." Moore and Robinson, *Partners for Democracy*, 331. See also Charles L. Kades, "The American Role in Revising Japan's Imperial Constitution," *Political Science Quarterly* 104, no. 2 (Summer 1989): 227.

84. See Kyoko Inoue, *MacArthur's Japanese Constitution: A Linguistic and Cultural Study of Its Making* (Chicago: University of Chicago Press, 1991).

85. MacArthur, *Reminiscences*, 301.

86. Akira Iriye, *The New Cambridge History of American Foreign Relations: The Globalizing of America, 1913–1945* (Cambridge: Cambridge University Press, 2013), 214.

87. Moore and Robinson, *Partners for Democracy*, 94–95.

88. Masumi Junnosuke, *Postwar Politics in Japan, 1945–1955,* trans. Lonny E. Carlile (Berkeley, CA: Institute of East Asian Studies, 1985), 61–66.

89. Nakamura Masanori, *The Japanese Monarchy*, 108.

90. There are many unresolved questions regarding Ashida's role in regard to Article 9. See John Swenson-Wright, *Unequal Allies? United States Security and Alliance Policy toward Japan, 1945–1960* (Stanford, CA: Stanford University Press, 2005), 261n7.

91. Kades later wrote that "I believed it was unrealistic to ban a nation from exercising its inherent right of self-preservation." See Kades, "The American Role," 236.

92. Susan J. Pharr, "The Politics of Women's Rights," in *Democratizing Japan: The Allied Occupation*, ed. Robert E. Ward and Sakamoto Yoshikazu (Honolulu: University of Hawai'i Press, 1987), 226.

93. Sirota was despondent: "They started to cut out the women's social welfare rights one by one. With each cut I thought they were adding to the misery of Japanese women. Such was my distress, in fact, I finally burst into tears. That Col. Kades, whom I respected so much, should fail to accept my point of view was a major disappointment. While I wept he patted me on the back, but he remained adamant." Beate Sirota Gordon, *The Only Woman in the Room* (Tokyo: Kodansha, 1997), 116.

94. Inoue, *MacArthur's Japanese Constitution*, 33–35.

95. Moore and Robinson, *Partners for Democracy*, 329.

96. Robert Ekladh, *The Great American Mission: Modernization and the Construction of an American World Order* (Princeton, NJ: Princeton University Press, 2010).

97. "Two Billion Dollar Failure in Japan: An Economic Report," *Fortune* 39, no. 4 (April 1949): 204.

98. Rovere and Schlesinger, *General MacArthur and President Truman*, 88.

99. R. P. Dore, *Land Reform in Japan* (New York: Oxford University Press, 1959), 132.

100. Ibid., 149.

101. "It was the restructuring of Japan that formed the main model for future American initiatives outside Europe." Odd Arne Westad, *The Global Cold War: Third World Interventions and the Making of Our Times* (Cambridge: Cambridge University Press, 2007), 24.

102. Dower, *Embracing Defeat*, 71.

103. Quoted in Roger Buckley, *US-Japan Alliance Diplomacy, 1945–1990* (Cambridge: Cambridge University Press, 1992), 4.

104. *In the Beginning, Woman Was the Sun: The Autobiography of a Japanese Feminist—Hiratsuka Raichō,* trans. Teruko Craig (New York: Columbia University Press, 2006), 312–313. As Jeremi Suri writes, "Nation building can work only when the people own it. . . . Too often Americans [acting abroad] have made authority the starting, and therefore, restricting, point for beginning reforms abroad. . . . The problem is . . . the desire to achieve a quick, rigid, and final solution to the problems of disorder," Suri, *Liberty's Surest Guardian,* 41–42.

105. John Whitney Hall, *Government and Local Power in Japan, 500 to 1700: A Study Based on Bizen Province* (Princeton, NJ: Princeton University Press, 1966), 11–13.

106. Marotti, *Money, Trains, and Guillotines,* 49.

107. Dower, *Cultures of War,* 240.

108. J. W. Dower, "Reform and Reconsolidation," in *Japan Examined: Perspectives on Modern Japanese History,* ed. Harry Wray and Hilary Conroy (Honolulu: University of Hawai'i Press, 1983), 345.

5. The Subordination of Japan

1. John Lewis Gaddis, *The United States and the Origins of the Cold War, 1941–1947* (New York: Columbia University Press, 1972), 30–31.

2. John Gerard Ruggie, *Winning the Peace: America and World Order in the New Era* (New York: Columbia University Press, 1996), 29–39.

3. John Lewis Gaddis, quoted in Robert A. Pollard, *Economic Security and the Origins of the Cold War, 1945–1950* (New York: Columbia University Press, 1985), 10.

4. Robert Dallek, *The Lost Peace: Leadership in a Time of Horror and Hope, 1945–1953* (New York: Harper Collins, 2010), 59.

5. Robert Dallek, *Franklin D. Roosevelt and American Foreign Policy, 1932–1945* (New York: Oxford University Press, 1979), 523–527. See also John Lewis Gaddis, *The Long Peace: Inquiries into the History of the Cold War* (New York: Oxford University Press, 1987), 30.

6. Aaron L. Friedberg, *In the Shadow of the Garrison State: America's Anti-Statism and Its Cold War Grand Strategy* (Princeton, NJ: Princeton University Press 2000), 208.

7. George F. Kennan, "The Sources of Soviet Conduct," *Foreign Affairs* 25 (July 1947): 566–582.

8. George F. Kennan, *The Kennan Diaries,* ed. Frank Costigliola (New York: Norton, 2014), 211.

9. Quoted in Gaddis, *Long Peace,* 58.

10. Ibid.

11. Kennan and the Policy Planning Staff minutes are quoted in Melvyn P. Leffler, *A Preponderance of Power: National Security, the Truman Administration, and the Cold War* (Stanford, CA: Stanford University Press, 1992), 253–255.

12. Robert D. Eldridge, *The Origins of the Bilateral Okinawa Problem: Okinawa in Postwar U.S.-Japan Relations, 1945–1952* (New York: Garland, 2001), 187. See also Leffler, *A Preponderance of Power*, 253–255.

13. Michael Schaller, *The American Occupation of Japan: The Origins of the Cold War in Asia* (New York: Oxford University Press, 1985), 125.

14. George F. Kennan, *Memoirs: 1925–1950* (Boston: Little, Brown, 1967), 391.

15. Ibid.

16. John W. Dower, *Embracing Defeat: Japan in the Wake of World War II* (New York: Norton, 1999), 544, 647n42.

17. Schaller, *American Occupation*, 179.

18. Nicholas Evans Sarantakes, *Keystone: The American Occupation of Okinawa and U.S.-Japanese Relations* (College Station: Texas A&M Press, 2000), 43.

19. George F. Kennan, *Memoirs: 1950–1963* (Boston: Little, Brown, 1972), 2:53. The document was dated August 11, 1950.

20. John W. Dower, "A Rejoinder," *Pacific Historical Review* 57, no. 2 (May 1988): 207.

21. W. D. Miscamble, *George F. Kennan and the Making of American Foreign Policy, 1947–1950* (Princeton, NJ: Princeton University Press, 1992), 273.

22. Ibid., 271. See also Leffler, *A Preponderance of Power*, 335.

23. Alger Hiss, a high-ranking State Department official charged with spying for the Soviet Union, was found guilty of perjury in January.

24. Ernest R. May, *American Cold War Strategy: Interpreting NSC 68* (Boston: Bedford / St. Martin's, 1993), vii.

25. Leffler, *A Preponderance of Power*, 356.

26. Miscamble, *George F. Kennan and the Making of American Foreign Policy*, 273.

27. Richard H. Immerman, *John Foster Dulles: Piety, Pragmatism, and Power in U.S. Foreign Policy* (Wilmington, DE: Scholarly Resources, 1999), 17–18.

28. Ibid., 20–23.

29. Richard B. Finn, *Winners in Peace: MacArthur, Yoshida, and Postwar Japan* (Berkeley: University of California Press, 1992), 270–272.

30. John W. Dower, *Japan in War and Peace: Selected Essays* (New York: New Press, 1993), 187–189.

31. Quoted in Michael Schaller, *Altered States: The United States and Japan Since the Occupation* (New York: Oxford University Press, 1997), 27.

32. David W. Mabon, "Elusive Agreements: The Pacific Pact Proposals of 1949–1951," *Pacific Historical Review* 57, no. 2 (May 1988): 147–177.

33. Ronald W. Pruessen, *John Foster Dulles: The Road to Power* (New York: Free Press, 1982), 480.

34. John W. Dower, *Empire and Aftermath: Yoshida Shigeru and the Japanese Experience, 1878–1954* (Cambridge, MA: Council on East Asian Studies, Harvard University, 1978), 439.

35. Kōsaka Masataka, *Saishō Yoshida Shigeru* (Tokyo: Chūōkōronsha, 1968), 5.

36. Leffler, *A Preponderance of Power*, 393.

37. Yonosuke Nagai, "U.S.-Japan Relations in the Global Context" (unpublished paper, 1983).

38. William J. Sebald, *With MacArthur in Japan: A Personal History of the Occupation* (New York: W. W. Norton, 1965), 257–258; Dower, *Empire and Aftermath*, 383.

39. Igarashi Takeshi, "Sengo Nihon 'gaikō jōsei' no keisei," *Kokka gakkai zasshi*, nos. 5–8 (1984): 486.

40. Chihiro Hosoya, "Japan's Response to U.S. Policy on the Japanese Peace Treaty," *Hitotsubashi Journal of Law and Politics* 10 (1981): 18.

41. Robert D. Eldridge, *Secret Talks between Tokyo and Washington: The Memoirs of Miyazawa Kiichi, 1949–1954* (Lanham, MD: Rowman & Littlefield, 2007), 92–93.

42. Miyazawa Kiichi, *Tokyo-Washington no mitsudan* (Tokyo: Jitsugyō no Nihonsha, 1956), 160.

43. John Swenson-Wright, *Unequal Allies? United States Security and Alliance Policy toward Japan, 1945–1960* (Stanford, CA: Stanford University Press, 2005), 62–63.

44. Ibid., 75.

45. Dulles wanted South Korea representation in order to begin building a new relationship between the former colonists and their occupier, but Yoshida vehemently opposed it, not wanting to give Sygman Rhee claim on any post-treaty gains. Dulles backed down, and, as a consequence, Koreans resident in Japan were soon deprived of the prospect of citizenship. Takemae Eiji, *The Allied Occupation of Japan* (New York: Continuum, 2003) 510. The Japanese government expressed its objection to South Korea's attendance on the grounds that "this country, not having been in a state of war or belligerency with Japan, cannot be considered an Allied Power." Yoshida told Dulles that he wanted to repatriate Koreans in Japan because most of them were communists and caused social disruption. See Hirofumi Hayashi, "The Japanese Military 'Comfort Women' Issue and the San Francisco System," in *The San Francisco System and Its Legacies: Continuation, Transformation, and Historical Reconciliation in the Asia-Pacific*, ed. Kimie Hara (London: Routledge, 2015), 165–166.

46. Leffler, *A Preponderance of Power*, 393.

47. Swenson-Wright, *Unequal Allies?*, 63.

48. Ibid., 278n.

49. Ibid., 99.

50. Article 11 reads: "Japan accepts the judgments of the International Military Tribunal for the Far East and of other Allied War Crimes Courts both

within and outside Japan, and will carry out the sentences imposed thereby upon Japanese nationals imprisoned in Japan. The power to grant clemency, to reduce sentences and to parole with respect to such prisoners may not be exercised except on the decision of the Government or Governments which imposed the sentence in each instance, and on recommendation of Japan. In the case of persons sentenced by the International Military Tribunal for the Far East, such power may not be exercised except on the decision of a majority of the Governments represented on the Tribunal, and on the recommendation of Japan."

51. In light of the emperor's new constitutional status, his involvement in policymaking was striking, as was his apparent willingness to sacrifice the sovereignty of the Okinawans. See Kenneth J. Ruoff, *The People's Emperor: Democracy and the Japanese Monarchy, 1945–1995* (Cambridge, MA: Harvard University Press, 2001), 96–97.

52. See the memorandum of conversation between Dulles and Shigemitsu, US Department of State, *Foreign Relations of the United States, 1955–1957, Japan,* vol. 23, pt. 1 (Washington, DC: Government Printing Office, 1991), 202–204. The complex Japanese-Soviet negotiations in 1955–1956 are the subject of an extensive literature. See inter alia Tsuyoshi Hasegawa, *The Northern Territories Dispute and Russo-Japanese Relations,* 2 vols. (Berkeley: University of California Press 1998); Kimie Hara, *Cold War Frontiers in the Asia-Pacific: Divided Territories in the San Francisco System* (London: Routledge, 2007); Schaller, *Altered States,* 114–123; Marc Gallicchio, "The Kuriles Controversy: U.S. Diplomacy in the Soviet-Japan Border Dispute, 1941–1956," *Pacific Historical Review* 60, no. 1 (February 1991): 69–101; Swenson-Wright, *Unequal Allies?,* 212–222; and Donald C. Hellmann, *Japanese Foreign Policy and Domestic Politics: The Peace Agreement with the Soviet Union* (Berkeley: University of California Press, 1969).

53. James Chace, *Acheson: The Secretary of State Who Created the American World* (New York: Simon & Schuster, 1998), 321.

54. Ibid., 319–320.

55. Roger Buckley, *US-Japan Alliance Diplomacy, 1945–1990* (Cambridge: Cambridge University Press, 1992), 78.

56. Howard B. Schonberger, *Aftermath of War: Americans and the Remaking of Japan, 1945–1952* (Kent, Ohio: Kent State University Press, 1989), 265.

57. Ibid., 267; Takemae, *Allied Occupation,* 506.

58. Victor Cha, *Powerplay: The Origins of the American Alliance System in Asia* (Princeton, NJ: Princeton University Press, 2016), 183–184. Also Mabon, "Elusive Agreements," 164.

59. Victor Cha, "Powerplay: Origins of the U.S. Alliance System in Asia," *International Security* 34, no. 3 (Winter 2009 / 10): 159.

60. G. John Ikenberry, *Liberal Leviathan: The Origins, Crisis, and Transformation of the American World Order* (Princeton: Princeton University Press, 2011), 215–219.

61. Fred Greene, *U.S. Policy and the Security of Asia* (New York: McGraw-Hill, 1968), 74.

62. See Ōtake Hideo, *Adenaua—to Yoshida Shigeru* (Tokyo: Chūō kōronsha, 1986).

63. John Welfield, *An Empire in Eclipse* (London: Athlone Press, 1988), 97–98.

64. Richard J. Samuels, *"Rich Nation, Strong Army": National Security and the Technological Transformation of Japan* (Ithaca, NY: Cornell University Press, 1994), chap. 5.

65. Samuels records that by resisting the temptation to nurture a large arms industry, Yoshida "played a brilliant game." Ibid., 52.

66. Welfield, *Empire in Eclipse,* 107.

67. See Richard J. Samuels, "Politics, Security Policy, and Japan's Cabinet Legislation Bureau: Who Elected These Guys Anyway?" (JPRI Working Paper No. 99, March 2004).

68. Hiroshi Nara, ed., *Yoshida Shigeru: Last Meiji Man* (Lanham, MD: Rowman & Littlefield, 2007), 221–222.

69. See US Department of State, *Foreign Relations of the United States, 1950, East Asia and the Pacific,* vol. 6 (Washington, DC: Government Printing Office, 1976), 1166–1167.

70. Iokibe Makoto, "The Japan-U.S. Alliance as a Maritime Alliance," in Ito Kenichi et al., *Japan's Grand Strategy for the 21st Century: From an Insular Nation to a Maritime Nation,* Japan Forum on International Relations, 2000, http://www.jfir.or.jp/e/special_study/seminar2/conversation.htm.

71. Swenson-Wright, *Unequal Allies?,* 200.

72. Takeo Doi, *The Anatomy of Dependence* (Tokyo: Kodansha, 1973).

73. See Akira Iriye, "Japan Returns to the World: Yoshida Shigeru and His Legacy," in *The Diplomats: 1939–1979,* ed. Gordon Craig (Princeton, NJ: Princeton University Press, 1994), 322.

74. Quoted in Okazaki Hisahiko, ed., *Rekishi no kyōkun* (Tokyo: PHP kenkyūjō, 2005), 162–163.

75. Yoshihide Soeya, *Japan's Economic Diplomacy with China, 1945–1978* (Oxford: Clarendon Press, 1998), 21.

76. Quoted in Schaller, *Altered States,* 71.

77. Quoted in Tetsuya Kataoka, *Price of a Constitution: The Origins of Japan's Postwar Politics* (New York: Crane Russak, 1991), 122–123.

78. Quoted in Schonberger, *Aftermath of War,* 266–268.

79. In his review of patterns of alliances from 1815 to 1945, Paul Schroeder found that many did not function solely for purposes of aggregated power, but rather served as tools for control and management of another country. Paul W. Schroeder, "Alliances, 1815–1945: Weapons of Power and Tools of Management," in *Historical Dimension of National Security Problems,* ed. Klaus Knorr (Lawrence: University Press of Kansas, 1976), 227. See also Jeremy Pressman, *Warring Friends: Alliance Restraint in International Politics* (Ithaca, NY: Cornell University Press, 2008).

80. George Ball, "We Are Playing a Dangerous Game with Japan," *New York Times Magazine,* June 25, 1972.

81. Correspondent Fred Hiatt, reported comments of Major General Henry C. Stackpole III in the *Washington Post,* March 27, 1990.

82. Iokibe Makoto, "The Japan-U.S. Alliance as a Maritime Alliance."

83. Quoted in Kent E. Calder, *Pacific Alliance: Reviving U.S. Japan Relations* (New Haven, CT: Yale University Press, 2009), 33.

6. For the Soul of Japan

1. See the essay by Justin Jesty, "Tokyo 1960: Days of Rage & Grief: Hamaya Hiroshi's Photos of the Anti-Security-Treaty Protests," *Asia-Pacific Journal/ Japan Focus* 13, issue 9, no. 2 (March 2, 2015), https://apjjf.org/2015/13/8 /Justin-Jesty/4291.html.

2. Ernest May, ed., *American Cold War Strategy: Interpreting NSC 68* (Boston: Bedford / St. Martin's, 1993), 25–26; also see Melvyn P. Leffler, *A Preponderance of Power: National Security, the Truman Administration, and the Cold War* (Stanford, CA: Stanford University Press, 1992), 355.

3. See John W. Dower, *The Violent American Century: War and Terror Since World War II* (Chicago: Haymarket Books, 2017), 100.

4. Daikichi Irokawa, *The Age of Hirohito: In Search of Modern Japan* (New York: Free Press, 1995), 6, 26–27.

5. Junji Banno and Jirō Yamaguchi, *The Abe Experiment and the Future of Japan: Don't Repeat History* (Kent, UK: Renaissance Books, 2016), 40.

6. Komiya Ryūtarō, "Ureubeki migi senkai," *Gendai keizai* 6 (Spring 1979): 71–84.

7. The statement was published in the December 1950 issue of *Sekai.* An abbreviated translation of this statement is found in the first issue of the *Journal of Social and Political Ideas in Japan* (April 1963). See also the discussion in John Dower, "Peace and Democracy in Two Systems," in *Postwar Japan as History,* ed. Andrew Gordon (Berkeley: University of California Press, 1993), 3–33.

8. John W. Dower, *Embracing Defeat: Japan in the Wake of World War II* (New York: Norton, 1999), 487–490. See also Richard H. Minear, ed., *War and Conscience in Japan* (Lanham, MD: Rowman and Littlefield, 2011); and Andrew E. Barshay, *State and Intellectual in Imperial Japan: The Public Man in Crisis* (Berkeley: University of California Press, 1988).

9. Karube Tadashi, *Maruyama Masao and the Fate of Liberalism in Twentieth-Century Japan* (Tokyo: International House of Japan, 2008), 132.

10. Maruyama Masao, *Senchū to sengo no aida* (Tokyo: Misuzu shobō, 1976), 305. See also Masao Maruyama, "Theory and Psychology of Ultra-Nationalism," in *Thought and Behavior in Modern Japanese Politics,* ed. Ivan Morris (New York: Oxford University Press, 1963).

11. Karube, *Maruyama Masao,* 103.

12. Quoted in Andrew E. Barshay, "Imagining Democracy in Postwar Japan: Reflections on Maruyama Masao and Modernism," *Journal of Japanese Studies* 18, no. 2 (1992): 384.

13. J. Victor Koschmann, "The Debate on Subjectivity in Postwar Japan," *Pacific Affairs* 54, no. 4 (1981): 628.

14. Maruyama, "Theory and Psychology of Ultra-Nationalism," 152.

15. Michael Schaller, *Altered States: The United States and Japan Since the Occupation* (New York: Oxford University Press, 1997), 63.

16. Bundy, *Danger and Survival,* 215.

17. Quoted in Joel H. Rosenthal, *Righteous Realists: Political Realism, Responsible Power, and American Culture in the Nuclear Age* (Baton Rouge: Louisiana State University Press, 1991), 102. Emphasis was Dulles's.

18. McGeorge Bundy, *Danger and Survival: Choices about the Bomb in the First Fifty Years* (New York: Vintage, 1990), 256.

19. Aaron L. Friedberg, *In the Shadow of the Garrison State: America's Anti-Statism and Its Cold War Grand Strategy* (Princeton, NJ: Princeton University Press 2000), 71.

20. Walter LaFeber, *The Clash: A History of U.S.-Japanese Relations* (New York: Norton, 1997), 316.

21. Barton C. Hacker, *Elements of Controversy: The Atomic Energy Commission and Radiation Safety in Nuclear Weapons Testing, 1947–1974* (Berkeley: University of California Press, 1994), 140.

22. William Tsutsui, *Godzilla on My Mind: Fifty Years of the King of Monsters* (New York: Palgrave MacMillan, 2004), 19.

23. Roger Dingman, "Alliance in Crisis: The Lucky Dragon Incident and Japanese-American Relations," in *The Great Powers in East Asia, 1953–1960,* ed. Warren I. Cohen and Akira Iriye (New York: Columbia University Press, 1990), 195. See also Matthew Jones, *After Hiroshima: The United States, Race and Nuclear Weapons in Asia, 1945–1965* (Cambridge: Cambridge University Press, 2010), 187–192.

24. John Swenson-Wright, *Unequal Allies? United States Security and Alliance Policy toward Japan, 1945–1960* (Stanford, CA: Stanford University Press, 2005), 199.

25. John M. Allison, *Ambassador from the Prairie—or Allison Wonderland* (Boston: Houghton Mifflin, 1973), 265.

26. John W. Dower, *The Violent American Century: War and Terror Since World War II* (Chicago: Haymarket Books, 2017), 33.

27. Ralph E. Lapp, *The Voyage of the Lucky Dragon* (New York: Harper and Brothers, 1957), 99.

28. James J. Orr, *The Victim as Hero: Ideologies of Peace and National Identity in Postwar Japan* (Honolulu: University of Hawai'i Press, 2001), 52.

29. Ibid., 61–62.

30. Ibid., 50.

31. Mari Yamamoto, *Grassroots Pacifism in Post-War Japan: The Rebirth of a Nation* (London: Routledge, 2004), 158–170.

32. Orr, *The Victim as Hero,* 51.

33. Monica Braw, *The Atomic Bomb Suppressed: American Censorship in Occupied Japan* (Armonk, NY: M. E. Sharpe, 1991), 140.

34. Orr, *The Victim as Hero,* 38–39.

35. Herbert Passin, "Japan and the H-Bomb," *Bulletin of the Atomic Scientists* 11, no. 8 (October 1955), 289–292.

36. Orr, *The Victim as Hero,* 227n93.

37. Ibid., 59.

38. John W. Dower, "The Bombed: Hiroshimas and Nagasakis in Japanese Memory," in *Hiroshima in History and Memory,* ed. Michael J. Hogan (Cambridge: Cambridge University Press, 1996), 117.

39. George F. Kennan, *The Cloud of Danger: Current Realities of American Foreign Policy* (Boston: Little, Brown, 1977), 109.

40. John Lewis Gaddis, *The Cold War: A New History* (New York: Penguin, 2005), 161–165.

41. Matthew Jones, *After Hiroshima: The United States, Race and Nuclear Weapons in Asia, 1945–1965* (Cambridge: Cambridge University Press, 2010), 220–221.

42. Ibid., 229.

43. Ibid., 223.

44. Kent E. Calder, *Pacific Alliance: Reviving U.S.-Japan Relations* (New Haven, CT: Yale University Press, 2009), 244n21.

45. Thomas R. H. Havens, *Fire across the Sea: The Vietnam War and Japan, 1965–1975* (Princeton, NJ: Princeton University Press, 1987), 85.

46. Swenson-Wright, *Unequal Allies?,* 229.

47. Schaller, *Altered States,* 123.

48. See Richard J. Samuels, *Machiavelli's Children: Leaders and Their Legacies in Italy and Japan* (Ithaca, NY: Cornell University Press, 2003), 226.

49. Kishi was adopted by his uncle and took his uncle's family name.

50. Schaller, *Altered States,* 136. See also LaFeber, *The Clash,* 318.

51. Schaller, *Altered States,* 135ff.

52. Walter LaFeber, *The Clash: A History of U.S.-Japanese Relations* (New York: Norton, 1997), 326.

53. Schaller, *Altered States,* 136.

54. Professor Kitaoka writes that "it has been revealed that both ruling and opposition parties were receiving secret financial assistance from the USA, the Soviet Union or other countries." Shinichi Kitaoka, "The Secret Japan-US Security Pacts: Background and Disclosure," *Asia-Pacific Review* 17, no. 2 (2010): 14.

55. Jennifer M. Miller, "Fractured Alliance: Anti-Base Protests and Postwar U.S.-Japanese Relations," *Diplomatic History* 38, no. 5 (2014): 953–986.

56. *Asahi shinbun,* April 9, 2013.

57. John O. Haley, "Waging War: Japan's Constitutional Constraints" (Washington University School of Law Faculty Working Paper Series, June 26, 2006).

58. Shigenori Matsui, *The Constitution of Japan: A Contextual Analysis* (Oxford, UK: Hart Publishing, 2011), 243.

59. Swenson-Wright, *Unequal Allies?*, 143.

60. See Sakamoto Kazuya, "Japanese Diplomacy in the 1950s," in *The Diplomatic History of Postwar Japan*, ed. Iokibe Makoto (London: Routledge, 2011), 75.

61. Kitaoka, "The Secret Japan-US Security Pacts," 10–25. As Schaller writes, "At the insistence of the Defense Department, [Ambassador] MacArthur was authorized to reach a secret understanding with Kishi that allowed American naval vessels and aircraft 'transiting' Japan to carry nuclear weapons. (Nuclear weapons on Okinawa were unaffected.) These and related secret agreements resulted in bombs and components occasionally being stored on barges located near American naval bases. The Japanese government would assert that since Washington had never requested permission to introduce nuclear weapons, and since Tokyo granted no permission, no nuclear weapons were in Japan." *Altered States*, 141.

62. Quoted in George R. Packard III, *Protest in Tokyo: The Security Treaty Crisis of 1960* (Princeton, NJ: Princeton University Press, 1966), 230–231.

63. Wesley Sasaki-Uemura, *Organizing the Spontaneous: Citizen Protest in Postwar Japan* (Honolulu: University of Hawai'i Press, 2001), 16–17.

64. The point is made well in Sasaki-Uemura, *Organizing the Spontaneous*.

65. Rikki Kersten, *Democracy in Postwar Japan: Maruyama Masao and the Search for Autonomy* (London: Routledge, 1996), 220.

66. Yoshikuni Igarashi, *Bodies of Memory: Narratives of War in Postwar Japanese Culture, 1945–1970* (Princeton, NJ: Princeton University Press, 2000), 142.

67. John Stuart Mill wrote of such circumstances, "When a people has had the misfortune to be ruled by a government under which the feelings and the virtues needful for maintaining freedom could not develop themselves, it is during an arduous struggle to become free by their own efforts that these feelings and virtues have the best chance of springing up. Men become attached to that which they have long fought for and made sacrifices for, they learn to appreciate that on which their thoughts have been much engaged." Michael W. Doyle, *The Question of Intervention: John Stuart Mill and the Responsibility to Protect* (New Haven, CT: Yale University Press, 2015), 224.

7. A Peculiar Alliance

1. G. John Ikenberry, *Liberal Leviathan: The Origins, Crisis, and Transformation of the American World Order* (Princeton, NJ: Princeton University Press, 2011), 161.

2. Geir Lundestad, "Empire by Invitation? The United States and Western Europe, 1945–1952," *Journal of Peace Research* 23, no. 3 (1986): 263–277.

3. Dan Kurzman, *Kishi and Japan: The Search for the Sun* (New York: Ivan Oblensky, 1960), 255–256.

4. Notable studies of the role of cultural relations drawing the elites of Japan and the United States together are Kent Calder, *Pacific Alliance: Reviving U.S.-Japan Relations* (New Haven, CT: Yale University Press, 2009); and Michael R. Auslin, *Pacific Cosmopolitans: A Cultural History of U.S.-Japan Relations* (Cambridge, MA: Harvard University Press, 2011).

5. Office of the Press Secretary, The White House, November 6, 2017.

6. See John W. Dower, foreword to *Soft Power and Its Perils: U.S. Cultural Policy in Early Postwar Japan and Permanent Dependency,* by Takeshi Matsuda (Washington, DC: Woodrow Wilson Center Press; Stanford, CA: Stanford University Press, 2007), xvi.

7. Noriko Aso, "Sumptuous Re-past: The 1964 Tokyo Olympics Art Festival," *Positions: East Asian Cultures Critique* 10, no. 1 (2002): 7–38.

8. Ellis S. Krauss and Robert J. Pekkanen, *The Rise and Fall of Japan's LDP: Political Party Organizations as Historical Institutions* (Ithaca, NY: Cornell University Press, 2011), 217.

9. Gordon Wood, *The Idea of America: Reflections on the Birth of the United States* (London: Penguin, 2011), 332.

10. Quoted in Christina Klein, *Cold War Orientalism: Asia in the Middlebrow Imagination, 1945–1961* (Berkeley: University of California Press, 2003), 127.

11. Ibid.

12. Ibid., 53–54.

13. Arthur M. Schlesinger, Jr., *The Vital Center: The Politics of Freedom* (Boston: Houghton Mifflin, 1949), 248, 235.

14. See John Lewis Gaddis, foreword to *Modernization as Ideology: American Social Science and "Nation Building" in the Kennedy Era,* by Michael E. Latham (Chapel Hill: University of North Carolina, 2000), ix.

15. Jeremi Suri, *Henry Kissinger and the American Century* (Cambridge, MA: Belknap Press of Harvard University Press, 2007), 93–103.

16. Kissinger, not yet an insider and ever sensitive to his Jewish immigrant background, soon soured on the New Frontier and resigned, remarking later that the patrician Bundy, the president's national security advisor, "tended to treat me with the combination of politeness and subconscious condescension that upper-class Bostonians reserve for people of, by New England standards, exotic backgrounds and excessively intense personal style." Suri, *Henry Kissinger,* 176.

17. George Packard, *Edwin O. Reischauer and the American Discovery of Japan* (New York: Columbia University Press, 2010), provides a good account of Reischauer's early life. For my review of this biography, see Kenneth B.

Pyle, "Japan and the United States: An Unnatural Intimacy," *Journal of Japanese Studies* 37, no. 2 (2011): 377–395.

18. T. Fujitani, "The Reischauer Memo: Mr. Moto, Hirohito, and Japanese American Soldiers," *Critical Asian Studies* 33, no. 3 (2001): 379–402.

19. Edwin O. Reischauer, *Wanted: An Asian Policy* (New York: Knopf, 1955), 192–213.

20. Edwin O. Reischauer, "The Broken Dialogue with Japan," *Foreign Affairs* 39, no. 1 (October 1960): 11–26.

21. See the reminiscence of Nathaniel Thayer, who was Reischauer's press attaché in the embassy: Akira Iriye and Robert A. Wampler, eds., *Partnership: The United States and Japan 1951–2001* (Tokyo: Kodansha, 2001), 71.

22. Packard, *Edwin O. Reischauer and the American Discovery of Japan,* 136.

23. Edwin O. Reischauer, *My Life between Japan and America* (New York: Harper & Row, 1986), 6–7, 88.

24. Ibid., 163.

25. Ibid., 196.

26. Quoted in Walter LaFeber, *The Clash: U.S.-Japan Relations throughout History* (New York: Norton, 1997), 335.

27. Reischauer, *My Life,* 196.

28. See Edwin O. Reischauer, "What Went Wrong?," in *Dilemmas of Growth in Prewar Japan,* ed. James W. Morley (Princeton, NJ: Princeton University Press, 1971), 489–510.

29. Packard, *Edwin O. Reischauer and the American Discovery of Japan,* 209.

30. Reischauer, *My Life,* 265.

31. See Nakashima Shingo, *Sengo Nihon no bōei seisaku: "Yoshida shisen" o meguru seiji, gaikō, gunji* (Tokyo: Keiōgijuku daigaku shuppankai, 2006), 182–184.

32. Fukunaga Fumio, *Ōhira Masayoshi* (Tokyo: Chūō kōronsha, 2008), 242–244. See also Tanaka Akihiko, *Anzen hoshō: Sengo 50nen no mosaku* [National security: Fifty years of postwar struggle] (Tokyo: Yomiuri shimbunsha, 1997), 284ff.

33. Packard, *Edwin O. Reischauer and the American Discovery of Japan,* 217.

34. George F. Kennan, *The Cloud of Danger: Current Realities of American Foreign Policy* (Boston: Little, Brown, 1977), 109.

35. Quoted in John Whittier Treat, *Writing Ground Zero: Japanese Literature and the Atomic Bomb* (Chicago: University of Chicago Press, 1995), 368–370.

36. Ibid., 369–371.

37. Thomas R. H. Havens, *Fire across the Sea: The Vietnam War and Japan, 1965–1975* (Princeton, NJ: Princeton University Press, 1987), 85.

38. Ibid., 133.

39. Ibid., 207.

40. Takafusa Nakamura, *The Postwar Japanese Economy: Its Development and Structure* (Tokyo: University of Tokyo Press, 1981), 80–81.

41. US Department of State, *Foreign Relations of the United States, 1964–1968,* vol. 29, part 2, *Japan* (Washington, DC: Government Printing Office, 2006), 56.

42. Ibid., 70. Also see *Japan Times,* May 25, 1998, 1.

43. Fukuda Takeo, the LDP's secretary general, raised a public storm of protest from the progressive parties and their supporters when he said on December 14, 1967, that "the majority of the Liberal Democrats see the need to outgrow the *'nuclear allergy.'"* Selig Harrison, ed., *Japan's Nuclear Future: The Plutonium Debate and East Asian Security* (Washington, DC: Carnegie Endowment, 1996), 7.

44. *Japan Times,* June 11, 2000, 1.

45. Harrison, *Japan's Nuclear Future,* 9.

46. Eric Heginbotham and Richard J. Samuels, "Mercantile Realism and Japanese Foreign Policy," *International Security* 22, no. 4 (Spring 1998)," 198. One of the authors of the secret study that Satō commissioned, the political scientist Nagai Yōnosuke, later explained the strategic stance that Japan was adopting. Building on the Yoshida Doctrine, strategic planning should concentrate on a limited but highly sophisticated defense posture, depending on advanced high technology such as lasers, precision-guided missiles, radar, and the like. Diplomacy should preserve the US-Japan alliance, but should the United States increase its pressure on Japan on economic and defense issues, Japan always had leverage in the form of a potential nationalist response: revision of the constitution, conversion of its industry and technology to military purposes, development of nuclear weapons, and so on. This threat gave Japan bargaining power to preserve its strategic concentration on developing its economic power. In this way, "the Yoshida Doctrine will be permanent (*eien de aru*)," Kenneth B. Pyle, *The Japanese Question: Power and Purpose in a New Era,* 2nd ed. (Washington, DC: AEI Press, 1996), 40–41.

47. See discussion in Robert Gilpin, *War and Change in World Politics* (Cambridge: Cambridge University Press, 1981), 215.

48. Harrison, *Japan's Nuclear Future,* 17–18.

49. Ibid., 11–13.

50. See the excellent essay by Richard J. Samuels and James L. Schoff, "Japan's Nuclear Hedge: Beyond Allergy and Breakout," in *Strategic Asia 2013–14: Asia in the Second Nuclear Age* (Seattle, Washington, and Washington, DC: National Bureau of Asian Research, 2013), 233–266.

51. See Pyle, *The Japanese Question,* 131–136.

52. Richard J. Samuels, "Politics, Security Policy, and Japan's Cabinet Legislation Bureau: Who Elected These Guys Anyway?" (JPRI Working Paper No. 99, March 2004), 3.

53. Ibid., 6–7.

54. Nishio Kanji, "Senryaku to shite mo 'sakoku' e no ishi," *Seiron,* January 1988.

55. Quoted in John Welfield, *An Empire in Eclipse* (London: Athlone Press, 1988), 251.

56. "Nori-okure gaikō no susume," *Chūō kōron,* March 1980.

57. Tahara Soichirō, "Ōkita gaikō nihyaku-gojūichi no hi," *Ushio,* October 1980.

58. Miyazawa Kiichi, quoted in Tahara Soichirō, "Soren wa kowai desu ka," *Bungei shunjū,* March 1980.

59. Amaya Naohiro, "Chōnin koku Nihon tedai no kurigoto," *Bungei shunjū,* March 1980; for a partial translation of this essay, see *Japan Echo* 7, no. 2 (1980): 53–62. See also Amaya Naohiro, "Nichi-Bei jidōsha mondai to chōnin kokka," *Bungei shunjū,* June 1980; and Amaya Naohiro, "Sopu nashonarizumu o haisu," *Bungei shunjū,* July 1981. Amaya's essays were collected in *Nihon chōnin kokka ron* (Tokyo: PHP bunko, 1989).

60. Iokibe Makoto, *Sengo Nihon gaikōshi* (Tokyo: Yuhikaku, 1999), 171.

61. Congressional Research Service, *Japan-US Relations: Issues for Congress,* February 20, 2014, 23–24.

62. *Japan Digest,* February 25, 2000. Kanemaru told his colleague Takeshita Noboru that he coined the term after reading that the Duke of Wellington had once said that "a great general should be considerate about the conditions of his soldiers' boots."

63. See "Omoiyari yosan' to iemasen," *Asahi shinbun,* January 22, 2012, 4.

64. Herman Kahn, *The Emerging Japanese Superstate: Challenge and Response* (Englewood Cliffs, NJ: Prentice-Hall, 1970), 165.

65. February 16, 1968, US Department of State, *Foreign Relations of the United States, 1964–1968,* vol. 29, part 2, *Japan,* 263–264.

66. Ibid., 297.

67. Richard M. Nixon, "Asia After Vietnam," *Foreign Affairs* 46, no. 1 (October 1967): 113–125.

68. US Department of State, *Foreign Relations of the United States, 1969–1976,* vol. 1, *Foundations of Foreign Policy, 1969–1972* (Washington DC: Government Printing Office, 2003), Document 59: Memorandum From the President's Special Assistant (Buchanan) to President Nixon.

69. Ibid.

70. Welfield, *Empire in Eclipse,* 242.

71. John Lewis Gaddis, *Strategies of Containment: A Critical Appraisal of Postwar American National Security Policy* (New York: Oxford University Press, 1982), 281.

72. Quoted in ibid., 280.

73. Quoted in ibid.

74. Michael Schaller, *Altered States: The United States and Japan Since the Occupation* (New York: Oxford University Press, 1997), 196.

75. George W. Ball, *The Past Has Another Pattern: The Memoirs of George W. Ball* (New York: Norton, 1982), 196.

76. In light of the strong sensitivities about the experience of the atomic bomb, the government chose for decades to prevaricate and keep from the

public the essence of its nuclear policy. Although the security treaty did not permit the introduction of nuclear weapons to US bases, in 1960 secret protocols established between the two countries allowed planes and ships to transit weapons through the country. (Maintenance of nuclear weapons on Okinawa was not affected.) Prime ministers and senior members of the Foreign Ministry, however, persisted in denying the existence of such an agreement, even as late as 2009, and despite the fact that American officials had openly reported the agreement since the 1970s. Instead, for decades after the agreement was reached, the Japanese officials dissembled by replying to inquiries in the Diet or the media about nuclear weapons at American bases that they trusted the Americans would inform them if they wanted to transit nuclear weapons; and since the Americans had not consulted them, they assumed it was not occurring. They knew the statement could never be verified, because it was well known that American policy was not to confirm, deny, or comment on the location of such weapons. Critics responded by subsequently labeling the policy Two-and-a-Half Non-Nuclear Principles.

77. Shinichi Kitaoka, "The Secret Japan-US Security Pacts: Background and Disclosure," *Asia-Pacific Review* 17, no. 2 (September 2011): 10–25. See also Yukinori Komine, "Okinawa Confidential, 1969: Exploring the Linkage between the Nuclear Issue and the Base Issue," *Diplomatic History* 37, no. 4 (2013): 807–840; Wakaizumi Kei, *The Best Course Available: A Personal Account of the Secret U.S.-Japan Okinawa Reversion Agreements,* ed. and trans. John Swenson-Wright (Honolulu: University of Hawai'i Press, 2002), especially 273–276.

78. Schaller, *Altered States,* 224.

79. Sadako Ogata, *Normalization with China: A Comparative Study of U.S. and Japanese Processes* (Berkeley: Institute of East Asian Studies, University of California, 1988), 104–105.

80. Robert Hoppens, *The China Problem in Postwar Japan: Japanese National Identity and Sino-Japanese Relations* (London: Bloomsbury, 2015), 100.

81. Schaller, *Altered States,* 236.

82. Yoshinori Komine, "The 'Japan Card' in the U.S. Rapprochement with China, 1969–1972," *Diplomacy and Statecraft* 20, no. 3 (2009): 499. See also Yoshinori Komine, *Secrecy in US Foreign Policy: Nixon, Kissinger and the Rapprochement with China* (Hampshire, UK: Ashgate, 2008), chaps. 7–8.

83. Quoted in Robert Hoppens, "The China Problem in Postwar Japan: Japanese Nationalism and Sino-Japanese Relations, 1971–1980" (PhD dissertation, University of Washington, 2009), 133.

84. William Bundy, *A Tangled Web: The Making of Foreign Policy in the Nixon Presidency* (New York: Hill and Wang, 1998), 236.

85. William Burr, ed., "Negotiating U.S.-Chinese Rapprochement," The National Security Archive, https://nsarchive2.gwu.edu/NSAEBB/NSAEBB70/.

86. LaFeber, *The Clash,* 355–358.

87. Henry Kissinger, *Years of Renewal* (New York: Simon & Schuster, 1999), 150.

88. Henry Kissinger, *Years of Upheaval* (Boston: Little, Brown, 1982), 693.

89. William Burr, ed., *The Kissinger Transcripts* (New York: New Press, 1998), 91.

90. Kissinger, *Years of Upheaval*, 693.

91. George Ball, "We Are Playing a Dangerous Game with Japan," *New York Times Magazine*, June 25, 1972; Robert C. Christopher, *The Japanese Mind* (New York: Ballantine Books, 1983), 55.

92. Henry Kissinger to Ambassador Ellsworth Bunker, Memorandum of Conversation, August 31, 1972, Kissinger Transcripts, 1968–1977 (Washington, DC: The National Security Archive), Digital National Security Archive accession no. KT00549.

93. Lord Lytton, charged by the League of Nations in 1932 to investigate the Manchurian Incident, wrote to his wife from Shanghai: "The Chinese are so articulate—they talk beautiful English and French and can express themselves clearly. With the Japanese it was a surgical operation to extract each word." Quoted in Ian Nish, *Japan's Struggle with Internationalism: Japan, China and the League of Nations, 1931–1933* (London: Kegan Paul International, 1993), 240.

94. Kennan, *Cloud of Danger*, 108.

95. Bartholomew Sparrow, *The Strategist: Brent Scowcroft and the Call of National Security* (New York: PublicAffairs Press, 2015), 473–474.

96. John Nathan, *Sony: The Private Life* (Boston: Houghton Mifflin, 1999), 81n.

97. Kissinger, *Years of Upheaval*, 735.

98. Schaller, *Altered States*, 212.

99. Walter Isaacson's 600-page study of Kissinger's diplomacy offers only one page reference to Japan in its index. Walter Isaacson, *Kissinger: A Biography* (New York: Simon & Schuster, 1992).

100. U. Alexis Johnson, *The Right Hand of Power* (Englewood Cliffs, NJ: Prentice Hall, 1984), 521; Marvin Kalb and Bernard Kalb, *Kissinger* (Boston: Little, Brown, 1974), 255.

101. Don Oberdorfer, "Japan and the United States: Reflections of a Diplomatic Correspondent," *IHJ Bulletin* 17, no. 2 (Summer 1997).

102. Kissinger, *Years of Upheaval*, 738.

103. Kalb and Kalb, *Kissinger*, 77.

104. Oberdorfer, "Japan and the United States."

105. Kissinger, *Years of Upheaval*, 738.

106. Ibid., 743.

107. Ibid.

108. Nathan, *Sony*, 77.

109. Ibid., 80–81.

110. Ibid., 88–89.

111. Ibid., 218.

112. Kissinger, *Years of Upheaval*, 737–738.

113. Henry Kissinger, *White House Years* (Boston: Little Brown, 1979), 324.

114. John Nathan, *Japan Unbound: A Volatile Nation's Quest for Pride and Purpose* (New York: Houghton Mifflin, 2004), 14.

115. See Chalmers Johnson, "Reflections on the Dilemma of Japanese Defense," *Asian Survey* 26, no. 5 (1986): 559. As Mishima's biographer observed, his suicide struck a responsive chord among Japanese who were "deeply traumatized" by the constitution that was forced on them and that required the abandonment of ancient traditions of martial valor, replaced by materialist and merchant values. Mishima, who had organized a small army of rightist students, was privately helped by Satō Eisaku, the prime minister, and Nakasone Yasuhiro, who was at that time director-general of the Japan Defense Agency. Satō's connections to right-wing businessmen facilitated financial support for Mishima's small militia, and Nakasone made it possible for it to train at a Self-Defense base. Satō, Nakasone, and many other prominent Japanese sympathized with Mishima's effort. Henry Scott Stokes, "Lost Samurai: The Withered Soul of Postwar Japan," *Harper's Magazine*, October 1985. Shortly before his suicide, Mishima had written that Japan must recover the essence of its culture, which he defined as *miyabi*, "courtly elegance" as epitomized in *The Tale of Genji*. John Nathan, *Mishima: A Biography* (New York: Da Capo Press, 2000), 232–233.

116. US Department of State, *Foreign Relations of the United States, 1964–1968*, vol. 29, part 2, *Japan*, 273.

117. Kōsaka Masataka, "Tsūshō kokka Nihon no unmei," *Chūō kōron*, November 1975.

118. Kōsaka Masataka, "Yaruta tasisei: Yonju-nen: Nihon gaikō no kijiku wa dō kawaru ka," *Chūō kōron*, January 1985. See also Kōsaka Masataka, *Bunmei ga suibō suru toki* (Tokyo: Shinchosha, 1981), 268.

119. Tadokoro Masayuki, "The Model of an Economic Power: Japanese Diplomacy in the 1960s," in *Diplomatic History of Postwar Japan*, ed. Makoto Iokibe (London: Routledge, 2011), 105.

8. Competing Capitalisms

1. See the debates the Japanese had over what was necessary to borrow from the West, discussed in Kenneth B. Pyle, *The New Generation in Meiji Japan: Problems of Cultural Identity, 1885–1895* (Stanford, CA: Stanford University Press, 1969).

2. See the discussion in Kenneth B. Pyle, "Meiji Conservatism," in *The Cambridge History of Japan*, ed. Marius B. Jansen (New York: Cambridge University Press, 1989), 5:674–720.

3. G. B. Sansom, *Japan: A Short Cultural History*, rev. ed. (New York: Appleton-Century Crofts, 1943), 15.

4. Albert M. Craig, "Kido Koin and Ōkubo Toshimichi: A Psychohistorical Analysis," in *Personality in Japanese History*, ed. Albert M. Craig and Donald H. Shively (Berkeley: University of California Press, 1970), 279.

5. Kenneth B. Pyle, "Advantages of Followership: German Economics and Japanese Bureaucrats, 1890–1925," *Journal of Japanese Studies* 1 (1974): 127–164.

6. See Gerhard Lehmbruch, "The Institutional Embedding of Market Economies: The German 'Model' and Its Impact on Japan," in *The Origins of Nonliberal Capitalism: Germany and Japan in Comparison,* ed. Wolfgang Streeck and Kozo Yamamura (Ithaca, NY: Cornell University Press, 2001), 39–93.

7. An excellent analysis in comparative perspective is found in Robert Gilpin, *Global Political Economy: Understanding the International Economic Order* (Princeton, NJ: Princeton University Press, 2001). As Gilpin writes, "The term 'developmental state capitalism' best describes the essence of the system, because this characterization conveys the idea that the state must play a central role in national economic development and in the competition with the West" (158).

8. Kozo Yamamura, "Bridled Capitalism and the Economic Development of Japan, 1880–1980," in *The Wealth of Nations in the Twentieth Century: The Policies and Institutional Determinants of Economic Development,* ed. Ramon H. Myers (Stanford, CA: Hoover Institution Press, 1996), 54–79.

9. Michael Spence, *The Next Convergence: The Future of Economic Growth in a Multispeed World* (New York: Farrar, Straus and Giroux, 2011), 14.

10. Quoted in Kenneth B. Pyle, *The Japanese Question: Power and Purpose in a New Era,* 2nd ed. (Washington, DC: AEI Press, 1996), 44.

11. Mark Mazower, *Governing the World: The History of an Idea* (New York: Penguin, 2012), 343.

12. David Calleo, *The Imperious Economy* (Cambridge, MA: Harvard University Press, 1982), 1.

13. G. John Ikenberry, *After Victory: Institutions, Strategic Restraint, and the Rebuilding of Order after War* (Princeton, NJ: Princeton University Press, 2001), 187.

14. Jerome B. Cohen, *Japan's Economy in War and Reconstruction* (Minneapolis: University of Minnesota Press, 1949), 427.

15. Kozo Yamamura, *Economic Policy in Postwar Japan: Growth versus Economic Democracy* (Berkeley: University of California Press, 1967), 1.

16. John W. Dower, *Embracing Defeat: Japan in the Wake of World War II* (New York: Norton 1999), 538.

17. Saburō Ōkita, *Japan's Challenging Years: Reflections on My Lifetime* (New York: George Allen and Unwin, 1985), 26.

18. Ibid., 32.

19. Bai Gao, "Arisawa Hiromi and His Theory for a Managed Economy," *Journal of Japanese Studies* 20 (Winter 1994): 125.

20. Saburō Ōkita, *Postwar Reconstruction of the Japanese Economy* (Tokyo: University of Tokyo Press, 1992), 91.

21. Ibid., 139.

22. Quoted in Mark Metzler, *Capital as Will and Imagination: Schumpeter's Guide to the Postwar Japanese Miracle* (Ithaca, NY: Cornell University Press, 2013), 68.

23. Laura Hein, *Fueling Growth: The Energy Revolution and Economic Policy in Postwar Japan* (Cambridge, MA: Harvard University Press, 1990), 113.

24. Scott O'Bryan, *The Growth Idea: Purpose and Prosperity in Postwar Japan* (Honolulu: University of Hawai'i Press, 2009), 34.

25. Dower, *Embracing Defeat,* 538.

26. Ibid., 539.

27. Ōkita, *Postwar Reconstruction,* 128.

28. See O'Bryan, *Growth Idea,* chap. 2.

29. Ibid., 186.

30. Chalmers Johnson, *MITI and the Japanese Miracle: The Growth of Industrial Policy, 1925–1975* (Stanford, CA: Stanford University Press, 1982), 210.

31. See the argument of Gene Park, *Spending without Taxation: FILP and the Politics of Public Finance* (Stanford, CA: Stanford University Press, 2011).

32. Leon Hollerman, "International Economic Controls in Occupied Japan," *Journal of Asian Studies* 38, no. 4 (August 1979): 719.

33. Kozo Yamamura and Jan Vandenberg, "Japan's Rapid Growth Policy on Trial," in *Law and Trade Issues of the Japanese Economy,* ed. Gary R. Saxonhouse and Kozo Yamamura (Seattle: University of Washington Press, 1986), 238–278.

34. Bai Gao, *Economic Ideology and Japanese Industrial Policy: Developmentalism from 1931 to 1965* (Cambridge: Cambridge University Press, 1997), 43.

35. Sakakibara Eisuke and Noguchi Yukio, "Ōkurashō—Nichigin ōchō no bunseki," *Chūō kōron,* August 1977, 113.

36. Ibid.

37. Ibid. See also Kozo Yamamura, "The Role of Government in Japan's 'Catch-up' Industrialization: A Neoinstitutionalist Perspective," in *The Japanese Civil Service and Economic Development,* ed. Hyung-ki Kim et al. (Oxford: Clarendon Press, 1995), 112.

38. Thomas P. Rohlen, "Learning: The Mobilization of Knowledge in the Japanese Political Economy," in *The Political Economy of Japan: Cultural and Social Dynamics,* ed. Shumpei Kumon and Henry Rosovsky (Stanford, CA: Stanford University Press, 1992), 327.

39. Richard J. Samuels, "Reinventing Security: Japan Since Meiji," *Daedalus* 120, no. 4 (Fall 1991): 54.

40. See Eric Heginbotham and Richard J. Samuels, "Mercantile Realism and Japanese Foreign Policy," *International Security* 22, no. 4 (Spring 1998): 177.

41. Quoted in Donald C. Hellmann, "Japanese Politics and Foreign Policy: Elitist Democracy within an American Greenhouse," in *The Political Economy of Japan,* vol. 2, *The Changing International Context,* ed. Takashi Inoguchi and Daniel I. Okimoto (Stanford, CA: Stanford University Press, 1988), 361.

42. John W. Dower, *Ways of Forgetting, Ways of Remembering* (New York: New Press, 2012), 199.

43. William S. Borden, *The Pacific Alliance: United States Foreign Economic Policy and Japanese Trade Recovery, 1947–1955* (Madison: University of Wisconsin Press, 1984), 178–180.

44. US Department of State, *Foreign Relations of the United States, 1958–1960,* vol. 18, *Japan, Korea* (Washington, DC: Government Printing Office, 1994), Document 190, June 24, 1960.

45. US Department of State, *Foreign Relations of the United States, 1964–1968,* vol. 19, part 2, *Japan* (Washington, DC: Government Printing Office, 2006), 18.

46. Stephen D. Krasner, "Vision, Interest, and Uncertainty," in *A Vision of a New Liberalism: Critical Essays on Murakami's Anticlassical Analysis,* ed. Kozo Yamamura (Stanford, CA: Stanford University Press, 1997), 53.

47. Fukuzawa Yukichi, *An Outline of a Theory of Civilization,* trans. David Dilworth and G. Cameron Hurst (Tokyo: Sophia University, 1973), 2.

48. Quoted in *The Cambridge History of Japan,* vol. 6, *The Twentieth Century,* ed. Peter Duus (New York: Cambridge University Press, 1989), 389.

49. I discuss the early Meiji debates in *The New Generation in Meiji Japan.*

50. Yamamura, "Bridled Capitalism," 54–79.

51. Edward J. Lincoln, *Japan's New Global Role* (Washington, DC: Brookings Institution, 1993), 59–62; Edward J. Lincoln, "Japanese Trade and Investment Issues," in *Japan's Emerging Global Role,* ed. Danny Unger and Paul Blackburn (New York: Lynn Reiner, 1993), 135.

52. Quoted in Samuel P. Huntington, "Why International Primacy Matters," *International Security* 17, no. 4 (Spring 1993): 76.

53. Book review of *Japan as Number One: Lessons for America,* by Ezra F. Vogel, *Monumenta Nipponica* 34, no. 3 (Autumn 1979): 380–381.

54. Ezra F. Vogel, *Japan as Number One: Lessons for America* (Cambridge, MA: Harvard University Press, 1979), 97.

55. Ibid., 230–238.

56. Amy Borovoy, "Robert Bellah's Search for Community and Ethical Modernity in Japan Studies," *Journal of Asian Studies* 75, no. 2 (May 2016): 489.

57. Book reviews of *Japan as Number One: Lessons for America,* by Ezra F. Vogel, *Journal of Japanese Studies* 6, no. 2 (Summer 1980): 416, 427.

58. Iida Tsuneo, *Nippon-teki chikara-tsuyosa no sai-hakken* (Tokyo: Nihon keizai shinmbunsha, 1979), 206.

59. *Kokuminsei no kenkyū dai 7-kai zenkoku chōsa* (Tokyo: Tōkei sūri kenkyūjō 1984).

60. Robert Gilpin, *The Political Economy of International Relations* (Princeton, NJ: Princeton University Press, 1987), 391–392.

61. See my survey of the Western critiques of Japanese economic policy in Pyle, *The Japanese Question.* See also Ōkita Saburō, *Amerika no ronri Nihon no taiō : Nichi-Bei masatsu 20-nen no kiroku* (Tokyo: Japan Times, 1989).

62. Chalmers Johnson, *MITI and the Japanese Miracle: The Growth of Industrial Policy, 1925–1975* (Stanford, CA: Stanford University Press, 1982).

63. T. J. Pempel, "The Legacy of Chalmers Johnson," *Pacific Review* 24, no. 1 (March 2011): 9–14. Johnson revised some of the positions he took in *MITI* in a retrospective essay: "Japanese 'Capitalism' Revisited" (JPRI Occasional Paper No. 22, August 2001).

64. Murakami Yasusuke, *Han koten no seiji-keizaiaku* (Tokyo: Chūō kōronsha, 1992), which was translated as *An Anticlassical Political-Economic Analysis* (Stanford, CA: Stanford University Press, 1996).

65. See the various essays discussing Murakami's ideas contained in Kozo Yamamura, ed., *A Vision of a New Liberalism? Critical Essays on Murakami's Anticlassical Analysis* (Stanford, CA: Stanford University Press, 1997).

66. See Kenneth B. Pyle, "The World Historical Significance of Japan," in Yamamura, *A Vision of a New Liberalism? Critical Essays on Murakami's Anticlassical Analysis*, 208–240.

67. Chalmers Johnson, *Japan: Who Governs?* (New York: W. W. Norton, 1995), 8.

68. Kozo Yamamura, "Germany and Japan in a New Phase of Capitalism: Confronting the Past and Future," in *The End of Diversity? Prospects for German and Japanese Capitalism*, ed. Kozo Yamamura and Wolfgang Streeck (Ithaca, NY: Cornell University Press, 2003), 115–116.

69. Takeo Hoshi in the *Journal of Japanese Studies* 41, no. 2 (Summer 2015): 452.

70. Yasusuke Murakami, *An Anti-Classical Political Economic Analysis: A Vision for the Next Century* (Stanford, CA: Stanford University Press, 1996), 191.

71. Ibid., 226.

72. Quoted in Edward J. Lincoln, review of *Choose and Focus: Japanese Business Strategies for the 21st Century,* by Ulrike Schaede, *Journal of Japanese Studies* 36, no. 1 (Winter 2010): 104.

73. See *Japan's "Lost Decade": Causes, Legacies and Issues of Transformative Change,* ed. W. Miles Fletcher III and Peter W. von Staden (London: Routledge, 2013), 53.

74. W. Miles Fletcher III, "Dreams of Economic Transformation and the Reality of Economic Crisis in Japan: Keidanren in the Era of the 'Bubble' and the Onset of the 'Lost Decade', from the mid-1980s to the mid-1990s," *Asia Pacific Business Review* 18, no. 2 (April 2012): 149–165.

75. Ulrike Schaede, *Choose and Focus: Japanese Business Strategies for the Twenty-First Century* (Ithaca, NY: Cornell University Press, 2008).

76. Ulrike Schaede, "From Developmental State to the 'New Japan': The Strategic Inflection Point in Japanese Business," *Asia Pacific Business Review* 18, no. 2 (April 2012): 177.

77. Ibid., 176.

78. Mark Metzler, "Introduction: Japan at an Inflection Point," *Asia Pacific Business Review* 18, no. 2 (April 2012): 139.

79. For an excellent exploration of the interplay of issues of convergence and diversity, see Kozo Yamamura and Wolfgang Streeck, eds., *The End of Di-*

versity? Prospects for German and Japanese Capitalism (Ithaca, NY: Cornell University Press, 2003).

80. Steven K. Vogel, "The Reorganization of Organized Capitalism: How the German and Japanese Models Are Shaping Their Own Transformations," in Yamamura and Streeck, *The End of Diversity?*, 332–333.

81. Schaede, *Choose and Focus*, 18.

82. Ibid., 258–259.

83. Metzler, "Introduction," 143.

84. Steven K. Vogel, *Japan Remodeled: How Government and Industry Are Reforming Japanese Capitalism* (Ithaca, NY: Cornell University Press, 2006), 203–224.

9. Japan's Nonconvergent Society

1. Odd Arne Westad, *The Global Cold War: Third World Interventions and the Making of Our Times* (Cambridge: Cambridge University Press, 2007), 20–21.

2. Elizabeth Borgwardt, *A New Deal for the World: America's Vision for Human Rights* (Cambridge, MA: Harvard University Press, 2005), 70.

3. Douglas MacArthur, *Reminiscences* (New York: McGraw-Hill, 1964), 283.

4. Mary Ann Glendon, *A World Made New: Eleanor Roosevelt and the Universal Declaration of Human Rights* (New York: Random House, 2002), chap. 12.

5. Lynn Hunt, *Inventing Human Rights: A History* (New York: Norton, 2007).

6. Mark Mazower, *Governing the World: The History of an Idea* (New York: Penguin Press, 2012), 318.

7. Glendon, *A World Made New*, 221–222. See also Mazower, *Governing the World*, 317ff.

8. Ray A. Moore and Donald L. Robinson, *Partners for Democracy: Crafting the New Japanese State under MacArthur* (New York: Oxford University Press, 2002), 129.

9. John W. Dower, *Embracing Defeat: Japan in the Wake of World War II* (New York: Norton, 1999), 215–216.

10. John W. Dower, "Preface," in Takemae Eiji, *Allied Occupation of Japan* (New York: Continuum, 2003), xx.

11. George F. Kennan, *The Cloud of Danger: Current Realities of American Foreign Policy* (Boston: Little, Brown, 1977), 109.

12. Sheldon Garon, *Molding Japanese Minds: The State in Everyday Life* (Princeton, NJ: Princeton University Press, 1997).

13. Lisa Yoneyama, "Liberation under Siege: U.S. Military Occupation and Japanese Women's Enfranchisement," *American Quarterly* 57, no. 53 (September 2005): 893.

14. Yanagita Kunio, *Nihonjin* (Tokyo: Mainichi shimbunsha, 1976), 1–2; Maruyama Masao, *Senchū to sengo no aida* (Tokyo: Misuzu shobō, 1976), 346–348.

15. Kenneth B. Pyle, *The New Generation in Meiji Japan: Problems of Cultural Identity, 1885–1895* (Stanford, CA: Stanford University Press, 1969).

16. Ernest R. May, *American Cold War Strategy: Interpreting NSC 68* (Boston: Bedford / St. Martin's, 1993), 26–27.

17. Alexis de Tocqueville, *Democracy in America: A New Translation* (New York: Doubleday Anchor, 1969), 508. See also Kyoko Inoue, *MacArthur's Japanese Constitution: A Linguistic and Cultural Study of Its Making* (Chicago: University of Chicago Press, 1991), 222ff.

18. Daniel Walker Howe, *Making the American Self: Jonathan Edwards to Abraham Lincoln* (New York: Oxford University Press, 1997), 260.

19. Ibid., 107.

20. Quoted in Albert Craig's introductory essay in Albert M. Craig and Donald H. Shively, *Personality in Japanese History* (Berkeley: University of California Press, 1970), 18.

21. Robert N. Bellah et al., *Habits of the Heart: Individualism and Commitment in American Life* (New York: Harper & Row, 1985), 142.

22. Reinhold Niebuhr, *The Irony of American History* (Chicago: University of Chicago Press, 1952), 13.

23. Quoted in Bellah, *Habits of the Heart,* 143.

24. Robert J. Smith, "A Pattern of Japanese Society: Ie Society or Acknowledgment of Interdependence," *Journal of Japanese Studies* 11, no. 1 (Winter 1985): 29–45. See also Robert J. Smith, *Tradition, Self, and the Social Order* (Cambridge: Cambridge University Press, 1983), chap. 3.

25. Smith, "A Pattern of Japanese Society," 37–39.

26. Andrew E. Barshay, *The Social Sciences in Modern Japan: The Marxian and Modernist Traditions* (Berkeley: University of California Press, 2004), 225.

27. Edward Fowler, *The Rhetoric of Confession: Shishosetsu in Twentieth-Century Japanese Fiction* (Berkeley: University of California Press, 1988), 82.

28. A translation of Sōseki's "Watakushi no kojinshugi" by Jay Rubin is found in *Kokoro and Selected Essays by Natsume Sōseki* (Lanham, MD: Madison Books, 1992).

29. Ibid., 303–304.

30. Ibid., 311–314.

31. Wilbur M. Fridell, "Government Ethics Textbooks in Late Meiji Japan," *Journal of Asian Studies* 29 (August 1970): 831.

32. See Otto D. Tolischus, *Tokyo Record* (New York: Reynal and Hitchcock, 1943), 406.

33. Robert N. Bellah, *Imagining Japan: The Japanese Tradition and Its Modern Interpretation* (Berkeley: University of California Press, 2003), 116.

34. Hajime Nakamura, *Ways of Thinking of Eastern Peoples: India-China-Tibet-Japan,* ed. Philip P. Wiener (Honolulu, HI: East West Center Press, 1964), 350.

35. S. N. Eisenstadt, *Japanese Civilization: A Comparative View* (Chicago: University of Chicago Press, 1995), 7.

36. Barshay, *The Social Sciences in Modern Japan,* 224.

37. Bellah, *Imagining Japan*, 6.

38. Moore and Robinson, *Partners for Democracy*, 4.

39. Ray A. Moore, *Soldier of God: MacArthur's Attempt to Christianize Japan* (Portland, ME: Merwin Asia, 2011), 60–63, 122.

40. Ibid., 123.

41. Ibid., 111.

42. Takemae, *Allied Occupation*, 378.

43. Takeshi Matsuda, *Soft Power and Its Perils: U.S. Cultural Policy in Early Postwar Japan and Permanent Dependency* (Washington, DC: Woodrow Wilson Center Press; Stanford, CA: Stanford University Press, 2007), 143.

44. See *War and Conscience in Japan: Nambara Shigeru and the Asia-Pacific War*, ed. and trans. Richard H. Minear (Lanham, MD: Rowman & Littlefield, 2011), 27n23, 11.

45. Mark B. Williams, *Endō Shūsaku: A Literature of Reconciliation* (London: Routledge, 1999), 33.

46. *Yomiuri shimbun*, May 30, 2008.

47. Robert Kisala, "Japanese Religions," in *Nanzan Guide to Japanese Religions* (Honolulu: University of Hawai'i Press, 2006), 9.

48. Ian Reader, "Folk Religion," in *Nanzan Guide to Japanese Religions*, 71. For an enlightening study of the definition of religion in modern Japan, see Jason Ananda Josephson, *The Invention of Religion in Japan* (Chicago: University of Chicago Press, 2012).

49. Mark R. Mullins, "Japanese Christianity," in *Nanzan Guide to Japanese Religions*, 124.

50. "The marriage of Crown Prince Akihito to a commoner and Christian, Shōda Michiko in 1959 received extensive media coverage and created a 'Michiko boom.'" Takemae, *Allied Occupation*, 519.

51. Dower, *Empire and Aftermath*, 306, 547n3.

52. John Breen, "'Conventional Wisdom' and the Politics of Shinto in Postwar Japan," *Politics of Religion* 4, no. 1 (2010): 68–82.

53. Katherine Sansom, *Sir George Sansom and Japan: A Memoir* (Tallahassee, FL: Diplomatic Press, 1972), 154.

54. Takemae, *Allied Occupation*, 348.

55. Ibid., 349.

56. Ibid., 352.

57. Edward R. Beauchamp and James M. Vardaman, Jr., eds., *Japanese Education Since 1945: A Documentary Study* (Armonk, NY: M. E. Sharpe, 1994), 82–85.

58. See, for example, the reflections of Gordon Bowles in Gary H. Tsuchimochi, *Education Reform in Postwar Japan, the 1946 U.S. Education Mission* (Tokyo: University of Tokyo Press, 1993), 309–313.

59. Beauchamp and Vardaman, *Japanese Education Since 1945*, 109–111.

60. Thomas P. Rohlen, *Japan's High Schools* (Berkeley: University of California Press, 1988), 67.

61. Teruhisa Horio, *Educational Thought and Ideology in Modern Japan: State Authority and Intellectual Freedom* (Tokyo: University of Tokyo Press, 1988), 401–402.

62. Ibid., 215.

63. Rohlen, *Japan's High Schools,* 135.

64. Amy Borovoy, "What Color Is Your Parachute? The Post-Degree Society," in *Social Class in Contemporary Japan: Structures, Sorting and Strategies,* ed. Hiroshi Ishida and David H. Slater (London: Routledge, 2009), 171.

65. Horio, *Educational Thought and Ideology,* 3.

66. Rohlen, *Japan's High Schools,* 68.

67. Ibid., 109.

68. Ibid., 209.

69. Christopher P. Hood, *Japanese Education Reform: Nakasone's Legacy* (London: Routledge, 2001), 172. See also Mark Lincicome, *Imperial Subjects as Global Subjects: Nationalism, Internationalism, and Education in Japan* (Lanham, MD: Rowman & Littlefield, 2009), xv; Leonard James Schoppa, *Education Reform in Japan: A Case of Immobilist Politics* (London: Routledge, 1991).

70. Kariya Takehiko, "The Two Lost Decades in Education: The Failure of Reform," in *Examining Japan's Lost Decades,* ed. Yoichi Funabashi and Barak Kushner (London: Routledge, 2015), 101–117.

71. Quoted in Yoneyama, "Liberation under Siege," 890.

72. Quoted in Yoneyama, "Liberation under Siege," 892.

73. Courtney Whitney, *MacArthur: His Rendezvous with History* (New York: Knopf, 1956), 290.

74. See Susan J. Pharr, "The Politics of Women's Rights," in *Democratizing Japan: The Allied Occupation,* ed. Robert E. Ward and Sakamoto Yoshikazu (Honolulu: University of Hawai'i Press, 1987), 226.

75. Ibid., 222.

76. Ibid., 225.

77. Key members of SCAP involved in the changes of the civil code make clear that Japanese participants had considerable influence in making the changes that often were opposed by Japanese conservatives. See Alfred C. Oppler, *Legal Reform in Occupied Japan: A Participant Looks Back* (Princeton, NJ: Princeton University Press, 1976), 11–120. See also Kurt Steiner, "The Occupation and the Reform of the Japanese Civil Code," in Ward and Sakamoto, *Democratizing Japan,* 188–220.

78. Robert J. Smith, "Gender Inequality in Contemporary Japan," *Journal of Japanese Studies* 13 (Winter 1987): 13.

79. Sheldon Garon, "State and Family in Modern Japan: A Historical Perspective," *Economy and Society* 39, no. 3 (August 2010): 324–325.

80. Amy Borovoy, "Japan as Mirror: Neoliberalism's Promise and Cost," in *Ethnographies of Neoliberalism,* ed. Carol J. Greenhouse (Philadelphia: University of Pennsylvania Press, 2008), 64.

81. Amy Borovoy, *The Too-Good Wife: Alcohol, Codependency, and the Politics of Nurturance in Postwar Japan* (Berkeley: University of California Press, 2005), 4.

82. *Tokyo Shimbun*, April 10, 2016.

83. Leonard J. Schoppa, *Race for the Exits: The Unraveling of Japan's System of Social Protection* (Ithaca, NY: Cornell University Press, 2006), 158–160.

84. Ibid., 203.

85. Iwao Sumiko, *The Japanese Woman: Traditional Image and Changing Reality* (Cambridge, MA: Harvard University Press, 1993), 215.

86. Garon, *Molding Japanese Minds*, chap. 6.

87. A good example of women's often unrecognized role in supporting issues of concern to housewives is found in their important role in the Kōmeitō Party. See "Housewife Voters and Kōmeitō Policies," in *Kōmeitō: Politics and Religion in Japan*, ed. George Ehrhardt, Axel Klein, Levi McLaughlin, and Steven Reed (Berkeley, CA: Institute of East Asian Studies, 2014), 187–211.

88. *Asahi Shimbun*, October 24, 2014.

89. Smith, "Gender Inequality," 16.

90. Schoppa, *Race for the Exits*, 92–93.

91. Mary C. Brinton, *Women and the Japanese Economic Miracle: Gender and Work in Postwar Japan* (Berkeley: University of California Press, 1993), 229.

92. See, for example, Borovoy, *The Too-Good Wife*; and also Karen Kelsky, *Women on the Verge: Japanese Women, Western Dreams* (Durham, NC: Duke University Press, 2001).

93. Borovoy, *The Too-Good Wife*, 28.

94. Ibid., 88–89.

95. Iwao, *The Japanese Woman*, 281.

96. Borovoy, *The Too-Good Wife*, 175–176.

97. Schoppa, *Race for the Exits*, 74, 161, 182.

98. Iwao, *The Japanese Woman*, 26ff.

99. *Kokuminsei no kenkyū: Dai jūni-ji zenkoku chōsa* (Tokyo: Tōkei suri kenkyūjō, 2009), 94–95.

100. Schoppa, *Race for the Exits*, 202.

101. Borovoy, "Japan as Mirror," 68.

102. *Economist*, March 14, 2015.

103. Jesper Edman, "Foreign Firms in Japan," *Oriental Economist*, June 2016.

104. Quoted in Pyle, *Japan Rising*, 18.

105. Ibid.

106. Ian Buruma, "Becoming Japanese," *New Yorker*, December 23, 1996.

107. Andrew Gordon, "Consumption, Leisure and the Middle Class in Transwar Japan," *Social Science Japan Journal* 10, no. 1 (April 2007): 14.

108. Jordan Sand, *House and Home: Architecture, Domestic Space, and Bourgeois Culture, 1880–1930* (Cambridge, MA: Harvard East Asia Center, 2003), 373.

109. Yasusuke Murakami, "Ie Society as a Pattern of Civilization," *Journal of Japanese Studies* 10, no. 2 (1984): 340. See also Kenneth B. Pyle, "The World Historical Significance of Japan," in *The Vision of a New Liberalism? Critical Essays on Murakami's Anticlassical Analysis,* ed. Kozo Yamamura (Stanford, CA: Stanford University Press, 1997), 208–237.

10. Democracy in Japan

1. David M. Fitzsimons, "Tom Paine's New World Order: Idealistic Internationalism in the Ideology of Early American Foreign Relations," *Diplomatic History* 19, no. 4 (Fall 1995): 570. See also Felix Gilbert, *To the Farewell Address: Ideas of Early American Foreign Policy* (Princeton, NJ: Princeton University Press, 1961).

2. For a distinction between Paine and Kant, see Kenneth N. Waltz, *Man, the State, and War: A Theoretical Analysis* (New York: Columbia University Press, 1954), 103ff.

3. Quoted in Michael W. Doyle, *Ways of War and Peace: Realism, Liberalism and Socialism* (New York: Norton, 1997), 206.

4. Thomas C. Walker, "The Forgotten Prophet: Tom Paine's Cosmopolitanism and International Relations," *International Studies Quarterly* 44, no. 1 (March 2000): 66.

5. Michael Howard, *War and the Liberal Conscience* (London: Temple Smith, 1978), 112–113.

6. Douglas MacArthur, "A Fourth of July Message," *Life Magazine,* July 7, 1947.

7. Charles Tilly, *Democracy* (Cambridge: Cambridge University Press, 2007), 13–14.

8. John W. Dower, *Embracing Defeat: Japan in the Wake of World War II* (New York: Norton, 1999), 71.

9. Karube Tadashi, *Maruyama Masao and the Fate of Liberalism in Twentieth-Century Japan* (Tokyo: International House of Japan, 2008), 103.

10. Quoted in Roger Buckley, *US-Japan Alliance Diplomacy, 1945–1990* (Cambridge: Cambridge University Press, 1992), 4.

11. Dale M. Hellegers, *We, the Japanese People: World War II and the Origins of the Japanese Constitution,* 2 vols. (Stanford, CA: Stanford University Press, 2001), 1:242.

12. Ibid., 2:518.

13. Dower, *Embracing Defeat,* 347.

14. Kenneth Mori McElwain and Christian G. Winkler, "What's Unique about the Japanese Constitution? A Comparative and Historical Analysis," *Journal of Japanese Studies* 41, no. 2 (Summer 2015): 249.

15. Hellegers, *We, the Japanese People,* 2:546.

16. Chalmers Johnson, *MITI and the Japanese Miracle: The Growth of Industrial Policy, 1925–1975* (Stanford, CA: Stanford University Press, 1982), 43–44.

17. Jeremi Suri's comments are apt: "Nation-building can only work when the people own it. America's complicated domestic history reinforces that insight. Acting abroad, citizens often forget that fact. They define power as a constant dictated from above, rather than a changing phenomenon modified from below. This is a somewhat natural reaction to the immediacy of threats and the dizzying complexity of foreign societies. Although stable authority emerged from a nation-building process in the United States, embodied by our never-ending constitutional debates, policymakers have neglected this experience when advising other governments. Too often, Americans have made authority the starting, and therefore restricting, point for beginning reforms abroad." Suri, *Liberty's Surest Guarantee,* 41.

18. Mill's essay, "A Few Words on Non-Intervention," is found in Appendix 1 of Michael W. Doyle, *The Question of Intervention: John Stuart Mill and the Responsibility to Protect* (New Haven, CT: Yale University Press, 2015). The passage quoted is on page 224. See also Michael Walzer, *Just and Unjust Wars: A Moral Argument with Historical Illustrations* (New York: Basic Books, 1977), 86ff.

19. Walzer explaining Mill's views in *Just and Unjust Wars,* 87.

20. Quoted in Kyoko Inoue, *Individual Dignity in Modern Japanese Thought: The Evolution of the Concept of Jinkaku in Moral and Educational Discourse* (Ann Arbor: Center for Japanese Studies, University of Michigan, 2001), 83.

21. Quoted in Kyoko Inoue, *MacArthur's Japanese Constitution: A Linguistic and Cultural Study of Its Making* (Chicago: University of Chicago Press, 1991), 75.

22. The Occupation chose to keep the British principle of parliamentary supremacy. It was the system with which Japanese were familiar from the prewar period, and perhaps, too, there was concern that the American presidential style might produce too strong a leader. "The British principle of parliamentary supremacy seemed preferable because it was closer to Japan's extant system." Hellegers, *We, the Japanese People,* 2:524.

23. Inoue, *MacArthur's Japanese Constitution,* 267.

24. Chalmers Johnson, "Japan: Who Governs? An Essay on Official Bureaucracy," *Journal of Japanese Studies* 2 (Autumn 1975): 11.

25. Ethan Scheiner, *Democracy without Competition in Japan: Opposition Failure in a One-Party Dominant State* (Cambridge: Cambridge University Press, 2006).

26. Ellis S. Krauss and Robert J. Pekkanen, *The Rise and Fall of Japan's LDP: Political Party Organizations as Historical Institutions* (Ithaca, NY: Cornell University Press, 2011), 262.

27. See Donald C. Hellmann, "Japanese Politics and Foreign Policy: Elitist Democracy within an American Greenhouse," in *The Political Economy of Japan,* vol. 2, *The Changing International Context,* ed. Takashi Inoguchi and Daniel I. Okimoto (Stanford, CA: Stanford University Press, 1988).

28. John W. Dower, *Japan in War and Peace: Selected Essays* (New York: New Press, 1993), 67.

29. Richard J. Samuels, "Japan's 3.11 Master Narrative Still Under Construction," *East Asia Forum,* March 6, 2016, www.eastasiaforum.org/2016/03/06/japans-3-11-master-narrative-still-under-construction/.

30. Krauss and Pekkanen, *The Rise and Fall of Japan's LDP,* 280.

31. Ibid., 30–31.

32. John W. Dower, *Cultures of War: Pearl Harbor / Hiroshima / 9–11 / Iraq* (New York: Norton, 2010), 316.

33. Tilly, *Democracy,* xi–xii.

34. Ibid., 77–78.

35. Wesley Sasaki-Uemura, "Competing Publics: Citizens' Groups, Mass Media, and the State in the 1960s," *Positions* 10, no. 1 (Spring 2002): 95.

36. J. Victor Koschmann, "Authority and the Individual," in *A Companion to Japanese History,* ed. William Tsutsui (Malden, MA: Blackwell, 2007), 515.

37. *Asahi shimbun,* July 12, 2012.

38. Richard J. Samuels, *3.11: Disaster and Change in Japan* (Ithaca, NY: Cornell University Press, 2013), 200.

39. Patricia L. Maclachlan, review of *Politics and Volunteering in Japan,* by Mary Alice Haddad, *Journal of Japanese Studies* 35, no. 1 (Winter 2009): 224–228.

40. John Owen Haley, *Authority without Power: Law and the Japanese Paradox* (New York: Oxford University Press, 1991), 14.

41. Quoted in Dan F. Henderson, "Law and Political Modernization in Japan," in *Political Development in Modern Japan,* ed. Robert E. Ward (Princeton, NJ: Princeton University Press, 1968), 448.

42. Judith Shklar quoted in Haley, *Authority without Power,* 15.

43. Frank K. Upham, *Law and Social Change in Postwar Japan* (Cambridge, MA: Harvard University Press, 1987), 209.

44. Quoted in John O. Haley, "Rivers and Rice: What Lawyers and Legal Historians Should Know about Medieval Japan," *Journal of Japanese Studies* 36, no. 2 (2010): 347.

45. Thomas Rohlen, "Order in Japanese Society: Attachment, Authority, and Routine," *Journal of Japanese Studies* 15 (Winter 1989): 5–40.

46. For an insightful essay on the role of the moral compact in labor disputes in the early twentieth-century history of Japan, see "The Right to Benevolence," in *Native Sources of Japanese Industrialization, 1750–1920,* ed. Thomas C. Smith (Berkeley: University of California Press, 1988).

47. Haley, *Authority without Power,* 14.

48. John Owen Haley, *The Spirit of Japanese Law* (Athens: University of Georgia Press, 1998), 18.

49. Norma Field, *In the Realm of a Dying Emperor: A Portrait of Japan at Century's End* (New York: Pantheon Books, 1991), 133–134.

50. Quoted in Upham, *Law and Social Change in Postwar Japan,* 205–206.

51. Ibid., 206.

52. Haley, *Spirit of Japanese Law,* 22.

53. Daniel H. Foote, ed., *Law in Japan: A Turning Point* (Seattle: University of Washington Press, 2007), xxxv.

54. Daniel H. Foote, "Citizen Participation: Appraising the Saiban'in System," *Michigan State International Law Review* 22, no. 3 (2013–2014): 755–775.

55. Eric A. Feldman, "Law, Culture, and Conflict: Dispute Resolution in Postwar Japan," in Foote, *Law in Japan,* 72. In a preliminary study, two legal scholars have noted an impressive turn to litigation in the 1990s. See Tom Ginsburg and Glenn Hoetker, "The Unreluctant Litigant? An Empirical Analysis of Japan's Turn to Litigation," *Journal of Legal Studies* 35 (January 2006): 31–59.

56. John Dower observes: "In all likelihood Japan would have become democratic and pro-Western without the occupation, but in substance as well as form it would have become a different state with a different collective ethos." *Cultures of War,* 323.

57. Doyle, *The Question of Intervention,* 29.

58. Watanabe Akio, "Japan's Position on Human Rights in Asia," in *Japan and East Asian Regionalism,* ed. S. J. Maswood (London: Routledge, 2001); see also Watanabe Akio, "Toward a Middle Path in Human Rights Policy," *Japan Review of International Affairs* 11, no. 2 (Summer 1997); Watanabe Akio, ed., *Ajia no jinken; kokusai seiji no shiten kara* (Tokyo: Nihon kokusaimondai kenkyūjō, 1997), 1–27.

59. Kyoko Inoue, *Individual Dignity in Modern Japanese Thought: The Evolution of the Concept of Jinkaku in Moral and Educational Discourse* (Ann Arbor: Center for Japanese Studies, University of Michigan, 2001), 226, 230.

60. Haley, *Spirit of Japanese Law,* 199.

11. Japan in the Twilight of the American Century

1. Henry R. Luce, *The American Century* (New York: Farrar & Rinehart, 1941), 23–24, 32–33, 39.

2. Alan Brinkley, "World War II and American Liberalism," in *The War in American Culture: Society and Consciousness during World War II,* ed. Lewis A. Erenberg and Susan E. Hirsch (Chicago: University of Chicago Press, 1996), 324–325.

3. David M. Kennedy, "The Origins of American Hyperpower," in *The Short American Century: A Post Mortem,* ed. Andrew J. Bacevich (Cambridge, MA: Harvard University Press, 2012), 15–16. I have borrowed much of his wording in these paragraphs to express an interpretation that is somewhat different.

4. It is interesting to note that Henry Luce went against the tide of public opinion in the last year of the war and opposed the policy of unconditional surrender, arguing that if peace were negotiated before Russia entered the war and invaded Manchuria, then the Soviets could not challenge the United States for supremacy in the region. Robert E. Herzstein,

Henry R. Luce, Time, and the American Crusade in Asia (Cambridge: Cambridge University Press, 2005), 48–50.

5. Francis Fukuyama, "The End of History?," *National Interest*, no. 16 (Summer 1989), 3.

6. Quoted in Jeremi Suri, "American Grand Strategy from the Cold War's End to 9 / 11," *Orbis* 53, no. 4 (Fall 2009): 623.

7. *New York Times*, March 8, 1992.

8. Chairman of the Joint Chiefs of Staff, *Joint Vision 2020* (Washington, DC: Government Printing Office, 2000), www.pentagonus.ru/doc/JV2020.pdf.

9. Suri, "American Grand Strategy," 627.

10. Luce, *The American Century*, 9.

11. Odd Arne Westad, *The Cold War: A World History* (New York: Basic Books, 2017), 617–621.

12. Murakami Yasusuke, *Han-koten no seiji keizaigaku* (Tokyo: Chūokōron sha, 1992), 1:3–4, 202, 2:242, 504.

13. Sakakibara Eisuke, "The End of Progressivism," *Foreign Affairs* 74, no. 5 (September-October 1995): 8–14. See also Sakakibara Eisuke, *Shimposhugi kara no ketsubetsu* (Tokyo: Yomiuri shimbunsha, 1996).

14. This is my argument in Kenneth B. Pyle, *Japan Rising: The Resurgence of Japanese Power and Purpose* (New York: Public Affairs, 2007).

15. The disarray within the Japanese government during the Gulf War is well told in Iokibe Makoto, Itō Motoshige, and Yakushiji Katsuyuki, eds., *Okamoto Yukio: Genbashugi o tsuranuita gaikōkan* (Tokyo: Asahi Shimbun, 2008), chap. 5. See also Michael J. Green and Igata Akira, "The Gulf War and Japan's National Security Identity," in *Examining Japan's Lost Decades*, ed. Yoichi Funabashi and Barak Kushner (London: Routledge, 2015), 158–175.

16. Nakasone Yasuhiro and Kōsaka Masataka, "Atarashii Nippon no senryaku," *Voice*, March 1992.

17. Tahara Soichirō, "Nippon no fumi-e," *Bungei shunjū*, October 1990.

18. Ibid.

19. I formed this view of Miyazawa not only from his writings but also from an extensive interview that former US ambassador to Japan Michael Armacost and I conducted with him in the summer of 2000. Particularly useful sources for Miyazawa's views in addition to his writings are interviews conducted by Mikuriya Takashi and Nakamura Takafusa in *Politics and Power in Twentieth Century Japan: The Reminiscences of Miyazawa Kiichi*, trans. Timothy S. George (London: SOAS Studies in Modern and Contemporary Japan, 2015).

20. Miyazawa Kiichi and Kōsaka Masataka, *Utsukushii Nihon e no chosen* (Tokyo: Bungei shunjū, 1984).

21. *Asahi shimbun*, November 29, 1991; Ozawa Ichiro, "Wareware wa naze kaikaku o mezasu ka," *Bungei shunjū*, December 1992. See also Ichiro Ozawa, *Blueprint for a New Japan* (Tokyo: Kodansha, 1992).

22. Christian G. Winkler, "Right Rising? Ideology and the 2012 House of Representatives Election," in *Japan Decides 2012: The Japanese General Election,* ed. Robert Pekkanen, Steven R. Reed, and Ethan Scheiner (New York: Palgrave Macmillan, 2013), 207.

23. H. Fukui, "Twenty Years of Revisionism," in *The Constitution of Japan: Its First Twenty Years, 1947–1967,* ed. Dan F. Henderson (Seattle: University of Washington, 1969), 49. See also John M. Maki, trans. and ed., *Japan's Commission on the Constitution: The Final Report* (Seattle: University of Washington Press, 1980), 19–20.

24. Of Etō's prolific writings, see especially Etō Jun, *1946-nen kempō: Sono kōsoku* (Tokyo: Bungeishunjūsha, 1980). See also Ann Sherif, "The Politics of Loss: On Eto Jun," *Positions: East Asia Cultures Critique* 10, no. 1 (2002): 111–139. For other prominent writings of political nationalists, see Kenneth B. Pyle, *The Japanese Question: Power and Purpose in a New Era,* 2nd ed. (Washington, DC: AEI Press, 1996), 55–64.

25. Nakasone Yasuhiro, *My Life in Politics* (typescript, 1982).

26. Abe Shinzō, *Atarashii kuni e* (Tokyo: Bungei shunju, 2013), 254. This was a revision of a book titled *Utsukushii kuni e,* published during his first administration.

27. Winkler, "Right Rising?," 208.

28. For discussion of Nippon kaigi and its influence, see David McNeill, "Nippon Kaigi and the Radical Conservative Project to Take Back Japan," *Asia-Pacific Journal / Japan Focus* 13, issue 50, no. 4 (December 14, 2015), https://apjjf.org/-David-McNeill/4409. See also David McNeill, "Growing Influence of Japan Conference Reflects Resentment at Tokyo's Postwar Settlement with Washington," *Japan Times,* August 15, 2015; and Sugano Tamotsu, *Nippon kaigi no kenkyū* (Tokyo: Fusōsha, 2016).

29. James Babb, "The New Generation of Conservative Politicians in Japan," *Japanese Journal of Political Science* 14, no. 3 (September 2013): 355–378.

30. Ibid.

31. Ibid.

32. Mark R. Mullins, "The Neo-Nationalist Response to the Aum Crisis: A Return of Civil Religion and Coercion in the Public Sphere?," *Japanese Journal of Religious Studies* 39, no. 1 (2012): 99–125. See also John Breen and Mark Teeuwen, *A New History of Shinto* (Malden, MA: Wiley-Blackwell, 2010), chap. 6. Also see David McNeil, "Back to the Future: Shinto's Growing Influence in Politics," *Japan Times,* November 23, 2013.

33. Lawrence Repeta, "Japan's Democracy at Risk—The LDP's Ten Most Dangerous Proposals for Constitutional Change," *Asia-Pacific Journal / Japan Focus* 11, issue 28, no. 3 (July 14, 2013), https://apjjf.org/2013/11/28/Lawrence-Repeta/3969/article.html. The translation from the draft is Lawrence Repeta's.

34. Will Dunham, "Kerry Condemns Russia's 'Incredible Act of Aggression' in Ukraine," *Reuters,* March 2, 2014.

35. Ashley J. Tellis, *Balancing without Containment: An American Strategy for Managing China* (Washington, DC: Carnegie Endowment for International Peace, 2014), 13.

36. Nina Solove, "The Pivot before the Pivot: U.S. Strategy to Preserve the Power Balance in Asia," *International Security* 40, no. 4 (Spring 2016): 45–88.

37. Kurt M. Campbell, *The Pivot: The Future of American Statecraft in Asia* (New York: Hachette Book Group, 2016).

38. Nadège Rolland, *China's Eurasian Century? Political and Strategic Implications of the Belt and Road Initiative* (Seattle, WA: National Bureau of Asian Research, 2017), xi.

39. Ministry of Foreign Affairs of Japan, "Japan Is Back," February 22, 2013, http://www.mofa.go.jp/announce/pm/abe/us_20130222en.html.

40. See Adam P. Liff and Andrew S. Erickson, "From Management Crisis to Crisis Management? Japan's Post-2012 Institutional Reforms and Sino-Japanese Crisis (In)stability," *Journal of Strategic Studies* 40, no. 5 (2017): 604–638.

41. The three conditions provide that CSD can be exercised only when an attack on a closely aligned country poses a threat to Japanese survival, when there is no other appropriate means to repel an attack, and where the use of force is limited to the minimum necessary.

42. Christopher W. Hughes, "Japan's Strategic Trajectory and Collective Self-Defense: Essential Continuity or Radical Shift?," *Journal of Japanese Studies* 43, no. 1 (Winter 2017): 126.

43. See Ellis S. Krauss and Robert J. Pekkanen, *The Rise and Fall of Japan's LDP: Political Party Organizations as Historical Institutions* (Ithaca, NY: Cornell University Press, 2011), 216–218.

44. Richard J. Samuels and James L. Schoff, "Japan's Nuclear Hedge: Beyond 'Allergy' and Breakout," in *Strategic Asia 2013–14: Asia in the Second Nuclear Age*, ed. Ashley Tellis, Abraham Denmark, and Travis Tanner (Seattle, WA, and Washington, DC: National Bureau of Asian Research, 2013), 252.

45. Iokibe Makoto, "The Japan-U.S. Alliance as a Maritime Alliance," in Ito Kenichi et al., *Japan's Grand Strategy for the 21st Century: From an Insular Nation to a Maritime Nation*, Japan Forum on International Relations, 2000, http://www.jfir.or.jp/e/special_study/seminar2/conversation.htm.

46. When Prime Minister Nakasone in the 1980s ordered the budget director to go beyond 1 percent, "the latter's face twitched and turned pale." In the end, however, Nakasone was permitted only a 1.004 percent level for the year.

47. Katsuyuki Yakushiji, "The Abe Administration's 'Pragmatic Line,'" AJISS-Commentary (Association of Japanese Institutes of Strategic Studies, April 4, 2016). See also Hiroshi Nakanishi, "Reorienting Japan? Security Transformation under the Second Abe Administration," *Asian Perspective* 39 (2015): 417–419.

48. Quoted in Koji Sonoda, "The Quest to Revise Japan's Constitution," *The Diplomat,* June 2, 2016.

49. Aurelia George Mulgan, "Securitizing the TPP in Japan: Policymaking Structure and Discourse," *Asia Policy,* no. 22 (July 2016): 212.

50. Ibid., 215.

51. Yakushiji, "The Abe Administration's 'Pragmatic Line.'" Yakushiji is a former associate editor of political news at the *Asahi Shimbun* and is now on the faculty of Tokyo University. Hughes argues that a "strong revisionist ideology . . . [is] the principal driver of Japan's foreign and security policies." Christopher W. Hughes, *Japan's Foreign and Security Policy under the 'Abe Doctrine': New Dynamism or New Dead End?* (New York: Palgrave Macmillan, 2015), 9.

52. See my discussion of Japanese conservatism in *Japan Rising,* 41–55.

53. *Nikkei Asian Review,* December 7, 2017.

54. Shinzo Abe, "Asia's Democratic Security Diamond," Project Syndicate, December 27, 2012, https://www.project-syndicate.org/commentary/a -strategic-alliance-for-japan-and-india-by-shinzo-abe.

55. NHK News, January 18, 2018.

56. Quoted in Samuels and Schoff, "Japan's Nuclear Hedge," 261.

57. Maruyama Masao, *Senchū to sengo no aida* (Tokyo: Misuzu shobō, 1976), 347–348.

58. Jeffry A. Frieden, "From the American Century to Globalization," in Bacevich, *Short American Century,* 157.

59. I am indebted to Richard Ellings for the characterization of the regional power configuration in this paragraph.

60. See the discussion of this understanding in S. N. Eisenstadt, "Multiple Modernities," *Daedalus* 129, no. 1 (Winter 2000): 1–29.

61. See the remarks of Henry Kissinger, *World Order* (New York: Penguin Press, 2014), 8.

62. I am indebted to an unpublished paper, Donald C. Hellmann, "Managing an Increasingly Interdependent but Non-Convergent Global Political Economy: The Role of Emerging Countries," (2013).

Acknowledgments

My intention in writing this book is to gather my thoughts on the extraordinary relationship of the United States and Japan during the past century. Focusing on the American impact on Japan is a useful way of tracing central themes in the making of postwar Japanese history. My hope is that this book will contribute to a greater degree of self-awareness and a deeper understanding of the impact that we Americans have had on Japan's people and civilization.

The book grows out of an interdisciplinary course that I have been teaching for many years at the University of Washington entitled "The Emergence of Postwar Japan." Also important to the making of this book has been an honors seminar that I have taught on "The Decision to Use the Atomic Bomb." Students have an opportunity to debate the difficult and troubling issues raised by the Hiroshima decision and the reasons historians have come to sharply different interpretations. The seminar has drawn a remarkable group of students, and it has been a privilege for me to engage with them in their debates.

Writing this book took me back to my student days, my love of American history, and the opportunity I had to study with leading American historians—Ernest May, Arthur Schlesinger Jr., Frederick Merk, and C. Vann Woodward. It was Ernest May who inspired my interest in and writing on American foreign policy toward Japan and Asia. As for Japanese studies, my debt to Thomas Smith, my graduate school mentor, is always a pleasure to acknowledge. Much of what I write about is contemporary history to me. I first arrived in Japan a few months after the Anpo demonstrations. Reflecting on my experience then as a student in Japan, I feel fortunate to have studied with the intellectual historian Matsumoto Sannosuke and to have had the extraordinary opportunity to audit the seminar of Maruyama Masao and the lectures of Ienaga Saburo, two giants of the postwar period. Later, my friendship with the remarkable scholar Murakami Yasusuke and his colleagues was of importance to themes in this book.

The book manuscript was read at different stages by valued friends Dick Samuels, T. J. Pempel, John Haley, Rich Ellings, and Ezra Vogel, who all made valuable suggestions. In bringing my work to the attention of Harvard University Press, Ezra was like a patron saint, although he prefers the description *aniki*. Kathleen McDermott at Harvard University Press guided me skillfully through the publication process.

My work has benefited from my colleagues at the Henry M. Jackson School of International Studies at the University of Washington and the support of its director, Resat Kasaba. I profited from many discussions of the book's themes with my longtime colleague Don Hellmann. I am deeply grateful to Martha Walsh, the managing editor of the *Journal of Japanese Studies,* for the countless ways that she has helped me in my work over the years.

Research and writing of this book have benefited from the generous support of the Henry M. Jackson Foundation. My friendship, experiences, and travels in Asia with Senator Jackson remain one of the important and memorable influences on my study of US relations with Asia.

Involvement in the founding and development of the National Bureau of Asian Research (NBR) has given me an opportunity to explore contemporary issues of American policy in Asia that are dealt with in this book. At NBR, I have profited from the support of my colleagues, especially Rich Ellings, Michael Wills, Karolos Karnikis, and Roy Kamphausen.

Some parts of this book are a sequel to my *Japan Rising: The Resurgence of Japanese Power and Purpose,* published in 2007 by Public Affairs. Chapters 5, 7, and 11 of this new book are informed by *Japan Rising.* I also incorporate in this book my thoughts about the remarkable American ambassador to Japan Edwin Reischauer that first appeared in "Japan and the United States: An Unnatural Intimacy" (*Journal of Japanese Studies* 37, no. 2 [2011]: 377–395, © Society for Japanese Studies). I am grateful to these publishers for giving me the opportunity to introduce concepts that I build on in this new book.

Our children, Will and Annie, have given constant encouragement to this project. My greatest obligation, as it always has been, is to my wife, Anne, my companion and best friend for nearly six decades, for her constant support, inspiration, and love that have sustained my being. This book, as with all my work, is dedicated to her.

Index